MARSILIUS OF PADUA AT THE INTERSECTION OF ANCIENT AND MEDIEVAL TRADITIONS OF POLITICAL THOUGHT

VASILEIOS SYROS

Marsilius of Padua at the Intersection of Ancient and Medieval Traditions of Political Thought

UNIVERSITY OF TORONTO PRESS
Toronto Buffalo London

Toronto Buffalo London
www.utppublishing.com

ISBN 978-1-4426-4144-0

Library and Archives Canada Cataloguing in Publication

Syros, Vasileios
Marsilius of Padua at the intersection of ancient and medieval traditions of political thought / Vasileios Syros.

Includes bibliographical references and indexes.
ISBN 978-1-4426-4144-0

1. Marsilius, of Padua, d. 1342. 2. Political science – Philosophy – History – To 1500. 3. Philosophy, Ancient – Influence. 4. Philosophy, Medieval – Influence. I. Title.

JC111.S97 2012 320.01 C2012-906817-9

University of Toronto Press acknowledges the financial assistance to its publishing program of the Canada Council for the Arts and the Ontario Arts Council.

University of Toronto Press acknowledges the financial support of the Government of Canada through the Canada Book Fund for its publishing activities.

Contents

Bibliographical Note vii

Acknowledgments ix

Introduction 3
- Sources 3
- Outline of Chapters 5

1 Marsilius's Life and Works 15

2 Major Intellectual Influences on Marsilius 19
- Albertino Mussato and Paduan Politics 19
- Peter of Abano and Late Medieval Natural Philosophy and Medicine 21
- Averroes Goes West: John of Jandun 22
- Muslim and Jewish Influences 24

3 Marsilius's Political Theory 25
- Marsilius and Aristotelian Teleology 25
- The Origins of Social Life 28
- Rhetoric and the Genesis of Civil Life 36
- The Purpose of the Political Community 46
- The Peace and Tranquility of the Political Community 47
- The Unity of the Political Community 53
- The Organization of the Political Community 56
  - *Marsilius's Classification of Human Acts* 56
  - *Marsilius and Aristotle* 57

Marsilius and Aquinas 58
Marsilius and Maimonides 59
Plato Transformed, Avicennian Echoes, and the Ideal Social Organization 61
The 'Circle of Justice' and Functional Specialization 64
The Idea of the Mean and the Parts of the Political Community 68
The Emergence of Religion and the Civic Function of the Sacerdotal Part 70
Marsilius's Notion of Citizenship 75

4 Marsilius's Legal Theory 80
The Definition of Law 80
Giants on the Shoulders of Dwarfs: Legislation and a Well-ordered Political Community 85
Cyclopes with Many Eyes: Laws and Collective Prudence 88
The *legislator humanus* 91
Legislation and Sovereignty 94
Medieval Echoes 96
Beyond Aristotle 97

5 Marsilius's Theory of Government 100
The Taxonomy of Constitutions 100
The Five Modes of Establishing Monarchy 102
The Appointment of the Government 105
The Political Community as a Living Organism 108

Conclusions 114

Appendix 117

Notes 119

Selected Bibliography 223

Index of Subjects 301

Index of Places and Proper Names 303

Bibliographical Note

References to the *Defensor pacis* (henceforth *DP*) are to the edition Marsilius von Padua, *Defensor pacis*, ed. Richard Scholz (= Fontes iuris Germanici antiqui in usum scholarum ex Monumentis Germaniae Historicis separatim editi; 7) (Hanover: Hahn, 1932/33). Citations will be to discourse, chapter, and paragraph.

References to Aristotle's *Politics* (henceforth *Pol.*) are, unless otherwise indicated, to William of Moerbeke's Latin translation: *Aristotelis Politicorum libri octo; cum vetusta translatione Guilelmi de Moerbeka*, ed. Franz Susemihl (Leipzig: B.G. Teubner, 1972). The abbreviations used for the other works of Aristotle follow *The Oxford Classical Dictionary*, ed. Simon Hornblower and Antony Spawforth (Oxford: Oxford University Press, 3rd rev. ed., 2003), xxxi:

An. post.	*Analytica posteriora*
De an.	*De anima*
De motu an.	*De motu animalium*
Eth. Nic.	*Ethica Nicomachea*
Gen. an.	*De generatione animalium*
Gen. corr.	*De generatione et corruptione*
Metaph.	*Metaphysica*
Ph.	*Physica*
Rh.	*Rhetorica*

References to the original Greek texts of Aristotle and Plato are to the Teubner editions. I have relied on the English translations of some of the Arabic, ancient and Byzantine Greek, medieval French, Hebrew, medieval and Renaissance Italian, and Latin sources mentioned throughout this book with some amendments.

Acknowledgments

After almost fifteen years of studying the history of medieval and early modern political thought, I remain greatly indebted to Jürgen Miethke, my former supervisor at the University of Heidelberg, for initiating me into Marsilius of Padua's ideas. I am likewise grateful to Kari Palonen for his mentoring and keen interest in the project over the years and to Cary Nederman and Bernardo Bayona for reading and commenting on early drafts of the manuscript. Clifford Angell Bates, Jr, Tony Black, Gianluca Briguglia, Marica Costigliolo, Andrew Gow, Tom Izbicki, Jules Janssens, Klaus-Frédéric Johannes, Roberto Lambertini, Oliver Leaman, Maurizio Merlo, Paul Rahe, Georgios Steiris, Miguel Vatter, and Ron Witt offered valuable suggestions and criticisms. Special thanks are also due to Jean-Pierre Rothschild for his invitation to deliver a series of lectures on some of the topics discussed in this book and the history of Jewish political thought at the École Pratique des Hautes Études in May 2011 as well as for his input on the sections dealing with the ties of Marsilius's political theory to the Jewish tradition. The three anonymous readers for the University of Toronto Press provided crucial feedback that led me to make several improvements in the final version.

The bulk of the present study originated and was completed during a two-year teaching appointment in the Committee on Social Thought at the University of Chicago from 2008 to 2010 and a one-year appointment as a senior fellow at the Martin Marty Center for the Advanced Study of Religion at the University of Chicago during the academic year 2010/11. I wish to thank the Committee and its faculty, especially David Nirenberg and Nathan Tarcov, as well as the Marty Center, and most particularly William Schweiker and Paul Mendes-Flohr, for providing a stimulating environment in which to bring this project to fruition.

The staff of the University of Chicago Library, especially Beth Bidlack and Frank Conaway, have been most helpful in securing materials. Thanks are also due to Juleen Eichinger and Catherine Plear for assistance with revisions and copy editing as well as to Suzanne Rancourt and Barb Porter for expert editorial advice. Finally, I would like to acknowledge the generous support provided by the Finnish Centre of Excellence in Political Thought and Conceptual Change, the Academy of Finland, and the Marty Center during the course of writing this book.

MARSILIUS OF PADUA AT THE INTERSECTION OF ANCIENT AND MEDIEVAL TRADITIONS OF POLITICAL THOUGHT

Introduction

Sources

What gained Marsilius of Padua notoriety in his time and a well-deserved position in modern narratives on the history of European political ideas is his interest in laying bare and combating the unique cause of the strife and dissension that afflicted the cities of central and northern Italy in his own time, i.e., the papacy's attempts to interfere in temporal affairs. My study of Marsilius has led to the notion that he was a strong advocate of secularization and that his model for political organization has enduring relevance for ongoing debates on social organization and the comparative study of diverse traditions of political thought.

Marsilius's political theory has attracted increasing research interest in recent years.[1] Previous scholarship has brought out the specific differences between Aristotle and Marsilius. The present work, however, focuses on Marsilius's model of political organization, identifying his sources and exploring how he articulates his program. It also situates him within broader debates on political phenomena in the Christian as well as in Islamic, Jewish, and Byzantine traditions. I will investigate Marsilius's reception of Aristotle's political doctrines, will consider alternative classical sources that Marsilius may have used, and will identify a variety of intellectual forces at work in the Paduan's thought. My intention is to highlight links between Marsilius's political theory and the medieval Muslim and Jewish traditions and demonstrate how Marsilius anticipates certain ideas and concepts that underlie the evolution of modern political thought. Ultimately, I advocate a fresh approach to the study of Marsilius's ideas, seeking to establish his importance as a purveyor of various intellectual strains and cultures of learning.

The present study builds partly on the findings of my monograph *Die Rezeption der aristotelischen politischen Philosophie bei Marsilius von Padua: Eine Untersuchung zur ersten Diktion des Defensor pacis* [= *The Reception of Aristotelian Political Philosophy in Marsilius of Padua: A Study on the First Dictio of the Defensor pacis*] (hereafter *Rezeption*), published by Brill in 2007. In the *Rezeption* I undertook a comparative exploration of Marsilius's and Aristotle's political ideas, investigating the ways in which Marsilius adopts and reworks Aristotle's theory of the *polis* as the foundation of his own political theory. A recurring theme in the *Rezeption* was Marsilius's challenge of the moral and teleological dimensions of Aristotle's thinking. I showed how Marsilius distances himself from Aristotle's teleological vision of the workings of social life and instead uses efficient causality as an analytical device to explore the mechanics of social evolution. I also engaged in systematic textual analysis and elaborate comparisons between Marsilius's *Defensor pacis* (*Defender of the Peace*) and Aristotle's *Politics* and brought out crucial differences between Marsilius's and Aristotle's political ideas.

A major purpose of the *Rezeption* was to dispel the view of Marsilius as an Aristotelian. More generally, I tried to question the validity of the concept of 'Aristotelianism' as a distinct category frequently employed in the historiography of medieval political ideas.[2] Admittedly, Aristotle enjoyed a special *auctoritas* for medieval thinkers, but subterranean influences and constant conversation with other writers from diverse contexts also shaped their views. In this book I delve more deeply into Marsilius's application of Aristotle's ideas and, more importantly, inquire into alternative sources and possible links to medieval political authors, especially those from non-Christian traditions.[3]

Marsilius was novel in his use of Aristotelian ideas to articulate a system fundamentally different from that of his predecessor in both aim and scope. He was also unique in his openness to various readings of Aristotle's writings and of a wide range of ancient and medieval sources. William of Moerbeke's (1215–86) Latin translation of the *Politics* (ca. 1260) opened the door to a trove of questions related to the emergence and function of the political community.[4] But even before the recovery of the *Politics*, many political theorists in the Middle Ages looked to *The Philosopher* for inspiration.[5] Numerous works that had appeared before the circulation of the *Politics* set forth ideas contained not only in the *Politics* but also in other Aristotelian treatises, such as the *Nicomachean Ethics* and the *Rhetoric*.[6] This has led certain scholars to posit the existence of 'political Aristotelianism' as a distinct trend in medieval thought. But Aristotle's ideas passed into the medieval world in a convoluted fashion and were often amalgamated or blended with doctrines deriving from other sources, such as Roman law and Christian teaching.

While in the present monograph I rely on Marsilius's reception of the Aristotelian legacy as a fundamental frame of reference, I am also guided by the belief that Marsilius's political theory offers a kaleidoscopic view of the late medieval world and is rich in meaning and readings drawn from various traditions of learning that extend beyond the Aristotelian heritage. These multiple sources influenced Marsilius's reception of classical political thought and the development of his own political ideas. In particular, I will show that Marsilius was influenced by three traditions in addition to the ideas of Aristotle and of his medieval commentators:[7] the Ciceronian tradition, Stoicism, and Platonic political thought.[8] In fact, I will argue that Marcus Tullius Cicero's political ideas, as expounded in *De republica* and *De officiis*, had a much more extensive and profound influence on Marsilius than hitherto assumed. Stoic ideas filtered through Cicero's works to produce a blend of philosophical doctrines; in fact, an entire Stoic framework undergirds Marsilius's political theory. Marsilius also took over and adapted ideas from Plato's *Timaios* about functional specialization and the principle of the division of labour, which were mediated through the writings of Avicenna, Dominicus Gundissalinus, and Roger Bacon.

Finally, the present study evinces concern for a broader set of issues (for example, the civic function of religion) and influences at work in Marsilius's thinking (for example, Neoplatonism) that have been hitherto unexplored.[9] Ideas advanced by previous scholars have led to entrenched views that preclude study of these broader influences that shaped Marsilius's political thinking. My work seeks to redress this oversight by pointing to Jewish and Muslim writers whose thought seems to have provided inspiration for Marsilius's political theory.

Outline of Chapters

In chapter 1, I briefly review Marsilius's life, illustrate the intellectual coordinates of his *œuvre*, and explore the relation of his political theory to the major political events and currents of the thirteenth and fourteenth centuries. In chapter 2, I trace the major intellectual influences on Marsilius's thought. These include Albertino Mussato and Paduan political life, as well as Peter of Abano and John of Jandun. Late medieval traditions of natural philosophy and medicine also find expression in Marsilius's project, as do influences from the Muslim and Jewish traditions.

The third chapter of this book, 'Marsilius's Political Theory,' is divided into eleven parts. First I address the relationship between Marsilius and Aristotelian teleology. Marsilius views the emergence and evolution of human society as a natural phenomenon, thereby adopting Aristotle's teleology in a mitigated form. Accordingly, and as I discuss in the chapter's subsequent sections, Marsilius depicts the birth and gradual growth of human communities, government, and human civilization in general as a process leading from imperfection to perfection. The desirable social order rests on the principle that the rightness of every political event conforms to the order prevailing in nature. Another crucial aspect of Marsilius's methodology is his application of the organic analogy, especially in the context of his discussion about the ideal political organization: just as health is by nature the optimal condition for any natural being, so is tranquility the best condition for any form of human association established in accordance with human reason. The central thrust of Marsilius's political theory is to investigate the causative factors involved in political phenomena and to articulate a model of political organization based on a chain of efficient causes that generate the laws and the government.

In the subsection entitled 'The Origins of Social Life,' I delve into Marsilius's teaching about human social development. In contrast to most medieval accounts of the beginnings of communal life, Marsilius abandons the Aristotelian topos about the social nature of man and instead takes inspiration from the Augustinian view that human frailty is the element that drives men to form social bonds and work together for the sake of material self-sufficiency. Marsilius endorses the Aristotelian idea that all men naturally aspire to a materially adequate existence and seek to avoid that which may be detrimental to their existence. But he also invokes Cicero's dictum that every living organism has the natural ability to preserve itself, to avoid what can endanger its existence, and to obtain the means that will guarantee its safety. In this belief, Marsilius harks back to the Platonic principle that men need to band together to meet their own individual needs and so must institute rules in order to assure peaceful coexistence. These ideas reverberate in a *risāla* (treatise) *On Government*, which was produced in Arabic and attributed to Themistios as well as in the in the work of another late antique thinker, Nemesios of Emesa, whose *On the Nature of Man* – translated into various languages including Arabic, Syriac, and Latin – highlights human necessity as the principal cause that induces humans to enter into society. Nemesios writes on the origins of social life from a perspective informed by Galen's medical teaching: the human body is composed of the four elements and is thus susceptible to the changes which these elements go through, i.e., division, change, and flux. As a result, man needs food, drink, clothing, and shelter for protection, and these needs lead to the emergence and development of diverse crafts and the exchange of products and knowledge. Marsilius's account of social genesis is reminiscent of the writings of Moses Maimonides, who echoes Aristotle's ideas; for example, his statement that man is a political animal by nature. Maimonides goes further, investing the standard Themistian formula with associations to Aristotle's concept of commutative justice. The ruler's task is to correct malefactors and inflict on them punishments proportionate to the gravity and nature of their delict. Maimonides recommends that every town have a judge and also a ruler to restrain people and fortify the authority of the judges. Finally, Ptolemy of Lucca set a precedent for Marsilius's ideas on social genesis in his *On the Government of Rulers* when he described the emergence of human associations as arising from human weakness.

In 'Rhetoric and the Genesis of Civil Life,' I explore Marsilius's ideas about the process whereby the first communities were established: prudent men (*prudentes*), by collective persuasion or exhortation, called together all heads of households (*patresfamilias*). I next look at how Marsilius's exposition of social genesis relates to previous accounts of the founding and function of human society. Medieval and early modern ideas on the emergence of social life can be classified into three main strands: one based on the Aristotelian notion of the founder of the political community; one grounded in Cicero's notion that men formed communities and appointed rulers on the basis of mutual consent; and one, also inspired by Cicero, in which joint efforts by the first heads of households and the primordial orators led to the initial formation of human communities and appointment of rulers.

The subsection entitled 'The Purpose of the Political Community' shows Marsilius arguing that differentiation of function is a prime prerequisite to a prosperous social life and a well-governed community. In

'The Peace and Tranquility of the Political Community,' I examine how the Marsilius's notion of domestic tranquility bears upon his views on the ideal form of social organization: the political community is made up of heterogeneous parts with varying dispositions and divergent interests and suffers from dissent and conflict, the resolution of which is indispensable for its viability; otherwise, the equipoise of the parts of the political community will be disrupted and the political community will fall apart. The perpetuation of social life requires a standard of justice and an agency responsible for implementing the laws, restraining malefactors, and dealing with internal and external threats. The Marsilian notion of the good life has far-reaching ramifications for his notions of peace and domestic tranquility and the ways they relate to the Aristotelian tradition. For Aristotle, peace and leisure are preconditions in the pursuit of felicity through speculative activity. Marsilius, in contrast, defines tranquility as the antithesis of discord, i.e., as the internal stability and equilibrium of the political community, and considers peace from a socioeconomic point of view, i.e., as the foundation for the mutual collaboration among the members of the political community. To explicate his notion of tranquility, Marsilius relies on Aristotle's organic imagery: he compares the political community to a living being, whose health and good disposition depend on the proportionate and symmetrical growth of its individual parts and organs. Marsilius here differs from most late medieval and Italian authors of his time, who, like Aristotle, related the conflicts that afflicted the Italian cities to the antagonism between rich and poor and accentuated the economic causes of factional discord.

In 'The Unity of the Political Community,' I demonstrate that the Marsilian concept of domestic unity is influenced strongly by the Ciceronian definition of the commonwealth as an association of men united by a common sense of right and by a community of interest. Marsilius argues that it is necessary for the political community to have a single supreme governmental agency with respect not to person but to office, clearly allowing for the possibility of a legitimate government comprising more than one individual, as is the case with the aristocracy and polity.

In 'The Organization of the Political Community,' I show how Marsilius articulates his model of social organization by advancing a categorization of human acts into 1) transient (transitive) acts, which are generated by the external organs or limbs of the human body for the benefit or harm of someone other than the doer; and 2) immanent acts, such as thoughts, emotions, and desires, that are not exercised by the external organs of the human body and do not affect any person other than the agent himself. The *legislator humanus*, the supreme instance and ultimate source of legislative and governmental authority within the political community cannot control or regulate them, nor can it settle by means of human law the conflicts and disputes that may arise from immanent passions. Marsilius considers it one of the foremost tasks of the ruling party to moderate the excesses of the transient acts and to reduce them to equality or due proportion. In this subsection, I also explore the relationship, similarities, and differences between Marsilius, Aristotle, Aquinas, and Maimonides. Once again, Marsilius's distinction of human acts had a precedent in Maimonides' classification of the commandments as set out in his *Guide of the Perplexed*. I claim that Maimonides is a likely candidate for being one of the direct sources of the Marsilian teaching about human acts. As a sequel to his classification of human acts, Marsilius goes on to bring out the connection between the acts of the member of the community and the segments of the body politic: the various sections of the community moderate the activities which spring from the parts of the soul – for instance, the agricultural part moderates the acts emanating from the nutritive part. The practitioners of the mechanical arts are responsible for the moderation of the human senses. Lastly, the function of the ruling and sacerdotal parts of the community consists in moderating the 'transient' and 'immanent' human acts, respectively.

In 'Plato Transformed, Avicennian Echoes, and the Ideal Social Organization' and 'The Idea of the Mean and the Parts of the Political Community,' I investigate how Marsilius builds on ideas found in Plato's *Timaios*, which proposes the strict regimentation of the civic body into four groups: priests; craftsmen; shepherds, hunters and ploughmen; and warriors. Every citizen must be allocated an occupation in accordance with his natural abilities. Marsilius's application of the principle of the specialization of labour must be seen against a long tradition, especially in medieval Islamic political writing: the 'circle of justice.' This tradition assumes that a lasting political community is contingent on the ability of each social group to fulfil its proper function, but it also reflects a vivid awareness of the mutual dependency of the members of the body politic.

Avicenna, for example, deems one of the lawgiver's central concerns to be the division of the members of society into three parts: rulers, artisans, and guardians. Avicenna's ideas on social organization were taken over by a number of Christian writers, such as Dominicus Gundissalinus and Roger Bacon. Marsilius holds that the political community is made up of disparate groups with divergent interests that need to be satisfied if the social organism is to be preserved. Moreover, he explains, the preponderance of one of these parts causes disequilibrium or diseases in the body politic. Christine de Pizan expressed similar ideas, as did Niccolò Machiavelli and other Florentine political theorists in their analysis of the political and social conditions that prevailed in early modern Florence.

'The Emergence of Religion and the Civic Function of the Sacerdotal Part' elaborates upon Marsilius's ideas on the emergence and societal function of religion. I specifically explore how Marsilius draws on pagan examples to illustrate the political aspects of religion. Al-Fārābī, for instance, in his summary of Plato's *Laws*, elaborates on Plato's account of Athenian religious festivals, adding that their purpose was to subserve the education and training of the members of the city. In the same spirit, Averroes in his *Incoherence of Incoherence* notes that the 'philosophers' considered the idea of resurrection instrumental for safeguarding order among men, which is indispensable for human existence and can lead to ultimate felicity. Similarly, Maimonides notes that by studying the doctrines and worship of the Sabians he gained valuable insights into the rational grounds for the existence of divine commandments as well as into the value of divine precepts as a means to ensure the morality of human deeds. In a similar vein, Marsilius contends that the first philosophers spoke of virtuous men in this world who were placed in the heavenly firmament and of certain stars and constellations named after them. They taught that the souls of evildoers entered the bodies of various brutes according to the grade of human vices, they mentioned various kinds of torments for malefactors (such as eternal thirst and hunger, as in the case of Tantalos), and they described the infernal regions as deep and dark. Out of fear, men refrained from wrongdoing and were driven to perform virtuous works of piety and mercy. Marsilius articulates the notion of religion as a 'law' (*lex*), i.e., a set of rules designed to regulate and channel the behaviour of the members of society.

Marsilius's ideas on the civic dimension of religion found a close echo in a number of Renaissance thinkers. Pietro Pomponazzi, for instance, suggests that a consensus exists about the societal benefits of religious belief and rites. Paolo Sarpi, following in the same tradition, conceptualizes the state as the generator and sustainer of social life and looks upon religion as an institution that is subservient and renders assistance to the governing authority. Sarpi defines religion as a body of rules and commands intended to regulate social relations, evoking an intriguing link to Marsilius's idea of religion as *lex*. Just as Marsilius sees the genesis of religion as a phenomenon coeval with the establishment of laws in the first communities, Sarpi maintains that society, the state, and religion have existed as long as man has existed.

In the eleventh and final subsection of chapter 3, 'Marsilius's Notion of Citizenship,' I analyse Marsilius's ideas on citizenship, manual occupations, and the hierarchy of ends. Most classical writers take a critical stance towards the mechanical crafts and recommend that these occupations be assigned solely to slaves or foreigners (*metics*). Marsilius, in contrast, articulates an inclusive model of social organization premised on the idea that all parts of society are equally important for a materially sufficient life and the preservation of the whole. Marsilius's notion of civic participation is evocative of classical Athenian democracy as Aristotle presents it in his *Politics*. The perfect community, according to Marsilius, is characterized by the existence of laws, which serve as a *regula iustorum*, i.e., as a binding standard according to which human acts are regulated. In this subsection I also review briefly Marsilius's use of the concepts of 'law' and 'judge' before turning to his twofold conception of the law. On the one hand, it denotes in general what is just or unjust, beneficial or harmful. In this meaning it is called the science or doctrine concerning what is right or just. On the other hand, the law is characterized by the fact that there exist precepts for executing and observing it which can be enforced through rewards and punishments in the present world. Marsilius defines the law as a text that originates from human prudence and reason and constitutes an arrangement about what is just and has punitive power.

Chapter 4, 'Marsilius's Legal Theory,' is divided into six subsections. 'The Definition of Law' discusses how Marsilius's formalization of the concept of law has important implications for his legal theory. First, unlike Aristotle, Marsilius attributes no importance to unwritten laws. Second, his concept of justice is modeled on the Aristotelian notion of commutative justice. And third, unlike Aristotle, Marsilius identifies the law, not friendship, as the bond that holds the various forces within the community in the right balance. As I show in 'Giants on the Shoulders of Dwarfs: Legislation and a Well-ordered Political Community,' Marsilius ascribes a dual function to the law: first, it allows the ruler to pronounce right judgments; second, it supports the ruler, especially in the case of a hereditary king, thereby guaranteeing the rightful and effective exercise of governmental authority. Marsilius starts from the Stoic premise that there is an inbuilt tendency in man to secure the means for his self-preservation and the maintenance of social life. From this Marsilius infers that citizens seek the means that are conducive to the general interest, such as laws designed with an eye to the benefit of the entire community. This does not work in practice, however, with a judge whose inner disposition is easily corruptible. In the subsection entitled 'Cyclopes with Many Eyes: Laws and Collective Prudence,' I expound upon Marsilius's use of Aristotle's theory of progress in the context of his discussion about the evolution of civil legislation. Marsilius argues that the 'first inventors' of the laws and everything that all persons of the same era have discovered about laws, based on their own experience, is inadequate. Laws are brought to perfection over subsequent generations, through additions to it. All that a single man discovers, Marsilius maintains, is imperfect in comparison to the accumulated wisdom of several generations.

Next I turn to Marsilius's notion of the *legislator humanus*. The primary (first) legislator (*legislator primus*) and specific efficient cause of the laws is, according to Marsilius, the body of the citizens – or their 'weightier part' (*valencior pars*) – by their vote or volition, which is expressed in the civil assembly. Aristotle holds that the doctrine of the sovereignty[10] of the multitude applies to a civic body that is not vile. Marsilius mentions the qualifications stipulated by Aristotle with regard to the doctrine of the sovereignty of the multitude only in passing. One of Marsilius's most distinctive arguments in favour of the sovereignty of the multitude rests on the assumption that the majority of men are simply not wicked and irrational and, in most matters, are not lacking in judgment, nor are they ignorant or irresponsible. To the contrary: they display sound human understanding and reason; and their natural desire to live in association with others and to obtain the necessities for their sustenance (such as laws and other statutes or customary rights) is only just. Marsilius appeals to another Aristotelian argument: the quantitative superiority of those who wish the endurance of a particular type of constitution vis-à-vis those who contest it. Marsilius argues, in Aristotelian vein, that the general principle for the perpetuation of any type of human association is that the segment of the population which desires the longevity of the civil order be quantitatively superior to that which desires the opposite. It would be contrary to nature if those who are opposed to the existence of the political community are so numerous that they surpass the part of the citizenry which wishes the continuance of the political community. By expressing such a strong belief in the ability of most men to exhibit collective insight and have a share in the process of decision making, Marsilius differs from a number of medieval writers such as Peter of Auvergne and Nicolas de Vaudémont.

In Chapter 5, 'Marsilius's Theory of Government,' I first detail 'The Taxonomy of Constitutions.' Marsilius's outline of the six major forms of constitution is patterned after the one in the *Politics*, although it diverges from Aristotle's constitutional theory in a number of respects: unlike Aristotle, Marsilius is concerned not with setting a universal standard of justice, but rather with the legitimacy of a regime and its acceptance by the citizenry. In keeping with his position that a well-structured polity presupposes the concordant interaction among its constituent parts, he dispenses with the Aristotelian term 'just' for the designation of the correct and rightly ordered forms of constitution. Instead, he opts for the term 'well-mixed constitution,' which he presents as the antithesis of *vitiatum*. This is explained against the medical background of the Marsilian vision of a well-instituted political community as the replica of a sound and symmetrically grown living organism, whose parts stand in a proportionate relationship to one another. Marsilius subdivides the various governmental types into 'well blended' and 'diseased.' In the first type, the ruler exercises leadership with an eye to the common good and in accordance with the assent of the citizenry, whereas this is not the case with the corrupt forms. Kingship, aristocracy, and polity belong to the first type; to the second belong the tyranny, oligarchy, and democracy.

'The Five Modes of Establishing Monarchy,' is devoted to Marsilius's treatment of the process whereby the various types of monarchical government come into being. In particular, he describes five distinct methods of establishing kingly monarchy: 1) functional monarchy; 2) hereditary despotic monarchy; 3) elective tyranny; 4) heroic monarchy; and 5) *dominus* monarchy. An important criterion for discerning the legitimacy of a royal regime is, for Marsilius, that the monarch – whether elected or non-elected – rule over willing subjects.

In 'The Appointment of the Government,' I look at Marsilius's ideas about the relationship between the *legislator humanus* and the government or the ruler. Following the Neoplatonic tradition, Marsilius depicts the *legislator humanus* as the primary cause and the government as the secondary cause. At the same time, as I show in 'The Political Community as a Living Organism,' Marsilius draws on Aristotle's biology to depict the function of the *legislator humanus* as analogous to that of the soul during the process of the generation and growth of a living organism: the *legislator humanus* appoints the government, which is in charge of setting up, differentiating, and sustaining the other parts of the body politic just as the heart is in charge of creating the other members and organs of a physical organism. Marsilius differs from most medieval thinkers by being rather unconcerned with the question of the best type of regime, although he does mention in passing that kingship might be the best one. He is instead concerned with providing the contours of a universal model of political organization that is valid for all time and all places and adaptable to changing social exigencies.

In the Conclusions, I describe how this volume challenges previous scholarship that portrays Marsilius as a staunch Aristotelian. I recapitulate some of the central arguments made in the various chapters and demonstrate that Marsilius was more profoundly influenced by Cicero and by Jewish and Muslim political thinkers than has been heretofore acknowledged. I close with a call for future scholarship to place Western political thinkers in dialogue with writers from other traditions, to identify patterns in the cross-cultural study of medieval political thought, and to explore the non-Christian sources of other seminal European political writers.

Chapter One

Marsilius's Life and Works

Marsilius (Marsiglio) dei Mainardini was born between 1270 and 1290 in Padua, in the Veneto region of Northern Italy.[1] The scion of a family of notaries, he departed from the family's tradition by choosing to study medicine instead of law. The friend of his youth, the prominent Paduan poet and historiographer Albertino Mussato, advised him and stood by him in this decision. All that we know about Marsilius's early life derives from the poem *Ad Magistrum Marsilium physicum Paduanum eius inconstantiam arguens*, which Mussato dedicated to Marsilius. In the poem, Mussato relates Marsilius's dilemma in a jocular tone and describes how he, Mussato, recommended medicine as the profession best suited for Marsilius, with the caveat that the profession be chosen out of honest motives.[2]

Marsilius went to Paris to study arts and medicine, most probably after an initial period of study under Peter of Abano at the University of Padua.[3] He was elected rector of the University of Paris for the period of December 1312 to March 1313. As a representative of the university, Marsilius had access not only to the council of the French king but also to the curia in Avignon.[4] In 1315, Marsilius was present as a witness in Peter of Abano's will, which was drawn up by Mussato in his capacity as notary.[5] John XXII's (ca. 1244–1334) appointment to the Avignon papacy in 1316 awoke in Marsilius the hope of an ecclesiastical career in his native Padua. Between 1316 and 1318, he received several promises from Pope John of an ecclesiastical benefice, but his hopes were never realized.[6]

Marsilius's interest in politics and his aspirations for a political career did not wither away, however: in 1319, he joined a delegation sent by the Milanese Signor Matteo I Visconti (1250–1322) to Charles, Count of La Marche (the later Charles IV of France or Charles le Bel, 1294–1328,

r. 1322–8), for the purpose of forging an alliance. Matteo had been excommunicated in 1317 by John XXII because of his opposition to Robert of Anjou (1278–1343, r. 1309–43), the king of Naples, whom John had appointed as vicar over the *regnum italicum*. With Cangrande I della Scala (1291–1329) of Verona, Matteo had made a stand against Robert and had petitioned Charles for support, offering him the leadership of the Ghibelline party in return.[7] The French declined this proposal, and Marsilius returned to his academic activities in Paris.[8]

On 24 June 1324,[9] Marsilius in Paris completed his magnum opus, the *Defensor pacis*, which he dedicated to Louis IV of Bavaria (1287–1347, r. 1314–47).[10] Although Marsilius claimed to be the sole author of the *Defensor pacis*,[11] the treatise was long considered to be the joint product of Marsilius and John of Jandun.[12] In support of this hypothesis, previous scholarship pointed to affinities between Marsilius's *Quaestiones super Metaphysicae libros I–VI* (*Questiones on the* [*First*] *Six Books of the Metaphysics*) and John's *Commentary on the Metaphysics*.[13] But there exist crucial differences between Marsilius's and John's ideas about human felicity; the final cause and structure of the political community; the nature and role of political authority; the distinction of human acts; the taxonomy of the various forms of rule; the notion of the lawgiver; and natural slavery, that render the assumption of their co-authorship of the work untenable.[14]

The publication of the *Defensor pacis* despite its polemic character had no immediate consequences for Marsilius or John. In 1326, Marsilius announced courses at the University of Paris and borrowed money from Italian students;[15] and in the summer of 1324, John signed a lifetime lease on a house in Paris.[16] This period of relative calm did not last long, however: in the summer of 1326, Marsilius and John fled from Paris to the court of Louis of Bavaria.

The arrival of Marsilius and John at Louis's court in Nuremberg led to even more strain on Louis's contest with the Avignon papacy.[17] And a curial reaction was not long in coming: on 9 April 1327, Marsilius and John were called before the papal court in Avignon to account for the publication of the *Defensor pacis*. When they did not obey John XXII's summon, the pope issued the bull *Licet iuxta doctrinam* on 23 October of the same year, which identifies five statements of the *Defensor pacis* (Jesus paid taxes to the Roman Emperor and not out of generosity, but because he was obligated to do so; Peter was not the head of the Church to a greater extent and did not possess more authority than the other apostles, and Jesus did not appoint any head for the Church nor did he designate any particular person as his representative; the emperor possesses the authority to correct, punish, appoint, and depose the pope; all priests stand on equal footing in terms of authority and jurisdiction; the pope or the clergy are not entitled to inflict coercive punishment on anyone, unless the emperor has granted them the authority to do so) as heretical and erroneous and condemns Marsilius and John, the alleged authors of the work, as heretics.[18] The *Defensor pacis* was influential in the time of the Great Schism (1378–1417).[19] Its *editio princeps* appeared in 1522 in Basel with the foreword of a Protestant writer, most probably Beatus Rhenanus (1485–1547)[20] and an English translation by William Marshall (fl. 1535) was published at Thomas Cromwell's (1485–1540) behest in 1535.[21]

In the spring of 1327, not long after the pope condemned the *Defensor pacis*, Louis of Bavaria launched his Italian expedition.[22] Marsilius and John accompanied Louis, and it is possible that Marsilius used his personal connections to the Ghibellines to back Louis's Italian venture.[23] In 1327, Marsilius was appointed *iudex clericorum et administrator archiepiscopatus Mediolani in temporalibus pro regia maiestate*.[24] A series of events in Rome hints at Marsilius's active involvement in the circumstances surrounding Louis's coronation as emperor in St. Peter's Cathedral in the name of the Roman people by the delegate of the people (*capitano del popolo*) Giacomo (Sciarra) Colonna on 17 January 1328; the deposing of John XXII proclaimed on 18 April 1328; and the appointment of the Friar Minor Peter of Corbara as antipope (Nicholas V) by the acclamation of the Roman people and by Louis's formal declaration on 12 May 1328.

Louis's success in Italy was short-lived, however; in 1329 political changes and increasing opposition forced Louis to leave Italy and return to Nuremberg. Marsilius accompanied Louis and spent the rest of his life as his personal physician. Marsilius's minor works[25] include the *De translatione imperii* (*On the Transfer of the Empire*) which deals with the transfer of imperial power from the Romans to the Greeks, from the Greeks to the Franks, and from the Franks to the Germans,[26] the *Defensor minor* (*Smaller* [or *Minor*] *Defender*,1342),[27] and two brief treatises, the *Forma divorcii matrimonialis* (*Form of the Dissolution of Marriage*) and the *De matrimonio* (*On Marriage*), that vindicate Louis's prerogative to annul the marriage between Margaret Maultasch (1318–69), countess of Tyrol and Carinthia, and John Henry of Luxembourg (1322–75), and approve a new marriage between Margaret and his son, Louis I, margrave of Brandenburg ([Louis V, Duke of Bavaria], 1315–61).[28]

The *Defensor minor* harks back to the *Defensor pacis* and offers a recapitulation of the central principles of Marsilius's political theory but, at the same time, it is a response to contemporary political developments. At the outset, Marsilius clarifies the term *iurisdictio* (jurisdiction). He then goes on to deny all coercive power of the clergy, of priests, of bishops, and of the pope. A substantial portion of the *Defensor minor* is devoted to the question of excommunication. At the end of the work, Marsilius sketches the profile of *the supremus legislator humanus* as the ultimate source of authority within the community of the faithful. A reference in a speech by Pope Clement VI (ca. 1290–1352, r. 1342–52) indicates that Marsilius died around 1342.

Chapter Two

Major Intellectual Influences on Marsilius

Marsilius's political theory was influenced by the writings and actions of several important figures of the intellectual and political life of his time.[1] Albertino Mussato provided not only career advice (as indicated earlier) but also access to the circle of the Paduan Prehumanists. With his translations of the works of Aristotle, Galen (129–ca. 216), and of Arab and Jewish writers not well known in Marsilius's time, Peter of Abano introduced Marsilius to key writings about natural philosophy and medicine. John of Jandun has been described by scholars as a simon-pure or rabid Averroist and the co-author of the *Defensor pacis*, but recent scholarship has challenged both of these assertions. Finally, there are intriguing affinities between Marsilius and such medieval Jewish and Muslim thinkers as Maimonides and Al-Fārābī (872–950), Avicenna (Ibn Sīnā, 980–1037), and Averroes (Ibn Rushd, 1126–1198).

Albertino Mussato and Paduan Politics

Albertino Mussato's works resonate with the traumatic experiences of tyranny under the rule of Ezzelino III da Romano (1194–1259, r. 1237–59), the leader of the Ghibelline faction in Padua, as well as with contemporary debates on of the fate of communal institutions and the rise of the *signoria*. Born in Padua in 1261, Mussato gave up his legal practice in order to serve in various government posts in Padua – as a member of the *Consiglio Maggiore* (Great Council) and numerous diplomatic missions.[2] As part of the Paduan delegation, he participated in Henry VII's (1278/79–1313, r. 1308–1313) coronation in Milan in 1312.

A salient aspect of Mussato's political activity were his feverish efforts to counteract the establishment of the *signoria* and halt the decline of the communal regime in Padua.[3] Following Giacomo da Carrara's (1264–1324) appointment as delegate of the people (*capitano del popolo*) in 1318,[4] Mussato was incarcerated for several months because of his political activities against the Carrara family. In 1325, he retired into exile. After Cangrande della Scala's seizure of Padua in 1328, Mussato made a plea to return to Padua but was unsuccessful; in 1329, he died in exile at Chioggia.

Mussato left behind a multifaceted literary and historical œuvre with a strong political intent.[5] Mussato's tragedy *Ecerinis* (1314/15),[6] written during his captivity in Vicenza, represents an effort to vilify Ezzelino's rule[7] and reflects a tendency of chroniclers in Mussato's time to depict Ezzelino as the archetypal tyrant. Such descriptions of Ezzelino's regime coalesced into the creation of the 'Myth of Ezzelino' that was propagated by apologists for communal ideals and was used as a means to denounce Padua's signorial past and to express alarm over the crisis of communal rule.[8] The 'Myth of Ezzelino' had a powerful impact on such works of Paduan historiography as Rolandino of Padua's (ca. 1200–76) *Cronica in factis et circa facta Marchie Trivixane* (*Ecerina* or *Rolandina*; *The Chronicles of the Trevisan March*; 1262), one of the most important sources for Padua's political history between 1200 and 1260 and Ezzelino's rule,[9] which was officially approved by the Faculty of Arts at the University Padua on 13 April 1262.[10]

Mussato's work draws lessons from Paduan history, but is also animated by the literary aspiration to emulate Seneca's tragedies.[11] In the wake of the discovery of the eleventh-century Etruscus codex with Seneca's dramas in the library of the Benedictine Abbey of Pomposa by Lovato (de') Lovati (Lupatus de Lupatis, 1240–1309), a leading member of the circle of Paduan Prehumanists,[12] Seneca's œuvre met with an enthusiastic reception within the circles of the Paduan *literati*. Lovato and Mussato found in Seneca a valuable source of inspiration for their reflections on the character and aims of poetry. Marsilius also seems to have taken a keen interest in contemporary debates on poetry and Seneca's works, as evidenced by a fictitious dialogue between Lovato and Mussato, the *Evidentia tragediarum Senece tradita magistro Marsilius philosopho Paduano ab Albertino Mussato Paduano poeta* (ca. 1315), which Mussato dedicated to him.[13]

The *Ecerinis* earned Mussato prominence in Padua's intellectual life, but also fame across Italy: in December 1315 he received the poetic laurel crown from the Paduan Faculty of Arts, and it was officially decided that the *Ecerinis* would be read in public once a year during Christmas.[14] One of the immediate aims of the *Ecerinis* was to raise the alarm among his fellow Paduan citizens about the rise of the signorial regime; Mussato also points to the hazardous effects of perpetual rule in general. In the end, Mussato was not able to galvanize the Paduans into action in the face of the imminent danger of Padua's conquest by Cangrande della Scala, the signore of Verona and Vicenza, whom Mussato saw as Ezzelino's counterpart.[15]

Mussato also produced a number of historiographical works following Livy's (Titus Livius, ca. 56 BC–AD 17) model.[16] His *Historia Augusta de gestis de Gestis Henrici VII Caesaris* and *De Gestis Italicorum post mortem Henrici VIII Caesaris*[17] offer an analysis of the political history of Italy during the period 1310 to 1316, in the aftermath of Henry's Italian expedition and a fulsome praise of Henry as the guarantor of communal freedom.[18] Mussato's literary activity was crowned by his historical work *Ludovicus Bavarus,* which deals with Louis's Italian expedition.[19] During the period of his final exile from Padua (1325–9), Mussato wrote the *Ludovicus Bavarus ad Filium,* an essay addressed to Louis of Bavaria that deals with the education of his son,[20] as well as the *Contra Casus Fortuitos* and *De lite Inter Naturam and Fortunam.*[21]

Peter of Abano and Late Medieval Natural Philosophy and Medicine

In assessing the main forces that shaped Marsilius's political thinking, it is instructive to dwell briefly on Peter of Abano's (ca. 1257–ca.1316) life and works.[22] During a stay in Constantinople, the capital of the Byzantine Empire, Peter devoted himself to the study of Greek and had access to a number of manuscripts on medicine and natural philosophy. After his return to Italy, Peter engaged in an ambitious project to translate writings of Aristotle, Galen, and Hippocrates.

One of Peter's major contributions to the transmission of Aristotle's natural philosophy in the medieval West was a commentary on the pseudo-Aristotelian *Problemata physica,* a collection of questions related to natural philosophy, under the title *Expositio problematum Aristotelis* which he completed in 1310 in Padua.[23] Peter's commentary is based on the Latin translation of the *Problemata* produced by Bartholomew of Messina (thirteenth century) at the court of King Manfred of Sicily (ca. 1232–66, r. 1258–66).[24]

The *Problemata* seems to have received scant attention from Aristotelian commentators. In the foreword to his commentary on the *Physics,* John of Jandun bemoans the lack of a commentary on the *Problemata.*[25] For the context of the present study, it is important to note that Peter sent a copy of his commentary to Jandun through Marsilius. John confirmed this in the foreword to his version of Peter's *Exposition of the Problemata*, with included his own comments, and it is probable that he used it as a compendium in his Paris lectures.[26]

Concurrent with his teaching activity in Paris (1290–1303/5), Peter worked on a Latin translation of the astrological texts of the Jewish writer Abraham (ben Meir) ibn Ezra (Avenarius) (1089/92–1164/7).[27] From 1307 until his death (ca. 1316), Peter taught medicine in Padua.[28] In 1310, he completed his *magnum opus*, the *Conciliator differentiarum philosophorum et praecipue medicorum*.[29] The *Conciliator* represents an ambitious project aimed to harmonize medicine and philosophy, although the central thrust of the work is to establish the primacy of medicine among the whole range of arts (*artes*). The *Conciliator* is in this respect a treasure trove of reflections on the status of medicine as *scientia*.[30] Peter also composed a number of astrological and medical treatises, including the *Lucidator dubitabilium astronomiae* (1310).[31]

Medieval discussions on the methodological principles of medicine often took their cue from Galen's *Tegni* (*Ars medica, Τέχνη ἰατρικῄ*).[32] The translations of this work (*Translatio antiqua* or *Translatio graeca*) from the Greek were included in the *Articella*. Another channel for the transmission of Galen's ideas on medicine was the Arabic translation of the *Tegni* by the Arab physician and astronomer Ali ibn Ridwân (Haly, ca. 998–ca. 1061).[33] The work was translated into Latin by Gerard of Cremona (ca. 1114–87) in the last years of his life and enjoyed a wide reception in the premier centers of medical learning in Italy (Salerno) and France (Paris and Montpellier).[34]

Peter turned to Haly's work as a foil for his interpretation of Galen's medical theory: he associates with Haly the *doctrina resolutiva* with Aristotle's *demonstratio quia.* He specifies that *resolvere* (to resolve) is used in normal usage for the (re)solution of the effect in causes just as a house can be broken down in various parts, i.e., its roof, walls, and foundation. For Peter, then, the starting point for scientific inquiry should be what is already known and not what is best known in the absolute sense. Peter touches here upon Aristotle's idea that the description of bare facts can serve as the fulcrum for the exploration of causal relations among natural phenomena.[35]

Averroes Goes West: John of Jandun

John of Jandun was born between 1285 and 1289 in Jandun (Champagne).[36] His first work, written while he was teaching on the Arts faculty in Paris, the *dissertatio* on the *sensus agens* (1310), dealt with a number of psychological and epistemological questions[37] and sparked a controversy with Bartholomy of Bruges (†1356), one of the leading Aristotelian commentators of the time.[38] It is possible that John formed a close friendship with Marsilius during the latter's stay in Paris. We also know that Peter of Abano, as noted above, sent a copy of his commentary on the *Problemata* to John through Marsilius.

In 1315, John was invited to teach at the Collège de Navarre, which had been founded by Joan I of Navarre (ca. 1270–1305), Philipp IV's wife, in 1304.[39] John produced a series of commentaries on various Aristotelian treatises, notably on the *Physics* (around 1315),[40] on *De anima* (between 1317 and 1319),[41] on the *Metaphysics* (between 1318 and 1325),[42] on *De coelo et mundo*,[43] the *Parva naturalia*, the *Rhetoric*, and the *Economics* (1319).[44] A salient feature of John's works is his endeavour to challenge the Scholastic tradition and his extensive use of Averroes's commentaries on Aristotle as a foil for the interpretation of Aristotelian philosophy. John's sympathy for Averroes has occasionally led past research to project John as a radical Averroist, along with Siger of Brabant (ca. 1240–ca. 1283),[45] and the founder of an Averroist school which included Marsilius and some of John's students, such as John of Göttingen.[46] However, recent scholarship on the reception of Averroes' philosophy in the Latin West has challenged this view.[47]

On 13 November 1316, Pope John XXII granted John a canonry in Senlis.[48] John took up the benefice and spent a short time there in 1323. He soon returned to Paris at the urging of a friend, whom he does not name, although it is possible that his allusion is to Marsilius.[49] John's decision to leave Paris for Senlis made him the target of criticism from the anonymous author of the treatise *Recommentatio civitatis Parisiensis*.[50] John responded with his *Tractatus de laudibus Parisius* (1323), an encomium of Paris, which is built around a detailed comparison between Senlis and Paris and, not surprisingly, describes Paris as superior to Senlis.[51] Given that John dedicated his *Tractatus* to King Charles IV, the *arrière-pensée* behind the composition of the work was most probably to gain the king's favour or ameliorate John's financial situation. The tract features a glowing description of the French capital: the university and its faculties;[52] parts of the city, such as the church of Notre-Dame, the chapel of the king, the Saint-Chapelle, and the royal palace;[53] and the professions, mores, physical characteristics, lifestyle, customs, and dietary habits of the Parisians.[54]

In 1327, John, together with Marsilius, joined Louis of Bavaria's expedition to Italy. On 1 May 1328, John was named by Louis bishop of

Ferrara, although he never took up the appointment.[55] John died at Montalto in September 1328, as Louis's army was marching northward through central Italy.[56]

Muslim and Jewish Influences

One of the greatest challenges associated with the interpretation of the *Defensor pacis* derives from the fact that Marsilius rarely reveals his medieval sources. The present study will identify potential sources of the *Defensor pacis* and cast fresh light on the ties between Marsilius's theory and the medieval Muslim and Jewish traditions of political thought.

As noted earlier, Marsilius has often been portrayed in past research as an 'Averroist,' a view based on the assumption of John of Jandun's active involvement in the composition of the *Defensor pacis*. Recent scholarship, however, has adduced new evidence against this assumption and disputes the existence of 'political Averroism' in general.[57] The notion that Marsilius was influenced by Averroes's political philosophy has come increasingly under critical scrutiny.

In Western Europe, Averroes's commentary on Plato's *Politeia* was first translated into Latin by Elia (Elijah) del Medigo (ca. 1460–97) in the second half of the fifteenth century,[58] and later in the sixteenth century by Jacob Mantinus (Mantino, d. 1549)[59] and the main sources for Averroes's political ideas available in Marsilius's time would have been his commentaries on the *Ethics* and the *Rhetoric*.[60] In addition, a comparative study of Marsilius's and Averroes's political ideas reveals crucial differences in their positions on the eternity of the world; the civic function of rhetoric; the purpose of social life; human felicity; the essential qualities and duties of the model ruler; the capacities for good government; the role and scope of legislation; and the definition of equity.[61] Following Shlomo Pines,[62] Jeannine Quillet argued that Marsilius was influenced not by Averroes but by Al-Fārābī's lost commentary on the *Ethics*, which was translated into Latin by Samuel ben Judah (of Marseilles) in 1321.[63] As attractive as Quillet's thesis may sound, there is no evidence that Marsilius had access to that commentary.

One of the questions thus far largely neglected by scholarly research on Marsilius's sources is that concerning his links with medieval Jewish philosophy, in particular Moses Maimonides' work.[64] The *Guide* had an enduring impact on medieval philosophy, especially on the works of Albert the Great and Thomas Aquinas. Maimonides may be considered to be a purveyor of Averroes's ideas and a pioneer in the use of pagan examples to explain the political dimension of religion.

Chapter Three

Marsilius's Political Theory

Marsilius and Aristotelian Teleology

Marsilius sees the genesis and evolution of the political community as a phenomenon parallel to the course of all natural processes. His notion of the relationship between social life and the natural order takes on a normative significance in this context. Marsilius adopts Aristotle's teleological view of the workings of social life in a mitigated form: in his view, all things man needs are provided by nature. Art has a complementary role to that of nature, which can be actualized through reason and made useful for man's survival. The birth and growth of human communities, government, and the various ways of life proceed from imperfection to perfection in a way that parallels the course of nature.

The creation and ordering of the political community reflect the relationship between social life and nature. Men are equipped by nature with various skills and dispositions. Nature has also not only endowed a single person but many with diverse talents and aptitudes for agriculture, the military, or for the judicial and advisory parts of the political community.[1] Nature produces the raw material that can be used for the purposes of the political community with the mediation of the governing part.[2]

The relationship between nature and social life has broader ramifications for the evolution of social life and the operation of the political community: a sustainable social organization is predicated on the principle that the rightness of every political event and every political decision is to be measured by the criteria of harmony with the order prevailing in nature. A fundamental condition for the endurance of the political community is, according to Marsilius, that the part of the citizenry that wishes its existence (*politizare*)[3] preponderates over the part that wishes the opposite. Marsilius infers from this that the majority of citizens seek the means that are conducive to the longevity and domestic stability of the political community, i.e., the law.[4] For it to be otherwise (i.e., if those in the political community who do not wish for its preservation exceeded those who seek the continued existence of the political community) would amount to an aberration of the natural order and render man's desire for a sufficient life futile.[5]

In the context of his discussion of the arguments in favour and against the existence of a supreme and universal government, Marsilius holds that the heavenly cause favours perhaps the existence of multiple governments in the various parts of the world which are separate from one another in terms of geographical location, language, and morals and customs, in order that the procreation of men does not become excessive. One might perhaps be inclined to think, Marsilius explains, that nature by means of wars and epidemics regulates the procreation of men and the other living beings so that the earth may suffice for their nourishment, which is a strong proof in favour of those who believe in eternal generation.[6]

This statement can be construed as evidence for Marsilius's endorsement of Averroes's doctrine of the eternity of the world.[7] However, this assumption is problematic, given that Marsilius's argument has a plainly hypothetical character. Marsilius does not adopt this idea apodictically, however, and refrains from taking an explicit stance on this question. He stresses instead that perhaps nature, by way of calamities, controls the procreation of the various living species on earth and that if this notion were true, the advocates of the idea of the eternity of the world would find support for their argument.

Marsilius is interested in the process which preceded the emergence of the first human associations: for a well-disposed political community to exist, it is essential that the entire body of the citizens or their *valencior pars* act as the efficient cause of the laws and the government, and that the government operate as the efficient cause of the other sections of the political community.[8] Any deviations from this model lead to anomalies and disturbances, which would lead to the disruption of social order and the destruction of the political community.

The central thrust of Marsilius's political theory is to explore the causal connections involved in natural phenomena and apply a 'genetic' mode of analysing the underlying causes of political events, in particular the creation and growth of political community.[9] Marsilius's challenge of Aristotle's teleology reaches its climax when he turns from the quest for final to efficient causality and gives priority to the efficient cause over the three other types of causes (final, material, and formal). The inquiry into efficient causes serves Marsilius as the starting point for a 'genetic' investigation of political phenomena. Thereby Marsilius anticipates modern ideas on the nexus between efficient causality and political theory.[10] Marsilius's emphasis on efficient causality reflects the methodological postulates of his political theory. The *Defensor pacis* is the work of a medically trained thinker associated with such important figures in the history of late medieval natural philosophy and medicine as Peter of Abano,[11] and a more detailed examination of the methodological principles of Marsilius's theory will illuminate his use of Aristotelian teleology and natural philosophy.[12]

Although Marsilius relies on efficient causality as an Archimedean point for exploring the dynamics of social life, he does not negate finality as perceived by Aristotle. On several occasions, he employs a teleological mode of explaining political phenomena to back up his own positions. He argues, for instance, that if laws are made without the consent of the body of the citizens, then the political community suffers from friction, since the citizens will oppose laws promulgated without their prior approval or consent and those who have made the laws will inevitably become into autocrats. This concept is of central importance for the interpretation of Marsilius's political thought. It is grounded not so much in the assertion of an 'organic' vision of the political community as in the investigation of the process whereby the government comes into being and the differentiation of the parts of the political community takes place.[13]

Another aspect related to Marsilius's methodology is the use of organic metaphors, especially in his exposition of the ideal political organization: just as health is the optimal condition for any living organism, so is tranquility the optimal condition for a stable and lasting social organization established in accordance with reason and presupposes that each part of the community carries out the particular function assigned to it for the sake of the public weal.[14] Just as the heart is responsible for the creation and growth of a living organism and the formation of its various parts and limbs, the entire body of the citizens or its *valencior par* operates as the counterpart of the soul and entrusts the government as the equivalent of the heart with the task to form and differentiate the other parts of the body politic.[15] Marsilius also appeals to the organic analogy to establish the necessity of a single government within the political community: if multiple principles were responsible for the operation of a living organism, the organism would receive conflicting instructions and would either be pulled in different directions or remain in a state of inertia. Likewise, the existence of multiple governments within a single political entity would cause its disintegration and ultimate collapse.[16]

The Origins of Social Life

Marsilius's narrative of the origins of social life is based on a blending of elements from the Augustinian, Stoic, and Aristotelian traditions. Although Aristotle's idea of human sociability formed the standard prelude to most medieval accounts on the origins of human associations, Marsilius dispenses with the Aristotelian topos about man's societal nature.[17] His theory is coloured by the Augustinian perspective and posits that men are confronted with natural dangers and regards mutual support among humans as the fundamental requirement for the acquisition of a complete and sufficient life.

Unlike Aristotle and Cicero, who see man as having a natural inclination to associate with others, Marsilius believes that human associations develop out of men's efforts to satisfy their material wants. Marsilius approximates here the Augustinian account of social origins. Thus Marsilius invokes Aristotle's theory of the origins of social life side by side with Augustine's theological explanation for the origin of human society and identifies the diversity in human desires and the necessity of mutual aid in meeting men's basic needs as the motives behind the formation of communal association.

In his account of the genesis of social life, Marsilius starts from the Aristotelian premise that all men have a natural propensity toward sufficient life and, unless not deformed or otherwise impeded, desire self-sufficiency and seek to avoid what can endanger their existence.[18] To reinforce this idea, Marsilius has recourse to Cicero's assertion that every living organism is endowed by nature with the ability to preserve itself, its body, and its life, to avoid things that seem harmful, and to seek and obtain the things that are necessary for its preservation.[19] This is a clear allusion to the Stoic *oikeiosis* teaching and the notion that man by nature is animated by an impulse for self-preservation and seeks the mans conducive to the preservation of its physical existence and the avoidance of harm.[20]

Marsilius quotes Cicero's dictum that man comes into the world not only for himself but also to serve his native land and his friends. The produce of the earth is intended for man's use, and each man has the obligation to follow the lead of nature and produce common utilities for the general good.[21] However, the primary emphasis of Marsilius's account of the beginnings of social life is on human weakness rather than confraternity and the cultivation of bonds of friendship among the members of society.[22] Marsilius endorses the Augustinian view of human community as the outcome of human frailty. In Marsilius's formulation, man is composed of contrary elements, whose contrary actions and passions work constantly to destroy human substance. Moreover, man is born bare and defenseless and is exposed to the influence of the surrounding air and other elements.[23] To overcome his inadequacy and protect himself from external influences and threats, man needs various kinds of arts, which can be invented, exercised, and developed not by a single individual but only by a number of men. For this reason, men banded together to attain what is beneficial through the exercise of these arts and to avoid what is harmful.[24]

Aristotle does not disregard this aspect of the process of the formation of human society: he defines the *polis* as an aggregate of individuals who aspire to a self-sufficient life.[25] In his view, man strives by nature for socialization since he seeks to provide for his basic needs and secure a good life and happiness through the exercise of moral virtues. Marsilius, by contrast, gives priority to the satisfaction of man's material needs as the basic purpose of human society. From this, Marsilius derives the necessity of the division of labour and the performance of diverse activities conducive to sufficient life, and identifies the ruling part as the agency in charge of monitoring and regulating the operation of the various parts and functional groupings of the community.

Marsilius here stands in a philosophical tradition, the roots of which reach down to Democritos's ideas on need as the prime mover behind the formation of human communities.[26] In Plato's *Protagoras*, Protagoras explains that unlike all other living creatures, man is born naked, unshod, and unarmed. In the presocial phase, men had to obtain knowledge of arts for their survival. They also instituted a religion, created a language, built houses, produced clothing, shoes, and food from the earth, but still lived scattered and isolated from one another and perished because they were unable to defend themselves against wild animals and still lacked political art and the art of warfare which is part of it. At some point, they strove to associate and protect themselves by forming communities. But as soon as they gathered together, they started inflicting injuries on one another and soon regressed to their original condition and started to perish. In order to ensure a harmonious social life, men had to cultivate mutual respect and justice.[27]

Similar ideas occur in Cicero's *De natura deorum* (*On the Nature of the Gods*),[28] and Plutarch's (AD 46–ca. 120) *Moralia* (*Morals*).[29] Origen (185–253/4) in his *Contra Celsum* (*Against Celsus*) contends that unlike animals, which find their food ready and enjoy natural protection, man has been created by God with various needs and is forced to discover and practice arts for his nourishment and protection. The need to obtain life necessities is the driving force behind the emergence of agriculture and the cultivation of vineyards and the arts of gardening, carpentry, and that of the blacksmith, which created tools for the arts aimed to provide for nourishment. Need for protection gave birth to the arts of weaving, wool-carding, spinning, and architecture. The need to transport goods generated the arts of sailing and navigation.[30]

Themistios (ca. 317–ca. 388), a late antique orator and author of commentaries on Aristotle, in an oration to the Byzantine emperor Julian, offers a similar rationale for the birth of the political community and the existence of laws, and his rationale was later reproduced, as will be shown below, by a number of medieval Islamic political theorists. For Themistios, reason is the element that sets humans apart from animals. But men are inferior to animals in terms of corporeal strength, speed, and the effectiveness of the senses. Solon, Lycourgos, Pittacos, Vias, and Cleovoulos were designated as sages not because of their ability to create syllogisms, engage in dialectic discussions about ideas, articulate sophisms, and determine the size of the sun or the motion of the moon, but because they devised and laid down laws and taught what one should do or not do, what to choose or avoid. They also demonstrated that man is not able meet his needs by living in isolation, but that he is a social and political creature and that, for this reason, it is his duty to care for his fatherland, the laws, and the polity.[31]

Ancient Greek theories of human social evolution passed into the medieval Arab world through a *risāla* (treatise or letter) *On Government* (*Risālat Dāmasṭiūs fī al-siyāsa*), which was attributed to Themistios. Although the authenticity of the *risāla* is questionable, its content shows close affinities to Themistios's ideas on the origins of social life which make his authorship quite probable.[32] The *risāla* indicates that human society arises in response to man's biological necessities and subtly de-emphasizes the factor of human gregariousness in the process of social genesis: man has been created by God (*Allāh*) to live within a society, but when people gathered together in cities and engaged in dealings with one another, their habits and ways of conducting themselves were very diverse. God then established laws and duties which they could regard as the ultimate authority. Moreover, he designated rulers as custodians of the laws with the purpose of upholding order, justice, and unity and suppressing strife.[33]

Another Greek thinker who identifies human necessity as the principal cause of the constitution of human society was Nemesios of Emesa (late fourth century). In his *Peri phuseōs anthrōpou* (*On the Nature of Man*), a work that was translated into Latin, Arabic, Syriac, Armenian, and Georgian,[34] Nemesios employs a biological/medical line of reasoning and points out that the human body is composed of four elements and is thus susceptible to all the changes which these elements go through.[35] As a result, man needs food, drink, clothing, shelter for protection from climatic conditions and wild animals as well as medical treatment because of the constant alteration of the qualities and the sensitivity with which the human body has been endowed. Nemesios refers to the Aristotelian idea that man is by nature a civic creature formed to live in a community, but hastens to explain that since no one can be self-sufficient in all respects, a number of men had to come together and found associations in order to join into bonds of social cooperation by practising diverse crafts and sciences, learn from one another, and share what is necessary for life.[36]

Nemesios of Emesa	*Marsilius of Padua*
Quia vero ex corpore est homo, omne autem corpus ex quattuor elementis consistit, necesse in easdem incidere passiones eum, in quas et elementa: in incisionem et transmutationem et fluxum, quae sunt solius corporis; transmutationem quidem quae est secundum qualitatem; fluxum vero evacuatione; transmutationem quidem quae est secundum qualitatem quae est alteratio, dealbatio et denigratio, frigiditas, caliditas et quae sunt	Unde propter ipsum consequendum concluserunt ipsi necessitatemm civilis communitatis, sine qua vivere hoc sufficiens obtineri non potest. Quorum eciam eximius Aristoteles 1° sue Politice cap. 1° dixit: *Omnes ‹homines› ferri ad ipsam, et secundum nature impetum propter hoc*. Quod quamvis experiencia sensata doceat, eius tamen causam quam diximus, inducere volumus distincte magis, dicentes, quod quia homo nascitur compositus ex contra-

talia; fluxum vero evacuatione: evacuatur enim semper animal et per invisibiles poros et per visibiles, de quibus postea dicemus. Necesse igitur aut his quae evacuantur reinferre paria, vel dissolvi animal idigentia eorum quae inducuntur. Siccis autem existentibus et humidis et spiritibus his quae evacuantur, necesse humido et sicco cibo indigere animal et spiritu. Est autem nobis cibus et potus per elementa ex quibus consistimus. Unumquodque enim familiari quidem et simili nutritur, contrario vero curatur (*De natura hominis; traduction de Burgundio de Pise,* 12).

Propter artes autem et disciplinas et eas quae ab his utilitates, nobis invicem indigemus. Sed propterea quia nobis invicem indigemus, in idem multi convenientes participamus a nobis invicem secundum vitae huius necessitates in permutationibus et negotiationibus, quam synodum et cohabitationem civitatem nominant, ut de prope et non a longe eas quae ad invicem sunt utilitates fructificemus. Natura enim gregarium et civile animal factus est homo ; unus enim nullus sufficiens est sibi ipsi ad universa. Manifestum est igitur quod civitates propter negotiationes et disciplinas constitutate sunt. (*De natura hominis; traduction de Burgundio de Pise,* 14).

riis elementis, propter quorum contrarias acciones et passiones quasi continue corrumpitur aliquid ex sua substancia; rursumque quoniam nudus nascitur et inermis, ab excessu continentis aeris et aliorum elementorum possibilis et corruptibilis, quemadmodum dictum est in sciencia naturarum, indiguit artibus diversorum generum et specierum ad declinandum nocumenta predicta. Que quoniam exerceri non possunt, nisi per ipsorum invicem communicacionem, oportuit homines simul congregari ad comodum ex hiis assequendum et incommodum fugiendum (*Defensor pacis* I.iv.3).

Like Marsilius and Nemesios, the great Muslim scientist and geographer al-Bīrūnī (ca. 973–1048) in his *Kitāb al-Jamāhir fī ma'rifat al-Jawāhir* (*Book on Precious Stones and Minerals*) holds that man is composed by nature of different qualities. The soul is most of the time subservient to the temperament of the body, and for this reason each person has a different character. 'Each' thing that comes into existence through the combination or blending of dissimilar elements is doomed to perish as soon as there is no uniting force in it and each element seeks dominate over the rest. All living creatures are subject to injuries and illnesses wrought by the collision of the external and internal elements. Given that man is exposed to external influences and has diverse needs that cannot be met by a one person alone, multiple individuals had to band together in cities. God has endowed each person with various dispositions and talents, otherwise uniformity would lead to the destruction of the species. Due to the disparity in men's intentions and desires, their occupations and crafts differ too.[37] Although all men come from the same ancestor, they are susceptible to contention and envy which stem from the differences in their temperaments and dispositions. Al-Bīrūnī establishes on the basis of these considerations the necessity of a ruler whose prime function consists in maintaining order and justice and eliminating strife.[38]

Similar sentimenst are echoed in Jewish philosophical discourse. In the *Guide of the Perplexed* (2:40; 3:27) Maimonides reiterates Aristotle's assertion of man's political nature.[39] At the same time, though, he employs a formula similar to that of Themistios: a man who exists in isolation loses control over his conduct, becomes like a wild animal, and will perish unless he by accident finds something to eat. Nourishment requires the exercise of some art and management that cannot be made perfect except through thought and perspicacity, as well as with the help of various tools and individuals, each one of whom engages in one single occupation. For this reason, humans need someone to rule and unify them so that their society should be orderly and have continued existence and so that the various individuals should assist each other (1:72).

Men, unlike animals, are, by Maimonides' account, characterized by diversity and form associations because of their need for mutual cooperation and aid. Just like his Muslim predecessors, Maimonides sees human society as the locus for cooperative labour and exchange of products for the sake of the common benefit. But he also recognizes that human diversity generates domestic strife and instability. From this, he deduces the necessity of a ruler whose duty is to guarantee the tranquility and internal order of the political community, curb excesses in human actions, and prescribe actions and moral habits (2:40).

Intriguingly, Maimonides invests the standard formula about human sociability with associations to Aristotle's concept of corrective (rectificatory) justice.[40] The ruler's chief duty, accordingly, is to redress grievances, to reduce that which is excessive, and to prescribe actions and moral habits that all individuals must always practice in the same way, so that the natural diversity between the members of the political community is concealed and that the community becomes well-ordered. Maimonides underscores the need for the ruler to mete out punishments to anyone who has done wrong to someone else and to give the offender the same treatment he gave to someone else. Moreover, he recommends appointing judges in every city and having a ruler who would be held in awe. The ruler would restrain his people by various means and enhance the authority of the judges; in his turn, he will draw strength from them (2:40).

Ptolemy of Lucca (Tolomeo da Lucca, ca. 1236–1327) adumbrated Marsilius's theory of the origins of human society in his continuation of Aquinas's (ca. 1225–74) *De regimine principum* (*On the Government of Rulers*, ca. 1300).[41] Ptolemy presents the emergence of human associations in terms very similar to those in the *Defensor pacis*: he rehearses the standard Aristotelian view of human sociability, but at the same time postulates human need to be the driving force that prompts men to seek intercourse with their fellow-beings, for the purpose of procuring the necessities of life.[42]

Like Marsilius, Ptolemy points out that human associations grow out of human frailty: animals are endowed by nature with the capacity to defend themselves and the instinct to avoid what is harmful and seek what is beneficial to their existence and, as such, they stand in no need of guidance. But men lack a natural instinct for what is proportionate to their nature and so need guidance about such things.[43] Unlike animals and plants, they are born naked and have needs that impel them to live together in order to to find shelter and cover their needs.[44] Finally, humans are often afflicted by diseases, and unlike animals that are equipped by nature with the ability to know which herbs and other things are conducive to their health, they need medical art, physicians, and the assistance of others.[45]

Marsilius considers the connection between male and female in creating the first household to be the first and smallest union of human beings and the one from which all others came into being. When procreation led to overcrowding within a single household, additional households were created. A number of households then came together to form villages or hamlets.[46] By drawing a line of demarcation between the house (*domus*), on the one hand, and the village (*vicus*) or settlements (*vicinia*) and the first community (*communitas*), on the other, Marsilius diverges from Aristotle,[47] who attributes the origin of the political community to the natural growth of social life beginning with the family, which he identifies as the first type of community.[48]

Consistent with his notion that the political community is a union of individuals intended to provide for a sufficient life, it is not accidental that Marsilius, unlike Aristotle, does not ascribe to the family the status of a community: due to the small number of its members, the household lacks differentiation of function and cannot supply all the material resources needed for a self-contented life. The family and the political community (*civilis communitas* or *perfecta communitas* or *civitas*)[49] differ with respect to their internal organization and the existence of an agency in charge of resolving disputes that break out among the citizens and are characteristic of every kind of human association.[50] For Marsilius, then, the main differences between the family and the community concern the number of inhabitants or the size of the territory they inhabit, and the specialization of function, which are the determinants of the progression to more complex forms of human association.

Another major *differentia* between the family and community noted by Marsilius is that the family is, in essence, the property of the *paterfamilias* and, as such, does not allow for civil relations within the household setting. The family is characterized by the absolute authority of the *paterfamilias* over the other members of the household. All the decisions over misdeeds occurring within the household was made according to the discretion or judgment of the *paterfamilias*.[51] In the village community, in contrast, the elder had to inflict punishments or compensations for the misdeeds that were committed or else strife and social disruption would occur. The elder had to rule on the affairs of the community and its utility according to a rational arrangement or according to a 'quasi-natural law' (*quasi-naturalis lex*); it appeared fair to everyone to act, according to a 'certain' *equitas*, without detailed investigation only according to the reason and a certain obligation of the society.[52] Marsilius understands 'quasi-natural law' to be an unwritten law that found validity only in the first phases of social coexistence.[53]

Rhetoric and the Genesis of Civil Life

Having established the differences between the family and the community, Marsilius proceeds to outline the process whereby the first communities were created: the heads of households (*patresfamilias*) were summoned not by the coercive authority of one or many individuals, but on the persuasion or exhortation of prudent men (*prudentes*). Those persons took the initiative to establish the first communities and were by nature endowed with a special inclination for that task. They tried to guide men gradually or all at once to a community created on the agreement of the majority.[54] The community is in this respect the conjoint product of the *prudentes* and the first *patresfamilias*, since the founding process is initiated by the *prudentes*, but the final decision for the formation of the community is made by the leaders of the households.[55]

In order to elucidate the premises that underpin Marsilius's account of social genesis, it will be instructive to look at how it relates to other medieval and early modern accounts of the beginnings of human society.[56] Medieval and early modern ideas on social genesis can be classified into three main strains: one that followed the ancient Greek notion of the founder of the political community; a second one grounded in Cicero's theory that men formed communities and appointed rulers based on mutual consent; and a third one, also inspired by Cicero, that ascribed the initial formation of human communities and appointment of rulers to the joint efforts of the first heads of households and the primordial orators.

Aristotle, particularly in his *Politics*, is committed to the idea of the founding of the *polis* through a heroic lawgiver (*nomothetēs*), such as Minos of Crete, Lycourgos of Sparta, and Theseus.[57] Thus, Aristotle dispenses with a detailed description of the process whereby the first cities were founded and confines himself to stating that the person who first instituted a political association is the best of benefactors, although he does not explicate the process whereby the first *poleis* were created.[58] In books 7 and 8 of the *Politics*, Aristotle sets out a series of conditions for the perfect city, such as a medium-sized population, a territory of a moderate size, protected by sea and land and suitable for importing commodities that it does not itself produce and to export its own surplus products, a certain amount of naval power, and people of high spirit, skill, and intelligence.[59]

The motif of the founder is a recurrent theme in medieval Arabic political writing. Al-Fārābī, for example, assigns to the creator of the city a range of tasks: from leading his citizens to virtue by monitoring and coordinating the various activities performed by the members of the city, to creating a language.[60]

In the Latin tradition, Thomas Aquinas exemplifies the group of medieval thinkers who subscribed to Aristotle's vision of the founder of the city. In his *De Regno* (*On Kingship*), Aquinas points out that a vital aspect of the office of the king is to found a city or kingdom. Similar to Aristotle, Aquinas presents miscellaneous recommendations for the ideal city: a temperate region conducive to health, military defense, and civil life; a region with healthful air; abundant food supplies through the fertility of the region; and a pleasant location (large fields in the plains, fruitful trees, conspicuous nearby mountains, agreeable glades, and good water irrigation) so that its inhabitants are not likely to desert it.[61]

The motif of the hero-founder forms a consistent thread in a number of early modern political writings. Niccolò Machiavelli (1469–1527) describes the founding of a republic or of a principality as the achievement of a single individual. As exempla of founders (*ordinatori di republiche*), he mentions Moses, Cyrus, Romulus, and Theseus.[62] The idea of the hero-founder was particularly influential on some of the proponents of the 'Myth of Venice,' i.e., the vision of the Venetian constitution as the harmonious blending of the monarchical, aristocratic, and democratic elements.[63] One of the writers to employ the notion of the founder of the state in connection with the 'Myth of Venice' was the Byzantine scholar George of Trebizond (1396–ca. 1472). George translated Plato's *Laws* in the early 1450s at the behest of Pope Nicholas V (1397–1455, r. 1447–55). In a letter to his former patron, the humanist Francesco Barbaro (ca. 1398–1454), in December 1451, George expressed the view that the founders of Venice had relied on the *Laws*, because the Venetian constitution was founded on Plato's maxim that the durability of a regime is contingent on the harmonious blending of the three principal forms of government: monarchy, aristocracy, and democracy. Barbaro advised George to add an introduction to the translation, to expand upon the affinities between the Venetian constitution and Plato's political ideas, and to dedicate the translation to the Venetian Republic so that he would thereby receive remuneration in return. In 1452, George presented a dedication to Barbaro and in the preface he depicted the constitution of the *Serenissima* as the embodiment of the ancient notion of the mixed constitution.[64] After Barbaro's death in 1454, George, in 1460, dedicated his translation to the

Doge and received by decree of the Senate the chair of humanities and rhetoric in the School of San Marco.

A substantial portion of George's discussion of Venice's constitutional arrangements is a eulogy of the 'founding fathers' of the *Serenissima*: they had Platonic erudition and prudently laid down procedures akin to those prescribed by Plato. Neither before Plato nor since Plato's time has there ever been introduced such complex voting procedures for the selection of the magistrates as the ones followed in Venice. Venice's founders read and understood Plato, for in those days almost all of Italy knew the Greek language. The men of the higher nobility who came together to found Venice and sought to avert the iniquities of the times were well versed both in Greek and Latin literature. The most stunning thing is that they implemented everything of which they had approved and did this with better results than Plato himself. George infers from this that the founders of the *Serenissima* had exceptional natural talent, learning, and practical experience and were endowed with every kind of virtue.[65]

As George phrases it, Plato had no hope that his laws would ever be applied unless the people were coerced to observe them by a tyrant who would install himself as a ruler with such self-control that, even while he was alive, his subjects would become accustomed to exercising this freedom.[66] The founders of Venice outshone all other men in every virtue as well as in civil science, inasmuch as they implemented the Platonic idea of the ideal city, not coerced by a tyrant but guided by their inner beliefs, and they eventually managed to create a city that was far better than the one envisioned by Plato.[67]

The theme of the founder reappears in Gasparo Contarini's (1483–1542) *De magistratibus et republica Venetorum* (*On the Magistrates and Republic of the Venetians*, 1543), the first systematic apologia for Venice's mixed constitution. Contarini traces the founding of the *Serenissima* to the union of some wise and virtuous men who came together driven by the desire to establish and expand their city without considering their personal glory or interest and prudently laid down institutions and laws that secured the long duration of Venice.[68] While one of George of Trebizond's and Contarini's dominant concerns was to shore up the political role of the Venetian nobility, hence the reference to multiple founders, the Florentine humanist Donato Giannotti (1492–1573), in his *Della Republica fiorentina* (*On the Florentine Republic*), put forward a variant of the theory of mixed constitution that emphasizes the value of the 'democratic' component.

Giannotti speaks of ancient lawgivers and institutors of states who, unlike reformers, encountered smaller difficulties when they endeavoured to rule people who had not previously been subject to any laws or who had abandoned their homelands and sought to dwell in other regions. In the former case, men lived like beasts and wandering beings. Thus, they accepted the laws proposed to them and agreed to constitute human associations for the sake of mutual convenience.[69] In the latter case, they agreed, after leaving their homelands, to abandon their old laws and to follow new ones. By contrast, the person who undertakes to organize an existing state with tested laws is confronted with great challenges. In promulgating laws, he needs to know not only what is beneficial for the citizens but also the defects of which he tries to rid them. An additional challenge for the reformer of a state derives from the fact that some persons insist on adhering to the old laws and oppose new ones. Lycourgos resorted to violence to break resistance against his laws, and Numa had to show to the Romans that his laws had been approved by God.[70]

For Giannotti, then, it is incumbent upon lawgivers and founders of states to provide for the maintenance of the state and be aware of the two causes that account for its downfall: dissension and disorder intrinsic to the state; and attacks from outside. Lawgivers and founders must also identify solutions for both the intrinsic and extrinsic causes by upholding a stable social order and building an efficient army, respectively. Sparta as founded by Lycourgos lasted for eight hundred years because no changes occurred within that city and the Spartans dealt successfully with external threats, whereas Romulus sought to ensure the durability of Rome by expanding the empire.[71] Giannotti compares the state to a natural body that is first produced by nature and then molded by art.[72] Accordingly, the sagacious founder of a republic operates like a physician who imitates nature[73] and sets himself the task of finding proper remedies for every ill of the republic.[74]

While Aristotle explains the creation of human associations as the work of a single individual, another matrix of the theory about the contractual origin of social life can be found in Cicero. Cicero's exposition of the emergence of the commonwealth can be summed up in the following formula that was employed in varying versions in medieval debates on the origin of human society: in the presocial condition, men lived dispersed but had various wants and needed to associate with others in order to sustain themselves and lead a sufficient life;[75] they subsequently formed communities based upon agreement about what is just and upon a communion of wellbeing; but faction and dissension occurred; therefore, men decided to institute a ruler who would protect them against those driven by greed and guarantee domestic stability.

In his *De re publica* (*On the Commonwealth*) I.39, Cicero has the Roman general Scipio Aemilianus (Scipio Africanus the Younger, ca. 184–129 BC) express the idea that a commonwealth (*res publica*) is the property of a people (*populus*); but a people is not a random congregation of human beings, but, rather, a multitude of men associated with each other in an agreement on justice and a share in the common utility.[76]

Cicero's theory encapsulates two elements that were used by a number of medieval and early modern political theorists who envisioned the genesis of human societies on the basis of a covenant: the agreement with respect to what is just (*consensus iuris*); and the share in the common advantage (*communio utilitatis*).[77] It served as the focus for the development of two sets of ideas concerning the emergence of human associations: a number of authors relied on Cicero and drew a link between the genesis and evolution of social life and the emergence of monarchical rule in consonance with natural law. Another group of thinkers employed the Ciceronian theory of the *raison d'être* of social life in a radically different direction to articulate a 'republican' vision of the ideal polity and depict the body of the citizens as the only legitimate source of political authority.

In the primeval condition, as delineated in Cicero's *De inventione* (*On Discovering Arguments*), men roamed the fields like beasts and lived on wild fare. They did nothing according to reason but relied primarily on physical strength. Life in the presocial stage was characterized by the total absence of divine worship, social duties, and the institution of marriage. No man regarded children as his own, nor did men realize the benefits of an equitable law.[78] Cicero's *Pro Sestio* ([*Speech in*] *Defense of Publius Sestius*) contains a similar account of life in the time before natural or civil law had been laid down, when men roved and lived dispersed all over the earth. They possessed solely the goods they acquired by physical force and violence and retained through murder and bloodshed. When those who at first appeared to excel in virtue and practical intelligence perceived that humankind can by nature be taught, they brought together into one place those who had been living scattered and led them from their bestial condition to one of justice and humanity. The discovery of divine and human law gave rise to things conducive to the public welfare, the creation of human associations, and the establishment of cities surrounded by walls.[79]

Cicero underscores the role of the orator as a catalyst in the process of founding a community. He sees man's innate tendency to live in association with others as rooted in the faculties of reason and speech.[80] Along these lines, Cicero conceives of the process whereby men band together into society as one of teaching and learning, communicating, discussing, and reasoning.[81] At a certain point, a great and wise man recognized the potential of the human mind if it could be develop and improved it by means of instruction. He assembled men who were previously living dispersed in the fields and hidden away in sylvan retreats. He subsequently introduced them to various occupations, although they initially resisted because the idea of such occupations was novel. By diligently using reason and eloquence, he captured men's attention and transformed them from wild savages into suave and gentle people.[82] Following the establishment of city life, laws and customs were instituted, and then the equitable distribution of private rights took place and a social system was set up.[83]

Cicero's scenario about the origins of social life is not confined to the phase that preceded the establishment of human associations. Oratory is not only important for the creation of the first communities but also constitutes a *conditio sine qua non* for the endurance of a well-run society. After the founding of the first cities, oratory was used to induce people to keep faith, to uphold justice, to become accustomed to obey others voluntarily, and to realize that they not only must work for the common advantage but must even sacrifice their lives in service to the commonwealth.[84]

Cicero sees a connection between the institution of the commonwealth and the protection of private property: as he phrases it, the main reason for the establishment of the commonwealth and government was to secure individual property rights. For, although men were guided by nature to join together and create communities, it was in the hope of safeguarding their possessions that they sought the protection of cities.[85] Cicero expresses the idea that men of integrity were appointed rulers so that the people might enjoy justice. Because the multitude was oppressed by the strong, they turned for protection to a man who excelled in virtue. That person prevented the mistreatment of the vulnerable members of society and laid down equitable conditions in order to ensure equality between strong and weak. The rationale behind the promulgation of laws was the same as that behind the appointment of kings: if the people secured their end at the hands of one just and good man, they were content with that, but when that did not happen, laws were invented that applied universally to all men and at all times.[86]

Cicero's ideas on the emergence of the commonwealth were transmitted to Latin Europe via two channels: Augustine's (354–430) *De civitate Dei* (*On the City of God*) and Isidore of Seville's (ca. 560–636) *Etymologiae* (*Etymologies*). Augustine found in Cicero's definition of the commonwealth a formidable weapon in his polemic against Rome's expansion: in his view, Rome had never been a true *res publica*, because it lacked justice.[87] Isidore reproduces Cicero's proposition that the *populus* is an association of men formed by agreement on what is just and by willing association[88] and defined the *civitas* as a multitude of people held together by a bond of association.[89]

Within the group of thinkers who subscribed to Cicero's account of the creation of human association, I will distinguish two major strands: a number of authors followed Cicero and posited a link between the genesis and evolution of social life and the emergence of monarchical government in consonance with natural law. Another group of thinkers employed the Ciceronian theory of the *raison d'être* of social life in a startlingly different direction to articulate a 'republican' vision of the ideal polity and elevate the body of the citizens to the sole legitimate source of authority within the political community.

One of the first thinkers to rely on Cicero to picture the creation of the political community in contractual terms was John Duns Scotus (ca. 1265–1308). Although Aristotle's idea of man's natural sociability forms the standard prelude to most medieval accounts on the origins of human associations,[90] Scotus carries on the Augustinian tradition and presents the political community as a remedy for sin (*remedium peccati*). He then expatiates on the differences between paternal (*auctoritas paterna*) and political authority (*auctoritas politica*): the former derives its jurisdiction from natural law; the latter can be exercised by a single person or a group of persons on the basis of a social pact. Scotus conceives of the first human communities as resulting from a pact among individuals who previously were not related by consanguinity or in any other way. 'Strangers' gathered together to found and live in a city. After realizing that they could not be well ruled without some kind of authority, they amicably agreed to entrust their community to a person or to a group. Just positive laws are made by a man who has prudence in himself or in his counselors and has acquired authority in one of the aforementioned ways.[91]

In his *De regia potestate et papali* (*On Royal and Papal Power*, 1302/3),

John of Paris (Quidort) (ca. 1255–1306) built on Cicero's *De inventione* to depict the formation of the first communities in contractual terms, while articulating a justification of kingship as deriving from natural law (*ius naturale*) and the law of nations (*ius gentium*).[92] John restates the Aristotelian dictum that man is by nature a political and civil creature, as shown by his insufficiency with regard to food, clothing, and shelter and from speech which is directed to one another.[93] Man is naturally made for living in a community, especially one that can be sufficient for all human needs, as is the case with a city or kingdom. Before the time of Belus and Ninus, people lived in the manner of beasts, without any rule. Men who had a greater capacity for using reason and were driven by compassion for others undertook by arguments to persuade their fellow men to live in a cooperative society under a ruler. Once people established communities, they complied with specific laws which are called the 'law of nations.'[94] A community in which each of its members pursues his own self-interest is susceptible to sedition and ultimately doomed to fall apart unless directed at the common interest by a single person, just like the human body decays unless there is a common force in it to direct it to the common good of its various organs and members.[95]

In his *De ortu et fine imperii Romani* (*On the Rise and End of the Roman Empire*) (around 1312) Engelbert of Admont (ca. 1250–1332) follows Cicero and explains the genesis of kingdoms (*regna*) and principalities (*principatus*) according to the order of nature: in the first age of the world, men were induced by nature and reason and compelled by the experience of natural needs to dwell together in secure locations and territories and live with the same language, way of life, and customs. They selected and appointed someone from among themselves who excelled in reason and intellect to guide, protect, and preserve the rest of the multitude. The members of the first community obeyed this chosen leader and agreed by a pact and bond of subjection (*pactum et vinculum subiectionis*) to be ruled by him and to live under his protection.[96]

The most analytically refined account of the birth of the political community was articulated by Giles of Rome (Aegidius Romanus). In his *De regimine principum* (*On the Government of Rulers*, written between 1277 and 1280), Giles enumerates three modes in which political communities and kingdoms emerged: 1) an increase in progeny led to the expansion of the household to a village, a number of villages established a city, and a number of cities united to establish the first kingdoms; 2) an agreement (*concordia*) among those who created a city or a kingdom; 3) a violent seizure of power and authority by a tyrant. With regard to the first mode, Giles refers to Aristotle's *Politics* (1252b22–24) and notes that, in the old times, people lived dispersed.[97] At some point, they agreed to establish a city in order to attain a sufficient life. In the course of time, a number of cities and encampments joined together and agreed, driven by fear of enemies, to unite under a king. According to Giles, this is the most natural way in which political communities and kingdoms emerge. The scheme of evolution household-hamlet-city-kingdom conforms to the dictates of nature and reaches its apex in the establishment of kingship. The natural impetus to secure self-sufficiency and form human associations led men to set up an authority and to establish kingship in order to lead a peaceful life and to protect themselves from external enemies. The second mode whereby power and authority came into being is also natural: it involves mutual agreement among men who are inclined by nature to communal living. Communities that are not governed by a king, Giles observes, suffer from wars and are susceptible to civil strife and discord. This gives rise to the third mode – violence. When men lived scattered, some among them rose up and sought to rule by tyrannical means and force over the others. Such men forced others to unite and establish a city. By using violence, they assumed authority, took over other cities, and installed themselves as kings.[98]

In his *De ecclesiastica potestate* (*On Ecclesiastical Power*, 1302), Giles speaks of a primordial condition in which there was no private possession fixed by law but which, instead, was governed by mutual agreement, which concerned solely the partitioning and division of the earth. As the number of men increased, it became necessary to broaden the scope of such pacts and agreements. At a later stage, when men began to exercise dominion over the earth and became kings, laws were laid down to contain all this and include additional arrangements.[99]

Cicero's teaching about the emergence of social life formed the basis for an extensive body of political literature that presents the emergence of social life and the subsequent establishment of authority as a process initiated by rhetorically gifted individuals who assembled their fellow men and persuaded them to band together and create a community.[100] As early as the twelfth century, Thierry of Chartres (1085–ca. 1155) reproduced Cicero's exposition of the primal condition of humankind: there was a certain time at the beginning of the world, during which men lived in an original condition like wild animals. They did not engage in the study of wisdom, nor did they exercise reason; instead, they relied solely on their physical strength. Eventually, a wise and eloquent man altered the original state. He brought people together to live in conformity with law and instructed the assembled persons to live according to right laws.[101]

This conception of the genesis of human associations gained wide currency in the Italian context. Indicative of the increasing importance attached to oratory as an essential ingredient of the civil life of central and northern Italy is the production of an extensive body of advice literature intended for the chief municipal magistrates (*podestà*) and officials of the communes in the thirteenth century.[102] These developments were stimulated by two factors: the circulation of Cicero's *De inventione* and the pseudo-Ciceronian *Rhetorica ad Herennium* which was attributed to Cicero;[103] and the emergence of the *ars dictaminis* in the late eleventh and early twelfth centuries as a branch of rhetoric concerned with the composition of letters and public documents that was destined to become an integral part of the communal administration and often served as a model for epistles in Latin within the circles of early humanists.[104]

A large number of treatises and manuals on the art of letter-writing, which were produced since the beginning of the twelfth century by letter-writers and instructors (*dictatores*), contain sample speeches and letters for various occasions and reflections on the civic function of oratory.[105] The civic dimension of rhetoric forms a prominent theme of the *podestà* literature as well.[106] The *Oculus pastoralis* (written by an anonymous author in 1180/90)[107] and John of Viterbo's *Liber de regimine civitatum* (ca. 1228, *Book on the Government of Cities*)[108] contain model speeches for various occasions.[109] The most enthusiastic advocate of the notion of rhetoric as an ingredient of efficient government was Brunetto Latini (ca. 1220–94). In his *Li Livres dou Tresor* (*The Books of the Treasure*, ca. 1266), Latini invokers Cicero's view that rhetoric is the most important science related to the government of the city and identifies oratory as a prime condition for the formation of every form of human association as well as for the application of justice and harmonious social interaction.[110] In Latini's opinion, the first cities were formed to offer protection against those people who coveted their neighbours' goods or, driven by pride, sought to overpower the weak. People began building houses, cities, and fortresses and enclosed them with walls and ditches.[111] They also instituted customs, laws, and rights that were common to all the members of the city.[112]

Drawing on Cicero, Latini imagines that in the beginning, men lived dispersed in caves like wild animals, without houses, without knowledge of God, without heed to marriage, and without knowing father or son. At some point, a wise man spoke to his fellow men, showed them the greatness of man and the dignity of reason, and instructed them how to live in one place and to maintain reason and justice. With his eloquence and good sense, he was like a second God who created the world through the order of human companionship.[113] As an example, Latini mentions Amphion, the founder of Athens, who with his good words brought men together in that city.[114]

The bond between oratory and wisdom is for Latini of paramount significance not only for the creation of human society but also for its duration. Latini declares discord and internecine strife to be constant features of every type of human association, which generate conflict and can cause the ultimate demise of the political community. The perils and conflicts involved in human social activity can be forestalled if the head of the city tries to impress upon the citizens the importance of domestic peace and alerts them to the nefarious effects of war, and demonstrates that civic concord is the foundation of a healthy and flourishing society.[115]

Marsilius omits the part of Cicero's account that deals with human condition prior to the emergence of social life. He begins his narrative of the rise of human associations with the creation of the first families. He draws on Cicero's account of social genesis to depict the emergence of the first communities as the result of synergistic action by rhetorically gifted individuals who took the initiative to summon the *patresfamilias* and persuaded them to enter into communal life. Likewise, he echoes Cicero's description of the organization of the first communities in his description of the village and the birth and evolution of human associations on the basis of a convention for the sake of mutual advantage; and his notion of the political community as an assemblage of persons who are united by mutual commitment to serve the common good and share an agreement with respect to justice.

The Purpose of the Political Community

The political community is, according to Marsilius, the necessary precondition for a complete and self-sufficient life. The necessities of life can only be obtained by a number of persons. Marsilius reckons the establishment of different orders (*ordines*) or professions (*officia*) to be a prerequisite for a sufficient life.[116] The community also needs various conveniences, repairs, and the preservation of material supplies both in times of peace as well as in war. Men need to cooperate in order to secure the benefits of a division of labour and enjoy material sufficiency. The existence of a cohesive and prosperous political community thus requires the harmonious interchange of functions among the citizens (*communicatio ipsorum invicem suorum operum*).[117]

The political community is composed of dissimilar groupings with differing interests and dispositions and suffers from internecine conflict and disputes, the settlement of which is indispensable for its preservation. Social harmony depends on the existence of mechanisms and a set of rules designed to regulate the interaction among the members of society as well as on an agency in charge of enforcing the laws, restraining malefactors, and repelling internal and external menaces.[118]

Marsilius's definition of the purpose of the political community as the satisfaction of material needs and functional division of labour has little in common with Aristotle's ideas about the good life and the ultimate end of the city. The political community must provide for human felicity not only in the temporal or earthly life, but also in the eternal life and the world to come. Accordingly, it entrusts certain persons with the spiritual instruction of the citizens.[119] For Aristotle on the other hand, true happiness involves contemplative activity. The political community has accordingly to make sure that all citizens are able to devote themselves to a theoretical (contemplative) life.[120]

The Peace and Tranquility of the Political Community

Marsilius's notion of the good life has far-reaching ramifications for his ideas on peace and domestic tranquility. For Aristotle, peace and leisure are preconditions in the pursuit of supreme felicity through the development of speculative activity.[121] Marsilius in contrast defines tranquility (*tranquillitas*) as the antithesis of discord (*discordia*), i.e., as the internal stability and equilibrium of the political community.[122] Unlike Aristotle, Marsilius looks upon peace from a socioeconomic point view, i.e., as the foundation for the harmonious coexistence of the members of society.[123]

Leisure is for Marsilius a prerequisite for a) those who are older and experienced in practical affairs, i.e., the *prudentes*, to discover the laws (I.xii.2); b) liberal activities (*opera libera*) (I.xiii.4); c) cultivating the essential virtues of rulership (I.xvi.21); and d) inquiring into and deciding issues related to the common good (I.xvii.4). Marsilius certainly does not downplay the importance of leisure as a requirement for active involvement in civic affairs, but he disassociates leisure and contemplation. Leisure (*scholē*) presupposes the same activities which those who are constantly concerned with fulfilling their daily needs by labour simply cannot pursue.[124] There may be a faint echo of the Ciceronian notion of the linkage between leisure and engaged civic involvement.[125]

To explicate his notion of tranquility, Marsilius, like Aristotle, has recourse to organic imagery: he analogizes the political community to a living organism, whose health depends on the uniform growth of its individual parts and organs.[126] Just as health is the optimal condition of a living organism, so is tranquility the best condition of a political community that operates in conformity with human reason. Given that the political community is composed of various parts with diverse functions, it resembles a living organism whose well-being and proper functioning depends on the unhindered collaboration among its constituent parts.[127]

Marsilius's deployment of the body metaphor in the context of the discussion of civic tranquility and peace involves crucial departures from Aristotle. Marsilius is primarily interested in the functional implications of the organic analogy and by placing such a strong emphasis on the mutual dependency of the segments of the body politic, he takes issue with Aristotle's teaching concerning the hierarchy of ends. Marsilius differentiates the parts of the political community according to the criterion of their functions, arguing that the lower functions direct and create the basic requirements for the existence of those 'parts,' which strive after higher goals. However, Marsilius does not go so far as to construct a rigid hierarchy among them and advocates instead an inclusive notion of citizenship that encourages broad participation in civic affairs.[128]

Marsilius argues that those parts that perform noble or more complete activities depend on those that exercise a less complete function. Once again, Marsilius relies on the biological metaphor to challenge the notion of the hierarchy of ends and illustrate the functional interrelationship among the various parts of society; an idea which, as will be shown later, is central to his vision of the desirable social organization and his account of the criteria for citizenship: the eye is a more perfect organ than the hands or feet, because it performs a more perfect function; however, it needs the hands and feet and receives action or motion from them. At the same time, the hands and feet depend on the eye, because they need its guidance toward the goal to which they move or are moved. In similar fashion, the government and the lower parts of the body politic are interconnected, since the government is dependent on the activities of the lower parts of the community and the latter depend on the operation of the reigning part.[129]

Second, unlike Aristotle, Marsilius divests the concept of social tranquility from any moral connotations. Marsilius sees social peace as coterminous with the harmonious coexistence of the various segments of the body politic, so that all its members can satisfy their material needs. Marsilius does not consider tranquility, however, to be a prerequisite for the existence of a political community devoted to a moral end, as Aristotle and his Scholastic interpreters did.[130]

Aristotle uses two different terms to designate political unrest and constitutional transmutation: 1) *metavolē* (*transmutatio*), which signifies constitutional transformation or the overthrow of the existing constitution and its replacement with another one;[131] and 2) *stasis* (*seditio*), 'faction.'[132] The *stasis* concept has strong biological connotations and signifies the dysfunction of an organism because of an illness. Aristotle's transposes it to the context of constitutional change to indicate the decay of the body politic due to the disproportionate increase or decrease of a social group.[133]

Aristotle compares the relationship among the various social groupings to the one among the limbs and members of a physical organism. The political community is thus conceived of as a replica of a natural or physical body, whose health and integrity depend on the proper functioning of its individual parts.[134] Thus, just as the different combinations of the bodily parts and organs generate various kinds of animals, in likewise fashion the various combinations of the parts of the political community produce a variety of constitutional forms.[135] Constitutional changes originate, in Aristotle's opinion, from the asymmetrical growth of a part of the body politic, especially without its being noticed, just as the disproportionate increase of a bodily member in terms of size and quality disturbs the symmetry and function of the entire organism.[136]

Aristotle identifies the wealthy and the poor as the two main constituent parts of the political community.[137] Accordingly, he identifies the asymmetrical growth of the segments of the body politic as one of the seven principal causes of civil disturbances and constitutional change.[138] Contention between rich and poor for political power is a persistent feature of any type of community and affects the nature of the constitution, giving rise to democracy or oligarchy.[139] For Aristotle, permanent stability in any form of government is contingent on the existence of a middle class numerically exceeding the two extreme classes together, or just one of them, because the well-off are unlikely to ally with the poor against the middle class, as neither class wishes to be subject to the other and will never take turns governing because they distrust each other.[140] Large cities are devoid of factions because they have a strong middle class, unlike small cities in which the population can easily be divided into two groups.[141]

The relationship between these two groups determines the specific configuration and the social and political organization of the community. Aristotle thus recommends in his discussion of the extreme form of democracy[142] the financial aid of the poor – with the proviso that the distribution of revenue among the poor must happen in such a way that all classes agree to.[143] For Aristotle, then, the existence of a strong middle class is the key to domestic stability and political security, as it can be instrumental in upholding the fragile balance between the quantitatively superior lower class and the qualitatively superior strata and neutralizes, soothes, or mitigates social tensions.[144] Aristotle sees the existence of a strong middle class as a remedy against revolution, for where the middle class is dominant, the less likely it is that insurrections and strife occur.[145]

Marsilius concurs with his Aristotle on the view that inequality is one of the prime causes of disharmony and strife within human society, since groups that are unequal do not share power equally. But at the same time, he dissents from Aristotle's theory of *stasis* in setting forth a novel explanation for the causes of the social maladies that afflicted the Italian city states of his time against the background of the papacy's claims to intervene in temporal affairs, which Marsilius identifies as the unique and hidden cause of the discord in his own day which neither Aristotle nor any other ancient philosopher could have foreseen or anticipated.[146]

With this assessment, Marsilius stands apart from most of the Italian authors of his time who emphasize the economic motives of civic discord. Like Aristotle, late medieval writers ascribe the factionalism that pervaded the political life of the Italian city states to the rivalry between rich and poor. An interesting example is Benzo d'Alessandria (fl. 1310–30), who served as chancellor for Cangrande della Scala at Verona. In his *Chronicon*, he touches upon the reasons for domestic turbulence in some of his contemporary Italian cities such as Milan, Pavia, Lodi, Padova, Vercelli, Genoa, and Bergamo. Benzo comes to the grim conclusion that discord and social degeneracy had permeated the civic life of most Italian city states so deeply that there was no remedy.[147]

Strife and internal division were the major political ills that gripped Padua, one of the last bastions of Italy's communal tradition, at the turn of the thirteenth century. In the wake of the emergence of the *signoria,* a form of despotic and permanent one-person rule, in most cities of northern Italy in the second half of the thirteenth century,[148] Italian writers engaged in sustained reflection on the origins of the friction and social crisis that afflicted late medieval Italy and resulted in the eclipse of communal government.[149] The Paduan jurist and chronicler Giovanni da Nono (1276–ca. 1346) points in his *De generatione aliquorum civium urbis Padue, tam nobilium, quam ignobilium,* the third part of his chronicle *Liber ludi fortunae* (ca. 1318), to avarice and moral dissolution as the principal causes of the erosion of civil life and the decay of the Paduan society in his own day.[150] A number of authors and *literati,* especially in Padua, looked to Aristotle's œuvre as a repository of observations on constitutional change and the various manifestations of societal crisis and as a frame of reference for addressing socio-economic problems. For instance, Geremia da Montagnone's (1250/60–1320/1) moral florilegium *Compendium moralium notabilium* (≈ *Anthology of Noteworthy Instances of Moral Conduct,* 1295) or *Epitoma sapientie* (*Epitome of Wisdom*) abounds with references to Aristotle's *Ethics* and the *Politics.*[151]

The siege of Padua by Cangrande della Scala prompted Albertino Mussato to meditate on the causes of the crisis of Padua's communal regime and identify internecine strife as the prime cause of the emergence of tyranny – just as had been the case during Ezzelino da Romano's retrograde regime. In the twelfth book of his chronicle *De gestis Italicorum post Henricum VII Caesarem* and his dialogue *De lite inter Naturam et Fortunam,* an analysis of the political history of Padua at the end of the thirteenth and the beginning of the fourteenth century, Mussato worked out analytical devices for explaining the causes and occasions of the constitutional changes that occurred in Padua.

Mussato's theory about the sequence of constitutional forms is based on a conflation of materials drawn from Aristotle's *Politics* and Livy's work on Rome's political history.[152] Following Sallust's lead and similar to Giovanni da Nono, Mussato highlights the moral aspects of the decline of communal government and sees one of the main causes of Padua's political and social maladies in the avarice (*avaritia*) of its civic body.[153] In his *De Lite inter Naturam et Fortunam,* Mussato follows in Aristotle's footsteps and develops a scheme of the rise, growth, and decay of the political community that conforms to the biological pattern of birth, acme, and decline. In Mussato's interpretation, Padua went through a cycle of constitutional transmutation in analogy with the aging process of the human organism: first there was a forty-year period in which the city was ruled by virtuous citizens. This form of government gave way to an interlude of oligarchic rule (*oligaricia*) brought forth by the vices of the rich citizens. The oligarchic regime was overturned by the common people (*plebs*), who subsequently established democratic rule (*democratia*). The radicalization of democracy gave rise to factional conflict. Everything was paralysed after twenty years in a lethal disease, which, as Mussato explains, was still not overcome in his time.

Like Aristotle and Mussato, Marsilius deploys the organic metaphor and compares the various parts of the body politic to the organs of a living animal and associates domestic tranquility with the harmonious interaction and collaboration among the various sections of the political community. Marsilius concurs with Aristotle in identifying the inordinate growth of the parts of the body politic as a prime cause of internal dissension and constitutional change, noting that the unnoticed increase in the number of the poor in the case of democracy is one of the major sources of constitutional transformation.[154]

More importantly, unlike many of his contemporary writers, Marsilius does not ascribe primacy to economic or moral motives behind the political crisis that occurred in late medieval Italy. Marsilius is not oblivious to the conflicts between the magnates. But at least in Padua, relations between the local clergy and the commune did not necessarily pose a greater threat than the conflicts between the wealthy and the common people. In the 1270s and 1280s, the commune passed legal measures aimed at curtailing the legislative and economic privileges of the local clergy. Such efforts were met with strong resistance on the part of the local bishop, Giovanni Forzate (1256–83), and resulted in a prolonged period of friction between the communal authorities and the local clergy that led to even harsher measures, such as the abolition of clerical immunity from the laws of the city and the drastic reduction of the legal penalties for the murdering priests.[155] Marsilius differs from Albertino Mussato in that he considers the political health and cohesion of society not against the background of the party struggles and the tensions that prevailed in late medieval Italy, but instead from the viewpoint of the relations between clergy and government.[156] He attributes the discord prevailing in his contemporary Italy not to the conflicts between nobles and the people, but to the political claims of the papacy.[157]

The Unity of the Political Community

From Aristotle's perspective, the *polis* is composed not just of a number of individuals but also of individuals who differ in their essence. Taking a polemical turn against Plato, Aristotle stresses that the political community differs, for instance, from a military alliance or a tribe.[158] The political community is a composite entity (*suntheton*) that consists of diverse parts.[159] The constitution is a basic determinant of the political community's identity and serves as its unifying bond.[160] As a result, constitutional transmutation leads to general changes within the political community, just as stones, bricks, and wood form the material of the house and can be arranged differently each time and assume different forms, depending on how they are designed by the architect.[161] To explicate his notion of relationship between the nature of the political community and the constitution, Aristotle also invokes the example of a chorus that appears in a comedy or a tragedy, although it often is composed of the same persons.[162]

The tenor of Marsilius's discussion of the unity of the political community, on the other hand, is influenced by the Ciceronian definition of the commonwealth as an association of men united by a common sense of right and by community of interest, although Marsilius refrains from adopting the Stoic idea of universal brotherhood. Taking their cue from Aristotle, the majority of medieval writers subscribe to the notion of the political community as a moral band, the unity of which is contingent on the agreement of its members regarding its end. Marsilius, in contrast, is concerned with the functional, not the moral, dimensions of the concept of unity.

As Marsilius expresses it, the unity of a city or kingdom is a 'unity of order,' not an absolute or total unity. Specifically, the political community is an aggregate of individuals who can be reckoned to be one in number not because they are one in number formally by virtue of an inherent natural form (as is the case with a mixture), but because they are all related to one thing in number, i.e., the government toward which they are ordered. Marsilius infers from this that it is necessary for the political community to have a single supreme government or a single ruler with respect not to person but to office. Accordingly, Marsilius allows for the possibility of a healthy government being composed of more than one person, as is the case with the aristocracy and polity, who form a single government with respect to office and by virtue of the numerical unity of their actions, judgments, and decisions based on the common decree and voluntary consent of all of them or their weightier part. Although such a unity of action is necessary for the effective functioning of the ruling part, it is not a requirement for the operation of the parts of the community, as the individuals who compose them produce a multiplicity of actions while following the commands or decrees of the government.[163] For Marsilius, this 'unity of action' represents the principle of order in the government, whether made up of one or several persons. At the same time, however, he regards it to be the determining hallmark of the ruling part compared to all the other sections of the political community, in which different acts emanate from different persons and therefore, for these classes, a 'unity of action' is not requisite and can, in fact, have pernicious effects for their individual members and the community as a whole.[164]

According to Marsilius, in large cities and political entities comprising a multitude of cities or provinces there must be *one* supreme government, to which all the other governments are subordinate, in charge of supervising the function of all governing agencies and local rulers.[165] Unlike many medieval writers who commend kingship as a guarantee of social cohesion and unity, Marsilius insists that it is perfectly possible to have multiple persons in government and still achieve unity in each act issuing from them,[166] as is the case with the aristocracy and polity, both of which are administered by more than one person. At the same time, the unity of every act, such as a court decision or judicial sentence, must be preserved. This unity cannot be enacted by *one* member of the government; it requires the unanimous decision (*consensus*) of the persons enlisted in the government or their 'weightier part' (*valencior pars*), in accordance with the laws.[167]

For a better understanding of the relationship between Marsilius's and Aristotle's doctrine of the unity of the political community, it will be necessary first to review briefly Aristotle's concept of unity. Aristotle equates unity with friendship. Concord among the citizens differs from mere agreement of opinions which can exist among strangers or from agreement among persons who think in the same way about a particular issue. Genuine concord, according to Aristotle, exists when the members of the political community agree as to their interests, are unanimous in their actions, and carry out common decisions, e.g., when the citizens unanimously decide that the offices will be elective.[168]

Marsilius's notion of unity, in contrast, is intimately tied to his idea that the political community is founded upon a general agreement about the common good and justice. As a result, Marsilius is unconcerned with friendship as one of the pillars of domestic unity[169] and lays emphasis on the significance of laws as a medium for regulating the relations among the citizens. This novel definition of unity is a corollary to Marsilius's belief that the specialization of functions within the community is an important precondition for a sufficient life.

To enunciate his idea of civic unity, Marsilius relies on Aristotle's *De motu animalium* (*On the Movement of Animals*) and adopts the analogy between the political community and an animal organism: the motion of the living organism presupposes the existence of a single moving principle in charge of communicating motion to the several members and organs.[170] If, however, multiple such principles exist, giving conflicting orders simultaneously, then the organism will inevitably be shifted in various directions or remain in a condition of inertia. The lack of a single moving principle threatens the survival of the living organism. In a well-organized political community, too, the plurality of such principles contravenes the natural order and would appear to be superfluous, indeed even harmful.

Marsilius sees common agreement on what is just and beneficial for the entire community as the guarantee of domestic unity. Accordingly, he accentuates three distinct aspects essential to creating unity: 1) the enforcement of justice; 2) the assembly of the citizenry for the purpose of discussing and deciding matters of common concern; and 3) the division of labour and assignment of different functions to the citizens.

The first aspect of unity is the firm and equitable administration of justice: if there are multiple governments that are not subordinate to a single supreme government, then the judgment and discussion of matters affecting the common good will fail, because there will be no authority to restrain malefactors and apply justice. This situation would result in infighting, friction, and the ultimate breakdown of social order. Transgressors of the laws cannot be brought to justice unless they are summoned before the ruler for an examination of the charges against them. Moreover, evildoers will either not obey the calls or will be called before several rulers simultaneously. If a transgressor decides to appear before one ruler, he will be considered in contempt of the others. But even if he appears before different governments, it is possible that they will not all reach the same verdict; and even if he is convicted by multiple rulers, it is possible that he will receive different punishment from each. Considering these possibilities, malefactors may choose not to appear before any ruler.[171]

The second aspect relevant to unity concerns the gathering of the citizens in the process of public decision making: the assembly of the citizens would also be complicated by a multiplicity of governments, which would have harmful implications for the common good. A ruler often needs to convene an assembly of the citizens, especially those having leisure, for the purpose of discussing and deciding matters that pertain to the public welfare and taking preventive measures for dangers posed by internal or external foes. Only when the citizens are called to gather in one specific place or at one point in time can an assembly be effective. Clearly it would be impossible for all the citizens to attend multiple assemblies taking place in different places.[172]

The third theme Marsilius touches upon in his treatment of domestic unity is functional specialization. Consistent with his conviction that the existence of a serene and unified society is contingent on each part's performing its proper function for the public interest, Marsilius points out that if one part of the citizenry opts to obey one regime but another part obeys another regime, then discord and division are likely to break out. And at the same time, conflict among the various regimes is likely to erupt, as each would claim primacy over the rest and there would be no supreme judge to assess the legitimacy of each regime. Each regime then will turn against the citizens who refuse to obey it.[173]

If there is no one supreme governing agency to which the other parts of the political community are subordinate, then there can be no unity. A situation in which each citizen would choose for himself whatever office or offices he wishes without the approval of a governing authority charged with the apportionment of the various social functions to the citizens would lead to havoc within the political community.[174] The authority for appointing the various officeholders and assigning functions to the members of society rests solely with the government, whose duty it is to execute the decisions of the *legislator humanus*.[175]

The Organization of the Political Community

Marsilius's Classification of Human Acts

The classification of human acts is integral to Marsilius's exposition of the parts of the political community and his theory of law. Marsilius distinguishes two categories of human acts: the first includes those acts which are the effect of natural causes apart from human knowledge, such as acts which result from the contrariety of the elements composing the human body, through their intermixture, e.g., the acts of the nutritive faculty.[176] To the second category belong those human acts and passions which are performed through the cognitive and appetitive faculties. Marsilius divides this second group further into two classes: 1) transient acts (*actus transeuntes*[177] or *actus civiles* or *politici*),[178] which are performed by the limbs and can be done for benefit or harm of someone other than the doer;[179] and 2) immanent acts (*actus immanentes* or *monastici*[180] or *spirituales*),[181] such as human thoughts and desires, which are not exercised by external organs or limbs of the human body and do not affect any person other than the agent himself.[182]

Marsilius considers it one of the prime tasks of the governing part to moderate the excesses of the transient acts and to reduce them to equality or due proportion.[183]As for the immanent acts, the *legislator humanus*, the supreme instance and ultimate source of legislative and governmental authority within the political community cannot control or regulate them, nor can he resolve by means of civil legislation the conflicts and disputes that may arise from immanent acts. As Marsilius explains, immanent acts cannot be proved to be present or absent in someone. But such acts cannot be concealed from God, whom philosophers feigned to be the maker of such laws, under the threat of punishment for wrongdoers and with the promise of eternal reward for those who perform virtuous deeds. Marsilius deduces from this that the function of the sacerdotal part is to moderate the immanent human acts.[184]

Marsilius's typology of human acts contains elements similar to those set forth by Aristotle and other medieval thinkers, but it is unique in the way it combines those elements to propose an entirely new classification. As a preliminary to a closer discussion of Marsilius's theory of human acts, we shall first provide a brief survey of similar distinctions proposed by Aristotle, Thomas Aquinas, and Maimonides and explore how Marsilius's relates to previous ideas on human acts.

Marsilius and Aristotle

Aristotle speaks of 'contractual relations' (*sunallagmata*),[185] which are the object of the commutative (corrective) justice, by ensuring that these are just.[186] In this context, he draws the distinction between voluntary and involuntary actions. To the first class belong those acts which are performed based on free decision.[187] Aristotle remarks in the *Rhetoric*[188] that deliberate choice is based on full knowledge of the individual circumstances and that their motivating principle is located in the agent alone.[189] A difference between *actus transeuntes* and *actus immanentes* is foreign to Aristotle. Furthermore, Aristotle's and Marsilius's views on voluntary and involuntary acts are fundamentally different. Marsilius even qualifies acts that Aristotle designates as 'involuntary' as voluntary *actus transeuntes*.

Marsilius and Aquinas

In order to illuminate the background of Marsilius's doctrine of human acts, it is necessary to look at those medieval writings in which the distinction of *actus transeuentes* and *actus immanentes* occurs. Thomas Aquinas, for instance, refers in the foreword to his *Commentary on the Politics* to *actus transeuntes* and *actus manentes*. In his view, political science is explicitly involved with human acts, even those whose effect is confined to the agent alone, whether the agent only considers something, makes a decision, or actually makes an effort (*actus manentes*). Aquinas contrasts the *actus manentes* with the *actus transeuntes* and the *operationes quae sunt ad alterum*,[190] which in Marsilius's *Defensor pacis*, in contrast, are defined as acts of the production and creation of the objects of the *artes mechanicae*.[191]

Drawing on Aristotle, Aquinas maintains that the human soul performs two kinds of activities: first are those which extend to external material, for example weaving, building, and sawing. According to Aquinas, these acts are a means to an end, e.g., the manufacturing of woven clothing or the construction of a house. The 'immanent' activities of the soul are subsumed under the second type and affect the agent alone. Felicity, for instance, is an activity, not a product. 'Immanent' acts aim at the perfection of the acting person, in contrast to the 'transient' acts.[192] Virtues, on the other hand, represent principles of action, and their effect is limited to the acting subject. Similar views occur in Peter of Auvergne's (1240s–1304) *Questiones super Politicum* (*Questions on the Politics*)[193] and in John of Jandun's *Commentary on the Metaphysics*, which discusses the relationship between of *operationes immanentes* and politics. John's conception of immanent acts, however, is closer to Aquinas's theory than to Marsilius's.[194]

Aquinas, like Marsilius, invests the distinction of human acts with political implications: in his view, laws are enacted in relation to those things which can be judged. External acts fall under the purview of civil legislation, but human laws cannot control or regulate internal acts in an adequate manner, and to this end, it was necessary that divine law came into being.[195] In contrast to Marsilius, however, Aquinas and the other Aristotelian commentators define virtue as the purpose of government and law.[196]

Marsilius and Maimonides

An important precedent for the Marsilian distinction of human acts, and one that is, in fact, rather significant in content as regards terminology, can be found in Maimonides' (1135–1204) *Guide of the Perplexed*.[197]

Around 1242–4, after the burning of the Talmud in Paris, there appeared a Latin translation of the first sections of part II of Maimonides' *Guide of the Perplexed* (*Moreh nevukhim, Dalālat al-ḥā'irīn*) and an almost complete one under the title *Dux neutrorum* which was made from the Harizi Hebrew translation.[198] It is possible that during his stay in Paris, Marsilius was exposed to contemporary discussions on Maimonides' work or that he even had access to one of the copies of the Latin translation of the *Guide* that were extant in libraries of French capital as early as the mid-thirteenth century. The two oldest manuscripts of the *Dux neutrorum* were located in the Sorbonne. Another two manuscripts dated from about the thirteenth century are extant in the Vatican and at Todi, and there are also references to two manuscripts of the same period that were in the possession of theologians in Paris. Two manuscripts (Munich and Graz) are dated to the turn of the fourteenth century, whereas three manuscripts (Saint-Omer, Cambridge, and Oxford) were produced in the first half of the fourteenth century.[199] It is also noteworthy that Peter of Abano's *Conciliator differentiarum philosophorum et praecipue medicorum* (ca. 1310) and *Lucidator dubitabilium astronomiae* contain a number of references both to the *Dux neutrorum* and Maimonides' medical writings, which enjoyed a wide reception at the universities of Montpellier, Bologna, and Padua as early as the thirteenth century.[200]

In order to gain a fuller understanding of Maimonides' ideas on the political relevance of religion and to demonstrate the points of convergence between his political ideas and those of Marsilius, it is crucial to turn to a closer analysis of chapter forty-one of the second part of the Latin translation of the *Guide of the Perplexed*. Following Aristotle's view of humans as being political by nature, Maimonides affirms that humans, as opposed to animals, are characterized by great diversity and are impelled to form associations due to the need for mutual cooperation and assistance, which is an indispensable condition for control over the body and can be realized only within a political association.

Maimonides stands on common ground with Marsilius in maintaining that the human community is composed of diverse individuals coming together to seek their mutual advantage. Moreover, Maimonides comes remarkably close to Marsilius in considering that the natural diversity of the members of this community generates internecine tension, instability, and fragmentation. Accordingly, he underscores the need for the existence of a political authority that can serve as a prophylactic against discord and disorder, as well as a ruler whose primary function is to guarantee the concord and the domestic order of the political community, ward off excesses in the conduct of the members of society, and prescribe actions and moral habits.[201]

In the third part of the *Dux neutrorum*, Maimonides classifies the commandments into fourteen classes but, at the same time, draws a more general distinction between transgressions between men and transgressions between man and God. He goes on to specify that some of commandments of the third class and those included in the fifth, sixth, and seventh classes concern relations among men, whereas all the rest refer to the relationship between man and God.[202] The commandments of the third group refer to moral qualities which are conducive to the perfection of human society.[203] The commandments of the fourth group relate to giving alms, lending, and bestowal of gifts.[204] The fifth group comprises commandments designed to prevent injustice and injuries.[205] The commandments of the sixth class refer to punishments for criminals such as thieves, robbers, and false witnesses. Maimonides is emphatic regarding the importance of laws against the various crimes and delicts and argues that punishments should follow the principle that the offender receives exactly the same treatment that he has given to somebody else.[206] The seventh class includes the laws of property that govern the transactions of the members of society; for instance, loans and trade activities.[207]

Maimonides writes that the categories of commandments often overlap, since commandments concerning the relations between man and God can affect relations between men. But the effect is only indirect, and only in a certain respect; it does not necessarily deter a person from engaging in actions that might harm his fellow men.[208] Marsilius's and Maimonides' ideas on the typology of human acts are indicative of their effort to draw a clear line of distinction between human and divine law.[209] Marsilius refers to divine law as the *lex evangelica*,[210] the *lex gratiae*,[211] the new law (*nova lex*),[212] and the law of eternal salvation (*lex salutis eterne*).[213] In one sense, divine law can be defined as 'justice,' inasmuch as it constitutes a standard of human deeds, evaluating whether are they performed rightly or wrongly in the present world. However, the coercive power for this, Marsilius says, comes only in the future world: the punishments or rewards that it metes out are distributed in the life to come.[214] Herein exists the difference between divine and human law: human law is designated as a mandatory rule in the domain of transient acts for the present world.[215] Marsilius explains, however, that in those cases in which certain things are permitted by human law but not by divine law and vice versa, it is preferable to follow divine law rather than human law.[216]

Plato Transformed, Avicennian Echoes, and the Ideal Social Organization

As a sequel to his distinction of human acts, Marsilius proceeds to establish a connection between the parts of the soul and the various parts of the community:[217] the parts of the community moderate the activities which emanate from the parts of the soul – for instance, the agricultural part has to moderate the acts of the nutritive part.[218] The mechanics are responsible for the moderation of the human senses.[219] Lastly, the function of the ruling and sacerdotal parts of the community consist in regulating the 'transient' and 'immanent' human acts, respectively.[220]

The view of the link between the parts of the soul and the various sections of the political community can ultimately be traced back to Plato's *Politeia*. In Plato's proposed city, every citizen must be allocated an occupation in accordance with his natural abilities. Plato identifies three parts in the human soul – the rational, the spirited, and the appetitive[221] – and sets forth a scheme of social classification based on three parts: the philosophers, who correspond to the element of wisdom; the guardians or warriors, who represent the virtue of bravery; and the farmers and tradesmen, who exemplify the appetitive component.[222] Though as indicated previously, the *Politeia* was not extant in the Latin West, Plato's *Timaios* sets forth a model of social division into three main social groupings, i.e., priests, warriors, and labourers that correspond to the rational, courageous, and volitional parts of the soul, respectively.[223]

Marsilius, on the other hand, places a distinct emphasis on the government's role in allocating the various functions within the body politic with an eye to the dispositions and abilities of the citizens. While in the first communities one person could fulfil different functions simultaneously and be ruler and farmer or shepherd, as was the case with Abraham, the hallmark of a full-fledged and properly constituted society is the differentiation and coordination of its various parts for the sake of a sufficient communal life.[224] Marsilius insists that in a well-governed polity, no one, especially a foreigner, is allowed to choose an office or function for himself, as this could generate social friction and deprive the community of sufficient life.[225] Accordingly, Marsilius believes that one of the ruler's foremost duties involves assigning to the offices of the political community individuals who perform the functions appropriate to them and cultivate the habits to which they are by nature inclined.[226]

Plato's ideas on the functional differentiation of the body politic as a pivotal condition for civic harmony had a considerable following among several medieval thinkers.[227] Avicenna, for example, holds one of the lawgiver's central concerns to be the division of society into three parts: rulers, guardians, and artisans. Each estate is to be administered by a leader, under whom there will be subordinate masters over smaller groups in a hierarchical order. A well-organized society, then, is one in which each person performs the specific function assigned to him and contributes to the common welfare, so that no one remains indolent.[228] Likewise, Averroes in his *Commentary on Plato's Politeia* alludes to the Platonic principle that justice consists in each citizen's carrying out the activity for which he is best equipped by nature.[229] Just like Avicenna, Averroes insists that each member of the political community should pursue a single occupation, since a situation in which the citizens engage in multiple occupations and move between different occupations or ranks gives rise to social conflict, wrongdoing, and ultimately, injustice. The effects of this kind of mobility, adds Averroes, are not so much evident in the practical crafts, but rather when people transfer from one social group to the other, as is the case when a person who is parsimonious and wealthy is assigned by virtue of his parsimony to the warrior or ruling class.[230]

A number of Christian authors in the Early Middle Ages, especially in the eleventh century, put forward a tripartite scheme of social organization based on three estates (orders): *oratores* (those who pray, i.e., the clerics); *bellatores* (fighters), who are in charge of defense; and *laboratores* (workers), who are engaged in manual occupations.[231] This scheme exhibits distinct affinities to Platonic ideas on occupational specialization and social division which permeated philosophical discourse in the Middle Ages through various channels, especially the Latin translations of the *Timaios* (17A–53C) by Chalcidios (fourth century) in the twelfth century and of Avicenna's *Metaphysics.*[232]

One of the first Christian writers to elaborate on Avicenna's views about the structure of the ideal polity was Dominicus Gundissalinus (ca. 1110–after 1190), who produced a Latin translation of Avicenna's *Metaphysics,* in his *De divisione philosophiae* (*On the Division of Philosophy,* ca. 1150). The main purpose in laying down laws, writes Gundissalinus, is to organize the city into three parts: administrators, ministers, and legal experts. In each estate, there should be a supervisor, and under him, subordinate supervisors who follow his orders, and after these, others, so that no citizen remains idle and refrains from exercising a function beneficial to the entire community. In Gundissalinus's vision of the ideal political order, there is no room for leisure and idleness and persons who do not have someone above them or who do not obey somebody else.[233]

Similar ideas occur in Roger Bacon's (ca. 1219–92) *Opus maius.*[234] According to Bacon, the second branch of moral philosophy deals with the internal ordering of the political community and the laws and ordinances concerning the relations among men. Laws follow a certain sequence: laws about marriages; laws which order subjects to prelates and rulers; laws which concern the appointment of experts on the various sciences and arts as well as of those assigned to perform military service and entrusted with the administration of justice and the correction of malefactors. Bacon quotes Avicenna in support of the view that the primary goal in framing laws is to organize the political community into three groups: administrators, executors, and experts on laws. Bacon draws on Avicenna to establish the need to appoint a superintendent for each group, with other officials subordinate to him and, after him, others, so that no one leads a parasitic life or shirks work and so that each member of the community performs a distinctive function conducive to the communal advantage. Along these lines, Bacon believes that one of the ruler's foremost duties must be to proscribe idleness and leisure and to banish the unruly.[235]

The Platonic notion of functional specialization had a distinguished career in Byzantine economic and political literature as well. The sixth-century anonymous treatise *Peri stratēgias* (*On Strategy*) outlines a model of social organization that includes writers, public orators, physicians, agriculturalists, and others with similar professions. The treatise mentions the sacerdotal part; lawyers; merchants, including those dealing with grain, wine, meat, iron, and copper: workers; and the unproductive segment of the population, including the infirm, elderly, and children, who are unable to contribute to the needs of society. In addition to these parts, the treatise refers to another one which it designates the 'leisure part': it is not engaged in any particular activity. The treatise points to the corrosive effects of idleness, unemployment, and of social evils such as licentiousness, thievery, and other kinds of social ills. It also stresses that every member of society should be appointed to that station for which he is best fitted and that just as in the human body there is no part or organ that does not perform any function, in a properly arranged polity, there is no room for people who albeit able to contribute to public welfare, refrain from work.[236]

Marsilius's Byzantine contemporary, Thomas Magister (? 1275–1350/51), in his *Peri Vasileias* (*On Kingship*), highlights the importance of arts and crafts for a right social order. He specifically recommends that each citizen pursue a single occupation and be registered with the prefect of Constantinople, who monitored the operation of the guilds of craftsmen and tradesmen.[237] In a similar fashion, George Gemistos Plethon (Pletho, d. 1452), in two memoranda for the reorganization of the Peloponnese which he addressed to Theodoros II Palaiologos (1396–1448, r. 1407–43), Despot of Mystra, in 1416,[238] and Emperor Manuel II Palaiologos (1350–1425, r. 1391–1421) in 1418,[239] proposes a division of work which he sees as the key to the effective functioning of the ideal polity: each member of society should be assigned a specific function in accordance with his natural disposition and abilities.[240] In line with Plato, Plethon stipulates the regimentation of the population into three groups: the most necessary class, composed of farmers and shepherds; the class of craftspeople and merchants; and the ruling group, which stands directly under the authority of the ruler.[241]

The 'Circle of Justice' and Functional Specialization

Marsilius's application of the principle of the division of labour must be seen against a long tradition, especially in the medieval Islamic context, that espoused the ideal of the 'circle of justice.' The concept of the 'circle of justice' (or 'circle of power') originally goes back to two popular dicta attributed to Aristotle and Ardashīr, ruler of Persia (224–41) and founder of the Sassanid dynasty, which present the ideal polity as composed of four distinct parts, i.e., the ruler, soldiers, tax collectors, and farmers and highlight the interconnectedness of the various segments of the body politic.[242] In the saying ascribed to Aristotle, the world is presented as a large garden administered by the state; the state signifies authority based on the law; the law is a way of ruling applied by the king, who acts like a shepherd; the king is supported by the army, the sustenance of which depends on tax revenues; tax revenues are sustenance procured by the subjects; subjects are slaves provided for by justice, which is the element that guarantees the proper function of the world. Ardashīr is reported to have said that government is contingent on the existence of men; men in their turn need money; money comes from cultivation of the land; and cultivation can only take place as long as there is justice and healthy rule.[243]

Underlying the notion of the 'circle of justice' is the assumption that the existence of a stable and lasting social order is contingent on the ability of each group to fulfil its functions, but it also reflects a vivid awareness of the functional interdependence of the various segments of the body politic. In his *'Uyūn al-Akhbār* (*The Founts of Information*), Ibn Qutaybah (828–89) adumbrated later interpretations and uses of the 'circle of justice' by distinguishing four occupational classes of society: 1) the learned, who are the bearers of religion; 2) the horsemen, who are charged with the protection of the seat of power; 3) the writers, who are the ornament of the kingdom; and 4) the farmers, who cultivate the land.[244]

The interrelationship of the parts of society is a dominant theme in a number of Byzantine political treatises, such as the *Taktika* (lit. *Tactical Constitutions*, ca. 905), a work on the conduct of war written by the Byzantine emperor Leo VI ['the Wise'] (866–912, r. 886–912):[245] agriculture provides for the maintenance of the army, and an essential aspect of the function of an able military leader is to defend and protect the farmers, who provide food supplies.[246] Leo highlights the importance of noncombatants such as physicians, slaves, and merchants for the sustenance of the military.[247] Military officers should concentrate on organizing their troops and be free from all other activities and, thus, must have assistants engage in agricultural labour and provide the required equipment to the army.[248] If, during winter time, the army lacks provisions such as horses and military equipment and does not have access to supplies in a particular region, a capable military commander ought to make sure that goods are available for sale by traders so as not to burden the local population.[249] Traders should receive just treatment; otherwise, they might discontinue providing supplies to the military[250] and the army should refrain from marching through lands under cultivation, whether they are small farms, vineyards, or gardens.[251]

The notion of the mutual dependency of the constituent parts of human society was brought out most emphatically in Christine de Pizan's (1364–1430) *Livre du corps de policie* (*The Book of the Body Politic*, 1407). Christine posits an intimate link between the corporeal analogy and an inclusive notion of civic participation that stresses the indispensability of all the parts of the community: just as a body lacking any of its members is defective or deformed, so in a healthy civil body, all its estates operate in harmony and correct proportion with one another. Christine identifies mutual assistance and harmonious collaboration among the various social groups as a prerequisite to the efficient functioning of the body politic, just as all the members of a living organism are necessary for its nourishment and proper functioning.[252] The function of the ruler is, by implication, to cater to the needs of the citizens and to make sure that they perform their duties.[253]

The notion that rigid division of labour is a prime condition for a lasting social order entails a strong emphasis on law as the cement of society. At the basis of this line of reasoning lies the proposition that the members of society are assigned distinct but complementary or mutually dependent functions for which they are fitted by nature and that each segment of the body politic is confined to its sphere and does not impinge on the function of the others.[254] Just as the preponderance or overgrowth of a part of the body causes imbalance, thereby leading to disturbances, so too do immoderate increase and predominance of a particular social group over the others lead to disequilibrium and, ultimately, the collapse of the social order.[255] This notion also implies that the political community encompasses diverse groups with competing claims and interests that need to be satisfied for the sake of the preservation of the entire social organism, and that the predominance of one part over the rest is a cause of disequilibrium or disease in the social organism.[256]

This idea, which reflects an inclusive vision of citizenship and acknowledges the contribution of all the sections of the community to the public good, occurs in a number of late medieval authors such as Jean Gerson (1363–1429) and Philippe de Mézières (1327–1405).[257] But while Marsilius and Christine de Pizan advocated the idea of the interdependence of the parts of the body politic in Aristotelian garb, early modern Florentine political debates on the interaction among the various social groups took their cue from Galen's humoural theory. This development must be seen against the background of the political crisis and social turbulence that beset early modern Florence.

As opposed to their classical predecessors, most Florentine writers were not looking for a perfect state. Rather, they were preoccupied with proposing measures that would suppress or prevent internecine strife and with instituting mechanisms that would balance the ever-present struggles among diverse social groups. One of the most important insights and modes of theorizing stable political arrangements that early modern political theorists borrowed from the theory of four humours (yellow bile, blood, black bile, phlegm) is that one of the central functions of salutary and successful rule is to handle factional disputes and to balance and satisfy the manifold, and often opposing, needs and claims of all the segments of the body politic and to avert the dominance of a particular part over the rest.[258]

This line of thought is most vividly exemplified by Niccolò Machiavelli. In his treatment of the ruler's modes of conduct with his subjects and friends or supporters, Machiavelli declares his intention to put aside) those things that concern a prince and are imaginary (*imaginate*) and discuss those that are real (*vere*). He thus sets himself apart from previous writers who envisioned republics and principalities which have never been seen or known to have existed in reality, given that there is a crucial difference between the way one lives and the way in which one ought to live and the person who disregards what is generally done and focuses on what ought to be done ends up working towards his ruin rather than his preservation and success.[259]

Moreover, Machiavelli makes extensive use of the bodily humours motif as an analytical device in his discussion of the political and social conditions that prevailed in various forms of political organization.[260] First he uses the bodily humours trope to signify the various social categories. The Roman patriciate contained three humours (the patricians, the plebeians, and the army); Florence's civic body comprised two humours, the *grandi* and the *popolo*; Venice's humours were the noblemen and the *popolo*; and Romagna, Naples, and Lombardy were composed of two humours, i.e., the noblemen and the people. Second, humours denote the desires, claims, and aspirations of the various social groups. Third, humours connote the activities emanating from the interaction among the various social groups, such as the conflicts and discord in Florence, which Machiavelli attributes to the humours of that city. Fourth, humours are the criteria for the taxonomy of regimes given that each regime is the outcome of the conflict of it constituent humours or of their combination. The first two uses of humours are a recurrent motif in Machiavelli's discussion of the social composition of the state and underlie his emphasis on harmonizing the needs of the different social parts as a pivotal condition for a well-managed and prosperous society.

Similarly, Francesco Guicciardini (1483–1540) argues that the challenge was not to excogitate an imaginary government that is more likely to appear in books than in practice (like Plato's *Politeia*), but rather to establish a viable government after considering the nature, quality, conditions, inclinations, and characteristics – in essence, the humours – of the city and of the citizens, which could be instituted by persuasion and, once established, could be tolerated and maintained according to the people's predilections. Such a strong concern with theorizing remedies for the pathological phenomena that afflict civil life pervades Guicciardini's political writings. As Guicciardini phrases it, one should follow the example of a physician who, albeit entitled to prescribe for his patients any medicines he wishes, does not give what he deems good and recommended but only what the patient is capable of tolerating according to his own constitution and other factors.[261]

The Idea of the Mean and the Parts of the Political Community

Marsilius relies on Aristotle's concept of moderation, as expounded in the *Nicomachean Ethics* in connection with the Aristotelian theory of virtue. The principle of the mean is of central significance in Hippocrates' medical theory.[262] Plato, too, in the *Timaios*, sees corporeal and spiritual health as being dependent on the symmetrical relationship between body and soul.[263] Aristotle associates virtue with *mesotēs*, i.e., the middle between two extremes, as moderation. This idea harks back to Aristotle's natural philosophy, according to which the mean is the hallmark of a proportionally grown living organism.[264] Just as a healthy and properly adjusted natural body is one where limbs and organs are created according to proper measure, a well-balanced community, as construed by Marsilius, is one in which each part is proportionally formed and performs its proper function in relation to the good of the whole.

The idea about the nexus between the mean and the moral edification of the members of the political community occupies a prominent place in medieval Muslim and Jewish philosophy.[265] For Avicenna, for example, one of the lawgiver's essential tasks is to lay down rules regarding morals and customs that promise justice, which consists in the mean.[266] Maimonides pictures moral decay as a disease of the soul and the result of the lack of the mean.[267] Shem-Ṭov ben Joseph ibn Falaquera (1225–ca. 1290), in his *Book of the Seeker*,[268] defines virtue as the mean between two vices, excess and deficiency.[269] In Falaquera's view, a pious man who possesses ten portions of every noble quality operates according to the mean and flees from extremes.[270]

While Aristotle and most medieval writers are concerned with the moral connotations of the concept of the mean, Marsilius is primarily focused on its functional dimensions. Accordingly, he highlights its value for the right balance of the acts of the citizens, the interaction among the component parts of the community, and, ultimately, the proper functioning of the body politic.

Aristotle offers two schemes of social organization: the first schema involves eight main parts: 1) farmers; 2) artisans; 3) merchants; 4) day workers; 5) soldiers; 6) the judiciary and councilmen; 7) the wealthy (the so-called propertied), who with their wealth are willing and ready to assist the political community; and 8) those who serve as public officials.[271] Aristotle, however, challenges Plato's teaching about functional specialization and concedes that a citizen can take up more than one function.[272] Accordingly, he proposes a second and more elastic classification which involves six functional categories and underlies Marsilius's exposition of the parts of the political community:[273]

1) The first part is made up of those who engage in agricultural activities and animal husbandry. Their primary task is to exercise the arts that are necessary for nourishment and, thus, moderate the acts generated by the nutritive part of the human soul.[274]
2) The second part, i.e., the mechanics, is responsible for the equilibrium of the actions and passions caused by the influence of the elements that surround the human body. Marsilius also deals with the general class of the mechanical arts, the *artes*, as he designates them following Aristotle, e.g., spinning, leather making, shoemaking, all arts involved in house building, and in general all other mechanical arts that moderate man's senses and assist the other sections of the community. Marsilius, in an Aristotelian manner, differentiates between arts that aim at life necessities and those that provide pleasure and the good life. He mentions the art of painting as an example of the latter and, following Aristotle, he defines medicine as a mechanical art.[275]
3) The third segment of the political community is the judiciary, or the ruling and deliberative parts. Its function is to moderate the excesses of the transient acts (i.e., acts performed by the limbs through knowledge and desire) and reduce them to equality or due

proportion and settle matters related to justice and the common good.[276]

4) The military is the fourth part. Its task is to protect the political community from both internal and external threats. In addition, the military is charged with enforcing the government's decisions and suppressing strife.[277]
5) The function of the financial part (*pars pecuniativa*) is to administer the finances and collect and store goods (wine, oil, etc.). This part of society is also supported by other parts of the political community.[278]
6) The sixth part, the 'sacerdotal,' differs from the other parts in that men do not perceive it to be necessary in the same way as the other parts. The true and primary necessity of the priestly class cannot be established through demonstration and is not self-evident. However, all nations agree that it is necessary to appoint a group of people for divine worship so as to gain benefit for both the present and future world.[279]

The Emergence of Religion and the Civic Function of the Sacerdotal Part

Marsilius illustrates the genesis of religion and the civic function of the sacerdotal part in the following way: unlike laws, which are the outcome of collective effort and prudence, the emergence of religion is the result of well-thought-out planning by an individual or a group of persons. Marsilius holds that the first philosophers, such as Hesiod and Pythagoras,[280] were aware of the fact that religion was believed to be essential to social life even though the causes for its existence were not rationally demonstrable. Those philosophers argued that divine laws or religions were essential for the preservation of life in the present world, since they can guarantee the goodness of both private and civil human acts and could thus contribute to political serenity. In propagating their teachings, some of the founders of religions contrived myths in order to instill in men reverence for and fear of God and the desire to cultivate virtues and avoid vices. For instance, although they did not believe in human resurrection and life after death, they tried to persuade others that it exists and that pleasures and pain in the afterlife depend on human deeds in the present one.[281]

Pagan examples were often invoked by medieval philosophers as a means to illustrate the civic function of religion.[282] Al-Fārābī, for instance, in his summary of Plato's *Laws*, glosses on Plato's views on Athenian religious festivals and explains that their purpose is to serve the education of the citizens. If the legislator had commanded people to refrain from pleasures, his laws would not have found acceptance given human propensity for pleasure. As a result, he reserved specific times for religious festivals which were intended for leisure and repose from work.[283]

A similar idea can be found in Averroes's *Tahāfut al-Tahāfut* (*The Incoherence of the Incoherence*) where he refutes Al-Ghazzālī's (1058–1111) idea that philosophers deny the doctrine of bodily resurrection. The crux of Averroes's argument is that resurrection had been mentioned in various religions for at least a millennium. The philosophers, Averroes explains, deemed the idea of resurrection instrumental for safeguarding order among men, which is indispensable for human existence and can lead to ultimate felicity.[284]

Maimonides writes that by studying the doctrines and worship of the Sabians, he gained insights into the rational grounds for the existence of divine commandments and into the importance of divine precepts in ensuring the morality of human actions and averting the destabilization of the social order.[285] The Sabians, according to Maimonides, erected golden and silver images for the stars, the sun, the moon, attributed the metals and the climates to the influence of the planets, and assumed that a certain planet was the god of a certain zone. They built temples, placed images in them, and believed that the stars sent forth their influence upon these images, which were thereby enabled to comprehend and to inspire human beings and to instruct them about what is useful to them.[286]

The Sabians believed that the earth would become peopled and the ground fertilized through the worship of the stars. The most wise and pious among them taught the people that agriculture, which is a *conditio sine qua non* for the perpetuation of humankind, would become perfect and satisfy the basic human needs only if the people worshipped the stars and the sun and refrained from disobeying and thereby provoking them; otherwise their cities would wither and eventually perish.[287] Tillers of the ground were praised in the religion of the Sabians, because they cultivated the land according to the desire of the stars. The Sabians also respected cattle because of their use in agriculture and prohibited their slaughter because they combined strength and the willingness to carry out man's work of tilling the soil.[288] Their priests instructed the people who met in the temples that as a result of certain religious acts, rain would come down, the trees of the field would yield their fruit, and the land would be fertile and populated. Similarly, all ancient wise men commanded the people to play certain instruments before the images during the religious festivals, in order to please the deities and receive their reward, such as long life, exemption from great bodily deformities, protection against diseases, and bountiful harvests.[289]

Like Marsilius, Maimonides suggests that the ancient wise men did not believe in the myths they propagated. However, they told their fellow men that a certain plague would befall those who did not perform the acts whereby faith is supported and confirmed forever, or that it may even one day accidentally befall a person, and that person would then direct his attention to the performance of those acts of faith. Capitalizing on the fact that people fear most the loss of their children and property, the worshippers of fire spread the tale that if anyone did not pass his son and daughter through the fire, the children would die. Therefore, everyone performed this action out of pity and apprehension for their children and because of the trifling character of the action and its ease.[290]

The first philosophers, Marsilius explains, spoke of virtuous men in this world who were placed in the heavenly firmament and of certain stars and constellations named after them. They declared that the souls of miscreants entered the bodies of various brutes according to the grade of human vices. They mentioned various kinds of torments for evildoers (such as eternal thirst and hunger, as in the case of Tantalos), and described the infernal regions as deep and dark.[291] Out of fear, men refrained from wrongdoing and were driven to perform virtuous works of piety and mercy. This way, men were internally well-disposed both internally and toward others and eschewed wrongdoing.[292]

Marsilius's ideas on the civic dimension of religion will emerge more clearly through a brief presentation of his ideas on the various meanings of 'law' (*lex*). Marsilius notes that in its third sense, 'law' denotes the standard containing admonitions for voluntary deeds. Laws shape and regulate human conduct. Aristotle, Marsilius adds, called religions 'laws.' The Mosaic Law was partly called a law. The evangelic law is called law in its entirety; and all religions, such as Islam and Zoroastrianism, are called 'laws in whole or in part.'[293]

Marsilius perceives religion to be a *lex* operating with practices and commands, and he advances a naturalistic explanation of the emergence of religious rites that evokes an intriguing link to Peter of Abano's views on the causal link between the movement of celestial bodies and the course of natural events. Peter of Abano postulates a causal connection between the major conjunction of Saturn and Jupiter (after a period of every 960 years) and the appearance of major historic figures, including political leaders and 'founders of religions,' e.g., Nebuchadrezzar, Moses, Alexander the Great, Jesus, and Muḥammad.[294]

This naturalistic notion of religion as invention originates in an Averroist matrix and forms a consistent thread in early modern philosophical writing that can be traced through Pietro Pomponazzi (1462–1525) and Paolo Sarpi (1552–1623). In his *Kitāb al-milal wa-al-duwal* (*Book of Religions and Dynasties*), which was translated into Latin by John of Spain under the title *De magnes coniunctonibus* (*On the Great Conjunctions*) in the twelfth century, the Arab astrologer Abū Ma'shar (787–886) (known in the West as Albumasar) describes three kinds of conjunctions of the two superior planets, Saturn and Jupiter: 1) the greatest occurs in the spring tropical sign every 960 solar years and causes the emergence of new religions; 2) the middle takes place every 240 solar years and leads to political changes, such as change of dynasty; and 3) the minor occurs every 20 years and results in revolutions and similar events.[295]

These ideas are echoed in Epistle 36, 'On Revolutions and Cycles,' of the Ikhwān al-Ṣafā' (Brethren of Purity, tenth century). The epistle contains an elaborate classification of astronomical cycles into five types of revolutions, six kinds or 120 species of conjunctions, and fours species of 'Thousands,' the largest of which is that of 360,000 years. The epistle specifies that revolutions and conjunctions occur in a long or short duration.[296]

The notion of a causal connection between the genesis of the various religions and the conjunctions of planets or configurations of stars had a considerable following among writers in the medieval West as well.[297] Roger Bacon ascribes the emergence of religions to the conjunction of the planets. Likewise, Cecco d'Ascoli (ca. 1257–1327), professor of mathematics and astronomy at the University of Bologna, draws on the astrological theories of Hippocrates and Zoroaster to state that the Mosaic Law ended with the Christian religion, which then was ended by the Antichrist.

In his *Tractatus de immortalitate animae* (*Treatise on the Immortality of the Soul*, 1516), Pomponazzi employs a phrasing very similar to Marsilius's to demonstrate that, notwithstanding any differences among various religions, there is a consensus on the social value of religious creeds. Pomponazzi believes that most people perform good deeds because they are driven more by fear of eternal punishment than by hope of eternal good, since men are more familiar with punishments than eternal goods. Given man's proclivity to evil and for the sake of common good, the lawgiver (*legislator*) ought to decree the immortality of the human soul in order to induce men to virtue. As indicated earlier, Marsilius claims that the first philosophers did not themselves believe in the truth of the teachings they spread. Pomponazzi holds that the statesman (*politicus*) need not care for truth but only for righteousness; just as a physician invents many things in the course of healing a patient, so too a successful statesman creates fables in order to keep the members of society on the right path. For if men were entirely healthy, the physician would not need to use such fictions.[298]

Another intriguing parallel to Marsilius's account of religion can be found in Paolo Sarpi's *Pensieri filosofici* (*Philosophical Thoughts* [or *Reflections*]).[299] Pretty much like Marsilius, Sarpi looks upon the state as the agency that generates and sustains social life and accords to religion the status of an institution that is subservient and renders assistance to the governing authorities.[300] Sarpi's understanding of religion as a body of laws intended to set the parameters for healthy social conduct evokes a specific link to Marsilius's idea of religion as *lex*: Sarpi explains the emergence of religion (*Torà* being a generic designation for all religions) as a natural phenomenon and ascribes to it a medicinal function: it is a remedy for defects and evils in human nature.[301] Sarpi also intersects with Marsilius on the insight that human insufficiency is the chief reason for the emergence of social life and that religion provides an authority that can prevent human depravity. In this sense, the state (*repubblica*) is the proprietor of man, but religion (*Torà*) is a proprietor of the state in that it provides things which the state cannot. Just as Marsilius sees the genesis of religion as a phenomenon coeval with the establishment of laws in the first communities, Sarpi holds that society, the state, and religion have existed since the creation of humankind.[302]

In establishing the social desirability and political significance of religion, Marsilius carries on an established trend of medieval political writing. Aristotle emphasizes the societal function of myths as a means to guide the people and uphold social order.[303] The civic function of myths and religious teachings is a prominent theme in medieval Islamic political thought as well, For Al-Fārābī, religion consists of opinions and acts, determined and limited by conditions, laid down to the people by their ruler as he seeks to achieve a specific goal.[304] Similarly, Averroes mentions that religions are, according to the philosophers, obligatory, since they lead towards wisdom in a way universal to all human beings. Philosophy only leads a certain number of intelligent people to the knowledge of happiness, whereas religions seek to instruct the mass.[305]

Marsilius regards religion as *ancilla politicae* and, like Aristotle, he highlights the status of the sacerdotal part as an integral part of the community.[306] With the specialization of labour, clerics evolve into a section of the community. Priests were appointed in the first communities and were entrusted with the administration of the sanctuaries of the temples and all duties associated with the divine cult.[307] Intriguingly, Marsilius passes over the differences between the ancient and medieval priesthood and adopts Aristotle's criteria for the selection of those appointed as priests. The selection process for the priests was rigorous. Their duty included honouring the gods and administering their sanctuaries, so not just any person – e.g., labourers or artisans who had to practice lower professions – could belong to the priesthood. The priests were men of advanced age and devoid of passions. After long service in the military, judiciary, and advisory offices, these virtuous and proven citizens had withdrawn from the political scene.[308]

For Marsilius, priests cannot be drawn from the ranks of farmers or artisans; the sacerdotal offices should be assigned only to men who have relinquished their civic duties due to their advanced age. In his treatment of the civic function of the sacerdotal part, Aristotle seems to orient himself in the realities which prevailed in the Athens of his time: priests fulfil an administrative function, and the persons entrusted with sacerdotal duties often held other public offices.[309] In Aristotle's view, activities in the service of the city correspond to the various stages of human life: the office of priest is the sequel to a successful *vita politica* that begins in the time of youth and physical strength, is honed in the military, and is followed in maturity by experience in the advisory and judicial organs of the political community.[310]

Marsilius's Notion of Citizenship

In Marsilius's view, the military, ruling, and sacerdotal parts constitute the *honorabilitas* (honourable class), i.e, the upper ranks of the citizenry, and are to be taken as parts of the community in the strict sense, whereas the other three groups (agricultural, artisanal, and financial) constitute the *vulgas* (common folk) and can be counted as parts only in the broad sense of the term.[311] The term *honorabilitas*, rendered with the Greek expression *timēma*, is obviously a mistranslation by William of Moerbeke.[312] In connection with the division of constitutions, Aristotle employs this term to designate the taxable income of the citizens.[313]

Marsilius's account of the parts of the political community displays crucial differences from Aristotle's. While Aristotle identifies farmers and artisans as the necessary segments of the body politic, Marsilius states that the *vulgus* includes traders as well.[314]

Once again, Marsilius relies on the biological metaphor to challenge the notion of the hierarchy of ends and illustrate the mutual dependency among the various organs of the body politic, an idea which, as will be shown later, is so central to his vision of the desirable social organization. He explains that the eye is a more perfect organ than the hands or feet, for it performs a more perfect function; nevertheless, the eye is dependent on the hands and feet and receives action or motion from them. But at the same time, the hands and feet depend on the eye, because they need its guidance toward the goal to which they move or are moved. In analogous fashion, there is an interrelationship between the government and the lower parts of the body politic: the government is dependent on the activities of the lower parts of the community, and, conversely, the latter depend on the governing part to pronounce coercive judgments and protect them from injuries.[315]

Aristotle's depreciation of manual work is a corollary to his view of the hierarchy of ends and is a well-entrenched theme in ancient philosophical discourse.[316] Plato takes a critical stance towards trade and mechanical activities and recommends that these occupations ought to be assigned solely to slaves or foreigners.[317] In like manner, Aristotle holds that peasants and artisans provide the material necessities of the *polis*, i.e., the production of food and the exercise of crafts. Farming and menial occupations pertain solely to slaves, barbarians, and peasant farmers (*perioikoi*). Although Aristotle concedes that the concept of citizen does vary according to each constitutional form, he considers that admitting farmers and menial labourers to the citizenry – as is the case with democracy[318] – is a symptom of constitutional degeneration.[319] Physical labour inhibits the process of cultivating virtue and the quest for a good life.[320] Banausic trades and activities are incompatible with the practice of virtue, active engagement in civic affairs, and debase man's intellectual ability. For this reason, farmers, artisans, and day labourers live partly in a state of slavery and have no place in the citizenry of the ideal city.[321]

Aristotle offers three definitions of citizenship:

1) A citizen is someone who has the right to participate in the administration of justice and in the various offices.[322] Some offices are of

fixed duration, whereas others, such as those of the members of the jury or the assembly, are without limit of tenure.[323]

2) Citizenship is defined by participation in civic offices,[324] although this criterion does not apply to all constitutions.
3) Finally, Aristotle sets forth a more generic definition of citizenship, which rests on the right to participate in deliberative or judicial office.[325]

Aristotle's third definition of citizenship is the central pillar of Marsilius's notion of the citizen as the person who participates in the deliberative or judicial offices according to his rank.[326] Marsilius maintains that children, slaves, aliens, and women are excluded from citizenship. This holds true also for young men, although in another sense, for they are at least potentially citizens (*in propinqua potencia*).[327] But in contrast to Aristotle, Marsilius regards members of the *vulgus*, i.e., peasant farmers and craftspeople, as parts of the citizenry.[328] In particular, Marsilius takes over fundamental elements of the praxis of the Athenian democracy as described by Aristotle, but with a subtle difference: whereas for Aristotle the form of government determines the criteria for citizenship and, ultimately, the complexion of the body politic, Marsilius views citizenship as the constant and the form of government as the variable.

The Aristotelian concept of citizenship is predicated on the notion of active civic participation. For this reason, Aristotle reckons representation to be a sign of oligarchy and cautions against granting the citizen status to artisans and farmers. Marsilius, in contrast, accommodates the possibility of representative government. In line with his view that functional specialization constitutes a vital condition for the existence of a properly arranged polity, Marsilius recognizes the functional value of the artisans and farmers in fulfilling the material needs of the populace and proposes a balanced and integrated political and social order as the foundation of a healthy form of constitution. He takes into consideration the quality and the quantity of the citizens and is aware of the dangers associated with the exclusion of a large portion of the population from citizenship and public life in general.

Marsilius's ideal of citizenship encourages the participation of all parts of the community. It is possible that Marsilius's view of citizenship is undergirded by his experiences with the political organization of his native Padua or other Italian city states, where government was under the grip of the *comunanza*. A large part of Padua's population did not meet the criteria for admission into the *comunanza*, while influential and powerful individuals and families were excluded.[329] Essentially only one out of ten adult males was able to fulfil the requirements for membership in the *Consiglio Maggiore* and the lower offices.[330]

Marsilius's model of civic participation is strongly reminiscent of the praxis of the Athenian democracy, as described by Aristotle in the *Politics*. Medieval writers perceived affinities between the political organization of the Italian city states and that of the ancient Greek *poleis*, most notably classical Athenian democracy.[331] Albert the Great (1193–1280) readily associated the communes of Lombardy and Genoa with the radical form of democratic rule in which, according to Aristotle, sovereignty resided with the multitude and not with the law and in which the decrees of the popular assemblies overrode the laws. Ptolemy of Lucca pointed out that many cities in his contemporary Italy were being ruled by the many and in this respect they resembled or were patterned after classical Athens.[332]

Although, as mentioned above, Marsilius outlines an inclusive model of civic participation and accommodates the possibility of incorporating artisans and mechanics as members of the citizenry, his goal is not to justify of the unbridled rule of the *vulgus* and the suppression of the *honorabilitas*. It is precisely for this reason that it would be wrong to lay at Marsilius's door a variant of democratic rule founded solely on the majoritarian principle. Marsilius expressly characterizes democracy as a defective and flawed form of regime. He also stresses that the disproportionate increase of a particular part of the political community in terms of quantity or quality which occurs without being noticed is one of the principal causes of intergroup conflict and he mentions as an example the increase in the number of the poor in the case of democracy.[333] Marsilius suggests precautions against the usurpation of power by the wealthy. Therefore, he recommends that the would-be ruler assume coercive power only after his election; otherwise virtuous and capable but poor men would be excluded from rulership.[334]

Unlike Aristotle, Marsilius is not concerned with articulating a program for the preservation of any particular form of constitution. In his view, the durability of the political community depends upon the broad participation of the citizens in the law-making process. The citizens, he argues, are more likely to strive to maintain a polity in which they have an active share. Marsilius seems to be conscious of the special risks associated with the disenfranchisement of a large part of the population. He insists that the members of *vulgus* are citizens who enjoy the same rights as the members of the *honorabilitas*. He even makes the blunt statement that the authority to correct the ruler if he is neglectful or irresponsible does not reside with the clergy, but with the prudent or learned citizens and, preferably, to the artisans.[335] Although Marsilius is aware that citizens who possess leisure and expertise are more qualified to occupy the offices of the political community, he is adamant that the ultimate authority to appoint and remove the various officeholders lies with the entire body of the citizens.

Chapter Four

Marsilius's Legal Theory

The Definition of Law

The law is, according to Marsilius, one of the main characteristics of an orderly and full-fledged community. It serves as the *regula iustorum*, i.e., as a binding norm, according to which human acts are regulated. Before proceeding to a closer analysis of Marsilius's theory of law, it may be helpful to explore briefly his use of the concepts of 'law' and 'judge.'

For Marsilius, the term *lex* signifies a natural inclination toward a certain action or emotion.[1] In a second sense, *lex* indicates a productive *habitus* and, in general, any form that exists in the human mind and serves as a model or measure of the forms of things produced by art.[2] According to a third definition, *lex* is the standard that contains or embodies admonitions for voluntary human deeds according to which these are ordered toward reward and punishment in the hereafter. In this sense, the Mosaic Law, or at least part of it, and the evangelical law are designated as laws.[3] This definition applies to all religions, and Islam or the Zoroastrian religion in their entirety or in some parts are called laws, although only the Mosaic and the evangelical, i.e., Christian, law contain the truth. Marsilius invokes here two passages from Aristotle's *Metaphysics* which correspond to this definition of law: Aristotle refers to religions as 'laws'[4] and explains that religious doctrines were propagated in the form of myths in order to persuade men to abide by the laws.[5] Finally, Marsilius mentions a fourth definition of the term, which is decisive for his theory of law and conceives of the law in two respects. On the one hand, it denotes in general what is just or unjust, or beneficial or harmful. In this meaning it is called the science or doctrine of right. On the other hand, law is characterized by the fact that there exist precepts for its execution and enforcement through rewards and punishments in the present world.[6]

Marsilius also uses the terms 'judgment' and 'judge' in various ways.[7] In a general sense, the term 'judge' signifies a person who discerns or knows, especially in accordance with a theoretical or practical habit (*habitus*). In this sense, the geometer can be called a judge in that he judges figures and their attributes, and the physician discerns illnesses and judges about health, the prudent man judges with regard to what should be done or be avoided, and the architect judges on how to build a house. The word may be used in a second sense, referring to knowledge of the laws. Accordingly, one who possesses this knowledge is called in various countries, especially in Italy, *advocatus*.[8] Lastly, Marsilius mentions a third meaning of the term 'judge' which is fundamental for his conception of law. The ruler is designated as judge because he must make decisions and pronounce sentences according to the laws, which are vested with coercive power.[9] Marsilius relies on Aristotle to demonstrate that the members of the public assembly and the judges must decide specific cases,[10] explaining that Aristotle means the judges or the rulers.[11]

Marsilius envisions the prince as the supreme judge within the political community and defines his principal task as defending and ensuring justice.[12] In so doing, he follows the medieval political tradition that depicts the ruler as the guarantor of the laws, an idea which has its roots in canon law literature.[13] A necessary precondition for the tranquility and preservation of the political community is, in Marsilius's view, bringing malefactors and lawbreakers to justice.[14] Accordingly, he styles the ruler (or the rulers, in the case of the aristocratic constitution)[15] as the 'animate law' (*lex animata*):[16] laws have no soul and possess no executive moving principle to pronounce judgments and sentences and execute punishments and, as such, they need an animate subject or principle to command and regulate or judge human acts and to provide for the correction of transgressors.[17]

Marsilius defines the law as a pronouncement or ordinance which originates from political prudence and concerns matters related to civil justice and the common good and their opposites. The law is also vested with coercive power and its observance is guaranteed by a coercive command.[18] In this regard, it differs from religious texts such as the Bible in that it enjoys coercive power, i.e., *potencia coactiva*, an expression used by Marsilius as the Latin equivalent of Aristotle's *anagkastikē dunamis*.[19] All rules which concern justice and the common benefit –

such as customs (*consuetudines*), statutes (*statuta*), plebiscites (*plebiscita*), and decretals (*decretales*) – fall into this category.[20]

Marsilius's view of punitive authority as the hallmark of civil legislation stems from his preoccupation with the applicability of the laws and the government's judicial function in the process of enforcing the laws and punishing transgressors. But it is also a corollary to his overall project of drawing a clear line of demarcation between the temporal and religious spheres and of countering papal pretensions to political authority. Marsilius explains that all true concepts of just and expedient things are not *eo ipso* laws. What distinguishes the laws of the political community from all other kinds of laws and religions is the very fact that they are vested with coercive force by the *legislator humanus*. A correct or right notion of the just and beneficial is not a law unless its observance has been sanctioned by a coercive regulation. Although sound knolwedge of matters bearing on civil justice is a requirement for the creation of perfect laws, sometimes false judgments become laws and are vested with coercive power. Marsilius notes here that in certain barbarian lands, a murderer can be absolved of civil guilt and punishment if he pays a fine or penalty. Although such a law is unjust, it has the proper form, i.e., a coercive command concerning its observance.[21]

Marsilius challenges Aristotle's idea of justice arguing that even erroneous notions about justice and the common good can underpin civil legislation. In the section of the *Defensor pacis* which is devoted to the definition of the *legislator humanus*, Marsilius explains that the yardstick of the legitimacy of a law is not whether it is 'just' but, rather, whether it has been ratified by the body of the citizens. Therefore, should an individual or a group of citizens possess the authority to promulgate laws and impose them on the entire body of the citizens, they would thereby become tyrants and rule as autocrats over the rest of the citizenry regardless of whether their laws are right or not.[22]

Marsilius's formalization of the concept of law has important ramifications for his theory of civil legislation. First, unlike Aristotle, Marsilius de-emphasizes the significance of unwritten laws. Second, Marsilius's concept of justice is modeled on Aristotle's notion of commutative justice. And third, unlike Aristotle, Marsilius sees the laws, and not friendship, as the element that holds the various social forces in the right balance.

Aristotle distinguishes two kinds of law: 1) particular; and 2) general, i.e., laws based on nature. Particular laws are subdivided into 1) written; and 2) unwritten.[23] Unwritten (customary) laws owe their validity to custom and enjoy a higher status than written ones because they concern facts of fundamental importance.[24] Accordingly, Aristotle emphasizes that one of the lawgiver's prime tasks must be to infuse into the members of the political community respect for both unwritten and written laws, since the stability of the political community depends on the citizens' becoming accustomed to the existing constitution and receiving education through good laws.[25] Unlike Aristotle, Marsilius does not perceive the political community to be an entity pursuing moral ends but rather as the forum for the harmonious collaboration among its various parts for the sake of the common advantage. He attributes no particular importance to unwritten laws, explaining that they found acceptance in the first stages of the evolution of human communities but have no relevance for a full-fledged political community.[26]

Aristotle distinguishes two forms of (particular) justice. Distributive justice (*dianemētikon dikaion, iustitia distributive*) concerns the distribution of honour, wealth, and various kinds of goods among the members of society in equal or unequal shares.[27] Any distributive activity presupposes at least four elements, i.e., two persons who act as recipients of the objects at their disposal, as well as the two allotments to be apportioned. In this case, justice is realized when all parties receive equal shares according to geometrical proportion.[28] Injustice occurs when unequal shares are allotted among equal persons or equal shares among unequal persons.[29] Distributive justice is incumbent on the head of the political community in that he lays down general rules for the organization of civil life.[30]

The other kind of justice is the commutative or corrective justice (*diorthōtikon dikaion, epanorthōtikon dikaion, iustitia commutativa*), which applies a corrective principle in private transactions.[31] Aristotle's concept of commutative justice is of central importance for Marsilius's concept of law: according to Aristotle, corrective justice seeks to preserve or restore the arithmetical proportion, and in this process the status of the law-breaker is irrelevant, since the law is concerned with the nature and effects of the injury, treating the two parties as equal and seeking to identify the agent and the victim of an unjust act. Corrective justice is implemented through the intervention of a judge who acts as a middleman, adjudicating between two equal parties and restoring equality by taking away a part from the one and adding it to the other as a compensation for the harm the victim has suffered.[32]

The proportional retribution enforced through the intervention of justice constitutes, for Aristotle, one of the fundamental conditions for domestic unity: penalties are a medium for securing balance in the dealings (both voluntary and involuntary) between two partners in order to prevent the tyranny of the evil-minded and to ensure a balance for the injury that has occurred. Aristotle thereby draws a parallel between the punishment of the perpetrator and medical treatment: illnesses are often cured by opposites, which involve pain. Similarly, sensual desire in men or its excess, which is the cause of all evils, is rooted out and restored by means of punishment and spiritual health.[33] Aristotle stresses the need to lay down rules that regulate social life, as men are more amenable to fear, compulsion, and punishment than to a sense of honour and virtuous conduct. Accordingly, the lawgiver must inflict punishments on evildoers and banish those who are not amenable to correction.[34]

For Aristotle, commutative justice is crucial for the regulation of the relations among the members of society, but it does not reflect an ideal condition. Laws and penalties are intended as substitutes for the lack of genuine friendship among the citizens. Aristotle here echoes Plato's notion that in the ideal city there is no need for judges or physicians. For Aristotle, friendship is the binding force of the political community. For this reason, it seeks to attain harmony and suppress strife. For, if friendship reigned in the citizens' relations, then a legal order would be redundant.[35]

In Marsilius's survey of the different meanings of the term *ius*, distributive justice receives perfunctory treatment. For Marsilius, 'justice' designates the act and *habitus* of particular justice when someone strives for equality in the process of exchange or distribution.[36] Aristotle sees a correlation between the justice of laws and the nature of a constitution: laws in accordance with just constitutions are just, whereas laws prevailing in flawed or corrupt constitutions are unjust.[37]

The central focus of Marsilius's teaching on civil legislation is on commutative justice and the specific role of the ruler as a judge called to apply justice, uphold domestic tranquility, and prevent oppression.[38] Marsilius conceives of the law as the *regula* of transient deeds[39] and the bond that holds the political community together and guarantees a sufficient life and the endurance of the social order. Marsilius starts from the assumption that an equal relationship exists between the members of society, the preservation of which is a *conditio sine qua non* for the avoidance of disputes and internecine strife. The principal function of the government is, accordingly, to moderate the 'transient' acts of the citizens according to the law as the norm of justice[40] and bring malefactors to justice.[41]

Marsilius's depiction of the ruler as the agency responsible for preserving and restoring the delicate equilibrium among the various segments of the civil body is a logical development of his notion of the political community as the forum for collaboration among individuals who come together to meet their material needs and achieve a sufficient life. The function of government is to preserve the mean in the transient acts, which are performed to the benefit, or disadvantage, or harm of another in the present world. Otherwise, strife and division arise among the citizens, which can bring about the dissolution of the community.[42] The *pars principans* must, by his authority and in accordance with the law, prescribe the just and honourable and prohibit their contraries. Political tranquility involves keeping each part in its right condition and protected against injuries and interference. The ruler acts in this regard as a judge, as depicted by Aristotle, and metes out rewards or punishments for the merits or misconduct of the citizens.[43]

In an Aristotelian manner, Marsilius sees punishments as medicine for a transgression, i.e., as a cure for both the perpetrator of a particular offense and the victim of the injury. The victim receives compensation, which restores equality and proportion while conserving each part of the community in its proper being.[44] Marsilius perceives the ruler to be the efficient cause which grants matter its appropriate form. For Marsilius as well as Aristotle, the status of the offender is of no relevance in the administration of justice.[45]

Giants on the Shoulders of Dwarfs: Legislation and a Well-Ordered Political Community

From these considerations Marsilius deduces that the law has a dual function. First, it aims at the common good and the application of justice; second, it guarantees support for the ruler, especially in the case of hereditary monarchy, and guarantees the success, right function, and permanence of the government. Marsilius asserts that laws are necessary because without them, just judgments could not be carried out.[46]

Marsilius's reasoning in favour of civil legislation is premised on the notion of the ruler as judge. According to Marsilius, a right judicial decision depends on a) the right disposition of the judge, and b) full knowledge of the matters over which the judgment is to be pronounced.[47]

With regard to the first point, Marsilius relies on Aristotle's account of the criteria for the proper function of forensic rhetoric. Aristotle distinguishes three kind of rhetoric: deliberative, forensic, and epideictic. Deliberative rhetoric aims at what is expedient or harmful.[48] In the case of forensic rhetoric, he notes that the orator should appear to be of a certain character and the hearer should be disposed in a certain way, because men's opinions vary depending on their emotions. When someone is favourably disposed towards another person about whom he is pronouncing a judgment, it can appear to him that the accused has committed no injustice or that his offence is minor. However, if the man hates the person whom he must judge, the opposite might occur (*Rh.* II.1). For Aristotle, the methods employed by the deliberative and forensic types of rhetoric are identical, although the former is nobler and more relevant to the administration of civic matters, whereas the scope of the latter is confined to the transactions among the citizens. Furthermore, forensic rhetoric allows more room for trickery than does deliberative rhetoric, since the judges make decisions concerning their personal affairs. As a result, the judges focus on their own interests and listen for their pleasure, but do not pass right judgments.[49]

Aristotle conceptualizes the model ruler as surpassing the other members of the political community in virtue to such an extent that he, as the embodiment of the law and just government, cannot be bound to civil legislation. Aristotle concedes that such an individual is extremely rare and proclaims legislation to be applicable to a political community comprised of likes and equals.[50] But he goes a step further asserting that such a type of rule is inapplicable, given that the human soul is susceptible to perverse emotions and appetites such as hatred, love, or greed, which pervert human desire for the good and lead to erroneous judgments,[51] whereas the law is devoid of vices and insulated against the influence of human emotions.[52]

Marsilius parallels Aristotle in giving priority to the sovereignty of the law over the rule of a single person according to his discretion, since laws are not made to favour friends or harm foes. He grounds his theory of the necessity of civil legislation on the Stoic doctrine that there is a concomitant tendency in human nature to secure one's life and guarantee the perpetuation of social life. Consistent with this idea, Marsilius infers that the citizens seek to obtain the means conducive to the good of the community, such as laws that are made for the public welfare and not for a friend or an enemy. The judge's inner disposition, on the other hand, can be corrupted at any moment; he can look at the persons summoned in the court as friends or enemies and can by bribes or promises be beneficial or harmful. This can lead his judgment into error but so long as the judge (or the ruler) operates in strict accordance with the laws, the likelihood of his pronouncing unjust judgments is minimized.[53]

Ignorance on the judge's part can also corrupt of his judgment, however principled and well-intentioned he might be. For Marsilius, laws contain almost perfect and complete provisions and regulations concerning what is just or unjust, and expedient or harmful. Laws are not the product of either a single individual or a group of individuals, no matter how discerning he/they may be, but emanate from the collective judgment and experience of several generations over a long period of time. Everything that the 'first inventors' of the laws and everything that all persons of the same era have said about laws, based on their own experience, is imperfect. Laws are ameliorated over the course of time through additions and amendments made by successive generations. The body of knowledge produced by the first investigators or all the men of a particular era is limited and imperfect in comparison with the accumulated prudence and experience of several generations.[54] The perfection or refinement of the laws over several generations runs parallel to the evolution of sciences,[55] which find their perfection through mutual aid and additions to earlier findings and discoveries.[56]

To bolster his notion of the laws as the outcome of collective prudence and experience, Marsilius employs an argument from Aristotle's *Metaphysics*, which encapsulates the notion of the progressive evolution of human civilization: Timotheos's melodies would not have been so perfect had he not been acquainted with those invented earlier by Phrynes. To Marsilius, then, legislation resembles the development of the sciences. To illustrate the process of the perfecting of the sciences, he quotes a passage from Averroes's commentary on the *Metaphysics*: no one is capable of discovering the larger part of practical or theoretical knowledge, since these are completed only through the aid which earlier inventors offer to their successors.[57]

Aristotle reckons the analogy between arts and laws to be erroneous, since changing the ways an art is practiced is different from modifying an existing law. In his view, laws per se have no force to command obedience other than the force of custom that grows up over time. Altering existing laws or substituting new laws for old ones erodes their power.[58] Aristotle maintains that progress pertains to the evolution and cultivation of the arts, since everyone seeks to complete and add to what they lack, so time thereby becomes an 'inventor' (*sunergos*),[59] as is the case with the primordial founders of cities and lawmakers.[60]

Marsilius, however, subtly converts Aristotle's theory of progress to present the laws as the outcome of the collective prudence and experience of a number of generations and to highlight the analogy between the process of legislation and the evolution of the arts and human learning. Although the laws can be better made by the wise than by those who are less learned, the assembled multitude desires and can discern the common benefit to a greater extent than any part of it, however prudent or learned that part may be.[61] The multitude can be of vital help in this process when working together with those who are more learned or possess more experience; for, although it cannot by itself discover true and useful measures, it has, nevertheless, the ability to evaluate the measures discovered (invented) and proposed to it by others and to judge whether amendments, rescissions, alterations, or omissions are necessary.[62]

Marsilius asserts that many things which a man cannot invent by himself, he can nevertheless comprehend and bring to perfection after they have been explained to him by someone else. Drawing on Aristotle, Marsilius explains that although it is difficult to recognize the beginning, i.e., the truth proper to each science, when the beginning has been discovered, it is easy to augment it.[63] Although the principles of the sciences, arts, and other disciplines can only be discovered by the best most discerning or acute minds, those of humbler ability, albeit not being able to discover such principles by themselves, can make or propose additions to what has already been discovered (invented), and thus contribute to the perfection of the sciences.[64] Marsilius reinforces his idea of collective wisdom by quoting the Arabic translation of the *Metaphysics* to the effect that each of the inventors of the various arts and sciences, apprehends or perceives nothing or very little about the truth, but when the insights of those who have achieved some comprehension are combined and brought together, the outcome will be of considerable quality, as is the case with astrology.[65]

Cyclopes with Many Eyes: Laws and Collective Prudence

Aristotle's ideas on the nexus between the perfection of the arts and sciences and knowledge produced by successive generations had an important echo in the work of a number of medieval Muslim (e.g., Averroes) and Christian (e.g., Thomas Aquinas, Roger Bacon) thinkers.

Averroes, for instance, contends that the study of philosophy is brought to perfection through the successive investigations of multiple persons, as is the case with the mathematical sciences, since a single individual cannot discern or identify all the principles and produce the entire body of knowledge in the theoretical or practical sciences by himself.[66] Albert the Great relies on Aristotle and speaks of the arts as guides and precursors for later generations of philosophers. The same idea can be found in Roger Bacon. Art, for Bacon, results from progress in the domain of the different sciences, which consists in complementing previous discoveries.[67]

While most medieval Scholastic writers employ Aristotle's concept of progress in the context of debates on the evolution of human knowledge, Marsilius uses it in a novel way in order to establish the collective superiority of the entire body of the citizens and to emphasize the analogy between the process of promulgating laws and the evolution of science. A prominent instance of a similar use of Aristotle's doctrine of progress is Isaac Abravanel (1437–1508), who favours collective leadership by building on the Aristotelian theory of collective wisdom and cites the *Metaphysics* instead of the *Politics*. Although Moerbeke's Latin translation of the *Politics* was quite widespread in Abravanel's time, and although Abravanel had access to major libraries in Portugal, Castile, and later Italy, he does not seem to have had firsthand knowledge of the *Politics*, and his references to that work were mediated by Thomas Aquinas and other Scholastic theorists.[68]

Marsilius describes the law as an eye which consists of many eyes, i.e., the outcome of the accumulated insights and observation of multiple individuals or generations, that helps avoid errors in civil judgments and provides the framework for right civil decisions so that they can be preserved from the ignorance, perverted emotions, and bias of the judges.[69] To set the stage for his notion of the sovereignty of the multitude, Marsilius also relies on a passage in the *Politics* in which Aristotle holds that many persons judging with many eyes and ears and acting with many hands and legs perceive better than a single person who judges with the aid of only two eyes and two ears and acts with only two hands and legs.[70] However, Aristotle refers here to the preservation of the various constitutional forms and makes the point that a successful ruler ought to multiply his eyes, ears, hands, and feet, i.e., to extend the circle of his friends and supporters and foster their partnership in his regime.[71]

When Aristotle speaks of the lawgiver, he has in mind such figures as Solon and Lycourgos, who established and framed laws and constitutions. Aristotle is committed to the view of the legislator as a wise individual[72] who lays down the principles for the function of the political community and introduces a system of written and unwritten rules. In the second book of the *Politics*, Aristotle refers to early legislators and clears a prominent place for Solon as the ideal legislator,[73] and in several passages of the *Nicomachean Ethics* he equates the head of the political community with the legislator.[74]

With his concept of the lawgiver, Marsilius breaks away from Aristotle and the Islamic political tradition which insists on the equation of the ruler and the lawgiver.[75] Averroes, for instance, stresses that the ruler should embody the functions of a *princeps absolutus, conservator iustitiae,* and *servitor aequalitatis*. According to Averroes, assuming rule over a political community requires the perfection of the rational faculty and the powers of conceptualization whereby the philosopher-king and the prophet-ruler partake of the active intellect. Only an individual who has attained this state may, as the head of a virtuous city, possess unlimited power. The ruler's paramount task is to make just legal decisions, and he is granted the authority to apply justice[76] and impose rules. The existence of the political community presupposes the existence of a *vir strenuus,* who can be no other person than the king himself.[77]

But according to Marsilius, the law pursues an additional goal: the security and permanence of the government and constitutional stability, especially in the case of hereditary monarchy. For, if a ruler governs according to law, his judgment is immune to the dangers attendant upon ignorance, perverted emotions, and corruption, and as such he is regulated both in himself and in relation to his subjects, whereas if he acted or decided in his discretion, the government would suffer from sedition and, ultimately, decline. This constitutes for Marsilius the golden rule for the preservation of kingship: the political community then suffers fewer tensions, and the danger of the collapse of the government is minimized.[78] The physician Marsilius wishes thereby to offer, in the spirit of Aristotle's *Politics,* remedies for the internal causes of the decline of the monarchy: kingship, Aristotle contends, is rarely ruined by exogenous factors, and in most cases the forces of destruction spring from within the body politic. The demise of kingship occurs when kings quarrel with one another or when a king acts in a tyrannical manner and seeks to expand his sphere of power.[79]

Once again, though, Marsilius alters the meaning of the original source to support his thesis about the value of legislation as a means for preserving the various kinds of constitutions, especially kingship. A closer comparison between the passage Marsilius cites from Aristotle's *Politics* with the Greek original shows that Marsilius has omitted a part of the Aristotelian text to highlight the vulnerability of kingship and call attention to the internal causes of constitutional transformation: Aristotle deems kingship to be an enduring type of rule, because it is least frequently overthrown from outside. He suggests that kingship is destroyed primarily by external agency, and that if these did not exist, endogenous causes would then come into consideration, which would lead to internecine strife. Marsilius, on the other hand, de-emphasizes the importance of extrinsic causes in the process of constitutional transformation and argues instead for the supremacy of domestic factors, especially if a ruler governs without paying heed to the laws or the consent of the citizens.[80]

The *legislator humanus*

The primary legislator (*legislator primus*) and specific efficient cause of the law is, according to Marsilius, the body of the citizens – or their 'weightier part' (*valencior pars*) – through their vote or will expressed in discussions taking place in the civil assembly. Marsilius is adamant that the only legitimate lawgiver, the 'primary and proper efficient cause' of the laws, is the whole body of the citizens (*universitas civium*) or its 'weightier part,' which is defined according to the quality and quantity of the persons over which a law is made. The entire body of the citizens or its weightier part is the legislator regardless of whether it creates the laws directly by itself or assigns the task of making laws to a person or a group of persons who are not and cannot be the legislator in the absolute sense (*simpliciter*), but only in a certain aspect (*ad aliquid*) and for a specific period and in accordance with the authority of the primary legislator.[81] The authority for legislation falls upon the *legislator humanus*, but the drafting of laws should be assigned to the 'prudent,' i.e., those who have leisure, are older and experienced in practical affairs, rather than to the mechanics who are constantly engaged in tasks aimed at providing the necessities of life.[82]

Marsilius sketches out a generic model of political organization which has value in various places and under different circumstances. Marsilius's concept of the *valencior pars* is one of the knottiest themes in Marsilian scholarship. A number of previous studies have analysed the concept in relation to the majoritarian principle and construed it as the majority of the citizens. Another line of scholarship has emphasized its qualitative dimensions and interpreted the concept as the 'worthy' or the 'weightier' part.[83]

The *valencior pars* concept occurs in the *Defensor pacis* in connection with the founding of the first communities, which took place on the basis of a primordial agreement among the majority (*valencior pars*) of the *patresfamilias*.[84] Like Aristotle, Marsilius expresses the conviction that the preservation of the political community presupposes that the part of the citizenry which wishes the continuation of the polity must outweigh the part which wishes the opposite.[85] For if the majority of citizens engaged in seditious activities and challenged civil life, the human desire for self-preservation would be futile. Pursuant to his idea that men seek by nature the proper means to preserve their existence, Marsilius asserts that the majority of the individuals who make up the political community desire the law ('Vult ergo valencior multitudo civitatis legem [. . .]').[86]

Marsilius also concurs with Aristotle on the idea that the conservation of all constitutional forms is contingent on the principle that the part of the political community which desires the maintenance of the constitution, must be superior to or stronger than the one which desires the opposite.[87] This principle is valid, according to Aristotle, both for just and erroneous constitutional types, since the majority is always stronger.[88] Elsewhere, Marsilius notes that every whole is greater than a part of it ('[. . .] omne totum maius esse sua parte [. . .]');[89] and that the body of the citizens or their majority are in a better position to judge what is beneficial for the community ('Unde satis evidenter per necessitatem infertur, universitatem civium aut ipsius valenciorem multitudinem, que pro eodem accipienda sunt, magis posse quid eligendum et quid spernendum discernere, quacumque sui parte seorsum).'[90] In Moerbeke's translation of the *Politics*, which Marsilius quotes in the *Defensor pacis*, it reads, 'Oportet valenciorem esse partem civitatis volentem non volentem manere politiam'; 'totque multitudine esse eos qui in politeumate, ut sint valentiores his omnibus, unum aliquod impossibilium est.' In these passages Aristotle uses the word *kreitton* in the meaning of 'stronger' or 'mightier.'

The preceding account demonstrates that in the passages cited above, the term *valencior pars* indicates the numerical majority.[91] Marsilius's intention is not to advocate the unfettered rule of the *vulgus*, however.[92] Marsilius is disinclined to favour a democratic form of government,[93] because a constitution in which the majority of the poor suppresses the minority of the well-off would be a perverted one and would suffer from social friction. Marsilius, like several other Italian writers of his time, is aware of the hazardous effects of the *popolo*'s rise to political power in many Italian cities.[94] The social and political tensions that ensued with the *popolo*'s rise to power are two of the themes that dominated a large body of writings on the political history of Padua,[95] which witnessed the exclusion of the *magnates, potentiores,* and *magni homines,* i.e., of individuals who were considered too powerful in terms of wealth or influence, in accordance with the statutes.[96]

Marsilius stipulates that one should construe the *pars valencior* concept according to the honest use of constitutions (*policiarum consuetudinem honestam*) or define it according to *Politics*, book 6, chapter 2:[97] according to Aristotle, the extreme form of democracy is founded on the principle of justice pertaining to the democracy, i.e., all enjoy equality according to number: the poor do not have a greater share of power than the wealthy, nor does ultimate authority reside solely with the poor, but that all segments of the body politic rule equally.[98]

In Aristotle's view, every political community consists of the components of quality and quantity. Aristotle understands freedom, wealth, education, and good birth to correspond to quality, whereas numerical superiority represents the element of quantity. The multitude or the poor can surpass the nobility or the wealthy numerically but not in terms of quality. Aristotle is therefore of the opinion that both factors must respectively be weighed against each other.[99]

Aristotle also contrasts the multitude and the few experts.[100] The many when coming together can surpass a few virtuous men in virtue and insight because each has his stake therein. Consequently, the many together display collective wisdom and come together to form a single many.[101] Aristotle asserts that the many when coming together are in a position to render a better judgment on works of music and poetry.[102] All men can, according to Aristotle, assess or judge a rhetorical line of reasoning.[103] For this reason, he considers deliberative oratory more honourable and of greater relevance to civic affairs than forensic rhetoric, since the adjudicator must at the same time judge his own affairs.[104] Aristotle asserts that the many are less susceptible to emotions and feelings than a single person; therefore they can judge with more certainty, whereas a single person is more likely to yield to his emotions and form an erroneous judgment.[105]

These considerations serve Aristotle as a starting point for the discussion on the role of the multitude[106] as well as the election of the officeholders and their accountability in the Solonian constitution. In this way limitation of the authority of the *plēthos* in the election and accountability of magistrates was supposed to serve as a prophylactic against the devolution of the constitution.[107]

According to Aristotle, the ability of any single individual or a small group of experts to judge is more limited than that of the entire multitude. This is true at least in the condition that the multitude is not of slavish character.[108] Aristotle concedes that the theory of the collective wisdom does not apply universally; after all, if this principle were applicable to every nation and every people, then it must apply also to animals, because some nations do not differ from the latter.[109] Aristotle mentions an additional condition, i.e., the freedom of the multitude,[110] according to which farmers and the artisans are excluded from this process since they are engaged in activities that do not permit direct and active engagement in civic occupations.[111]

Aristotle's concept of collective wisdom concerns the selection, review, and correction of office holders. Aristotle, like other ancient political theorists, is acutely sensitive to the perils inherent in the unfettered rule of the multitude and thus not prepared to vindicate the multitude's right to cooperate in legislation. He criticizes the civil decisions (*psēphismata*) of the Athenian democracy. One of his main criticisms of Athenian democracy concerns the conflict between the rule of the *nomos* in the sense of a law imposing a general rule on the one hand and the decisions of the civil assemblies on the other.[112] The law must, Aristotle states, regulate civic affairs and comprise general rules;[113] at the same time, the authority of making decisions about particular cases must reside with the assembly of the citizens. Therefore, a democratic constitution in which the decrees of the assembly and not the laws govern is not genuine. As long as supreme sovereignty lies with the laws, the likelihood of the emergence of demagogues is minimized; whereas when the laws do not rule, the many act collectively like a monarch and succumb to despotic tendencies, and flatterers and demagogues gain influence.[114] Marsilius, by contrast, asserts that the body of the citizens or their 'weightier part' should have the final say in the most important matters within the political community.[115]

Legislation and Sovereignty

The primary legislator (*primus legislator*), i.e., the primary and proper efficient cause of the laws, can only be, according to Marsilius, the entire body of the citizens and/or their 'weightier part,' whether they promulgate the laws directly or assign the drafting of laws to one or multiple citizens who cannot be the legislator in an absolute sense (*qui legislator simpliciter non sunt nec esse possunt*) but only in a relative sense and for a specific period in accordance with the authority of the primary legislator. Through the election or will expressed in discussion in the general assembly of the citizens, the primary legislator commands or determines what needs to be done or omitted concerning human civil act under a punishment. As such, laws and anything that constitutes the outcome of election must be approved by the primary legislator. Likewise, any additions, omissions, modifications, or changes to the laws and their interpretation or suspension must take place only with the approval of the primary legislator according to the exigencies of time, place, and other factors. By the same authority, the laws must be announced or publicized after they have been ratified so that no citizen or alien who fails to observe them may be exculpated because of ignorance.[116]

Marsilius's concept of sovereignty – like Machiavelli's[117] – is markedly similar to the one used by Aristotle (*kurion*) in his definition of democracy as the form of constitution in which the multitude is sovereign ('dominant'). ('Est autem politia ordo civitatis aliorum principatuum et maxime dominantis omnium. Dominans quidem enim ubique est politeuma civitatis, politeuma autem est politia. Dico autem puta in democraticis quidem dominans populus, paucis autem e contrario in oligarchiis' – *Pol.* 1278b10–15.)[118]

Marsilius examines the question of the collective sovereignty of the citizens from an epistemological point of view. He specifically builds on Aristotle's doctrine of collective wisdom in support of the idea that any corporeal whole is greater both in mass and effective strength and activity (*activa virtus et accio*) than any part thereof considered separately. Thus, any deficiencies or lacunae in the drafts of the laws presented to the body of the citizens are more likely to be noticed by the whole body of the citizens or its weightier part rather than a small segment of the citizenry.[119] Marsilius asserts that a small group of prudent individuals can judge the drafts of the laws better than the rest of the citizens, yet a small number of nonexperts can be so superior that they could judge as well as or better than a small group of experts.[120] Likewise, Marsilius holds that no citizen or group of citizens is capable of judging what has been proposed and discovered by someone else or of discerning and deciding what must be added, subtracted, or amended, better than the entire body of the citizens. Marsilius and Aristotle agree that the many can even pass a just judgment over the quality of a picture, house, ship, or other works of art without necessarily being able to discover or produce them themselves.[121]

Marsilius also relies on Aristotle's principle that the entire body of the citizens comprises several persons, including the members of the civil assembly, of the judiciary, and of the upper classes, who when merged together are stronger than a single individual or a group, including the few who hold high government offices.[122] Marsilius's civil assembly (i.e., farmers, artisans, and others of that sort), the judiciary (i.e., jurists in the service of the government such as lawyers, legal experts, and notaries), the *honorabilitas* (i.e., those who hold senior government posts), or any other segment of the body politic taken *per se* cannot surpass all the groups of the political community taken together and cannot form a judgment which is safer than that of the entire body of the citizens.[123]

As indicated earlier, Aristotle holds that the doctrine of the sovereignty of the multitude applies to a multitude that is not depraved. Marsilius refers to Aristotle's qualifications only in passing. His argument for the sovereignty of the multitude depends on the assumption that the majority of the citizens are neither wicked nor undiscerning.[124] To the contrary: they possess sound understanding and rational ability; and they are actuated by the desire for the political community and the means for its preservation, such as the laws.[125]

To bolster his argument about the sovereignty of the body of the citizens, Marsilius appeals to another Aristotelian principle: the quantitative superiority of those who wish the endurance of the constitution vis-à-vis those who oppose it. In Marsilius's view, a stable and lasting social organization depends on whether the fraction which desires the conservation of the political community is quantitatively superior to that which desires the opposite.[126] For, it would be contrary to nature if those who are averse to social life are so numerous that they surpass in power that part of the populace which wishes the well-being and continuance of the community.[127]

Medieval Echoes

By expressing such a high estimate of the ability of most men to exhibit collective prudence and have a share in the process of decision making, Marsilius differs from a number of medieval writers. Peter of Auvergne, for instance, agrees with Marsilius that a community is run more efficiently when the fundamental locus of sovereignty in the process of appointing and correcting a ruler rests in the entire body of the citizens, and not just a small group of virtuous and prudent individuals. However, Peter specifies that this doctrine does not apply to a vile and beastlike multitude. Peter distinguishes between a bestial multitude (*multitudo bestialis*), which is obdurate, intractable, and impervious to persuasion and lacks political understanding, wisdom, and virtue;[128] and a well-ordered multitude (*multitudo bene ordinata*), which can partake of virtue, is pliable and amenable to persuasion, and consists of prudent men and the common folk. The well-ordered multitude, by contrast, deserves the right to elect, appoint, and punish the ruler, since it fulfils the fundamental conditions for stable government – notably prudence and the power to repel external threats. This type of multitude should be ruled by a wise and virtuous individual who receives authority by the assent of the other members of the community through election.[129]

Similar ideas occur in the *Quaestiones super octo libros politicorum Aristotelis* (*Questions on Aristotle's Politics*), which until recently had been falsely attributed to John Buridan (1300–58). The author of the *Questions*, Nicolas de Vaudémont, who taught at the Faculty of Arts in Paris in the second half of the fourteenth century, follows Peter of Auvergne's lead and distinguishes between a well-ordered multitude, which consists of strong, virtuous, and wise men, and a vile multitude. The bestial multitude can be classified into the one that is bereft of rational ability and the one that can potentially be induced to reason through persuasion. The bestial multitude is not entitled to elect or correct the ruler. The well-ordered multitude, by contrast, is characterized by prudence, affection, and loyalty toward the political community, and displays numerical strength. Therefore, an election in which the well-ordered multitude participates is conducive to domestic tranquility and stability and its outcome can be enforced as long as the multitude possesses the right to correct the ruler if he breaks or evades the laws.[130]

Beyond Aristotle

Marsilius is not concerned with prescribing a universal standard of justice, but rather with the extent to which laws emanate from and reflect the voluntary agreement of the body of the citizens. Unjust laws contain the seeds for slavery, oppression, and misery of the citizenry and lead to the destruction of the political community.[131] Thus, Marsilius asserts that the authority to promulgate laws cannot reside with a single individual or group of persons who are likely to be more attentive to their personal benefit than the public welfare, as is the case with oligarchic regimes and the decretals of the clergy.[132]

The natural tendency to strive after a self-sufficient life and avoid the contrary prompts men to band together in the political community which constitutes the necessary condition for the achievement of self-sufficient and commodious living. Marsilius builds here on the Stoic theory of *oikeiosis*: men gather together for a life in the community to lead a materially sufficient life and seek the means conducive to the preservation of social life and the creation of a flourishing community. By extension, they also seek to provide for the enactment of the laws, whereas the opposite would amount to a natural abnormality.[133]

Although Marsilius recognizes, as does Aristotle, the importance of 'good' laws for the proper ordering of human society, his primary focus is on whether and to what extent laws are supported by a consent of the citizens. For Aristotle, an excellent legal order (*eunomia*) requires obedience to the existing laws.[134] He compares the city in which just resolutions are passed and good laws are in effect, but not enforced, to an incontinent person; he compares the city which retains bad laws to a wicked man.[135] For Marsilius, the salient criterion defining a right law is its acceptance by the citizenry. Accordingly, he assigns legislative power to the body of the citizens, for only they hold the coercive power that is necessary for the enforcement of the laws.[136] A citizen will more readily and voluntarily follow a law in the promulgation of which he believes to have a share, and this is true only for laws enacted after the body of the citizens has heard and endorsed or approved them.[137]

How great an importance Marsilius attaches to consent is shown in his statement that it would be more reasonable to enact a less useful law according to these guidelines than to enact a better law which an individual or a group of citizens have passed pursuing their own private interests. In the latter case, a group of citizens in charge of making the laws would lapse into despots, causing the other citizens to oppose their laws and refuse to observe them.[138]

Marsilius cautions against frequent changes of the laws, because they erode their strength. Marsilius concurs with Aristotle on the importance of custom as the paramount feature of a stable legal order. Although Marsilius does not consider unwritten laws essential to a stable political order, he does emphasize the need to infuse in the citizens the *ésprit des lois* and generate obedience and respect for the existing legal order.[139] Marsilius also insists, with Aristotle, that minor violations of the laws emasculate their sovereignty and can ultimately lead to the disintegration of the political community, just as small overexpenditures can result in the dissipation of one's wealth.[140]

Chapter Five

Marsilius's Theory of Government

The Taxonomy of Constitutions

Following Aristotle, Marsilius distinguishes two kinds of government (*principatus*).[1] In the *Nicomachean Ethics,* Aristotle speaks of three basic kinds of constitutions and an equal number of deviant types. The basic forms are monarchy, aristocracy, and timocracy, which involves the rule of those who possess property. Their corresponding perversions are tyranny, oligarchy, and democracy.[2] In the *Politics,* Aristotle proposes a broader division of the various regimes based on whether they are oriented toward the common good or toward the interest of a particular group: those aiming at the common benefit conform to the absolute concept of justice, whereas those that promote the self-interest of the ruler or rulers involve an element of despotism and constitute perversions of the right constitutional types.[3]

Marsilius's classification of the various constitutions is modeled on the one in the *Politics,* but differs from Aristotle's typology in a number of respects. Marsilius dispenses with the concept of 'just' constitutions.[4] He is concerned not with setting a universal standard of justice but, rather, with the legitimacy of a regime and its acceptance by the citizenry. In accordance with his idea that the existence of an orderly and prosperous society is contingent on the harmonious interrelation of its constituent parts, Marsilius uses the term 'well-mixed constitution' as the antithesis of *vitiatum*. This is explained against the medical background of the Marsilian vision of a properly functioning political community as the analogue of a symmetrically grown living organism, whose parts stand in a proportional relationship to one another.[5]

Marsilius divides the forms of government into 'well-tempered' (*bene temperate*) and 'diseased' (*vitiati*): in the first case, the ruler exercises leadership with an eye to the general welfare and in accordance with the will (*voluntas*) or consent (*consensus*) of the governed, whereas this is not the case with the deviant forms. Kingship, aristocracy, and polity belong to the first type; to the second belong the tyrannical monarchy, oligarchy, and democracy.[6] Kingship is a temperate form of single-man rule which rests on citizen consent and is directed to the common benefit. Tyranny is a vicious regime type in which a single individual rules only in his own interest and against the consent of the subjects. Aristocracy is a temperate form of government that is based on the rule of the honourable class (*honorabilitas*), involves citizen consent, and seeks to foster the general good. In its degenerate allied form, oligarchy, the wealthier or more powerful govern in defiance of the consent of the other citizens and for private gain. In the polity (*policia*) all citizens serve in the government or perform a deliberative function according to their rank and ability to serve the public interest and in accordance with the will or consent of the body of the citizens. In the corrupt variant of polity – democracy – rule is exercised by the mass (*vulgus*), by the multitude of the poor, against the will or without the consent of their fellow citizens and not for the common good.[7]

In his scheme of constitutional classification, Marsilius adopts from Aristotle the numerical criterion, i.e., the number of persons who exercise supreme authority and the size of the governing part. Like Aristotle, he also employs the criterion of whether a particular constitution aims towards the benefit of those in power. However, he introduces an additional criterion of distinction, i.e., the process (*modus institucionis*)[8] whereby every form of regime comes into existence, i.e., with or without the citizens' consent.[9]

In his discussion of the various forms of kingship, Aristotle refers to the consent of the ruled as the element that determines their legitimacy:[10] tyrannical rulers are compelled to rely on foreign troops for their security, whereas kings who govern according to law and over willing subjects select their guards from among their people.[11] Aristotle mentions that the third type of kingship, the *aisumnēteia*, is a hybrid form of rule, because it combines features of both tyranny and elective kingship and operates in accordance with the consent of the subjects.[12] Aristotle also describes a fourth form of kingship that prevailed in the heroic times, and was exercised over willing subjects in the manner of hereditary succession and according to the laws.[13] But, alhough Aristotle mentions consent as one of the factors conducive to the legitimacy and longevity of a regime, his categorization of constitutional forms is coloured by the teleological orientation of his political thought and is based on the notion of finality as the criterion for the quality of a particular constitution.[14]

While most medieval political writers rely on Aristotle's constitutional taxonomy, Marsilius goes beyond Aristotle and his medieval predecessors in that he introduces the element of consent into his analysis of the various forms and modes of rule and elevates it to the criterion that determines the character and legitimacy of a constitution.[15] In his view there are two prime criteria on which such a classification is based: 1) the consent of the citizens (*subditorum consensus*); and 2) and the extent to which government authority is exercised in accordance with laws laid down for the common good. Marsilius grants primacy to the consent of the citizens as the determining, or the most important, factor for the legitimacy of a constitution.[16] This shift of perspective is readily explained in view of Marsilius's preoccupation with the factors and causes involved in political phenomena. The legitimacy of any form of government can be tested, Marsilius argues, by ascertaining the value that a regime attaches to the citizens' consent. Healthy systems of government incorporate the consent of the citizens as an essential element, while the evil forms of constitution deny such consent.[17]

The Five Modes of Establishing Monarchy

Marsilius's concern with the process whereby the various constitutions come into being has an important bearing on his discussion of the various kinds of kingship. In particular, he delineates five 'modes of establishing' kingly monarchy (*modi instituendi regaliem monarchiam; modi institutionis regalis monarchiae*) that may be described as follows: 1) functional monarchy; 2) hereditary despotic monarchy; 3) elective tyranny; 4) heroic monarchy; and 5) *dominus* monarchy.[18]

A monarch is appointed for a specific function, such as the command of the army, either with hereditary succession or for his own lifetime only. As an example, Marsilius mentions Agamemnon, who was entrusted with the command of the army.[19] A ruler might be elected for the sole purpose of taking charge of the armed forces,[20] as is the case with the captaincy (*capitaneatus*) or the constabulary (*constabiliria*).[21] Such a leader does not have any judicial authority in peacetime, but possesses absolute authority to punish or put to death malefactors during military operations or war.[22]

Kings in Asia typify the second variant, i.e., hereditary despotic monarchy. They receive their authority through hereditary succession and rule according to a despotic law that is aimed at their own benefit. Various nations in Asia accept such a rule without protest because of their barbaric and slavish nature and the influence of custom. This kind of rule is regal in that it is native to the country and is exercised over voluntary subjects, because the ruler's ancestors were the first to inhabit the region. But at the same time, it exhibits tyrannical features in that its laws are intended not for the common good but, rather, for the king's interest.[23]

This idea of a link between geography and methods of government is not unique to Marsilius. Ptolemy of Lucca, for example, points out that people of certain regions are by nature slavish; as such, they need tyrannical government, whereas others have a courageous heart and trust in their intelligence.[24] These ideas ultimately go back to Aristotle, who traces the servile character of Asian nations[25] to geographic and climatic conditions as well as to physical appearance, temperament, and lifestyle.[26] Similarly, and along with Avicenna, Peter of Abano highlights the effect of climatic and astrological factors on human physique and temperament.[27]

Following Aristotle, Marsilius designates the third type of monarchy as an 'elective tyranny' (*electa tyrannida*): this comes into being through election but operates according to a law which is concerned with the interest of the ruler, like the law of tyrants ('quasi-tyrannical' law).[28]

The fourth chief mode whereby a royal regime comes into being presupposes that the ruler is elected with subsequent hereditary succession and governs in accordance with the laws and with an eye to the well-being of the whole community. This procedure, Marsilius notes in agreement with Aristotle,[29] was followed in the 'heroic times,' which were called so because the stars produced men who were regarded as 'heroes' ('divine') on account of their outstanding virtue; or because they acquired ruling power through displaying exceptional virtues or performing beneficial deeds, such as gathering a number of men who previously lived dispersed and guiding them into social life; liberating the region from oppressors; or acquiring the land by some legitimate method and dividing it among their subjects.[30]

Marsilius's reference to the nexus between the emergence of the rulers of the heroic times and favourable stellar conjunctions offers an important clue about his views on the influence of astrological phenomena on civic affairs and evokes a link to Peter of Abano and other

Italian political authors and historians. It is also indicative of Marsilius's interest in astrology that on 17 November 1327, he handed over to Simone Moroni in Milan the canon of an astronomical table drawn up in Paris by John of Linerius.[31]

The use of astrological motifs is a prominent aspect of historical writing in late medieval Padua. Peter of Abano's teaching at the University of Padua must have contributed to the spread of astrological theories in early fourteenth-century Padua and seems to have had a major impact on Paduan writers[32] such as Rolandino of Padua[33] and Albertino Mussato. Mussato evinced strong interest in sidereal phenomena as evidenced by the extensive use of astrological motifs in the *Ecerinis*. With the aid of astrology, he sought to articulate an explanatory model for important historical events such as the decline of Rome and the downfall of Padua's communal government. Mussato posits a connection between historical cycles and astrological influences, as documented in *De lite inter Naturam et Fortunam*.[34]

Similarly, the Italian chronicler Giovanni Villani (ca. 1280–1348) relies on astrology in his *Nuova Cronica* (*New Chronicle*) as a heuristic model to explain natural and historical phenomena. Villani's application of astrological motifs is underpinned by his belief in the value of history as a means to explore the political changes that occurred in Italy and other countries in the past and thus enable the readers of his work to predict the future. He specifically makes the point that during the 960 or 953 years that preceded the composition of his treatise, there occurred forty-eight conjunctions, and the very first and most important of them was followed by the collapse of the Roman Empire, the invasion of the Goths and Vandals in Italy, and a series of crises within the Holy Church.[35] Referring to a conjunction of Saturn, Jove, and Mars in the sign of Aquarius on 28 March 1345, Villani mentions that the conjunction of these planets brings about with God's consent major events in the world, wars, important political and historical changes, the advent of new nations, rulers, religions, prophets and heresies, famines, and various kinds of calamities.[36]

The fifth way of establishing monarchy resembles the rule of the head of the household (*paterfamilias*): the ruler acts as a lord (*dominus*) over the entire community and exercises dominion according to his own will.[37]

All five varieties of kingly monarchy can be classified on the basis of the aforementioned criteria. Marsilius distinguishes two general modes whereby a king/monarch is appointed: 1) through election and the consent of the subjects; or 2) without election, in which case a person is appointed king because he or his ancestors first inhabited the region or because he bought the land or acquired it by some other lawful method.[38] If the king is appointed through election, the appointment can only be valid for his lifetime and that of one or several of his successors, or for a fixed period. The king may have full jurisdiction or may be entitled to take up only a specific office, e.g., the command of the army.[39]

Marsilius introduces an additional criterion for the classification of the five types of monarchy. Elected and non-elected monarchs rule over voluntary subjects, although they differ in that non-elected kings rule over less-voluntary subjects and according to less 'politic' laws ('legibus minus politicis'), i.e., laws which are less conducive to the common benefit, as is the case with the political systems in certain parts of Asia. Elected monarchs, in contrast, rule more voluntary subjects and according to more 'politic' ('legibus politicis magis') laws.[40]

If one attempts to construct a scale which measures the justice of the five forms of kingly monarchy, then it is necessary, according to Marsilius, to ascertain the degree in which the aforementioned types reflect the consent of the subjects and to determine whether those types exist according to laws that consider the common good. The more a monarchical regime approximates the archetype of kingship, the more it comes into being and exists by the consent of the subjects and according to a law that considers the common welfare; and the more it deviates or recedes from the ideal form of royal government, the more it slides into tyranny.[41]

To reinforce the thesis that election is a prerequisite to the existence and preservation of the political community, Marsilius appeals to the following analogy: election can never fail so long as men are able to procreate.[42] The election of the *legislator humanus* – with rare exceptions – strives after and realizes, according to Marsilius, the common good. Election helps identify a perfect or at least adequate or competent ruler, whereas hereditary succession and dynastic perpetuation cannot yield the same result with the same degree of certainty.[43]

The Appointment of the Government

Marsilius assigns to the body of the citizens the efficient power and primary authority to elect, appoint, correct, and depose the ruler, but also to promulgate laws and propose or make changes, cancellations, additions, and amendments to the existing body of laws or laws under consideration.[44] Although Marsilius recognizes that the differences between different regions call for different constitutional arrangements, he vindicates the supreme authority of the whole body of the citizens or its weightier part as the locus of the highest authority within a healthy and well-organized polity.[45]

Marsilius provides the contours of a generally applicable model aimed at upholding the sovereignty of the *legislator humanus*. He insists that the election and appointment of the government are incumbent only upon the *legislator humanus*, i.e., the body of the citizens or their 'weightier part' (*valencior pars*).[46]

In order to illustrate the relationship between the *legislator humanus* and the government, Marsilius relies on a combination of Aristotelian and Neoplatonic motifs:

1. First, he refers to Aristotelian principle that art imitates nature and that the task of science is to determine both the form and matter, just as the physician is concerned with health and its constituents and the builder knows both the form of a building and the materials that need to be used for its construction.[47] Marsilius infers from this that the body of the citizens acts as the efficient cause and generates the form, i.e., the law, and determines the material and the subject of this form, namely the ruling part, which has to regulate the citizens' activities and apply justice.[48] The *legislator humanus* as the efficient cause promulgates the laws and appoints the government.[49]
2. Marsilius relies on the Neoplatonic scheme of first and second causes: the *legislator humanus* is the first efficient and actual cause (*prima et appropriata causa effectiva*) of the parts of the political community; the government serves as the second instrumental and/or efficient cause (*secundaria vero quasi instrumentalis seu executiva causa effectiva*). It receives its authority from the first cause and it is easier to entrust the execution of legal precepts to one or a few persons who act as representatives of the body of the citizens. For, it would be futile to entrust the entire community with the enforcement of the laws and to distract it from other duties that are necessary for its operation.[50]

Explicit discussion of primary and secondary causality in the context of a discussion of creation can be found in the widely disseminated Latin translation of the *Kalām fī maḥd al-khair* (*Discourse on the Pure Good*, compiled in the ninth century).[51] The Latin translation of the work was produced by Gerhard of Cremona (d. 1187) between 1167 and 1187 in Toledo under the title *Liber de expositione bonitatis purae* (*Book on the Exposition of Pure Goodness*), which was to become later widely known as *Liber de causis* (*Book of Causes*).[52]

The *Liber de causis* enjoyed an intense reception in late medieval philosophical discourse. Thomas Aquinas, however, called its authorship into question in his *Super librum de causis expositio*. On the basis of textual comparisons with Proclos's *Elementatio theologica*, which had been translated by William of Moerbeke in 1268 from the Greek into Latin,[53] Aquinas identified Proclos as its author.[54] The *Liber de causis* was the subject of commentaries by Albert the Great,[55] Roger Bacon,[56] (pseudo-) Henry of Ghent,[57] Siger of Brabant,[58] Giles of Rome,[59] and (pseudo-) Adam of Bocfeld.[60] In 1255 it was introduced as a component of the teaching curriculum of the Faculty of Arts in Paris.

One of the intriguing aspects of the *Liber de causis* is that it makes a claim to a doctrine that attributes creation solely to the first cause, while stressing that creation occurs only through intermediaries, in particular the intellect, as is the case with Plotinos's (ca. 204–70) theory of emanation.

Theories of causality and the doctrine of the first and second cause had an important influence on political debates throughout the Middle Ages. An outstanding example of the application of the principle *cessante causa, cessat effectus* ('when the cause ceases, the effect ceases') in the context of royal taxation is provided by Peter of Auvergne's *Quodlibet*, which was presented in Paris at Christmas 1298. Peter's focal point is the question of whether a ruler or his successors are entitled to maintain a tax introduced in a period of emergency after the emergency is over or abolish it and return to regular taxation.[61] Peter stresses the need to establish and safeguard the proportion and equality among the various orders of society. A ruler who introduces a tax must act according to the principles of equality and justice and terminate it as soon as the emergency is over. Relying on the principle that as soon as the cause ceases, the effect ceases too, Peter argues that as soon as the necessity that generates a particular cause ceases, so too must the tax promulgated in response to an extraordinary situation or exceptional circumstances be abolished. Peter concludes that a ruler who fails to abolish a tax that is unnecessary or obsolete commits a sin, since he seeks to collect revenue that is not intended for a particular emergency. In such a case, his subjects are entitled to refuse to pay such a tax.

Marsilius defends the idea that the *legislator humanus* as the efficient cause determines both the form (the law) as well as the material suitable for this form, i.e., the citizens assigned to the various parts of the community.[62] The *legislator humanus* acts as the first cause of the parts of the political community. The duty of setting up the individual parts resides with the government as the secondary cause of the *legislator humanus*. Marsilius assumes a causal nexus between the *legislator humanus* and the government in the same way that the secondary cause owes its strength to the prime cause. The activity of the *legislator humanus* is not confined to assigning to the government and/or to the ruler their specific operational power. It also upholds this operating power and is effectively present in the function of the ruling part, which serves as its executive agent.

The Political Community as a Living Organism

Marsilius sees the formation of the political community and its parts and the appointment of the government as a process analogous to the genesis and growth of a living organism. He acknowledges that the soul acts as the moving (efficient) cause and generates the heart, which subsequently produces the other organs of the natural body.[63] Following Aristotle, Marsilius asserts that the heart is the first part to be formed and that it is nobler and more perfect in its qualities and operation than the other organs and parts of the natural organism. The heart receives a natural virtue or power (*virtus seu potencia naturalis*) and a kind of heat as an active principle, both of which have a universal active causality and allow the heart to form, separate, and arrange the other parts of the organism, protect them against harm, and to sustain them if their function is inhibited by illnesses or other causes.[64]

Similarly, in a properly organized polity operating according to precepts of reason, the entire citizenry or its 'weightier part' takes on the role of the soul as efficient cause and appoints the government as the counterpart of the heart. The *legislator humanus* (≈ soul) imparts a certain virtue or form (*virtus seu forma*) universal in causality, i.e., the law, to the government, with the active power to establish the other parts of the political community, which translates into the authority to pronounce and enact judgments related to justice and the public welfare.[65] Just as the health of a physical organism depends on the proper functioning of the heart, so too is the long duration of the political community contingent on the existence the government, because without an agency to suppress strife and execute the laws, the political community would suffer from fragmentation and, ultimately, fall apart.[66]

Marsilius advocates that the ruling part have precedence vis-à-vis the other sections of the political community in its qualities, especially prudence and moral virtue.[67] The government is vested with authority that resembles the innate heat (*caliditas innata*) of the heart as well with an armed or coercive instrumental power (*armata seu coactiva potestas instrumentalis*) that corresponds to the spirit (*spiritus*). Both forms of power must be regulated and channeled by the law in the judgment, prescription, and execution of matters pertaining to what is just and expedient in civil life; otherwise the ruler cannot work toward the right objective, namely, the maintenance of the political community, since, as Marsilius explains, quoting Aristotle's *De generatione et corruptione*[68] and *De anima*,[69] fire has a 'worse' effect than tools ('deterius agit ignis quam organa').[70]

In his exposition of the process of the establishment of the government and the differentiation of the parts of the political community, Marsilius relies on Aristotle's *De partibus animalium* (*On the Parts of Animals*)[71] and Galen's *De Zogonia* (*De foetuum formatione, On the Formation of the Foetus*).[72] Marsilius draws on the ideas of Aristotle and Galen or pseudo-Galen to form a unique and coherent argument for the emergence and necessity of government, although his reference to Galen's *De Zogonia* is problematic, given that the *editio princeps* of the Greek text appeared in 1525, that the first Latin translations of the work by Johannes Bernardus Felicianus (ca. 1490–ca. 1552) (Basel, 1535), Janus Cornarius (1500–58) (Basel, 1536), and Johannes Guinterius Andernacus (1487–1574) (Paris, 1536) were published shortly thereafter, and that there is no evidence of earlier versions of the work in Syriac or Arabic.[73]

More importantly, Galen disputes the doctrine of his Stoic and Peripatetic predecessors that the heart is the first of the bodily organs to be formed in the development of the embryo and that it is responsible for the creation of the other parts.[74] Galen distinguishes three phases of embryonic development on the basis of the formation of the three principal organs, i.e., the liver, the heart, and the brain, which are the seats of the appetitive, nutritive, and vegetative parts of the soul, respectively. First come the arteries and veins, the chorion and the liver; in the second phase, the heart is formed and thereby begins the differentiation of the embryo; in the third phase, the brain and the facial features emerge. It is noteworthy that Isaac Abravanel offers an interesting application of Galenic physiology in his discussion of kingship and negates the precedence of royal rule and the analogies between the dominant function of the heart in the living organism by drawing on Galen's physiological theory to refute the primacy of any particular bodily organ and to establish the equality of the heart, brain, and liver.[75]

On the other hand, in his *De foetuum formatione* (*Peri kuoumenōn diaplaseōs*), Galen notes that in his *Peri spermatos* (*De spermate; On Sperm*) he suggests that the heart is formed in the first few days after conception, but that he subsequently changed his mind as it appears to him that the heart does not have any function in the initial stages of formation and that its formation is subsequent to that of the liver.[76] It is possible that Marsilius relies here on the (pseudo-) Galenic *De spermate*, which was translated into Latin as early as the eleventh century and enjoyed a wide circulation in Christian Europe,[77] although in his *Expositio Problematum* Peter of Abano contests the authenticity of the treatise.[78] It is also possible that Marsilius refers to another ancient Greek treatise that had been recovered in Constantinople or translated by Peter of Abano but has apparently left no other trace in the literature.[79]

Marsilius's statement that fire acts in ways inferior to instruments evokes a link to John Philoponos's (sixth century) interpretation of the *De generatione et corruptione* that fire has 'worse' effects than that of tools and human art in general.[80] Given that the Greek version of Philoponos's commentary and two Latin translations by Hieronymus Bagolinus and Andreas Sylvius were first published in Venice in the sixteenth century,[81] his interpretation was mediated by Averroes's middle commentary on the *De generatione et corruptione* which was translated by Michael Scotus (ca. 1175–ca. 1234) into Latin and served as a foil for Scholastic commentaries on that work.[82]

Following Philoponos, Averroes points out that the motive power of fire is worse than that of a tool ('motio ignis est vilior motione instrumenti'), since the tool cannot operate without the artisan, and when it does so with the artisan's intervention, it moves things toward generation; whereas when fire operates without the prime mover, it moves things toward corruption.[83] Likewise, Giles of Rome in his commentary on *De generatione et corruptione*, stresses that fire acts in a manner worse to instruments ('Propter hoc enim dicit Philosophus II *huius*, quod ignis sine virtute corporis caelestis deterius ageret quam instrumenta artis sine artifice').[84]

Marsilius treats armed force as an attribute of the model prince,[85] in addition to a set of intrinsic intellectual and moral virtues, i.e., prudence; moral virtue, notably justice; equity, and love (benevolence) for the community and the citizenry.[86] Marsilius stipulates that the ruler should receive it only after assuming his office. He also stresses that the ruler's military power must be subject to certain limitations, in order to avert malfeasance of authority and the degeneration of the government into despotism. He draws on Aristotle's discussion about the size of the ruler's military forces, an issue related to kingship, especially hereditary kingship, in the third book of the *Politics*. Aristotle prescribes that the military power of the king should exceed that of a single person or several taken together, but not that of the entire body of the citizens.[87] Marsilius borrows Aristotle's formula and specifies that the armed forces of the prospective ruler should exceed the force of each citizen separately or a group of citizens taken together, but not that of all or the majority of the citizens or the entire body of the citizens.[88]

Aristotle's account of the qualities requisite for those aspiring to senior offices was often misconstrued by commentators: for example, Aristotle's reference to the 'greatest capacity for administration,' such as military expertise, was erroneously rendered by William of Moerbeke as 'potentia maximorum operum principatus.'[89] Marsilius is adamant that military power, unlike the other qualities that are demanded of the ruler before his appointment, should be granted to him only after his appointment and upon the prior approval of the citizens and those charged with his election. If it were otherwise, the ruler might tamper with the laws and slide into despotic rule; moreover, poor but competent persons would be deprived of the opportunity to take over rulership.[90] The fact that Marsilius calls for the coercive power of the prince instead of an outstanding capacity for the management of civic affairs could be explained by reference to Moerbeke's mistranslation of the relevant passage of the *Politics*. But this divergence from Aristotle's text could also be a corollary of Marsilius's view that dissent and disorder are endemic problems of social life and that every form of social existence is fundamentally contingent on the existence of an agency in charge of enforcing the law and coercing malefactors. Marsilius is clearly aware of the significance of the balanced and judicious use of compulsive force by the ruler.

It is worth noting in this context that the coercive power of the law and of the would-be ruler occupied a prominent place on the agenda of issues of late medieval political philosophy. Peter of Auvergne, for example, includes coercive power among the cardinal attributes of the excellent ruler, thus elaborating on Aristotle's exposition of the qualities requisite in the occupants of the higher offices:[91] the ruler ought to combine prudence and virtue. In addition, he should possess the power necessary to compel the obedience of the citizens, restrain recalcitrant individuals and those who cannot be easily persuaded by means of reason and must be corrected, and fend off external foes. Like Marsilius, Peter urges that the ruler should receive power only after assuming his office and upon the prior consent of the people. He also recommends that the power of the prince should exceed that of one or more persons together; otherwise he would not be in a position to discharge and perform his duties and pursue justice. At the same time, the prince's power should not exceed that of the entire community; otherwise the ruler could degenerate into a tyrant.

In his account of the duties inherent in rulership, Marsilius, unlike Aristotle, attaches little importance to the moral upbringing of the youth.[92] He is more interested in the ruler's role as the guarantor of justice and regulator of society. Just as the activity of the heart in an organism must never cease, the government – in contrast to the other parts of the political community, such as the military, which is not always indispensable and can remain inactive – must constantly ensure that every part of the political community is kept in right order and protected from injuries[93] by inflicting penalties for transgressions of the laws.[94] In this way, the government provides the conditions for all the parts of the community to perform their functions.[95]

Marsilius's application of medical metaphors involves significant departures from the previous tradition: he does not assert the primacy of the king by way of analogy to the heart, thus challenging a notion that has permeated not only late medieval political discourse but also medical writing. Peter of Abano, for instance, in his *Lucidator* asserts the analogy between the position of the sun in the sky and the heart in the organism and agrees with Plato's idea that the sky resembles a large organism whose heart is located in the center, just like the prince is located in the center of his realm so that he can have a global overview.[96]

Marsilius is primarily interested in the efficient causes and factors involved in the formation and growth of the body politic. Most medieval accounts of the relationship between the political community and the living organism are focused on the analogies between the parts of the body politic and the various members and organs of the natural body, as evidenced, for example, by John of Salisbury's (1115/20–1180)

Policraticus (1159). Unlike Marsilius, John is not interested in the process of the formation and growth of the body politic, but seeks to illustrate the function of the various parts and occupational groupings of the community as counterparts of the organs of the human body: the clergy corresponds to the soul, the ruler to the head, the senate to the heart, and the judges and local governors operate as the eyes, ears, and mouth. The revenue collectors and soldiers are the analogue of the hands, the courtiers perform the function of the flanks, and the record keepers and those in charge of the treasury act as the stomach and intestines. Finally, the farmers and artisans are the feet of the body politic.[97]

Marsilius assigns precedence within the political community not to the king but to the *legislator humanus*. He does not share the promonarchical sympathies of his Scholastic predecessors because he does not endorse the view of monarchy as the best political form.[98]

Conclusions

The primary purpose of this book has been to offer an in-depth analysis of Marsilius of Padua's political ideas by focusing on his reception of Aristotle's political thought – but also, and more particularly, on the possible sources of Marsilian theory. Although the results and findings of this work do not deliver the *coup de grâce* to the thesis about the existence of political Aristotelianism in the history of medieval political thought, they do challenge earlier scholarly attempts to portray Marsilius as a staunch Aristotelian, bring out crucial differences between Marsilius's political ideas and those of his Greek predecessor, and call for a drastic reassessment of the notion of political Aristotelianism. More importantly, whereas previous scholarship has focused on Marsilius's ties to Aristotelian and Scholastic political thought, this volume represents the first systematic endeavour to appreciate his role as a purveyor of various ancient and medieval intellectual trends and cultures of learning, as well as the ways those conditioned his reading of classical and medieval sources.

One of my central claims is that Cicero's influence on Marsilius is much more profound and extensive than hitherto assumed. I explored the importance of Stoic ideas as mediated by Cicero for Marsilius's views on genesis and growth of social life, legislation, and the appointment of the government or the ruler. Moreover, I examined Marsilius's application of the Platonic principle of functional specialization as an essential condition for an orderly and prosperous society. I also revisited the question about the relations between Marsilius's theory and the medieval Arabic and Jewish traditions of political theorizing. Although I challenged assumptions about Marsilius's Averroism, I reconstructed a line of tradition which underpins a naturalistic understanding of the emergence of religious belief and rites, originates with Al-Fārābī and Averroes, passes through Marsilius to Pietro Pomponazzi and Paolo Sarpi in the Italian Renaissance, and emphasizes the societal benefits of religion. I also traced Marsilius's potential links to Moses Maimonides, especially with regard to the classification of human acts, the demarcation of the spheres of human and divine law, and the use of pagan examples as a heuristic device to explicate the political function of religion and its significance for a stable and lasting social order.

Whereas past scholarship has looked at Marsilius's ideas against the background of the political and social history of the Italian city states and church-state relations, my analysis breaks new ground in that it offers a novel interpretation of Marsilius's thought from a cross-cultural perspective. In particular, I explored the ways in which the Byzantine, Islamic, and Jewish political writers relied on classical political and ethical literature and engaged with some of the themes that lie at the core of Marsilius's thought, such as the functional specialization of the members of the political community, the interconnectedness of the various social groupings, the structure and constitutive features of the perfect polity, and the duties and attributes of the exemplary ruler. I also highlighted the ways in which Marsilius foreshadows and anticipates early modern writers such as Machiavelli and Guicciardini.

By examining and re-evaluating Marsilius's importance as a political thinker in a comparative framework, I have highlighted the complexity of his political thought. My investigation has been guided by the effort to place Marsilius in 'conversation' with representatives from other medieval and early modern political traditions and to show that interaction among these traditions has been much more intensive than typically assumed. Marsilius wrote in a context that saw other political writers deal with similar themes; medieval political writers often drew on the Aristotelian legacy and focused on the ideal political community and model prince. But Marsilius was novel in that he did not simply carry forward the ideas of his predecessors such as Aristotle, reproduce the ideas and doctrines of his contemporaries, or merely seek to ingratiate himself with the civil authorities in his time. Instead, he formulated a unique vision of the ideal political community and ruler that builds on various ancient and medieval sources. Further, Marsilius's political teaching challenged some of the theories about the emergence and proper structure of the political community that prevailed in his time and exhibits intriguing affinities to ideas found in the Islamic and Jewish traditions.

As this book shows, Marsilius relied on a combination of ideas deriving from various traditions and earlier strands of political thought to articulate the vision of the body of the citizens as the sole source of all legitimate authority. In so doing he parted company with previous thinkers who emphasized the role of the king as a prerequisite for stability and peace. And he set the foundation for intense debates on such issues as the role and scope of the government vis-à-vis the individual rights of the citizens and the optimal social organization that resonate with contemporary debates on the relations between government and citizens and the conditions for equitable and efficient government. The fact that a number of thinkers from the ancient Greek and Roman and Latin, Islamic, Jewish, and Byzantine traditions focused on similar questions indicates that the same issues are of perennial interest and makes it likely that they will be considered not only now, in the twenty-first century, but also in the future. Marsilius exemplifies an approach to such issues that is not narrow and dogmatic but is respectful of a broad array of predecessors while being creative and original. His call for a structured society, a clear body of laws, and a prudent ruler attentive to the needs and claims of various social groups is no less compelling today than it was in his own time.

Marsilius represents an excellent testing ground for the validity of the thesis concerning the evolution of medieval Aristotelianism, but my findings point to a crucial need to further explore the trajectories and implications of Aristotelian ideas for the evolution of Western political thought and to determine or extrapolate the main patterns of the dissemination of classical political ideas in general. Given the multiplicity of identities and intentions informing Marsilius's thinking, it behooves future scholarship to assess the applicability of the method followed in this book to the study of medieval political thought in terms of placing Western political thinkers in dialogue with writers from other Abrahamic traditions that dealt with similar topics and relied on the classical heritage; identifying patterns in the comparative investigation of medieval political ideas;[1] and delving into the non-Christian sources of early modern European thinkers such as Machiavelli.[2]

Appendix

Given that some of the topics discussed in this work have been dealt with in the *Rezeption*, though from the viewpoint of Marsilius's reception of Aristotle's political ideas and in the German language, I append below a table indicating correspondences between the two books. This is intended to help readers interested in pursuing a further reading of ancient and medieval sources and secondary literature that have not been included or discussed in detail in the present work.

Marsilius of Padua at the Intersection of Ancient and Medieval Traditions of Political Thought	*Rezeption*
Chapter 1. Marsilius's Life and Works	17–27
Chapter 2. Major Intellectual Influences on Marsilius	
Albertino Mussato and Paduan Politics	29–35
Peter of Abano and Late Medieval Natural Philosophy and Medicine	35–9
Averroes Goes West: John of Jandun	39–42
Muslim and Jewish Influences	8–11
Chapter 3. Marsilius's Political Theory	
Marsilius and Aristotelian Teleology	45–51, 53–60
The Origins of Social Life	} 63–81
Rhetoric and the Genesis of Civil Life	
The Purpose of the Political Community	81–7
The Peace and Tranquillity of the Political Community	87–99
The Unity of the Political Community	262–68
The Organization of the Political Community	
Marsilius's Classification of Human Acts	
Marsilius and Aristotle	102–4
Marsilius and Aquinas	104–7

Marsilius and Maimonides	107–14
Plato Transformed, Avicennian Echoes, and the Ideal Social Organization	
The 'Circle of Justice' and Functional Specialization	115–17
The Idea of the Mean and the Parts of the Political Community	115–17
The Emergence of Religion and the Civic Function of the Sacerdotal Part	121–7
Marsilius's Notion of Citizenship	128–36
Chapter 4. Marsilius's Legal Theory	
The Definition of the Law	171–82
Giants on the Shoulders of Dwarfs: Legislation and a Well-ordered Political Community Cyclopes with Many Eyes: Laws and Collective Prudence	183–93
The *legislator humanus* Legislation and Sovereignty Medieval Echoes Beyond Aristotle	193–212
Chapter 5. Marsilius's Theory of Government	
The Taxonomy of Constitutions	143–51
The Five Modes of Establishing Monarchy	151–70
The Appointment of the Government The Political Community as a Living Organism	248–62

Notes

Introduction

1 For a presentation of Marsilius as a thoroughgoing Aristotelian, see Dolf Sternberger, *Die Stadt und das Reich in der Verfassungslehre des Marsilius von Padua* (= Sitzungsberichte der Wissenschaftlichen Gesellschaft an der Johann-Wolfgang Goethe-Universität Frankfurt am Main; 18, 3) (Wiesbaden: Steiner, 1981), 87–147 – repr. in idem, *Die Stadt als Urbild: Sieben politische Beiträge* (Frankfurt a. M.: Suhrkamp, 1985), 76–142. On the other hand, there is a substantial body of scholarship calling for a more nuanced interpretation of Marsilius's reception of Aristotelian thought. See, e.g., Jürgen Miethke, 'Marsilius von Padua. Die politische Philosophie eines lateinischen Aristotelikers des 14. Jahrhunderts,' in *Lebenslehren und Weltentwürfe im Übergang vom Mittelalter zur Neuzeit: Politik-Naturkunde-Theologie*, ed. Hartmut Boockmann et al. (Göttingen: Vandenhoeck & Ruprecht, 1989), 52–76; Jeannine Quillet, 'L'aristotelisme de Marsile de Padoue,' in *Die Metaphysik im Mittelalter, ihr Ursprung und ihre Bedeutung*, ed. Paul Wilpert (Berlin: W. de Gruyter, 1963), 696–706; Cesare Vasoli, 'La *Politica* di Aristotele e la sua utilizzazione da parte di Marsilio da Padova,' in *Marsilio da Padova: Convegno internazionale (Padova, 18–20 settembre 1980)* [= *Medioevo* 5–6 (1979/80)] (hereafter *MPCI*), 533–42; Mario Grignaschi, 'Le rôle de l'aristotélisme dans le *Defensor Pacis* de Marsile de Padoue,' *Revue d'Histoire et de Philosophie Religieuses* 35 (1955): 301–40; Georges de Lagarde, 'Une adaptation de la politique d'Aristote au XIVe siècle,' *Revue Historique de Droit Français et Étranger* ser. 4, 11 (1932): 227–69; Max Guggenheim, 'Marsilius von Padua und die Staatslehre des Aristoteles,' *Historische Vierteljahresschrift* 7 (1904): 343–62.

2 On the history of 'political Aristotelianism,' see, e.g., Christoph Horn and Ada Neschke-Hentschke, eds., *Politischer Aristotelismus: Hauptstationen seiner Rezeption vom Hellenismus bis zum 19. Jahrhundert* (Stuttgart: Metzler, 2008); Alexander Fidora, Johannes Fried, Matthias Lutz-Bachmann, and Luise Schorn-Schütte, eds., *Politischer Aristotelismus und Religion in Mittelalter und Früher Neuzeit* (Berlin: Akademie, 2007); Salvador Rus Rufino, 'Aristotelismo político en la Europa Medieval y Moderna,' *Schede Medievali* 44 (2006): 19–76; Wolfgang Brückle, *Civitas terrena: Staatsrepräsentation und politischer Aristotelismus in der französischen Kunst, 1270–1380* (Munich and Berlin: Deutscher Kunstverlag, 2005); Christoph Flüeler, 'Politischer Aristotelismus im Mittelalter. Einleitung,' *Vivarium* 40 (2002): 1–13; Karl Ubl, *Engelbert von Admont: Ein Gelehrter im Spannungsfeld von Aristotelismus und christlicher Überlieferung* (Vienna and Munich: R. Oldenbourg, 2000); Francisco Bertelloni, 'Zur Rekonstruktion des politischen Aristotelismus im Mittelalter (Die Entwicklung der dreigliedrigen *philosophia practica* vor der Rezeption der aristotelischen *libri morales*),' in *Was ist Philosophie im Mittelalter?* ed. Jan A. Aertsen and Andreas Speer (Berlin and New York: W. de Gruyter, 1998), 999–1011; Ubaldo Staico, 'L'aristotelismo politico nel Medioevo. Pensiero politico medievale e problema storiografico,' *Studi Senesi* 99 (1987): 261–322.

3 See appendix.

4 See further Mary E. Sullivan, 'The Bond of Aristotelian Language Among Medieval Political Thinkers,' in *Communities of Learning in the Middle Ages: Networks and the Shaping of Intellectual Identity in Europe, 1100–1500*, ed. Constant J. Mews and John N. Crossley (Turnhout: Brepols, 2011), 213–28; Francsisco Bertelloni, 'Nähe und Distanz zu Aristoteles: Die neue Bedeutung von *civitas* im politischen Denken zwischen Thomas von Aquin und Nikolaus von Kues,' in *University, Council, City: Intellectual Culture on the Rhine (1300–1550)*, ed. Laurent Cesalli et al. (Turnhout: Brepols, 2007), 323–47; Peter Hallberg and Björn Wittrock, 'From *koinonìa politikè* to *societas civilis*: Birth, Disappearance and First Renaissance of the Concept,' in *The Languages of Civil Society*, ed. Peter Wagner (New York and Oxford: Berghahn Books, 2006), 28–51, esp. 33–8; Andrés Martínez Lorca, 'El lenguaje filosófico de Aristóteles en las versiones greco-latina de Moerbeke y árabo-latina de Escoto,' in *A recepção do pensamento greco-romano, árabe e judaico pelo Ocidente Medieval*, ed. Luis A. De Boni et al. (Porto Alegre: Pontificia Universidade Católica do Rio Grande do Sul, 2004), 39–53; Roberto Lambertini, 'Politische Fragen und politische Terminologie in mittelalterlichen Kommentaren zur *Ethica Nicomachea*,' in *Politische Reflexion in der Welt des späten Mittelalters*, ed. Martin Kaufhold (Leiden and Boston: Brill, 2004),

109–27, esp. 113–16; idem, 'La diffusione della *Politica* e la definizione di un linguaggio politico aristotelico,' *Quaderni storici* n. s. 102 (1999): 677–704; Diego Quaglioni, 'Il tardo Medioevo: confusione o pluralità di linguaggi politici?' *Il Pensiero Politico* 26 (1993): 79–84; Nicolai Rubinstein, 'The History of the Word *politicus* in Early Modern Europe,' in *The Languages of Political Theory in Early-Modern Europe*, ed. Anthony Pagden (Cambridge: Cambridge University Press, 1987), 41–56. Consider also Aude Mairey, 'Les langages politiques au Moyen Âge (xɪɪᵉ-xvᵉ siècle),' *Médiévales* 57 (2009) [= *Langages politiques, XIIᵉ–XVᵉ siècle*, ed. Alban Gautier and Aude Mairey]: 5–14; Antony Black, 'Political Languages in Later Medieval Europe,' in *The Church and Sovereignty c. 590–1918*, ed. Diana Wood (Oxford and Cambridge, MA: B. Blackwell, 1991), 313–28 – repr. in idem, *Church, State and Community: Historical and Comparative Perspectives* (Aldershot: Ashgate, 2003), no. XI; idem, *Political Thought in Europe, 1250–1450* (Cambridge: Cambridge University Press, 1992), 7–12. For an evaluation of Moerbeke's contribution to the medieval political lexicon and a comparison between his and Leonardo Bruni's (1369–1444) translations of the *Politics*, consult James Schmidt, 'A Raven with a Halo: The Translation of Aristotle's *Politics*,' *History of Political Thought* 7 (1986): 295–319.

5 Scholarly literature on the reception of Aristotle's political thought in medieval Europe is quite extensive and is constantly growing. Noteworthy contributions include *Comentarios a la 'Política' de Aristóteles en la Europa Medieval y Moderna (siglos XIII al XVII): La historia de un equilibrio inestable* (Madrid: Fundación Ignacio Larramendi, 2008); Salvador Rus Rufino, 'Significado e importancia de la *Política* de Aristóteles en la Europa Medieval y Moderna,' *Patristica et Mediaevalia* 26 (2005): 3–30; idem, 'Aristóteles y el aristotelismo: Una aproximación a la historia de la filosofía política europea medieval y moderna,' in *Historia, filosofía y política en la Europa Moderna y Contemporánea* (León: Universidad de León, Secretariado Publicaciones y Medios Audiovisuales, 2004), 119–58, esp. 119–33; Gert Sørensen, 'The Reception of the Political Aristotle in the Late Middle Ages (from Brunetto Latini to Dante Alighieri). Hypotheses and Suggestions,' in *Renaissance Readings of the Corpus Aristotelicum*, ed. Marianne Pade (Copenhagen: Museum Tusculanum, 2001), 9–25; Christoph Flüeler, 'Der Einfluß der aristotelischen *Politica* auf die philosophische Begründung von politischer Herrschaft,' in *Gewalt und ihre Legitimation im Mittelalter*, ed. Günther Mensching (Würzburg: Königshausen & Neumann, 2003), 65–78; idem, *Rezeption und Interpretation der aristotelischen Politica im späten Mittelalter*, 2 vols. (Amsterdam and Philadelphia, PA: B.R. Grüner, 1992 [on this work, see the critical remarks by Sabine Krüger, "Bemerkungen zu einem Buch

von Christoph Flüeler," *Deutsches Archiv für Erforschung des Mittelalters* 50 (1994): 215–21]); Roberto Lambertini, 'Lo studio e la recezione della *Politica* tra XIII e XIV secolo,' in *Il pensiero politico dell'età antica e medioevale: Dalla polis alla formazione degli Stati europei*, ed. Carlo Dolcini (Turin: UTET, 2000), 145–73; Gianfranco Fioravanti, 'La réception de la *Politique* d'Aristote au Moyen Âge tardif,' in *Aspects de la pensée médiévale dans la philosophie politique moderne*, ed. Yves Zarka (Paris: Presses Universitaires de France, 1999), 9–24; idem, 'La *Politica* aristotelica nel Medioevo: linee di una ricezione,' *Rivista di storia della filosofia* n.s. 52 (1997): 17–29; David Luscombe, 'Commentaries on the Politics: Paris/Oxford, XIII–XVth Centuries,' in *L'enseignement des disciplines à la Faculté des arts (Paris et Oxford, XIIIe–XVe siècles)*, ed. Olga Weijers and Louis Holtz (Turnhout: Brepols, 1997), 313–27; Francisco Bertelloni, 'Presupuestos de la recepción de la *Política* de Aristóteles,' in *Aristotelica et Lulliana*, Fernando Domínguez, Ruedi Imbach, Theodor Pindl and Peter Walter (Steenbrugge/The Hague: In Abbatia S. Petri/M. Nijhoff International, 1995), 35–54; Jürgen Miethke, 'Politische Theorie in der Krise der Zeit, Aspekte der Aristotelesrezeption im früheren 14. Jahrhundert,' in *Institutionen und Geschichte: Theoretische Aspekte und mittelalterliche Befunde*, ed. Gert Melville (Cologne and Vienna: Böhlau, 1992), 157–86; Georg Wieland, 'Die Rezeption der aristotelischen *Politik* und die Entwicklung des Staatsgedankens im späten Mittelalter: Am Beispiel des Thomas von Aquin und des Marsilius von Padua,' in *Rechts- und Sozialphilosophie des Mittelalters*, ed. Erhard Mock und Georg Wieland (Frankfurt a. M. and New York: P. Lang, 1990), 67–81; Jeannine Quillet, 'Présence d'Aristote dans la philosophie politique médiévale.' *Revue de philosophie ancienne* 2 (1984): 93–102 – repr. in eadem, *D'une cité l'autre: Problèmes de philosophie politique médiévale* (Paris: H. Champion, 2001), 35–41; Jean Dunbabin, 'The Reception and Interpretation of Aristotle's *Politics*,' in *The Cambridge History of Later Medieval Philosophy*, ed. Norman Kretzmann et al. (Cambridge: Cambridge University Press, 1982), 723–37; eadem, 'Aristotle in the Schools,' in *Trends in Medieval Political Thought*, ed. Beryl Smalley (Oxford: B. Blackwell, 1965), 65–85; Lowrie J. Daly, 'Medieval and Renaissance Commentaries on the *Politics* of Aristotle,' *Duquesne Review* 13 (1968): 41–55. Some older studies retain their value, especially Conor Martin, 'Some Medieval Commentaries on Aristotle's *Politics*,' *History* n.s. 36 (1951): 29–44; idem, 'The Commentaries on the *Politics* of Aristotle in the Late Thirteenth and Early Fourteenth Century, with Reference to the Thought and Political Life of the Time' (Diss., University of Oxford, 1949); Martin Grabmann, 'Die mittelalterlichen Kommentare zur *Politik* des Aristoteles,' *Sitzungsberichte der Bayerischen Akademie der Wissenschaf-*

ten zu München, Philos.-hist. Abt. 1941, II: 4–78 – repr. in idem, *Gesammelte Akademieabhandlungen*, ed. Grabmann-Institut der Univerität München (Paderborn: F. Schöningh, 1979), 2: 1725–1800; F. Edward Cranz, 'Aristotelianism in Medieval Political Theory: A Study of the Reception of the *Politics*' (Diss., Harvard University, 1938); Wilhelm Oncken, 'Die Wiederbelebung der aristotelischen Politik in der abendländischen Lesewelt,' in *Festschrift zur Begrüßung der vierundzwanzigsten Versammlung deutscher Philologen und Schulmänner*, ed. Historisch-philologischer Verein zu Heidelberg (Leipzig: W. Engelmann, 1865), 3–18.

6 See in particular the following studies by Cary J. Nederman: 'Aristotelianism and the Origins of "Political Science" in the Twelfth Century,' *Journal of History of Ideas* 52 (1991): 179–94; 'Aristotle as Authority: Alternative Aristotelian Sources of Late Medieval Political Theory,' *History of European Ideas* 8 (1987): 31–44 – repr. in idem, *Medieval Aristotelianism and its Limits: Classical Traditions in Moral and Political Philosophy, 12th–15th Centuries* (Aldershot and Brookfield, VT: Variorum, 1997), nos. II and XV, respectively; and 'The Meaning of "Aristotelianism" in Medieval Moral and Political Thought,' *Journal of the History of Ideas* 57 (1996): 563–85.

7 There is a good deal of scholarship on the relationship between Marsilius's political theory and the Scholastic tradition – see, e.g., *Rezeption*; Alan Gewirth, *Marsilius of Padua, The Defender of Peace*, vol. 1: *Marsilius of Padua and Medieval Political Philosophy* (New York and London: Columbia University Press, 1951); Felice Battaglia, *Marsilio da Padova e la filosofia politica del medio evo* (Florence: F. Le Monnier, 1928).

8 The Latin reception of Plato's political ideas is surveyed in Gian Carlo Garfagnini, 'Platone politico, ovvero il sogno di uno stato "divino",' in *I Decembrio e la tradizione della Repubblica di Platone tra Medioevo e Umanesimo*, ed. Mario Vegetti and Paolo Pissavino (Naples: Bibliopolis, 2005), 99–125; Stefano Perfetti, 'Immagini della *Repubblica* nei commenti medievali alla *Politica* di Aristotele: i casi di Alberto Magno e Tommaso d'Aquino,' ibid., 83–98, and with regard to Peter Abelard (1079–1142) is discussed in John Marenbon, 'Peter Abelard and Platonic Politics,' in *The Political Identity of the West: Platonism in the Dialogue of Cultures*, ed. Marcel van Ackeren and Orrin Finn Summerell (Frankfurt a. M.: P. Lang, 2007), 133–50. On the ways in which Plato's prescriptions for the community of women, children, and property, as well as his views on domestic unity, were dealt with by late medieval Scholastic thinkers, such as Henry of Ghent (1217–1293), Giles of Rome (Aegidius Romanus) (ca. 1243/7–1316), and Peter of Auvergne (†1304), consult Roberto Lambertini, 'Philosophus videtur tangere tres rationes. Egidio Romano lettore ed interprete della *Politica* nel terzo

libro del *De regimine Principum,' Documenti e studi sulla tradizione filosofica medievale* 1 (1990): 277–325, 313–16.

9 David E. Luscombe, 'Hierarchy in the Late Middle Ages: Criticism and Change,' in *Political Thought and the Realities of Power in the Middle Ages*, ed. Joseph Canning and Otto Gerhard Oexle (Göttingen: Vandenhoeck & Ruprecht, 1998), 113–26; Wilfried Kühn, 'Zur Kritik des politischen Platonismus im Mittelalter. Marsilius von Padua gegen Aegidius Romanus,' *Freiburger Zeitschrift für Philosophie und Theologie* 55 (2008): 98–128.

10 In the present study, the concept of sovereignty signifies the highest executive authority in the context of my analysis of Aristotle's and Marsilius's teaching on the rule and authority of the whole citizen body. I use the term 'sovereign' in connection with the reigning part of the political community that possesses the ultimate authority, but do not mean to associate it with how later political theorists, like Jean Bodin (1530–96), Hugo Grotius (1583–1645), and Thomas Hobbes (1588–1679), define and deploy it.

1 Marsilius's Life and Works

1 On Marsilius's life, see Bernardo Bayona Aznar, *Religión y poder: Marsilio de Padua: ¿La primera teoría laica del Estado?* (Madrid: Biblioteca Nueva, 2007), 25–43; Jürgen Miethke, *De potestate papae: Die päpstliche Amtskompetenz im Widerstreit der politischen Theorie von Thomas von Aquin bis Wilhelm von Ockham* (Tübingen: Mohr Siebeck, 2000), ch. 'Marsilius von Padua: *Defensor pacis*,' 204–47; Carlo Pincin, *Marsilio* (Turin: Giappichelli, 1967), 21–54; Carlo Dolcini, *Introduzione a Marsilio da Padova* (Rome and Bari: Laterza, 1995); Johannes Haller, 'Zur Lebensgeschichte des Marsilius von Padua,' *Zeitschrift für Kirchengeschichte* 48 (1929): 166–97 – repr. in idem, *Abhandlungen zur Geschichte des Mittelalters* (Stuttgart: Cotta, 1944), 335–68.

2 New critical edition in Jürgen Miethke, 'Die Briefgedichte des Albertino Mussato,' *Pensiero Politico Medievale* 6 (2008): 49–65. For further discussion, see Silvana Collodo, 'Marsilio da Padova e la polemica sul Papato nella testimonianza di Albertino Mussato,' in *Chiesa, vita religiosa. società nel Medioevo italiano*, ed. Mariaclara Rossi and Gian Maria Varanini (Rome: Herder, 2005), 237–51, at 240–9; Rosario La Terra Bellina, 'Albertino Mussato e Marsilio da Padova: un ricordo (*Ep*. XII, vv. 50–5),' *Pensiero Politico Medievale* 2 (2004): 189–94; Enzo Cecchini, 'Le epistole metriche del Mussato sulla poesia,' in *Tradizione classica e letteratura umanistica. Per Alessandro Perosa*, ed. Roberto Cardini et al. (Rome: Bulzoni, 1985), 1: 95–119.

3 Miethke, *De potestate papae*, 209.

4 *Chartularium Universitatis Parisiensis sub auspiciis consilii generalis facultatum*

Parisiensum. Ex diversis bibliothecis tabulariisque collegit cum authenticis chartis contulit, notisque illustravit, vol. 2: *Ab anno MCCLXXXVI usque ad annum MCCCL*. Ed. Heinrich Denifle and Emile Châtelain (Paris: Ex typis fratrum Delalain, 1891; repr. Brussels: Culture et Civilisation, 1964), nos. 698 (158) and 699 (158–9) (both dated 12 March 1313). For Marsilius's Parisian years, see William J. Courtenay, 'Marsilius of Padua at Paris,' in *A Companion to Marsilius of Padua*, ed. Gerson Moreno-Riaño and Cary J. Nederman (Leiden and Boston: Brill, 2012), 57–70; idem, 'University Masters and Political Power: The Parisian Years of Marsilius of Padua,' in *Politische Reflexion in der Welt des späten Mittelalters*, 209–23.

5 Tiziana Pesenti, 'Per la tradizione del testamento di Pietro d'Abano,' in *MPCI*, 533–42; Pincin, *Marsilio*, 245–9.

6 Sigmund Riezler, *Vatikanische Akten zur deutschen Geschichte in der Zeit Kaiser Ludwigs des Bayern* (Innsbruck: Wagner, 1891; repr. Aalen: Scientia Verlag, 1973), nos. 6 (5) (14.10.1316) and 100 (66) (5.4.1318); Miethke, *De potestate papae*, 210.

7 Charles W. Previté-Orton, 'Marsilius of Padua and the Visconti,' *English Historical Review* 44 (1929): 278–9.

8 Ludwig Schmugge, *Johannes von Jandun (1285/89–1328): Untersuchungen zur Biographie und Sozialtheorie eines lateinischen Averroisten* (Stuttgart: A. Hiersemann, 1966), 28–9.

9 *DP* III.iii.

10 In *DP* I.i.6, Marsilius addresses Louis as *imperator*, although it is probable that this is a later interpolation – see Miethke, *De potestate papae*, 221–2. The work has been translated into several European languages: [English] Marsilius of Padua, *The Defender of Peace* vol. 2: *Defensor pacis*, trans. Alan Gewirth (New York: Columbia University Press, 1956; repr. 2001); Marsilius of Padua, *The Defender of the Peace*, ed. and trans. Annabel Brett (Cambridge: Cambridge University Press, 2005); [French] *Le Défenseur de la paix*, trans. Jeannine Quillet (Paris: J. Vrin, 1968); [German] *Der Verteidiger des Friedens*, trans. Horst Kusch 2 vols. (Berlin: Rütten & Loening,1958); [Italian] *Il difensore della pace*, trans. Mario Conetti, Claudio Fiocchi, Stefano Radice and Stefano Simonetta 2 vols. (Milan: Rizzoli, 2001); *Il difensore della pace*, trans. Cesare Vasoli (Turin: UTET, 1960; rev. ed. 1975); [Portuguese] *O defensor da paz*, trans. José Antônio C.R. de Souza (Petrópolis: Vozes, 1997); [Spanish] *El defensor de la paz*, trans. Luis Martínez Gómez (Madrid: Tecnos, 1989). In my discussion of the *Defensor pacis*, I follow Gewirth's translation with occasional modifications.

11 *DP* I.i.6.

12 See, for instance, the bull of Pope John XXII *Licet iuxta doctrinam*

(23.10.1237) in *Const.* VI, no. 361, in which Marsilius and John as the alleged authors of the *Defensor pacis* are condemened as heretics. The authorship of the work has been the subject of a long-standing scholarly debate. The co-authorship has been advocated by Noël Valois, 'Jean de Jandun et Marsile de Padoue, auteurs du *Defensor pacis*,' *Histoire littéraire de la France* 33 (1906): 528–623. For a different view, see Alan Gewirth, 'Philosophy and Political Thought in the Fourteenth Century,' in *The Forward Movement of the Fourteenth Century*, ed. Francis L. Utley (Columbus, OH: Ohio State University Press, 1961), 125–64, 141–50; idem, 'John of Jandun and the *Defensor pacis*,' *Speculum* 23 (1948): 267–72; Carlo Dolcini, 'Marsilio da Padova e Giovanni di Jandun,' in *Storia della chiesa*, vol. 11: *La crisi del Trecento e il papato avignonese (1274–1378)* (Cinisello Balsamo: San Paolo [?], 1994), 435–46; Ephraim Emerton, *The Defensor pacis of Marsiglio of Padua:* A *Critical Study* (Cambridge, MA: Harvard University Press, 1920; repr. 1951), 17–19.

13 On Marsilius's *Questiones*, see Mario Grignaschi, 'Réflexions suggérées par une dernière lecture du *Defensor Pacis* de Marsile de Padoue,' in *Papers in Comparative Political Science – Estudios de Ciencia Politica Comparada*, ed. Manuel J. Peláez (Barcelona: [Cátedra de Historia del Derecho y de las Instituciones, Facultad de Derecho, Universidad de Málaga], 1990), 4507–28, esp. 4509–17; Piero Di Vona, 'L'ontologia di Marsilio da Padova nelle *Quaestiones I–II super IV librum Metaphysicae*,' *Atti dell'Accademia di Scienze Morali e Politiche (Napoli)* 89 (1978): 251–81; Jeannine Quillet, 'Brèves remarques sur les *Questiones super Metaphysice Libros I–VI* (Codex Fesulano 161 f° 1ra–41va) et leurs relations avec l'aristotélisme hétérodoxe,' in *Auseinandersetzungen an der Pariser Universität im XIII. Jahrhundert*, ed. Albert Zimmermann (Berlin: W. de Gruyter, 1975), 361–85; Helmut Riedlinger, 'Note sur les *Questions sur la Métaphysique* attribuées à Marsile de Padoue,' *Bulletin de la Societé Internationale pour l'Étude de la Philosophie Médiévale* 4 (1962): 136–7 – repr. in *Raimundi Lulli Opera Latina*, vol. 5: 154–5: *Opera Pariesiensia, anno MCCCIX composita*, ed. Helmut Riedlinger (Palma de Mallorca: Maioricensis Schola Lullistica, 1967), 62–6; Roberto Lambertini and Andrea Tabarroni, 'Le *Quaestiones super Metaphysicam* attribuite a Giovanni di Jandun. Osservazioni e problemi,' *Medioevo* 10 (1984): 41–106; Schmugge, *Johannes von Jandun*, ch. 'Johannes von Jandun und der *Defensor Pacis*,' 95–119; Mario Grignaschi, 'L'ideologia marsiliana si spiega con l'adesione dell'autore all'uno o all'altro dei grandi sistemi filosofici dell'inizio del Trecento?' in *MPCI*, 201–22, esp. 203–14. Marsilius's artistic writings also include two *sophismata*, although the authenticity of one of them is doubtful – see Roberto Lambertini, 'The *Sophismata* attributed to Marsilius of Padua,' in *Sophisms in Medieval Logic and Grammar*, ed. Stephen Read (Dordrecht and Boston: Kluwer, 1993), 86–102.

14 For further discussion, see *Rezeption*, 85–6, 105–6, 139–40, 144–5, 149, 191–2, 207–8, 226, 229; Dolcini, *Introduzione a Marsilio da Padova*, 113–21; Alan Gewirth, 'John of Jandun and the *Defensor pacis*,' *Speculum* 23 (1948): 267–72. Scholarly treatments of Jandun's political ideas include: Roberto Lambertini, '*Felicitas politica* und *speculatio*. Die Idee der Philosophie in ihrem Verhältnis zur Politik nach Johannes von Jandun,' in *Was ist Philosophie im Mittelalter*, 984–90; and Grignaschi, 'Il pensiero politico e religioso di Giovanni di Jandun.' Armand Llinarès, 'Un averroïste déclaré: Jean de Jandun,' *Anuario de estudios medievales* 4 (1967): 393–402, is also germane.

15 Carlo Pincin, *Marsilio da Padova, Il Difenditore della pace. Nella traduzione in volgare fiorentino del 1363* (Turin: Einaudi, 1966), 571.

16 Pincin, *Marsilio*, 54; Schmugge, *Johannes von Jandun*, 2, 25–6. Based on a re-interpretation of the sources, Frank Godthardt argues that Marsilius's and Jandun's departure from Paris was a premeditated decision to enter Louis's court and that it took place most probably in 1324 and not in 1326. See his 'The Life of Marsilius of Padua' [trans. from the German Cornelia Oefelein] in *A Companion to Marsilius of Padua*, 13–55 at 22–7. Godthardt's *Marsilius von Padua and der Romzug Ludwigs des Bayern: Politische Theorie und politisches Handeln* (Göttingen: Vandenhoeck & Ruprecht, 2011) arrived when my manuscript was near publication and I was not able to take his argument into fuller consideration.

17 Jürgen Miethke, 'Der Kampf Ludwigs des Bayern mit Papst und avignonesischer Kurie in seiner Bedeutung für die deutsche Geschichte,' in *Kaiser Ludwig der Bayer: Konflikte, Weichenstellungen und Wahrnehmung seiner Herrschaft*, ed. Hermann Nehlsen and Hans-Georg Hermann (Paderborn: Schöningh, 2002), 39–74; idem, *De potestate papae*, 227–8; Hilary S. Offler, 'Empire and Papacy: The Last Struggle,' *Transactions of the Royal Historical Society* 5th Ser. 6 (1956): 21–47; idem, 'Über die Prokuratorien Ludwigs des Bayern für die römische Kurie,' *Deutsches Archiv für Erforschung des Mittelalters* 8 (1951): 461–87 – both repr. in idem, *Church and Crown in the Fourteenth Century: Studies in European History and Political Thought*, ed. Anthony I. Doyle (Aldershot and Burlington, VT: Ashgate, 2000), nos. II and V, respectively. See, in general, also Richard Scholz, 'Politische und weltanschauliche Kämpfe um den Reichsgedanken am Hofe Ludwigs des Bayern,' *Zeitschrift für deutsche Geisteswissenschaften* 1 (1938): 298–316. For an outline, though not complete, of Marsilius's activities in Germany, see Richard Scholz, 'Marsilius von Padua und Deutschland,' in *Marsilio da Padova: Studi raccolti nel VI centenario della morte*, ed. Aldo Checchini and Norberto Bobbio (Padua: CEDAM, 1942), 3–35.

18 Heinrich Denzinger, *Enchiridion symbolorum definitionum et declarationum de rebus fidei et morum*, 43th ed., ed. Helmut Hoping and Peter Hünermann

(Freiburg i. Br.: Herder, 2010), nos. 941–6 (370–1). Papalist reactions to the *Defensor pacis* are discussed in Thomas Turley, 'The Impact of Marsilius: Papalist Reactions to the *Defensor pacis*,' in *The World of Marsilius of Padua*, ed. Gerson Moreno-Riaño (Tunhout: Brepols, 2006), 47–64; idem, 'Silbert of Beck's Response to Marsilius of Padua,' *Carmelus* 52 (2005): 81–104; Donato Del Prete, 'La confutazione nel *Defensor pacis* di Marsilio da Padova da Siberto da Beek, Guglielmo Amidani e Pietro da Lutra a Giovanni XXII,' *Annali del Dipartimento di Scienze Storiche e Sociali dell'Università degli Studi di Lecce* 1 (1983): 213–83.

19 Gregorio Piaia, *Marsilio da Padova nella Riforma e nella Controriforma: Fortuna ed interpretazione* (Padua: Antenore, 1977); Johannes Heckel, 'Marsilius von Padua und Martin Luther. Ein Vergleich ihrer Rechts- und Soziallehre,' *Zeitschrift der Savigny Stiftung für Rechtsgeschichte, Kanon. Abt.*, 44 (1958): 268–336 – repr. in idem, *Das blinde, undeutliche Wort 'Kirche": Gesammelte Aufsätze*, ed. Siegried Grundmann (Cologne and Graz: Böhlau, 1964), 49–110; Werner Krämer, *Konsens und Rezeption: Verfassungsprinzipien der Kirche im Basler Konziliarismus* (Münster: Aschendorff, 1980), 166–81; Hermann J. Sieben, *Die Konzilsidee des lateinischen Mittelalters (847–1378)* (Paderborn: Schönigh, 1984), 366–409.

20 Piaia, *Marsilio da Padova nella Riforma e nella Controriforma*, 7–77; idem, 'Beato Renano e il *Defensor pacis* agli inizi della Riforma,' *Studia patavina* 21 (1974): 28–79; Ernst Staehelin, 'L'édition de 1522 du *Defensor pacis* de Marsile de Padoue,' *Revue d'histoire et de philosophie religieuse* 34 (1954): 209–22. See also in general Thomas M. Izbicki, 'The Reception of Marsilius,' in *A Companion to Marsilius of Padua*, 305–33.

21 Marshall's translation bears the title *The defence of peace: lately translated out of laten in to englysshe, with the kynges moste gracyous privilege* (London 1535). On the reception of Marsilius's political ideas in early modern England, see J. Patrick Coby, *Thomas Cromwell: Machiavellian Statecraft and the English Reformation* (Lanham, MD: Lexington Books, 2009), 17–31; Stefano Simonetta, *Dal difensore della pace al Leviatano: Marsilio da Padova nel Seicento inglese* (Milan: UNICOPLI, 2000); idem, *Marsilio in Inghilterra: Stato e chiesa nel pensiero politico inglese fra XIV e XVII secolo* (Milan: LED, 2000); Shelley Lockwood, 'Marsilius of Padua and the Case for the Royal Ecclesiastical Supremacy,' *Transactions of the Royal Historical Society* 6th Ser., 1 (1991): 89–119.

22 Heinz Thomas, *Ludwig der Bayer (1282–1347): Kaiser und Ketzer* (Regensburg and Graz: Friedrich Pustet/Styria, 1993), 197–8; Martin Berg, 'Der Italienzug Ludwigs des Bayern. Das Itinerar der Jahre 1327–1330,' *Quellen und Forschungen aus italienischen Archiven und Bibliotheken* 67 (1987): 142–97;

Hermann O. Schwöbel, *Der Diplomatische Kampf zwischen Ludwig dem Bayern und der römischen Kurie im Rahmen des Kanonischen Absolutionsprozesses, 1330–1346* (Weimar: Böhlau, 1968).

23 Jürgen Miethke, 'Wirkungen politischer Theorie auf die Praxis der Politik im Römischen Reich des 14. Jahrhunderts: Gelehrte Politikberatung am Hofe Ludwigs des Bayern,' in *Political Thought and the Realities of Power in the Middle Ages*, 173–210, at 173–8.

24 Alberto Cadili, 'Marsilio da Padova amministratore della Chiesa ambrosiana,' *Pensiero Politico Medievale* 3–4 (2005/06): 193–225.

25 For a more detailed discussion of these works, see Gianluca Briguglia, 'The Minor Marsilius: The Other Works of Marsilius of Padua,' in *A Companion to Marsilius of Padua*, 265–303; Godthardt, *Marsilius von Padua and der Romzug Ludwigs des Bayern*, 94–107.

26 Edition and French trans. in Marsile de Padoue, *Œuvres mineures: Defensor minor, De translatione imperii*, ed. and trans. Colette Jeudy and Jeannine Quillet (Paris: Éditions du Centre national de la recherche scientifique, 1979), 369–433; Eng. trans. by Fiona Watson and Cary J. Nederman and Marsiglio of Padua, *Writings on the Empire: Defensor minor and De translatione Imperii*, ed. Cary J. Nederman (Cambridge: Cambridge University Press, 1993), 65–82; Portug. trans. José Antônio C.R. de Souza, 'Marsílio de Pádua, *Sobre a Translação do Império*,' *Veritas* 43 (1998): 703–23 – repr. in *A ciência e a organização dos saberes na Idade Média*, ed. Luis A. de Boni (Porto Alegre: EDIPUCRS, 2000), 299–313.

27 Edition and French trans. in Marsile de Padoue, *Œuvres mineures*, 169–311. See also *The Defensor Minor of Marsilius of Padua*, ed. C. Kenneth Brampton (Birmingham: Cornish Brothers, 1922). Translations of the *Defensor minor* in modern European languages include [English] *Writings on the Empire: Defensor minor and De translatione Imperii*; [French] *Œuvres mineures: Defensor minor, De translatione imperii*, 169–311; [Italian] *Il Difensore minore*, trans. Cesare Vasoli (Naples: Guida, 1975); [Portuguese] *O Defensor menor*, trans. José Antônio C.R. de Souza, in *Marsílio de Pádua e Jerônimo Savonarola – Escritos* (Petrópolis: Vozes, 1991), 115–66; [Spanish] *Sobre el poder del imperio y del Papa: El defensor menor; La transferencia del imperio*, trans. Bernardo Bayona and Pedro Roche Arnas (Madrid: Biblioteca Nueva, 2005), 87–159. On the *Defensor minor*, see Cary J. Nederman, 'From *Defensor Pacis* to *Defensor Minor*: The Problem of Empire in Marsiglio of Padua,' *History of Political Thought* 16 (1995): 313–29; as well the following studies by Carlo Dolcini, 'Osservazioni sul *Defensor Minor* di Marsilio da Padova,' *Atti della Accademia delle Scienze dell'Istituto di Bologna. Classe di Scienze Morali* 64 (1975/6): 87–102; 'Marsilio contro Ockham. Intorno a una recente edizione

del *Defensor minor,*' *Rubiconia Accademia dei Filopatridi* Quaderno 12 (1979) – both repr. in *Crisi di poteri e politologia in crisi: Da Sinibaldo Fieschi a Guglielmo d'Ockham* (Bologna: Pàtron, 1988), 251–67, and 269–89, respectively; and ch. 'Marsilio e Ockham. Il diploma imperiale *Gloriosius Deus,* la memoria politica *Quoniam scriptura,* il *Defensor minor,*' ibid., 292–426.

28 The treatises are edited in Pincin, *Marsilio,* 262–83. The *De matrimonio* is almost identical with chapters 13–15 of the *Defensor minor*. Portug. trans. 'Marsílio de Pádua, *Sobre a jurisdição do imperador em questões matrimoniais,*' [trans. José Antônio de C.R. de Souza], in *Estudos Sobre Filosofia Medieval,* ed. José Lourenço da Araujo and José Antônio de C.R. de Souza (São Paulo: Loyola, 1984), 175–87. On the circumstances surrounding the composition of these tracts, see, e.g., Jürgen Miethke, 'Die Eheaffäre der Margarete »Maultasch«, Gräfin von Tirol (1341/42). Ein Beispiel hochadliger Familienpolitik im Spätmittelalter,' in *Päpste, Pilger, Pönitentiarie,* ed. Andreas Meyer et al. (Tübingen: M. Niemeyer, 2004), 353–91; Hermann Nehlsen, 'Die Rolle Ludwigs des Bayern und seiner Berater Marsilius von Padua und Wilhelm von Ockham im Tiroler Ehekonflikt,' in *Kaiser Ludwig der Bayer,* 285–328; Mario Grignaschi, 'Il matrimonio di Margarete Maultasch e il *Tractatus de matrimonio* di Marsilio di Padova,' *Rivista di storia del diritto italiano* 25 (1952): 195–204.

2 Major Intellectual Influences on Marsilius

1 For general accounts of intellectual influences on Marsilius's thought, see Janet Coleman, *A History of Political Thought,* vol. 2: *From the Middle Ages to the Renaissance* (Oxford and Malden, MA: Blackwell, 2000), ch. 'Marsilius of Padua,' 134–68, at 153–8; Paolo Giuriati, 'Marsilio da Padova e il *Defensor pacis* al vaglio di una sociologia della conocenza,' *Studia Patavina* 27 (1980) [= *Marsilio, ieri e oggi,* ed. Gregorio Piaia]: 268–80.

2 On Mussato's life and works, see, e.g., John K. Hyde, *Padua in the Age of Dante* (Manchester and New York: Manchester University Press/Barnes & Noble, 1966), 295–306; Guido Billanovich, 'Il preumanesimo padovano,' in *Storia della cultura veneta,* vol. 2: *Il Trecento,* ed. Gianfranco Folena (Vicenza: Neri Pozza, 1976), 19–110; Manlio T. Dazzi, *Il Mussato preumanista (1261–1329): L'ambiente e l'opera* (Vicenza: Neri Pozza, 1964). For Mussato's year and place of birth, see Manlio T. Dazzi, *Intorno alla nascita di Albertino Mussato* (Venice: La R. Deputazione Editrice, 1930); idem, 'Intorno alla nascita di Albertino Mussato,' *Archivio Muratoriano* 16 (1915): 263–72.

3 On the history of the Carrara regime, see Oddone Longo, ed., *Padova carrarese* (Padua: Il Poligrafo, 2005); Benjamin G. Kohl, *Padua under the Car-*

rara, 1318–1405 (Baltimore, MD: Johns Hopkins University Press, 1998); idem, 'Government and Society in Renaissance Padua,' *Journal of Medieval and Renaissance Studies* 2 (1972): 205–21, esp. 205–10 – repr. in idem, *Culture and Politics in Early Renaissance Padua* (Aldershot: Ashgate, 2001), no. XI; Andrea Di Salvo, 'L'affermazione della signoria cittadina nella percezione dei contemporanei: L'esempio dei Carraresi a Padova nella prima metà del Trecento' (Tesi di dottorato, Università Ca' Foscari Venezia, 1997); Donato Gallo, 'L'epoca delle signorie: Scaligeri e Carraresi (1317–1405),' in *Monselice: Storia, cultura e arte di un centro 'minore' del Veneto*, ed. Antonio Rigon (Treviso: Canova, 1994), 173–89; Silvana Collodo, *Una società in trasformazione: Padova tra XI e XV secolo* (Padua: Antenore, 1990); Luigi Montobbio, *Splendore e utopia nella Padova dei Carraresi* (Venice: Corbo e Fiore, 1989).

4 Jacopo Zennari, 'Giacomo II da Carrara, signore di Padova 1345–1350,' *Bollettino del Museo Civico di Padova* 13 (1910): 101–23; 14 (1911): 1–55.

5 For further discussion, see Richard C. Cusimano, 'Albertino Mussato and the Politics of Early *Trecento* Padua: A Prehumanist in the Transition from Commune to *Signoria*' (Diss., University of Georgia, 1970).

6 Albertino Mussato, *Écérinide, Épîtres métriques sur la poésie, Songe*, ed. Jean-Frédéric Chevalier (Paris: Les Belles Lettres, 2000). On the *Ecerinis*, see Silvia Locati, *La rinascita del genere tragico nel Medioevo: l'Ecerinis di Albertino Mussato* (Florence: F. Cesati, 2006); Hubert Müller, *Früher Humanismus in Oberitalien: Albertino Mussato, Ecerinis* (Frankfurt a. M.: P. Lang, 1987); Daria Perocco, 'Albertino Mussato e l'*Ecerinis*,' in *Dal Medioevo al Petrarca* (Florence: L.S. Olschki, 1983), 337–49; Ezio Raimondi, 'L'*Ecerinis* di Albertino Mussato,' in *Studi ezzeliniani* (Rome: Istituto storico italiano per il Medio Evo, 1963), 189–203; Joseph R. Berrigan, 'The *Ecerinis*: A Prehumanist View of Tyranny,' *Delta Epsilon Sigma Bulletin* 12 (1967): 71–86.

7 On Ezzelino and his rule, see Giorgio Cracco, *Nato sul mezzogiorno: La storia di Ezzelino* (Vicenza: Neri Pozza, 1995); Marco Rapisarda, *La signoria di Ezzelino da Romano* (Udine: Del Bianco, 1965).

8 For further discussion, see Gherardo Ortalli, 'Fra leggenda e realtà: la lunga vita del mito ezzeliniano,' in *Ezzelini: Signori della Marca nel cuore dell'Impero di Federico II*, ed. Carlo Bertelli and Giovanni Marcadella (Milan: Skira, 2001), 215–19; idem, 'Ezzelino: genesi e sviluppi di un mito,' in *Nuovi Studi Ezzeliniani*, ed. Giorgio Cracco (Rome: Istituto storico italiano per il Medio Evo, 1992), 2: 609–25; idem, 'Ezzelino crudelissimo tiranno: genesi e sviluppo di un mito,' *La ricerca folklorica* 25 (1992): 89–98; Gina Fasoli, 'Ezzelino da Romano, fra tradizione chronachistica e revisione storiografica,' in *Storia e cultura a Padova nell'età di Sant'Antonio* (Padua: Istituto per la Storia Ecclesiastica Padovana, 1985), 85–101; Girolamo Arnaldi, 'Il mito

di Ezzelino da Rolandino al Mussato,' in *La rinascita della tragedia nell'Italia dell'umanesimo* (Viterbo: Agnesotti, 1980), 85–97 [first published in *La Cultura* 18 (1980): 155–65]; idem, Girolamo Arnaldi, *Studi sui cronisti della Marca Trevigiana nell'età di Ezzelino da Romano* (Rome: Istituto storico italiano per il Medio Evo, 1963); Raoul Manselli, 'Ezzelino da Romano nella politica italiana del sec. XIII,' in *Studi Ezzeliniani*, 35–79; Paolo Toschi, 'Ezzelino da Romano nella leggenda,' ibid., 205–23; and, in general, Marino Zabbia, 'Il Mito di Ezzelino. Le Cronache,' in *Ezzelini: Signori della Marca*, 227–31; Louis Green, 'The Image of Tyranny in Early Fourteenth-Century Italian Historical Writing,' *Renaissance Studies* 7 (1993): 335–51.

9 Rolandino, *Vita e morte di Ezzelino da Romano (Cronaca)*, ed. Flavio Fiorese (Rome and Milan: Fondazione Lorenzo Valla / A. Mondadori, 2004); *Rolandini Patavini Cronica in factis et circa facta Marchie Trivixane*, ed. Antonio Bonardi, in *Rerum Italicarum Scriptores* 2nd series (Città di Castello: Lapi, 1905), VIII/1: 5–174; Rolandino Patavino, *The Chronicles of the Trevisan March*, trans. Joseph R. Berrigan (Lawrence, KS: Coronado Press, 1980). On Rolandino, see Gianluca Briguglia, 'Il diletto del linguaggio. La scelta della lingua come spazio politico in alcuni testi politici e letterari della seconda metà del Duecento,' in *Thinking Politics in the Vernacular: From the Midlle Ages to the Renaissance*, ed. Gianluca Briguglia and Thomas Ricklin (Fribourg: Fribourg Academic Press, 2011), 43–56, at 43–8; Frances Andrews, 'Albertano of Brescia, Rolandino of Padua and the Rhetoric of Legitimation,' in *Building Legitimacy: Political Discourses and Forms of Legitimacy in Medieval Societies*, ed. Isabel Alfonso, Hugh Kennedy and Julio Escalona (Leiden and Boston: Brill, 2004), 319–40; John K. Hyde, 'La prima scuola di storici accademici, da Buoncompagno da Signa a Rolandino da Padova,' in *Storia e cultura a Padova nell'età di Sant'Antonio*, 305–23; Carlo Polizzi, 'Rolandinus Paduanus professor gramatice facultatis,' *Quaderni per la storia dell'Università di Padova* 17 (1984): 231–2. Rolandino's views on Ezzelino's rule are discussed in Gina Fasoli, 'Un cronista e un tiranno: Rolandino da Padova e Ezzelino da Romano,' *Atti della Accademia delle Scienze dell'Istituto di Bologna, Scienze Morali, Rendiconti* 72 (1984/5): 25–48; Girolamo Arnaldi and Lidia Capo, 'I Cronisti di Venezia e della Marca Trevigiana dalle origini alla fine del secolo XIII,' in *Storia della cultura veneta*, vol. 1: *Dalle origini al Trecento*, ed. Gianfranco Folena (Vicenza: N. Pozza, 1976), 387–423, esp. 411–23; Hyde, *Padua in the Age of Dante*, 287–8.

10 Nancy G. Siraisi, *Arts and Sciences at Padua: The Studium of Padua Before 1350* (Toronto: Pontifical Institute of Mediaeval Studies, 1973), 22–4.

11 On Mussato's reception of Seneca, see Carmen Cardelle de Hartmann, *Lateinische Dialoge 1200–1400: Literaturhistorische Studie und Repertorium*

(Leiden: Brill, 2007), 72–3; Pierpaolo Fornaro, 'Tragedia e *argumenta* senecani in Albertino Mussato,' in *Hommages à Carl Deroux*, vol. 5: *Christianisme et Moyen Âge, Néo-latin et survivance de la latinité*, ed. Pol Defosse (Brussels: Latomus, 2003), 396–407; Anastasios C. Megas, *Albertini Mussati argumenta tragoediarum Senecae: Commentarii in L.A. Senecae tragoedias fragmenta nuper reperta* (Thessalonike: n.p., 1969); idem, 'The Pre-humanistic Circle of Padua (Lovato Lovati–Albertino Mussato) and the Tragedies of L. A. Seneca' (Diss., Aristotle University of Thessalonike, 1967) [in Greek]; Alexander MacGregor, 'Mussato's Commentary on Seneca's Tragedies: 149 New Fragments,' *Illinois Classical Studies* 5 (1980): 149–62. On the reception of classical authors within the circle of the Paduan Prehumanists, see Guido Billanovich, 'Vetera vestigia vatum nei carmi dei preumanisti padovani,' *Italia Medioevale e Umanistica* 1 (1958): 155–243, at 158–9; and, in general, Giorgio Ronconi, *Le origini delle dispute umanistiche sulla poesia (Mussato e Petrarca)* (Rome: Bulzoni, 1976), esp. ch. 'Mussato,' 17–59.

12 On Lovato's life, works, and role in the recovery and circulation of Seneca's tragedies, see Ronald G. Witt, *The Two Latin Cultures and the Foundation of Renaissance Humanism in Medieval Italy* (Cambridge: Cambridge University Press, 2012), 457–67; Paul O. Kristeller, 'Umanesimo e Scolastica a Padova fino al Petrarca,' *Medioevo* 11 (1985): 1–18; Giuseppe Billanovich, 'Vetera vestigia vatum' nei carmi dei preumanisti padovani,' *Italia Medioevale e Umanistica* 1 (1958): 155–243, 158–9; *I primi umanisti e le tradizioni dei classici latini* (Freiburg i.d.S.: Edizioni Universitarie, 1953); Roberto Weiss, *The Dawn of Humanism in Italy: An Inaugural Lecture* (London: Lewis, 1947; repr. New York: Haskell, 1970); idem, 'Lovato Lovati (1241–1309),' *Italian Studies* 6 (1951): 3–28. On the Pomposa library and Seneca's tragedies, see especially Guido Billanovich, 'Il Seneca tragico di Pomposa e i primi umanisti padovani,' *La Bibliofilia* 85 (1983): 149–69; Alexander MacGregor, 'L'Abbazia di Pomposa, centro originario della tradizione 'E' delle tragedie di Seneca,' ibid., 171–85; Remigio Sabbadini, *Le scoperte dei codici latini e greci ne' secoli XIV e XV* (Florence: G.C. Sansoni, 1967). For Lovati's poems, see *Lupati de Lupatis, Bovetini de Bovetinis, Albertini Mussati necnon et Iamboni Andreae de Favafuschis carmina quaedam ex codice veneto nunc primum edita*, ed. Luigi Padrin (Padua: Tip. del Seminario, 1887). See also Cesare Foligno, 'Epistole inedite di Lovato de' Lovati e d'altri a lui,' *Studi Medievali* 2 (1906–7): 37–58; Remigio Sabbadini, 'Postille alle "Epistole inedite di Lovato,"' ibid., 255–62. The medieval reception of Seneca is discussed in Winfried Trillitzsch, 'Seneca tragicus: Nachleben und Beurteilung im lateinischen Mittelalter von der Spätantike bis zum Renaissancehumanismus,' *Philologus* 122 (1978): 120–36; Gordon Braden,

Renaissance Tragedy and the Senecan Tradition: Anger's Privilege (New Haven, CT: Yale University Press, 1985). On the history of Paduan Prehumanism, see Lino Lazzarini, *Paolo de Bernardo e i primordi dell'Umanesimo in Venezia* (Geneva: L.S. Olschki, 1930), 4–21.

13 Anastasios C. Megas, 'The Prehumanist Circle of Padua,' 113–44.

14 Henry A. Kelly, *Ideas and Forms of Tragedy from Aristotle to the Middle Ages* (Cambridge: Cambridge University Press, 1993), 141.

15 Giovanna M. Gianola, 'L'*Ecerinis* di Albertino Mussato tra Ezzelino e Cangrande,' in *Nuovi Studi Ezzeliniani*, 2: 537–74; eadem, 'Tra Padova e Verona: il Cangrande di Mussato (e quello di Dante),' in *Gli Scaligeri: 1277–1387*, ed. Gian Maria Varanini (Verona: Mondadori, 1988), 51–60; Antonio Zardo, *L'Ecerinis di Albertino Mussato sotto l'aspetto storico* (Turin: Fratelli Bocca, 1889).

16 On Mussato as a historian, see Ronald G. Witt, *'In the Footsteps of the Ancients': The Origins of Humanism from Lovato to Bruni* (Leiden: Brill, 2000), ch. 'Albertino Mussato and the Second Generation,' 117–73; Sante Bortolami, 'Da Rolandino al Mussato: tensioni ideali e senso della storia nella storiografia padovana di tradizione "repubblicana",' in *Il senso della storia nella cultura medievale italiana (1100–1350)* (Pistoia: Centro Italiano di Studi di Storia e d'Arte, 1995), 53–86; Manlio Dazzi, 'Il Mussato storico,' *Archivio Veneto*, ser. 5, 6 (1929): 357–471; idem, 'Albertino Mussato: un nuovo autografo e precisazioni biografiche,' *Italia Medioevale e Umanistica* 25 (1985): 189–208. Livius's reception in Trecento Padua is discussed in Giuseppe Billanovich, 'Il Livio di Pomposa e i primi umanisti padovani,' *La bibliofilia* 85 (1983): 125–48; idem, *Petrarca e il primo umanesimo* (Padua: Antenore, 1996), 22–3.

17 'Albertini Mušati Paduani Historiographi et Tragœdi de gestis Heinrici VII. Cæsaris *Historia Augusta*' and 'Albertini Mussati Historici Patavini de gestis Italicorum post mortem Henrici VII Cæsaris *Historia*,' in *Rerum Italicarum Scriptores*, ed. Lodovico A. Muratori (Milan: Societas Palatina, 1727), 10: cols. 9–568 and 571–768, respectively; *Sette libri inediti del 'De gestis italicorum post Henricum VII' di Albertino Mussato*, ed. Luigi Padrin (Venice: Società Veneta di Storia Patria, 1903); Walter Friedensburg, *Das Leben Kaiser Heinrichs VII. Berichte der Zeitgenossen über ihn* (Leipzig: Dyk, 1882; new ed. Roland Pauler, Neuried: Ars Una, 1999), 'Des Albertinus Mussatus Kaisergeschichte oder Geschichte Kaiser Heinrichs VII.,' 71–334 (cited according to the new edition); Maria E. Franke, *Kaiser Heinrich VII. im Spiegel der Historiographie: Eine faktenkritische und quellenkundliche Untersuchung ausgewählter Geschichtsschreiber der ersten Hälfte des 14. Jahrhunderts* (Cologne: Böhlau, 1992), 25–76. See, in general, Mauro Tosti-Croce, ed., *Il*

viaggio di Enrico VII in Italia (Città di Castello: Edimond, 1993); William M. Bowsky, *Henry VII in Italy: The Conflict of Empire and City-State, 1310–1313* (Lincoln, NE: University of Nebraska Press, 1960); Otto Felsberg, 'Beiträge zur Geschichte des Römerzuges Heinrichs VII.: Innere- und Finanzpolitik Heinrichs VII. in Italien' (Diss., University of Freiburg, 1886).

18 Franke, *Kaiser Heinrich VII. im Spiegel der Historiographie*, 309.

19 'Albertini Mussati Ludovicus Bavarus,' in *Geschichtsquellen Deutschlands* vol. 1: *Johannes Victoriensis und andere Geschichtsquellen Deutschlands im vierzehnten Jahrhundert*, ed. Johannes F. Boehmer (Stuttgart: Cotta, 1843; repr. Aalen: Scientia Verlag, 1969), 170–89. On Louis's image in late medieval Italian poetry, see Alessandro D'Ancona, 'La poesia politica italiana ai tempi di Lodovico il Bavaro,' in idem, *Varietà storiche e letterarie* (Milan: Fratelli Treves, 1885), 1: 75–113.

20 'Albertini Mussati Ludovicus Bavarus ad Filium,' in *Rerum Italicarum Scriptores*, 10: cols. 769–84.

21 Andrea M. Moschetti, 'Il *De lite inter Naturam et Fortunam* e il *Contra causos fortuitos* di Albertino Mussato,' in *Miscellanea di studi critici in onore di Vincenzo Crescini* (Cividale: Tipografia Fratelli Stagni, 1927 – repr. Milan: Erasmo, [1957?]), 567–99.

22 More detailed accounts include: Eugenia Paschetto, *Pietro d'Abano: Medico e filosofo* (Florence: Vallecchi, 1984); Francesco A. Barcaro, *Tre grandi Europei del Trecento: Pietro d'Abano, Jacopo e Giovanni de'Dondi dall'Orologio* (Padua: Panda, 1991); Luigi Olivieri, *Pietro d'Abano e il pensiero neolatino. Filosofia, scienza e ricerca dell'Aristotele greco tra i secoli XIII e XIV* (Padua: Antenore, 1988); Nancy G. Siraisi, 'Pietro d'Abano e Taddeo Alderotti, Two Models of Medical Culture,' *Medioevo* 11 (1985): 139–62 – repr. in eadem, *Medicine in the Italian Universities, 1250–1600* (Leiden: Brill, 2001), 79–99; Franco Alessio, 'Filosofia e scienza. Pietro da Abano,' in *Storia della cultura veneta*, vol. 2: *Il Trecento*, 171–206; Marie-Thérèse D'Alverny, 'Pietro d'Abano et les 'naturalistes' à l'époque de Dante,' in *Dante e la cultura veneta*, ed. Vittore Branca and Giorgio Padoan (Florence: L.S. Olschki, 1966), 207–19; Alexandre [Aleksander] Birkenmajer, 'Le rôle joué par les médecins et les naturalistes dans la réception d'Aristote au XII-e et XIII-e siècles,' in *La Pologne au VI-e Congrès International des Sciences Historiques, Oslo 1928* (Warsaw and Lviv: Société Polonaise d'Histoire, 1930), 1–15 – repr. in idem, *Études d'histoire des Sciences et de la Philosophie du Moyen Âge* (Wroclaw: Zakład Narodowy im. Ossoli skich, 1970), 73–87; Leo Norpoth, 'Zur Bio-, Bibliographie und Wissenschaftslehre des Pietro d'Abano,' *Kyklos* 3 (1930): 292–353.

23 On Peter's *Expositio problematum*, consult Gijs Coucke, 'The Needle in the

Haystack. In Search of the Model of Peter of Abano's *Expositio problematum,' Revue d'Histoire des Textes* n.s. 4 (2009): 179–214; Matthew Klemm, 'Medical Anthropology in the Late Middle Ages: Body, Soul, and the Virtues According to Peter of Abano (d. 1316)' (Diss., The Johns Hopkins University, 2007); idem, 'Medicine and Moral Virtue in the *Expositio Problematum Aristotelis* of Peter of Abano,' *Early Science and Medicine* 11 (2006): 302–35; Nancy G. Siraisi, 'The *Expositio Problematum Aristotelis* of Peter of Abano,' *Isis* 61 (1970): 321–39. For compelling evidence against the commonly held assumption that Peter produced a translation of the *Problemata*, see Pieter De Leemans, 'Was Peter of Abano the Translator of pseudo-Aristotle's *Problemata physica*?' *Bulletin de Philosophie Médiévale* 49 (2007): 103–18.

24 Gijs Coucke and Tine Swaenepoel, 'The Relation between Bartholomew of Messina's Translation of the *Problemata* and Peter of Abano's *Expositio Problematum,*' in *The Aristoteles Latinus: Past, Present, Future*, ed. Pieter De Leemans and Carlos Steel (Brussels: The Royal Flemish Academy of Belgium for Science and the Arts, 1999), 85–114. On Bartholomew of Messina's translation of the *Problemata*, see Gerardo Marenghi, 'Un capitolo dell'Aristotele medievale: Bartolomeo da Messina traduttore dei Problemata physica,' *Aevum* 36 (1962): 268–83; Rudolf Seligsohn, *Die Übersetzung der pseudo–aristotelischen Problemata durch Bartholomaeus von Messina. Text und textkritische Untersuchungen zum ersten Buch* (Berlin: E. Ebering, 1934). The medieval and Renaissance reception of the *Problemata* is surveyed in Pieter De Leemans and Michèle Goyens, eds., *Aristotle's Problemata in Different Times and Tongues* (Leuven: Leuven University Press, 2006); Iolanda Ventura, 'Quaestiones and Encyclopedias: Some Aspects of the Late Medieval Reception of Pseudo-Aristotelian Problemata in Encyclopaedic and Scientific Culture,' in *Schooling and Society: The Ordering and Reordering of Knowledge in the Western Middle Ages*, ed. Alasdair A. MacDonald and Michael W. Twomey (Leuven: Peeters, 2004), 23–42; Ann Blair, 'The Problemata as a Natural Philosophical Genre,' in *Natural Particulars: Nature and the Disciplines in Renaissance Europe*, ed. Anthony Grafton and Nancy Siraisi (Cambridge, MA and London: MIT Press, 1999), 171–204; John Monfasani, 'The Pseudo–Aristotelian Problemata and Aristotle's *De animalibus* in the Renaissance,' ibid., 205–47.

25 *Quaestiones super octos libros physicorum Aristotelis* (Venice, 1551; repr. Frankfurt a. M.: Minerva, 1969), Praefatio, end of secunda pars. See further Blair, 'The Problemata as Natural Philosophical Genre,' 178–9.

26 Stuart MacClintock, *Perversity and Error: Studies on the 'Averroist' John of Jandun* (Bloomington, IN: Indiana University Press, 1956), 128; Schmugge,

Johannes von Jandun, 26–7; Zdzislaw Kuksewicz, 'Les *Problemata* de Pietro d'Abano et leur 'rédaction' par Jean de Jandun,' *Medioevo* 11 (1985): 113–37.

27 Graziella Federici Vescovini, 'Pietro d'Abano e le fonti astronomiche greco-arabo-latine (a proposito del *Lucidator dubitabilium astronomiae o astrologiae*),' *Medioevo* 11 (1985): 65–96. For a full list of Peter's works, see Peter Schulthess and Ruedi Imbach, *Die Philosophie im lateinischen Mittelalter: Ein Handbuch mit einem bio–bibliographischen Repertorium* (Zurich: Artemis & Winkler, 1996; repr. Düsseldorf and Zurich: Patmos, 2000), 538–9.

28 On the study of medicine at the University of Padua, see Siraisi, *Arts and Sciences at Padua*; Charles B. Schmitt, 'Aristotelianism in the Veneto and the Origins of Modern Science: Some Considerations on the Problem of Continuity,' in *Atti del convegno internazionale su Aristotelismo veneto e scienza moderna* (Padua: Antenore, 1983), 104–23 – repr. in idem, *The Aristotelian Tradition and Renaissance Universities* (London: Variorum Reprints, 1984), no. I.

29 *Conciliator controversiarum, quae inter philosophos et medicos versantur* (Venice, 1565; Facsimile) ed. Ezio Riondato and Luigi Olivieri (Padua: Antenore 1985).

30 *Conciliator*, fol. 4r; Nancy G. Siraisi, *Medieval and Early Renaissance Medicine: An Introduction to Knowledge and Practice* (Chicago, IL: University of Chicago Press, 1990), 67–8. On late medieval views on the status of medicine as *scientia* or *ars*, see Daniella Mugnai Carrara, 'Epistemological Problems in Giovanni Mainardi's Commentary on Galen's *Ars parva*,' in *Natural Particulars*, 251–73, at 260–1.

31 *Il 'Lucidator dubitabilium astronomiae' di Pietro d'Abano; opere scientifiche inedite*, ed. Graziella Federici Vescovini (Padua: Programma e 1+1 Ed., 1988). Peter's views on astrology are discussed in Graziella Federici Vescovini, 'Peter of Abano and Astrology,' in *Astrology, Science and Society: Historical Essays*, ed. Patrick Curry (Woodbridge: Boydell Press, 1987), 19–39.

32 On the medieval reception and translations of this work, see Stefania Fortuna and Anna M. Urso, 'La tradizione latina dell'*ars medica* di Galeno: la *translatio antiqua* e il completamento di Burgundio,' in *Sulla tradizione indiretta dei testi medici greci: Le traduzioni*, ed. Ivan Garofalo, Stefania Fortuna, Alessandro Lami, and Amneris Roselli (Pisa: F. Serra, 2010), 137–68; Nicoletta Palmieri, ed., *L'Ars Medica (Tegni) de Galien: Lectures antiques et médiévales* (Saint-Étienne: Publications de l'Université de Saint-Étienne, 2008); Per-Gunnar Ottosson, *Scholastic Medicine and Philosophy:* A *Study of Commentaries on Galen's Tegni (ca. 1300–1450)* (Naples: Bibliopolis, 1984), 101; Neal W. Gilbert, *Renaissance Concepts of Method* (New York: Columbia University Press, 1960); and, in general, Jole Agrimi and Chiara Crisciani,

Edocere medicos: Medicina scolastica nei secoli XIII–XV (Naples: Guerini e associati, 1988); Pearl Kibre, 'Logic and Medicine in Fourteenth Century Paris,' in *Studi sul XIV secolo in memoria di Anneliese Maier*, ed. Alfonso Maierù and Agostino Paravicini Bagliani (Rome: Storia e letteratura, 1981), 416–20.

33 Timo Joutsivuo, *Scholastic Tradition and Humanist Innovation: The Concept of Neutrum in Renaissance Medicine* (Helsinki: Academia Scientiarum Fennica, 1999), 231–3.

34 Cornelius O'Boyle, *The Art of Medicine: Medical Teaching at the University of Paris, 1250–1400* (Leiden: Brill, 1998), 117–18; Eduard Seidler, *Die Heilkunde des ausgehenden Mittelalters in Paris: Studien zur Struktur der spätscholastischen Medizin* (Wiesbaden: Steiner, 1967).

35 *An. post.* 74ab5.

36 For additional details on John's life, see Jean-Baptiste Brenet, *Transferts du sujet: La noétique d'Averroès selon Jean de Jandun* (Paris: Vrin, 2003); 11–13; Schmugge, *Johannes von Jandun*, 1–38; Valois, 'Jean de Jandun,' 528–623.

37 'Les questions de Jean de Jandun au sujet du sens agent,' in Adrian Pattin, *Pour l'histoire du sens agent: La controverse entre Barthélemy de Bruges et Jean de Jandun, ses antécédents et son évolution* (Leuven: Leuven University Press, 1988), 111–234. Consider also Charles J. Ermatinger, 'John of Jandun in His Relations with Arts Masters and Theologians,' in *Arts libéraux et philosophie au Moyen Age* (Montreal/Paris: Institut d'études médiévales/J. Vrin, 1969), 1173–84.

38 Pattin, *Pour l'histoire du sens agent*; MacClintock, *Perversity and Error*, 10–50, 104–5. On Bartholomew's life and work, see the indispensable articles of Cornelius O'Boyle, 'An Updated Survey of the Life and Works of Bartholomew of Bruges (†1356),' *Manuscripta* 40 (1996): 67–95; Auguste Pelzer, 'Barthélemy de Bruges, philosophe et médecin du XIVe siècle (†1356),' *Revue néoscolastique de philosophie* 36 (1934): 459–74.

39 Schmugge, *Johannes von Jandun*, 8–14. On the history of the Collège de Navarre, see Nathalie Gorochov, *Le Collège de Navarre, de sa fondation (1305) au début du XV e siècle (1418): histoire de l'institution, de sa vie intellectuelle et de son recrutement* (Paris: H. Champion, 1997).

40 *Quaestiones super octos libros physicorum Aristotelis* (Venice, 1551; repr. Frankfurt a. M.: Minerva, 1969).

41 *Super libros Aristotelis De anima* (Venice, 1587; repr. Frankfurt a. M.: Minerva, 1966).

42 *Quaestiones in duodecim libros metaphysicae* (Venice, 1553; repr. Frankfurt a. M.: Minerva, 1966).

43 *Ioannis de Ianduno In libros Aristotelis De coelo et mundo quaestiones subtilissimae* (Venice, 1552).

44 For a detailed list of John's writings, see MacClintock, *Perversity and Error,* 117–29.

45 On Siger of Brabant's thought and role in the evolution of 'Latin Averroism,' see Pierre Mandonnet, *Siger de Brabant et l'averroïsme latin au XIIIme siécle* 2 vols. (Leuven: Institut supérieur de philosophie de l'Université, 2nd rev. ed. 1911).

46 For Jandun's students, see Zdzislaw Kuksewicz, *De Siger de Brabant à Jacques de Plaisance. La théorie de l'intellect chez les averroïstes latins des XIIIe et XIVe siécles* (Wrocław: Ossolineum, 1968); MacClintock, *Perversity and Error*, 130.

47 See pages 126–7, note 14.

48 Schmugge, *Johannes von Jandun*, 12–13, 23.

49 Schmugge, *Johannes von Jandun*, 23; C. Kenneth Brampton, 'Marsiglio of Padua,' *English Historical Review* 37 (1922): 501–15, at 508.

50 Latin text and parallel French translation: 'Recommentatio civitatis Parisiensis = Éloge de la cité de Paris,' in *Paris et ses historiens aux XIV et XVe siècles,* ed. Antoine J.V. Le Roux de Lincy and Lazare M. Tisserand (Paris: Imprimerie impériale, 1867), 22–9. On this work, see Hyde, 'Medieval Descriptions of Cities,' in idem, *Literacy and Its Uses: Studies on Late Medieval Italy*, ed. Daniel Waley (Manchester and New York: Manchester University Press, 1993), 1–32, at 22–3.

51 'Éloge de Paris, composé en 1323 par un habitant de Senlis, Jean de Jandun,' ed. Nicolas R. Taranne and Antoine J.V. Le Roux de Lincy, *Bulletin du Comité de la langue, de l'histoire et des arts de la France* 3 (1855/6): 505–40; Latin text and parallel French translation: 'Tractatus de laudibus Parisius = Traité des louanges de Paris,' in *Paris et ses historiens aux XIV et XVe siècles*, 32–79; partial English translation as 'A Treatise of the Praises of Paris,' in *In Old Paris: An Anthology of Source Descriptions, 1323–1790,* ed. Robert W. Berger (New York: Italica Press, 2002), 7–17. On Jandun's *De Laudibus Parisius,* see also Erik Inglis, 'Gothic Architecture and a Scholastic: Jean de Jandun's *Tractatus de laudibus Parisius,*' *Gesta* 42 (2003): 63–85; *In Old Paris,* 1–6; Hyde, 'Medieval Descriptions of Cities,' 23; Carl J. Classen, *Die Stadt im Spiegel der Descriptiones und Laudes urbium in der antiken und mittelalterlichen Literatur bis zum Ende des zwölften Jahrhunderts* (Hildesheim and New York: Olms, 1980), 64; Schmugge, *Johannes von Jandun,* 23–5.

52 'Éloge de Paris,' 510–6; 'Tractatus de laudibus Parisius,' 34–47.

53 'Éloge de Paris,' 516–21; 'Tractatus de laudibus Parisius,' 48–53.

54 'Éloge de Paris,' 521–36; 'Tractatus de laudibus Parisius,' 52–79.

55 Schmugge, *Johannes von Jandun,* 36–7; Karl Bosl, 'Die 'Geistliche Hofakademie' Kaiser Ludwigs des Bayern im alten Franziskanerkloster zu

München,' in *Der Mönch im Wappen: Aus Geschichte und Gegenwart des katholischen München* (Munich: Schnell & Steiner, 1960), 97–129, at 127.

56 Schmugge, *Johannes von Jandun*, Anhang II: Wo und wann ist Johannes gestorben? 121–2.

57 For further discussion, see Ana María C. Minecan, 'Introducción al debate historiográfico en torno a la noción de "averroísmo latino,"' *Anales del Seminario de Historia de Filosofía* 27 (2010): 63–85; Bernardo Bayona Aznar, 'La incongruencia de la denominación "averroísmo político,"' in *Maimónides y el pensamiento medieval: VIII Centenario de la muerte de Maimónides*, ed. José Luis Cantón Alonso (Cordoba: Servicio de Publicaciones, Universidad de Córdoba, 2007), 329–40; Julio A. Castello Dubra, 'Nota sobre el aristotelismo y el averroísmo político de Marsilio de Padua,' *Veritas* 42 (1997): 671–7; Gregorio Piaia, '"Averroisme politique": anatomie d'un mythe historiographique,' in *Orientalische Kultur und europäisches Mittelalter*, ed. Albert Zimmermann and Ingrid Craemer-Ruegenberg (Berlin and New York: W. de Gruyter, 1985), 288–300 [Italian version: '"Averroismo político": anatomia di un mito storiografico,' in idem, *Marsilio e dintorni: Contributo alla storia delle idee* (Padua: Antenore, 1999), 79–103]; idem, 'L'averroismo politico e Marsilio da Padova,' in *Saggi e ricerche su Aristotele, Marsilio da Padova, M. Eckhart, Rosmini, Spaventa, Marty, Tilgher, Omodeo, metafisica, fenomenologia ed estetica*, ed. Carlo Giacon (Padua: Antenore, 1971), 33–54. On the question of 'Political Averroism,' see Wolfgang Hübener, 'Unvorgreifliche Überlegungen zum möglichen Sinn des Topos "politischer Averroismus,"' in *Averroismus im Mittelalter und in der Renaissance*, ed. Friedrich Niewöhner and Loris Sturlese (Zürich: Spur-Verlag, 1994), 222–38; Charles E. Butterworth, 'What Is Political Averroism?' ibid., 239–50; Luca Bianchi, 'Filosofi, uomini e bruti. Note per la storia di un'antropologia averroista,' *Rinascimento* 32 (1992): 185–201; Mario Grignaschi, 'Indagine sui passi del 'commento' suscettibili di avere promosso la formazione di un averroismo politico,' in *L'Averroismo in Italia* (Rome: Accademia Nazionale dei Lincei, 1979), 237–78 – repr. in *Il pensiero politico del basso Medioevo: Antologia di saggi*, ed. Carlo Dolcini (Bologna: Pàtron, 1983), 273–312. Surveys of the history of medieval 'Averroism' include: Dragos Calma, 'La polysémie du terme averroïsme,' *Freiburger Zeitschrift für Philosophie und Theologie* 57 (2010): 189–98; Jean-Baptiste Brenet, ed., *Averroès et les averroïsmes juif et latin* (Turnhout: Brepols, 2007); André Bazzana et al., eds., *Averroès et l'averroïsme (XIIe–XVe siècle): Un itinéraire historique du Haut Atlas à Paris et à Padoue* (Lyon: Presses Universitaires de Lyon, 2005); Emanuele Coccia, *La trasparenza delle immagini: Averroè e l'averroismo* (Milan: B. Mondadori, 2005); Ruedi Imbach, 'L'averroïsme latin du XIIIe siècle,' in *Gli studi di filosofia medievale fra otto e novecento, contributo a un bilancio storiografico*, ed.

Ruedi Imbach and Alfonso Maierù (Rome: Storia e Letteratura 1991), 191–208 – repr. in idem, *Quodlibeta: Ausgewählte Artikel*, ed. Francis Cheneval et al. (Freiburg i. S.: Universitätsverlag Freiburg/Schweiz, 1996), 45–62; Jorge M. Ayala Martínez, ed., *Averroes y los averroísmos* (Zaragoza: Sociedad de Filosofía Medieval, 1999); Valeria Sorge, 'L'aristotelismo averroistico negli studi recenti,' *Paradigmi* 50 (1999): 243–63; *L'Averroismo in Italia*; Ludwig Hödl, 'Über die averroistische Wende der lateinischen Philosophie des Mittelalters im 13. Jahrhundert,' *Recherches de théologie ancienne et médiévale* 39 (1972): 171–204; *Averroismo e aristotelismo padovano* (Padua: CEDAM, 1939). For Marsilius in particular, see Hermann Ley, *Studie zur Geschichte des Materialismus im Mittelalter* (Berlin: Deutscher Verlag der Wissenschaften, 1957), ch. 'Politischer Averroismus bei Marsilius von Padua und Johannes von Jandun: Die Schrift *Defensor pacis*,' 445–62; and the following studies by Erminio Troilo: 'Lo spirito dell'averroismo padovano,' in *Il diritto dell'uomo al sapere e al libero uso di esso* (Padua: Liviana, 1954), 43–74; idem, 'L'averroismo di Marsilio da Padova,' in *Marsilio da Padova*, 49–77; and 'Per l'Averroismo Padovano o Veneto.' *Atti del Reale Istituto Veneto di Scienze, Lettere ed Arti* (Venezia) Parte II: Classe di Scienze morali e lettere 99 (1939–1940): 273–98 – repr. in *Ibn Rushd in the Western Tradition: Texts and Studies*, ed. Fuat Sezgin (Frankfurt a. M.: Institute for the History of Arabic-Islamic Science at the Johann Wolfgang Goethe University, 1999), 3: 357–82.

58 Averroè, *Parafrasi della 'Repubblica' nella traduzione latina di Elia del Medigo*, ed. Annalisa Coviello and Paolo E. Fornaciari (Florence: L.S. Olschki, 1992).

59 Published in *Francisci Philelphi, De morali disciplina libri quinque. Averrois paraphrasis in libros De de Republica Platonis. Francisci Robortelli in libros Libros politicos Politicos Aristotelis disputatio* (Venice, 1552), 89–166.

60 For Averroes' *Commentary on the Ethics*, see Noah [R.] Feldman, 'The Translators of Ibn Rushd's Commentary on the Nicomachean Ethics,' *Turjumān* 8 (1999): 69–85; idem, 'Reading the *Nicomachean Ethics* with Ibn Rushd' (Diss., University of Oxford, 1994). Its reception in the Latin West is surveyed in Péter Molnár, 'Une étape négligée de la réception d'Aristote en Occident: Averroès, le *Liber Nicomachie* et la science politique,' in *Averroès et l'averroïsme*, 265–73; Roberto Lambertini, 'Zur Frage der Rolle des Averroes in der praktischen Philosophie des Spätmittelalters: Vorbemerkung zur Rezeption seines Ethikkommentars,' in *Averroes (1126–1198) oder der Triumph des Rationalismus*, ed. Raif G. Khoury (Heidelberg: C. Winter, 2002), 243–53; Christoph Kummerer, *Der Fürst als Gesetzgeber in den lateinischen Übersetzungen von Averroes* (Ebelsbach: Gremer, 1989); as well as in the following studies by Jerzy B. Korolec: 'Mittlerer Kommentar von Averroes

zur *Nikomachischen Ethik* des Aristoteles,' *Mediaevalia philosophica Polonorum* 31 (1992): 61–118; 'Averroès et son Commentaire Moyen sur l'Ethique à Nicomaque,' *Internationale de l'Imaginaire* 17–18 (1991) [= *Le choc Averroès. Comment les philosophes arabes ont fait l'Europe*]: 66–77; 'Le Commentaire d'Averroès sur l'*Ethique à Nicomaque*,' *Bulletin de philosophie médiévale* 27 (1985): 104–7. For the Arabic version and reception of the *Nicomachean Ethics*, consult see *The Arabic Version of the Nicomachean Ethics, with an Introduction and Annotated Translation by Douglas M. Dunlop*, ed. Anna A. Akasoy and Alexander Fidora (Leiden and Boston: Brill, 2005); Ernst A. Schmidt and Manfred Ullmann, *Aristoteles in Fes: Zum Wert der arabischen Überlieferung der Nikomachischen Ethik für die Kritik des griechischen Textes* (Heidelberg: Winter, 2012).

61 *Rezeption*, 50, 80–1, 84, 190–1, 236.

62 Shlomo Pines, 'La philosophie dans l'économie du genre humain selon Averroès: une réponse à al-Fārābi?' in *Multiple Averroès*, ed. Jean Jolivet (Paris: Les Belles Lettres, 1978), 189–207; idem, 'The Limitations of Human Knowledge according to Al-Fārābī, Ibn Bājja, and Maimonides,' in *Studies in Medieval Jewish History and Literature*, ed. Isadore Twersky (Cambridge, MA: Harvard University Press, 1979), 1: 82–109 – repr. in idem, *Collected Works*, vol. 4: *Studies in the History of Jewish Thought*, ed. Warren Z. Harvey and Moshe Idel (Jerusalem: Magnes Press 1997), 404–31, esp. 404–5.

63 Jeannine Quillet, 'L'aristotélisme de Marsile de Padoue et ses rapports avec l'averroïsme,' in *MPCI*, 81–142; eadem, *La philosophie politique de Marsile de Padoue* (Paris: Vrin, 1970) 61–4. For information on Samuel ben Judah's life and works, see the indispensable study of Lawrence V. Berman, 'Greek into Hebrew: Samuel ben Judah of Marseilles, Fourteenth-Century Philosopher and Translator,' in *Jewish Medieval and Renaissance Studies*, ed. Alexander Altmann (Cambridge, MA: Harvard University, 1967): 289–320.

64 On the fortune of the *Guide of the Perplexed* in the medieval West, see Görge K. Hasselhoff, *Dicit Rabbi Moyses: Studien zum Bild von Moses Maimonides im lateinischen Westen vom 13. bis 15. Jahrhundert* (Würzburg: Königshausen & Neumann, 2004; 2nd extended ed., 2005), 88–93, 122–7; Mauro Zonta, 'Traduzioni e commenti alla *Guida dei perplessi* nell'Europa del secolo XIII: a proposito di alcuni studi recenti,' in *Maimonide e il suo tempo*, ed. Geri Cerchiai and Giovanni Rota (Milan: Franco Angeli, 2007), 51–60.

3 Marsilius's Political Theory

1 *DP* I.vii.1.

2 See also the discussions in Cary J. Nederman, *Community and Consent: The Secular Political Theory of Marsiglio of Padua's Defensor pacis* (Lanham, MD:

Rowman & Littlefield, 1995), 55–61; idem, 'Character and Community in the *Defensor Pacis*: Marsiglio of Padua's Adaptation of Aristotelian Moral Psychology,' *History of Political Thought* 13 (1992): 377–90; Marjorie Reeves, 'Marsiglio of Padua and Dante Alighieri,' in *Trends in Medieval Political Thought*, 86–104, 92–3.

3 On the meaning of the term *politizare* as living in a human association and its various uses as a synonym of and correlative to *civiliter vivere* in the medieval political lexicon, see Cranz, 'Aristotelianism in Medieval Political Theory,' 65.

4 *DP* I.xiii.2.

5 *DP* I.xiii.2. See also Gewirth, *Marsilius of Padua, The Defender of Peace*, 435–8; James G. Lennox, 'Nature Does Nothing in Vain,' in *Beiträge zur antiken Philosophie*, ed. Hans-Christian Günther and Antonios Rengakos (Stuttgart: F. Steiner, 1997), 199–214.

6 *DP* I.xvii.10.

7 For comments, consider also Alan Gewirth, *Marsilius of Padua, Defender of Peace*, vol. 1: *Marsilius of Padua and Medieval Political Philosophy* (New York and London: Columbia University Press, 1951), 85; idem, *Marsilius of Padua and Medieval Political Philosophy*, 126–31; Quillet, *La philosophie politique*, 67–8. For medieval debates on the eternity of the world, see Rolf Schönberger, 'Der Disput über die Ewigkeit der Welt,' in *Bonaventura, Thomas von Aquin, Boethius von Dacien, Über die Ewigkeit der Welt*, German trans. Peter Nickl (Frankfurt a. M.: Klostermann, 2000), vii–xxxii; Richard C. Dales, *Medieval Discussions of the Eternity of the World* (Leiden and New York: E.J. Brill, 1990); Richard C. Dales and Omar Argerami, eds., *Medieval Latin Texts on the Eternity of the World* (Leiden: E.J. Brill, 1991); Josef B.M. Wissink, ed., *The Eternity of the World in the Thought of Thomas Aquinas and His Contemporaries*, (Leiden: E.J. Brill, 1990). The Arabic and Jewish precedents are discussed in Herbert A. Davidson, *Proofs for Eternity, Creation and the Existence of God in Medieval Islamic and Jewish Philosophy* (Oxford: Oxford University Press, 1987); Ernst Behler, *Die Ewigkeit der Welt: Problemgeschichtliche Untersuchungen zu den Kontroversen um Weltanfang und Weltunendlichkeit im Mittelalter*, vol. 1: *Die Problemstellung in der arabischen und jüdischen Philosophie des Mittelalters* (Munich: Schöningh, 1965).

8 E.g., *DP* I.xii; xv.

9 See also Gewirth, *Marsilius of Padua and Medieval Political Philosophy*, 33–7, 52–3.

10 See Anneliese Maier, *Zwei Untersuchungen zur nachscholastischen Philosophie: Die Mechanisierung des Weltbilds im 17. Jahrhundert; Kants Qualitätskategorien* (Rome: Storia e letteratura, 2nd ed. 1968); Alexandre Koyré, *From the Closed World to the Infinite Universe* (New York: Harper, 1968); Herbert Butterfield,

The Origins of Modern Science, 1300–1800 (London: G. Bell, 1950); Marie Boas, 'The Establishment of the Mechanical Philosophy,' *Osiris* 10 (1952): 412–541; Jürgen Mittelstraß, *Neuzeit und Aufklärung: Studien zur Entstehung der neuzeitlichen Wissenschaft und Philosophie* (Berlin and New York: W. de Gruyter, 1970).

11 General treatments of the use of medical metaphors in medieval political writing include: Cary J. Nederman, 'Body Politics: The Diversification of Organic Metaphors in the Later Middle Ages,' *Pensiero Politico Medievale* 2 (2004): 59–87; Gianluca Briguglia, *Il corpo vivente dello Stato: Una metafora politica* (Milan: B. Mondadori, 2006); Jeffery Zavadil, 'Anatomy of the Body Politic: Organic Metaphors in Ancient and Medieval Political Thought' (Diss., Arizona State University, 2006); Takashi Shogimen, 'Treating the Body Politic: The Medical Metaphor of Political Rule in Late Medieval Europe and Tokugawa Japan,' *Review of Politics* 70 (2008): 77–104; Jacques Krynen, 'Naturel. Essai sur l'argumentation de la nature dans la pensée politique française à la fin du moyen âge,' *Journal des Savants* (April–June 1982): 169–90; Tilman Struve, *Die Entwicklung der organologischen Staatsauffassung im Mittelalter* (Stuttgart: Hiersemann, 1978); idem, 'Die Funktion des Organismusvergleichs in den mittelalterlichen Theorien von Staat und Gesellschaft,' in *Soziale Ordnungen im Selbstverständnis des Mittelalters*, ed. Albert Zimmermann (Berlin and New York: W. de Gruyter, 1979), 144–61 – repr. in idem, *Staat und Gesellschaft im Mittelalter: Ausgewählte Aufsätze* (Berlin: Duncker & Humblot, 2004), 12–28; Wolfgang Stürner, *Natur und Gesellschaft im Denken des Hoch- und Spätmittelalters: Naturwissenschaftliche Kraftvorstellungen und die Motivierung politischen Handelns in Texten des 12. bis 14. Jahrhunderts* (Stuttgart: Klett, 1975); August Nitschke, *Naturerkenntnis und politisches Handeln im Mittelalter: Körper-Bewegung-Raum* (Stuttgart: Klett, 1967); Ernst H. Kantorowicz, *The King's Two Bodies: A Study in Mediaeval Political Theology* (Princeton, NJ: Princeton University Press, 1957; repr. 1997), 199–206; Anton-Hermann Chroust, 'The Corporate Idea and the Body Politic in the Middle Ages,' *Review of Politics* 9 (1947): 423–52.

12 See also Gillian R. Evans, 'The Use of Mathematical Method in Medieval Political Science: Dante's *Monarchia* and the *Defensor pacis* of Marsilius of Padua,' *Archives Internationales d'Histoire des Sciences* 32 (1982): 78–94, esp. 89–91; Luigi Olivieri, 'Teoria aristotelica dell'opinione e scienza politica in Marsilio da Padova,' in *MPCI*, 223–35.

13 *DP* I.xii.5–7.

14 *DP* I.i.3; ii.3; 'Resumere autem oportet propter hec tranquillitatis et sui oppositi descripciones iam dictas 2° huius. Erat enim tranquillitas bona disposicio civitatis seu regni, qua potest unaqueque suarum parcium fa-

cere opera conveniencia sibi secundum racionem et suam institucionem. Ex qua siquidem descripcione apparet ipsius natura. Cum enim dicitur bona disposicio, notatur ipsius intrinseca quidditas generalis. In eo vero quod *per ipsam* dicitur *unaqueque parcium civitatis posse agere sibi opera conveniencia*, signifi catur eius fi nis, qui eciam ipsius propriam quidditatem seu differenciam intelligere facit. Ipsa vero, cum forma seu disposicio quedam sit civitatis aut regni, nec amplius una quam regnum et civitatem esse diximus 17° huius, parte 11a et 12a, non habet formalem causam; hoc enim proprium est compositorum. Ipsius autem agentem causam *sive* factivam comprehendere possumus ex dictis 15° huius et aliis, que ipsam necessario consecuntur in civitate vel regno: hec nempe sunt civium conversacio mutua et communicacio ipsorum invicem suorum operum, mutuumque auxilium atque iuvamentum, generaliterque suorum propriorum operum et communium exercendi ab extraneo non impedita potestas, participacio quoque communium commodorum et onerum secundum convenientem unicuique mensuram, et cum hiis cetera commoda et desiderabilia expressa in oracione Cassiodori, quam posuimus initium huius libri. Quorum quidem omnium aut precipuorum quorundam contraria, intraquillitatem seu discordiam illi oppositam, consecuntur' (*DP* I.xix.2).

15 *DP* I.xv.5, 6, 7, 8. On medieval views on the soul-body relationship, see, e.g., Romana Martorelli Vico, 'Anima e corpo nell'embriologia medievale,' in *Anima e corpo nella cultura medievale*, ed. Carla Casagrande and Silvana Vecchio (Tavarnuzze: SISMEL–Edizioni del Galluzzo, 1999), 95–106; Mario Vegetti, 'Anima e corpo,' in idem and Giuseppe Cambiano, *Il sapere degli antichi* (Turin: Boringhieri, 1985), 201–28. On the use of the heart and soul metaphor in late medieval political thought, see Roberto Lambertini, 'Il cuore e l'anima della città: Osservazioni a margine sull'uso di metafore organistiche in testi politici bassomedievali,' ibid., 289–303.

16 'Adhuc, sicut in composito animali primum precipiens et movens ipsum, motu eo qui secundum locum, est unum, ut in eo libro qui De Motibus Animalium apparet, quoniam pluribus nexistentibus hiis principiis et contraria vel diversa simul precipientibus, necesse foret animal aut in contraria ferri vel omnino quiescere et hiis carere, que per motum sibi necessaria queruntur et commoda; sicque in civitate convenienter ordinata, quam animali bene formato secundum naturam proporcionaliter habere diximus 15° huius. Ideoque velut in animali talium principiorum ociosa, quinimo nociva foret pluralitas, eodem modo in civitate firmiter opinandum. Idem autem videre est, intendere volendi de primo alterante in animali, quemadmodum de movente secundum locum, et in toto similiter ordine movencium et motorum. Hec autem pretermittantur, quoniam ad naturale

pertinent negocium magis; quantum autem suffi ciens est, de ipsis diximus ad presentem consideracionem' (*DP* I.xvii.8).

17 For a similar point, see Nederman, *Community and Consent*, 31; John P. Gibbons, 'Marsilius of Padua's Defense of the Peace' (Diss., Harvard University, 1981), 53.

18 *DP* I.iv.1; 2.

19 *DP* I.iv.2; Cicero, *De Officiis* I.iv.11.

20 On the Stoic theory of *oikeiosis*, see, e.g., Roberto Radice, *'Oikeiosis': Richerche sul fondamento del pensiero stoico e sulla sua genesi* (Milan: Vita e Pensiero, 2000); Troels Engberg-Pedersen, *The Stoic Theory of Oikeiosis: Moral Development and Social Interaction in Early Stoic Philosophy* (Aarhus: Aarhus University Press, 1990); Malcolm Schofield, 'Epicurean and Stoic Political Thought,' in *The Cambridge History of Greek and Roman Political Thought*, ed. Christopher Rowe and Malcolm Schofield (Cambridge: Cambridge University Press, 2000), 435–55, at 449–51; S.G. Pembroke, 'Oikeiōsis,' in *Problems in Stoicism*, ed. Anthony A. Long (London: Athlone Press, 1971), 114–49. On the dissemination of Stoic ideas in the Middle Ages, see Marcia L. Colish, *The Stoic Tradition from Antiquity to the Early Middle Ages*, 2 vols. (Leiden: E.J. Brill, 1985/90), and, in general, Steven K. Strange and Jack Zupko, eds., *Stoicism: Traditions and Transformations*, (Cambridge: Cambridge University Press, 2004).

21 *DP* I.i.4; Cicero, *De officiis*, I.vii.22.

22 For Augustinian influences on Marsilius's political theory, see Joanna Vecchiarelli Scott, 'Influence or Manipulation? The Role of Augustinianism in the *Defensor pacis* of Marsiglio of Padua,' *Augustinian Studies* 9 (1978): 59–79; Conal Condren, 'On Interpreting Marsilius' Use of St Augustine,' *Augustiniana* 25 (1975): 217–22; Mary A. Butts, 'The Political Doctrines of Augustine of Hippo and Marsilius of Padua: A Comparison' (Diss., University of Toronto, 1974); Daniel G. Mulcahy, 'Marsilius of Padua's Use of St. Augustine,' *Revue des Études Augustiniennes* 18 (1972): 180–90; idem, 'The Hands of Augustine but the Voice of Marsilius,' *Augustiniana* 21 (1971): 457–66. Augustine's reception in late medieval political thought is discussed in Roberto Lambertini, 'Jenseits des politischen Augustinismus: Zur Rezeption Augustins in der politischen Theorie des Spätmittelalters,' in *Augustinus – Recht und Gewalt*, ed. Cornelius Mayer (Würzburg: Augustinus bei Echter, 2010), 73–96.

23 *DP* I.iv.3; vi.10.

24 *DP* I.iv.3; I.v.4.

25 Aristotle, *Pol.* 1275b20–21. See further Nederman, *Community and Consent*, 53; Fritz Steinmetz, 'Staatengründung – aus Schwäche oder natürlichem

Geselligkeitsdrang? Zur Geschichte einer Theorie,' in *Politeia und res publica: Beiträge zum Verständnis von Politik, Recht und Staat in der Antike*, ed. Peter Steinmetz (Wiesbaden: F. Steiner, 1969), 181–99.

26 For further references, see Thomas Cole, *Democritus and the Sources of Greek Anthropology* (Atlanta: Scholars Press, 1990); as well as Wiktor Stoczkowski, *Explaining Human Origins: Myth, Imagination and Conjecture*, trans. Mary Turton (Cambridge: Cambridge University Press, 2002), 14–15; Arthur O. Lovejoy and George Boas, *Primitivism and Related Ideas in Antiquity* (Baltimore, MD: John Hopkins Press, 1935; repr. 1997); Origen, *Contra Celsum*, trans. Henry Chadwick (Cambridge: Cambridge University Press, 1953), 244.

27 Plato, *Protagoras* 321B–322D. For further discussion, see Juha Sihvola, *Decay, Progress, the Good Life?: Hesiod and Protagoras on the Development of Culture* (Helsinki: Societas Scientiarum Fennica, 1989).

28 II, 47, 121.

29 98D.

30 Origen, *Contra Celsum*, IV.76 (244–5).

31 Hugo Schneider, ed., *Die 34. Rede des Themistios (Peri tēs archēs)* (Winterthur: P.G. Keller, 1966), 56 and 58 (Greek text)/57 and 59 (German trans.); Wilhelm Dindorf, ed., *Themistii Orationes ex codice medioelanensi*, (Leipzig: K. Knobloch, 1832 – repr. Hildesheim: G. Olms, 1961), 444–72, at 444–6. On Themistios's political thought, see John Vanderspoel, *Themistius and the Imperial Court: Oratory, Civic Duty, and Paideia from Constantius to Theodosius* (Ann Arbor, MI: University of Michigan Press, 1995); Peter Heather, 'Themistius: A Political Philosopher,' in *The Propaganda of Power: The Role of Panegyric in Late Antiquity*, ed. Mary Whitby (Leiden: Brill, 1998), 125–50; Gilbert Dagron, 'L'Empire romain d'Orient au IVe siècle et les traditions politiques de l'hellénisme: le témoignage de Thémistios,' *Travaux et Mémoires du Centre de Recherche d'Histoire et Civilisation byzantines* 3 (1968): 1–242. The following section is based on Vasileios Syros, 'Shadows in Heaven and Clouds on Earth: The Emergence of Social Life and Political Authority in the Early Modern Islamic Empires,' *Viator* 43 (2012): 377–406, esp. 379–85.

32 John W. Watt, 'Julian's *Letter to Themistius* – and Themistius' Response?' in *Emperor and Author: The Writings of Julian 'The Apostate,'* ed. Nicholas J. Baker-Brian and Shaun Tougher (Swansea: Classical Press of Wales, 2011), 91–103; Francis Dvornik, *Early Christian and Byzantine Political Philosophy: Origins and Background* (Washington, DC: Dumbarton Oaks Center for Byzantine Studies, 1966), 2: 666–9; idem, 'The Emperor Julian's "Reactionary' Ideas on Kingship,' in *Late Classical and Mediaeval Studies in Honor of*

Albert Mathias Friend, Jr., ed. Kurt Weitzmann (Princeton, NJ: Princeton University Press, 1955), 71–81; Jeanne Croissant, 'Un nouveau Discours de Thémistius,' *Serta Leodiensia* 44 (1930): 7–30.

33 Paul L. Heck, *The Construction of Knowledge in Islamic Civilization: Qudāma b. Ja'far and his Kitāb al-Kharāj wa-šinā'at al-kitāba* (Leiden: Brill, 2002), 217; Irfan Shahid, 'Epistula de re publica gerenda,' in *Themistii orationes quae supersunt*, ed. Heinrich Schenkl (Leipzig: Teubner, 1974), 3:73–119, at 90–1. The political teaching of the *risāla* is helpfully digested by Maurice Bouyges, 'Notes sur les traductions arabes d'auteurs grecs,' *Archives de philosophie* 2 (1924): 1–23, at 15–23.

34 Moreno Morani, *La tradizione manoscritta del 'De natura hominis' di Nemesio* (Milan: Vita e pensiero, 1981). Nemesios's legacy in the Latin world is traced in Emil Dobler, *Zwei syrische Quellen der theologischen Summa des Thomas von Aquin: Nemesios von Emesa und Johannes von Damaskus: Ihr Einfluss auf die anthropologischen Grundlagen der Moraltheologie (S. Th. I-II, qq 6–17; 22–48)* (Fribourg: Universitätsverlag, 2000), esp. 59–93. The Arabic reception of Nemesios's *De natura hominis* is covered in Khalil Samir, 'Les versions arabes de Némésius de Homs,' in *L'eredità classica nelle lingue orientali*, ed. Massimiliano Pavan and Umberto Cozzoli (Rome: Istituto della Enciclopedia italiana, 1986), 99–151; Ursula Weisser, *Das 'Buch über das Geheimnis der Schöpfung' von Pseudo-Apollonios von Tyana* (Berlin and New York: W. de Gruyter, 1980), esp. 63–8. For the Syriac reception, consult Mauro Zonta, 'Nemesiana Syriaca: New Fragments from the Missing Syriac Version of the *De natura hominis*,' *Journal of Semitic Studies* 36 (1991): 223–58. In general, see also Beatrice Motta, *La mediazione estrema: L'antropologia di Nemesio di Emesa fra platonismo e aristotelismo* (Padua: Il Poligrafo, 2004).

35 Némésius d'Émèse, *De natura hominis; traduction de Burgundio de Pise*, ed. Gérard Verbeke and J.R. Moncho (Leiden: E.J. Brill, 1975), 12; Moreno Morani, ed., *Nemesii Emeseni De natura hominis*, (Leipzig: Teubner, 1987), 7–8; Nemesius, *On the Nature of Man*, trans. Robert W. Sharples and Philip van der Eijk (Liverpool: Liverpool University Press, 2008), 42; Nemesio di Emesa, *La natura dell'uomo*, trans. Moreno Morani (Salerno: Grafiche Moriniello, 1982), 18. For the Galenic precedents of this idea, see Eiliv Skard, 'Nemesiosstudien: II. Nemesios und Galenos,' *Symbolae Osloenses* 17 (1937): 9–25, 9–18; and, in general, Friedrich Lammert, 'Hellenistische Medizin bei Ptolemaios und Nemesios. Ein Beitrag zur Geschichte der christlichen Anthropologie,' *Philologus* 94 (1940): 125–41. Consider also the remarks by David S. Wallace-Hadrill, *The Greek Patristic View of Nature* (Manchester/ New York: Manchester University Press/Barnes & Noble, 1968), 53.

36 *De natura hominis; traduction de Burgundio de Pise*, 14; *De natura hominis*, 9; *On the Nature of Man*, 44; *La natura dell'uomo*, 19–20.
37 Takī ed Dīn al-Hilālī, *Die Einleitung zu Al-Bīrūnī's Steinbuch* (Leipzig: O. Harrassowitz, 1941), 6.
38 Al-Hilālī, *Die Einleitung zu Al-Bīrūnī's Steinbuch*, 26.
39 On Maimonides' views on human sociability, see Howard T. Kreisel, *Maimonides' Political Thought: Studies in Ethics, Law, and the Human Ideal* (Albany, NY: State University of New York Press, 1999), 189–223; Abraham Melamed, 'Maimonides on the Political Nature of Man: Needs and Responsibilities,' in *Minah le-Sarah: Mekhqarim be-Filosofiyah Yehudit ve-Qabbalah (= Sarah Heller Wilensky Jubilee Volume)*, ed. Mosheh Idel et al. (Jerusalem: Magnes Press, 1994), 292–333 [in Hebrew] – rev. English version as 'Aristotle's *Politics* in Medieval and Renaissance Jewish Political Thought,' in *Well Begun Is Only Half Done: Tracing Aristotle's Political Ideas in Medieval Arabic, Syriac, Byzantine, and Jewish Sources*, ed. Vasileios Syros (Tempe, AZ: Arizona Center for Medieval and Renaissance Studies, 2011), 145–86.
40 *Eth. Nic.* 1131a1ff.
41 Ptolemy of Lucca, *On the Government of Rulers = De Regimine Principum; with portions attributed to Thomas Aquinas*, trans. James M. Blythe (Philadelphia, PA: University of Pennsylvania Press, 1997), 1–5. On Ptolemy's life, works, and political ideas, see the following studies by James M. Blythe: *The Life and Works of Tolomeo Fiadoni (Ptolemy of Lucca)* (Turnhout: Brepols, 2009) (for the *De regimine pincipum*, 157–90); idem, *The Worldview and Thought of Tolomeo Fiadoni (Ptolemy of Lucca)* (Brepols: Turnhout, 2009); 'Aristotle's *Politics* and Ptolemy of Lucca,' *Vivarium* 40 (2002): 103–36; as well as Cary J. Nederman and Mary E. Sullivan, 'Reading Aristotle through Rome: History and Republicanism in Ptolemy of Lucca's *De regimine principum*,' *European Journal of Political Theory* 7 (2008), 223–4; Charles T. Davis, 'Tolomeus of Lucca and the Roman Republic,' *Proceedings of the American Philosophical Society* 118 (1974): 30–50 – repr. in *Renaissance Thought: A Reader*, ed. Robert Black (London and New York: Routlegde, 2001), 254–89.
42 *'De regno,'* in *S. Thomae Aquinatis Opuscula omnia necnon opera minora*, vol. 1: *Opuscula philosophica*, ed. Jean Perrier (Paris: P. Lethielleux, 1949), 364–5; Ptolemy of Lucca, *On the Government of Rulers* 4:2 (220).
43 *'De regno,'* 365; Ptolemy of Lucca, *On the Government of Rulers* 4:3 (220).
44 *'De regno,'* 365; Ptolemy of Lucca, *On the Government of Rulers* 4:4 and 4:5 (220–1).
45 *'De regno,'* 365; Ptolemy of Lucca, *On the Government of Rulers* 4:5 (221).
46 *DP* I.iii.3
47 *DP* I.iii.3. On this point, see also Nederman, *Community and Consent*, 32–8.

48 Aristotle, *Pol.* 1253b1–5. See, in general, D. Brendan Nagle, *The Household as the Foundation of Aristotle's Polis* (Cambridge: Cambridge University Press, 2006).
49 *DP* I.iii.5.
50 *DP* I.iii.4.
51 *DP* I.iii.4.
52 *DP* I.iii.4. A fuller treatment of the Marsilian notion of *quasi-naturalis lex* appears in Cary J. Nederman, 'Private Will, Public Justice: Household, Community and Consent in Marsiglio of Padua's *Defensor pacis*,' *Western Political Quarterly* 43 (1990): 699–717, at 705–7 and 713.
53 Compare Aristotle, *Rh.* 1375a31–32.
54 *DP* II.xxii.15.
55 *DP* I.iii.4. See also Nederman, *Community and Consent*, 63.
56 The following account is partly based on Vasileios Syros, 'Founders and Kings Versus Orators: Medieval and Early Modern Views on the Origins of Social Life,' *Viator* 42 (2011): 383–408.
57 See Wolfgang Leschhorn, *"Gründer der Stadt": Studien zu einem politisch-religiösen Phänomen der griechischen Geschichte* (Stuttgart: F. Steiner, 1984); Peter Weiss, 'Lebendiger Mythos: Gründungsheroen und städtische Gründungstraditionen im griechisch-römischen Osten,' *Würzburger Jahrbücher für die Altertumswissenschaft* n.s. 10 (1984): 179–208; W.G. Runciman, 'Origins of States: The Case of Archaic Greece,' *Comparative Studies in Society and History* 24 (1982): 351–77; Irad Malkin, *Religion and Colonization in Ancient Greece* (Leiden and New York: Brill, 1987); Andrew Szegedy-Maszak, 'Legends of the Greek Lawgivers,' *Greek, Roman and Byzantine Studies* 19 (1978): 199–209. Ancient ideas on the origins of social life are surveyed in Cole, *Democritus and the Sources of Greek Anthropology*; Sue Blundell, *The Origins of Civilization in Greek and Roman Thought* (London and Sydney: C. Helm, 1986); Steinmetz, 'Staatengründung – aus Schwäche oder natürlichem Geselligkeitsdrang?'; Anton-Hermann Chroust, 'The Origin and Meaning of the Social Compact Doctrine,' *Ethics* 57 (1946): 38–56; Harry E. Barnes, 'Theories of the Origin of the State in Classical Political Philosophy,' *The Monist* 34 (1924): 15–62. Consider also Nederman, *Community and Consent*, 44.
58 William K.C. Guthrie, *In the Beginning: Some Greek Views on the Origins of Life and the Early State of Man* (Ithaca, NY: Cornell University Press, 1957; repr. Westport, CT: Greenwood Press, 1986), 99–102; Ernest Barker, *The Political Thought of Plato and Aristotle* (London: Methuen, 1906; repr. New York: Dover Publications, 1959), 213, 234, 254–5, 293.
59 The other conditions are a social structure founded on the elements req-

uisite for the efficient functioning of the city: food; arts and crafts; arms; a certain supply of goods for domestic use and military purposes; worship of gods; a method of deciding what is most conducive to the common good and what is just in the private dealings of the citizens; a proper division of land; good planning with an eye to four factors (health; convenience for political activities; a secure location protected from external enemies; natural supply of waters and streams or large supplies of rainwater); a beautiful appearance; and the proper training of the youth. Aristotle, *Pol.*, 1325b35–1342b34. See also the work of Jeff Chuska, *Aristotle's Best Regime: A Reading of Aristotle's Politics VII. 1–10* (Lanham, MD: University Press of America, 2000). On Aristotle's ideas on city planning, consult Glanville Downey, 'Aristotle as an Expert on Urban Problems,' *Talanta* 3 (1971): 56–73.

60 Ralph Lerner and Muhsin Mahdi, eds., *Medieval Political Philosophy: A Sourcebook* (New York: Free Press of Glencoe, 1963), 85–6. On Al-Fārābī's views of the founding of human communities, see the discussion in Christopher Colmo, 'On the Prudence of Founders,' *Review of Politics* 60 (1998): 719–41, esp. 739–40.

61 Thomas Aquinas, 'De regno ad regem Cypri,' in *Sancti Thomae de Aquino opera omnia* (= Editio Leonina; 42), ed. Antoine Dondaine (Rome: Editori di San Tommaso, 1979), book II, chaps. 1–4 (464–8); Ptolemy of Lucca, *On the Government of Rulers*, 104–12. For further discusion, see José R. Pierpauli, 'El origen de la comunidad política en la Edad Media: Alberto Magno–Tomás de Aquino y Marsilio de Padua,' *Rivista internazionale di filosofia del diritto* 78 (2001): 47–75; Angelo Marchesi, 'Stato democratico e programmazione urbanistica nel pensiero politico dell'Aquinate,' in *Les philosophies morales et politiques au Moyen Âge*, ed. B. Carlos Bazán, Eduardo Andújar and Léonard G. Sbrocchi (New York: LEGAS, 1995), 3: 1542–54, esp. 1550–4.

62 Niccolò Machiavelli, *Il Principe*, chap. 6; idem, *Discorsi sopra la prima deca di Tito Livio*, book 1, chap. 9; *Il Principe*, chap. 26. References to *Il Principe* and the *Discorsi* are to Niccolò Machiavelli, *Opere*, ed. Corrado Vivanti (Turin: Einaudi-Gallimard, 1997), 1: 115–92 and 193–525, respectively. I have also consulted the following English translations: Harvey C. Mansfield, trans., *The Prince* (Chicago, IL, and London: University of Chicago Press, 2nd ed. 1998); Quentin Skinner and Russell Price, eds., *The Prince* (Cambridge: Cambridge University Press, 1988); Harvey C. Mansfield and Nathan Tarcov, trans., *Discourses on Livy* (Chicago, IL, and London: University of Chicago Press, 1996). See also the discussion in Hanna F. Pitkin, *Fortune Is A Woman: Gender and Politics in the Thought of Niccolò Machiavelli* (Chicago,

IL, and London: University of Chicago Press, 1999), 52–79; Barbara Silberdick Feinberg, 'Creativity and the Political Community: The Role of the Law-Giver in the Thought of Plato, Machiavelli and Rousseau,' *Western Political Quarterly* 23 (1970): 471–84.

63 On the medieval and early modern reception of the idea of the mixed constitution, see Marie Gaille-Nikodimov, ed., *Le Gouvernement mixte: De l'idéal politique au monstre constitutionnel en Europe (XIIIe–XVIIe siècle)* (Saint-Etienne: Publications de l'Université de Saint-Étienne, 2005); Maurizio Merlo, 'La sintassi del "regimen bene commixtum" e del "regimen politicum" fra Tommaso d'Aquino e Tolomeo da Lucca,' *Filosofia Politica* 19 (2005): 33–47; James M. Blythe, *Ideal Government and the Mixed Constitution in the Middle Ages* (Princeton, NJ: Princeton University Press, 1992); Wilfried Nippel, *Mischverfassungstheorie und Verfassungsrealität in Antike und früher Neuzeit* (Stuttgart: Klett-Cotta, 1980). On the 'Myth of Venice,' see Edward Muir, *Civic Ritual in Renaissance Venice* (Princeton, NJ: Princeton University Press, 1981); Craig Kallendorf, *Virgil and the Myth of Venice: Books and Readers in the Italian Renaissance* (Oxford: Clarendon Press, 1999); Robert Finley, 'The Immortal Republic: The Myth of Venice during the Italian Wars (1494–1530),' *Sixteenth Century Journal* 30 (1999): 931–44; Franco Gaeta, 'Alcune considerazioni sul mito di Venezia,' *Bibliothèque d'Humanisme et Renaissance* 23 (1961): 58–75; Gina Fasoli, 'Nascita di un mito,' in *Studi storici in onore di Gioacchino Volpe per il suo 80 compleanno* (Florence: Sansoni, 1958), 1: 445–79. On medieval and early modern accounts of the founding of Venice, see *Franco Gaeta, 'Storiografia,* coscienza nazionale e politica culturale nella Venezia del Rinascimento,' *Storia della cultura veneta* 3/I: *Dal primo Quattrocento al Concilio di Trento,* ed. Girolamo Arnaldi and Manlio Pastore Stocchi (Vicenza: N. Pozza, 1980), 1–91; Antonio Carile, 'Le origini di Venezia nella tradizione storiografica,' in *Storia della cultura veneta* 1: *Dalle origini al Trecento,* 134–66.

64 John Monfasani, ed., *Collectanea Trapezuntiana: Texts, Documents and Bibliographies of George of Trebizond* (Binghamton, NY: Medieval & Renaissance Texts & Studies, 1984), 198–202; George of Trebizond, 'Preface to His Translation of Plato's *Laws*,' trans. John Monfasani, in *Cambridge Translations of Renaissance Philosophical Texts* 2: *Political Philosophy,* ed. Jill Kraye (Cambridge: Cambridge University Press, 1997), 128–33 (on the history of the Preface and the ideas expressed there, see John Monfasani's introduction, ibid., 128–9). On George of Trebizond's political thought, see Thomas Berns, 'Construire un idéal vénitien de la constitution mixte à la Renaissance: L'enseignement de Platon par Trébizonde,' *Le Gouvernement*

mixte, 25–38; James Hankins, *Plato in the Italian Renaissance* (Leiden and New York: Brill, 1991), 1: 165–92; 2: 429–35, 445–8; John Monfasani, *George of Trebizond: A Biography and a Study of His Rhetoric and Logic* (Leiden: E.J. Brill, 1976), 171–4; Giorgio Ravegnani, 'Nota sul pensiero politico di Giorgio da Trebisonda,' *Aevum* 49 (1975): 310–29; Franco Gaeta, 'Giorgio da Trebisonda, le *Leggi* di Platone e la costituzione di Venezia,' *Bullettino dell'Istituto storico italiano per il medio evo e Archivio Muratoriano* 82 (1970): 479–501.

65 *Collectanea Trapezuntiana*, 200; 'Preface to His Translation of Plato's *Laws*,' 130.

66 *Collectanea Trapezuntiana*, 200; 'Preface to His Translation of Plato's *Laws*,' 130–1.

67 'Quare qui civitatem Venetam fundarunt, tanto ceteros omnes homines omni virtutis numero civilique scientia vicerunt quanto non a tyranno compulsi, sed a se ipsis inducti Platonice civitatis effigiem in rem ipsam verterunt. Et quod nullum mirandi excessum relinquit, multo meliorem etiam quam ipse dicit, vir Iove quoque ipso, ut gentiles dicerent, eloquentior, condiderunt.' *Collectanea Trapezuntiana*,' 201; 'Preface to His Translation of Plato's *Laws*,' 131.

68 Gasparis Contareni Cardinalis, *De Magistratibus et Republica Venetorum* (Venice, 1589), fol. 6r–v; Eng. trans. Gasper Contareno, *The Commonwealth and Government of Venice*, trans. Lewes Lewkenor Esquire (London: Imprinted by Iohn Windet for Edmund Mattes, 1599; repr. Theatrum Orbis Terrarum/Da Capo Press, 1969), 5–6; Gasparo Contarini, *La Republica e i Magistrati di Vinegia*, ed. Vittorio Conti (Florence: Centro editoriale toscano, 2003), 41–2. For Contarini's life and works, see Elisabeth G. Gleason, *Gasparo Contarini: Venice, Rome, and Reform* (Berkeley, CA: University of California Press, 1993); Gigliola Fragnito, *Gasparo Contarini. Un magistrato veneziano al servizio della Cristianità* (Florence: L.S. Olschki, 1988). His political ideas are discussed in Vittorio Conti, 'The Mechanization of Virtue: Republican Rituals in Italian Political Thought in the Sixteenth and Seventeenth Centuries,' in *Republicanism: A Shared European Heritage* 2: *The Values of Republicanism in Early Modern Europe*, ed. Martin van Gelderen and Quentin Skinner (Cambridge: Cambridge University Press 2002), 73–83; Giovani Silvano, *La 'Republica de' Viniziani': Ricerche sul repubblicanesimo veneziano in età moderna* (Florence: L.S. Olschki, 1993), 85–120; Alois Riklin, 'Die Venezianische Mischverfassung im Lichte von Gasparo Contarini (1483–1542),' *Zeitschrift für Politik* 37 (1990): 264–91; John G.A. Pocock, *The Machiavellian Moment: Florentine Political Thought and the Atlantic Republican*

Tradition (Princeton, NJ: Princeton University Press, 1975), 320–8; Hermann Hackert, *Die Staatsschrift Gasparo Contarinis und die politischen Verhältnisse Venedigs im sechzehnten Jahrhundert* (Heidelberg: Winter 1940).

69 'Tra gli antichi datori di leggi et introduttori di republiche, quelli hanno trovato minore difficultà nelle loro ordinazioni li quali hanno avuto a regolare uomini che non erano più ad altre leggi stati sottoposti o, abbandonati gli antichi paesi loro, erano in quelli di altri venuti ad abitare. Percioché quelli vivendo a caso et separati l'uno dall'altro a guisa di fiere, ogni forma di vivere umano che fu loro proposta, per la dolcezza sua, fu da essi approvata et ricevuta.' Donato Giannotti, *Republica fiorentina*, ed. Giovanni Silvano (Geneva: Droz, 1990), 103. On Giannotti's political thought, see Alexander Thumfart and Arno Waschkuhn, *Staatstheorien des italienischen Bürgerhumanismus. Politische Theorie von Francesco Petrarca bis Donato Giannotti* (Baden-Baden: Nomos, 2005), 251–72; Théa Picquet, 'Rome: un modèle pour Florence?' *Rinascimento* 41 (2001): 285–301; Pocock, *The Machiavellian Moment*, 272–320; Giorgio Cadoni, *Crisi della mediazione politica e conflitti sociali: Niccolò Machiavelli, Francesco Guicciardini e Donato Giannotti di fronte al tramonto della Florentina Libertas* (Rome: Jouvence, 1994); idem, *L'utopia repubblicana di Donato Giannotti* (Milan: Giuffrè, 1978). On the reception of the 'Myth of Venice' in Florentine political thought, see Piero Venturelli, 'Teorie e immagini del governo "misto" nel Cinquecento: i casi di Gasparo Contarini, Donato Giannotti, Paolo Paruta e Traiano Boccalini' (Diss., University of Bologna, 2009); Marie Gaille-Nikodimov, 'L'ideale del governo misto tra Venezia e Firenze. Un aristotelismo politico a doppia faccia,' *Filosofia Politica* 19 (2005): 63–76; Felix Gilbert, 'The Venetian Constitution in Florentine Political Thought,' in *Florentine Studies: Politics and Society in Renaissance Florence*, ed. Nicolai Rubinstein (Evanston, IL: Northwestern University Press, 1968), 463–500; Erdmann Blackstein, 'Der venezianische Staatsgedanke im 16. Jahrhundert und das zeitgenössische Venedig-Bild in der Staatstheorie des republikanischen Florenz' (Diss., University of Frankfurt a. M., 1973); Rudolf von Albertini, *Das florentinische Staatsbewusstsein im Übergang von der Republik zum Prinzipat* (Bern: Francke, 1955), 146–66; Felice Battaglia, 'La dottrina dello stato misto nei politici fiorentini del Rinascimento,' *Rivista internazionale di filosofia del diritto* 7 (1927): 286–304.

70 Giannotti, *Republica fiorentina*, 103–4.

71 'Tutti quelli che danno leggi a' popoli et ordinano republiche, è necessario che abbiano sempre l'animo diritto alla diuturnità dello stato che introducono. Et perché ciascuno stato ruina per due cagioni principali, l'una è intrinseca, come sono le dissensioni civili et altri disordini che nasconro

drento, l'altra è estrinseca, come sono gli assalti esterni, all'una col buono ordine et forma della republica, la quale si ingegnano introdurre, all'altra con la milizia bene ordinata, proveggono. Questi pensieri caddeno nella mente di Licurgo Lacedemonio, quando ordinò la sua republica la quale durò ottocento anni con le medesime leggi et non patì mai alcuna intrinseca alterazione et dagli assalti esterni si potette difendere. Romulo ancora, uomo sopra tutti gli altri sapientissimo, quando ordinò la republica, pensò, oltre le predette due cose, al propagare l'imperio.' Giannotti, *Republica fiorentina*, 153–4. See also ibid., 71, 81–2.

72 Donato Giannotti, *Della Repubblica de' Viniziani*, in idem, *Opere politiche*, ed. Furio Diaz (Milan: Marzorati, 1974), 1: 27–151, at 37–8.

73 Giannotti, *Republica fiorentina*, 163–4. See also Donato Giannotti, *Die Republik Florenz (1534)*, ed. Alois Riklin, trans. Daniel Höchli (Munich: Fink, 1997), 111.

74 Giannotti, *Republica fiorentina*, 212–13, 155–6.

75 On medieval views on the original condition of man, see the classic study by George Boas, *Primitivism and Related Ideas in the Middle Ages* (Baltimore, MD: Johns Hopkins University Press, 1948; repr. 1997).

76 'Est igitur, inquit Africanus, res publica res populi, populus autem non omnis hominum coetus quoquo modo congregatus, sed coetus multitudinis iuris consensu et utilitatis communione sociatus. eius autem prima causa coëundi est non tam inbecillitas quam naturalis quaedam hominum quasi congregatio.' On the medieval and Renaissance reception of Cicero's ideas on the emergence of human associations, see Matthew Kempshall, '*De Re Publica* I.39 in Medieval and Renaissance Political Thought,' in *Cicero's Republic* (= *Bulletin of the Institute of Classical Studies* Supplement 76), ed. Jonathan G.F. Powell and John A. North (London: Institute of Classical Studies, School of Advanced Study, University of London, 2001), 99–135. Also of value is Otto von Gierke, *Political Theories of the Middle Ages*, trans. Frederic W. Maitland (Cambridge: Cambridge University Press, 1958), 89–90, 187–8. On Cicero's notion of the *res publica* and his ideas on the origins of social life, see Malcolm Schofield, 'Cicero's Definition of *res publica*,' in idem, *Saving the City: Philosopher-Kings and Other Classical Paradigms* (London and New York: Routledge, 1999), 178–94; Werner Suerbaum, *Vom antiken zum frühmittelalterlichen Staatsbegriff: Über Verwendung und Bedeutung von res publica, regnum, imperium und status von Cicero bis Jordanis* (Münster: Aschendorffsche Verlagsbuchhandlung, 1961), 1–37; Rudolf Stark, 'Ciceros Staatsdefinition,' *La Nouvelle Clio* 6 (1954): 56–69 – repr. in *Das Staatsdenken der Römer*, ed. Richard Klein (Darmstadt: Wissenschaftliche Buchgesellschaft, 3rd ed. 1980), 332–47. The Aristotelian

background of Cicero's definition of the *res publica* is discussed in Dorothea Frede, 'Constitution and Citizenship: Peripatetic Influence on Cicero's Political Conceptions in the *De re publica*,' in *Cicero's Knowledge of the Peripatos*, ed. William W. Fortenbaugh and Peter Steinmetz (New Brunswick, NJ and London: Transaction Pub., 1989), 4: 77–100, at 84–6.

77 On medieval views of human society as the outcome of a founding compact, see, e.g., Arthur P. Monahan, *Consent, Coercion, and Limit: The Medieval Origins of Parliamentary Democracy* (Kingston: McGill-Queen's University Press, 1987); Mario Grignaschi, 'Le problème du contrat social et l'origine de la 'civitas' dans la scolastique,' *Anciens Pays et Assemblées d'Etats* 22 (1961): 67–85; Mario D'Addio, *L'idea del contratto sociale dai Sofisti alla riforma e il 'De principatu' di Mario Salamonio* (Milan: Giuffrè, 1954); John W. Gough, *The Social Contract: A Critical Study of Its Development* (Oxford: Clarendon Press, 1936); Otto von Gierke, *The Development of Political Theory*, trans. Bernard Freyd (New York: H. Fertig, 1966), 98–101, 125–6; Frédéric Atger, *Essai sur l'histoire des doctrines du contrat social* (Paris: F. Alcan, 1906), 44–90; and, in general, François Foronda, ed., *Avant le contrat social. Le contrat politique dans l'Occident médiéval XIII*[e]*–XV*[e] *siècle* (Paris: Publications de la Sorbonne, 2011).

78 'Nam fuit quoddam tempus cum in agris homines passim bestiarum modo vagabantur et sibi victu fero vitam progabant, nec ratione animi quicquam, sed pleraque viribus corporis administrabant; nondum divinae religionis, non humani offici ratio colebatur, nemo nuptias viderant legitimas, non certos quisquam aspexerat liberos, non, ius aequabile quid utilitatis haberet, acceperat. Ita propter errorem atque inscientiam caeca ac temeraria dominatrix animi cupiditas ad se explendam viribus corporis abutebatur, perniciosissimis satellitibus.' Cicero, *De inventione; De optimo genere oratorum; Topica*, trans. Harry M. Hubbell (Cambridge, MA/London: Heinemann/Harvard University Press, 1949), I.ii.2 – 4 and 6 (Latin text)/5 and 7 (Eng. trans.).

79 'Quodam tempore homines nondum neque naturali neque civili iure descripto fusi per agros ac dispersi vagarentur tantumque haberent, quantum manu ac viribus per caedem ac vulnera aut eripere aut retinere potuissent? Qui igitur primi virtute et consilio praestanti existerunt, ii perspecto genere humanae docilitatis atque ingenii dissipatos unum in locum congregarunt eosque ex feritate illa ad iustitiam atque ad mansuetudinem transduxerunt. Tum res ad communem utilitatem, quas publicas appellamus, tum conventicula hominum, quae postea civitates nominatae sunt, tum domicilia coniuncta, quas urbes dicimus, invento et divino iure et humano moenibus saepserunt.' Cicero, *The Speeches: Pro Sestio and In*

Vatinium, trans. Robert Gardner (London/Cambridge, MA: Heinemann/Harvard University Press, 1958), XLII.91–158 and 160 (Latin text)/159 and 161 (Eng. trans.).

80 Cicero, *De officiis*, trans. Walter Miller (Cambridge, MA/London: W. Heinemann/Macmillan, 1921), I.iv.11–12 – 12 and 14 (Latin text)/13 and 15 (Eng. Trans); xxx.107 (108/109). See also Cary J. Nederman, *Community and Consent*, 44–5.

81 Cicero, *De officiis*, I.xvi.50–2 and 54/53 and 55.

82 'Quo tempore quidam magnus videlicet vir et sapiens cognovit quae materia esset et quanta ad maximas res opportunitas in animis inesset hominum, si quis eam posset elicere et praecipiendo meliorem reddere; qui dispersos homines in agros et in tectis silvestribus abditos ratione quadam compulit unum in locum et congregavit et eos in unam quamque rem inducens utilem atque honestam primo propter insolentiam reclamantes, deinde propter rationem atque orationem studiosius audientes ex feris et immanibus mites reddidit et mansuetos.' Cicero, *De inventione*, I.ii.2 (4 and 6/5 and 7). See also Luciano Perelli, *Il pensiero politico di Cicerone: Tra filosofia greca e ideologia aristocratica romana* (Florence: La Nuova Italia, 1990) 17–33; idem, 'La definizione e l'origine dello stato nel pensiero di Cicerone,' *Atti della Accademia delle Scienze di Torino, 2. Classe di Scienze Morali, Storiche e Filologiche* 106 (1972): 281–309.

83 Cicero, *De officiis*, II.iv.15 (182/183).

84 'Age vero, urbibus constitutis, ut fidem colere et iustitiam retinere discerent et aliis parere sua voluntate consuescerent ac non modo labores excipiendos communis commodi causa, sed etiam vitam amittendam existimarent, qui tandem fieri potuit, nisi homines ea quae ratione invenissent eloquentia persuadere potuissent? Profecto nemo nisi gravi ac suavi commotus oratione, cum viribus plurimum posset, ad ius voluisset sine vi descendere, ut inter quos posset excellere, cum eis se pateretur aequari et sua voluntate a iucundissima consuetudine recederet quae praesertim iam naturae vim obtineret propter vetustatem.' Cicero, *De inventione*, I.ii.3 (6/7).

85 'Hanc enim ob causam maxime, ut sua tenerentur, res publicae civitatesque constitutae sunt. Nam, etsi duce natura congregabantur homines, tamen spe custodiae rerum suarum urbium praesidia quaerebant.' Cicero, *De officiis*, II.xxi.73 (248/249). See also the discussions in Neal Wood, *Cicero's Social and Political Thought* (Berkeley, CA: University of California Press, 1988), 129–32, 140–2; idem, 'The Economic Dimension of Cicero's Political Thought: Property and State,' *Canadian Journal of Political Science* 16 (1983): 739–56; and, in general, Julia Annas, 'Cicero on Stoic Moral

Philosophy and Private Property,' in *Philosophia togata: Essays on Philosophy and Roman Society*, ed. Miriam Griffin and Jonathan Barnes (Oxford: Clarendon Press, 1989), 151–73.

86 'Mihi quidem non apud Medos solum, ut ait Herodotus, sed etiam apud maiores nostros iustitiae fruendae causa videntur olim bene morati reges constituti. Nam cum premeretur inops multitudo ab iis, qui maiores opes habebant, ad unum aliquem confugiebant virtute praestantem; qui cum prohiberet iniuria tenuiores, aequitate constituenda summos cum infimis pari iure retinebat. Eademque constituendarum legum fuit causa, quae regum. Ius enim semper est quaesitum aequabile; neque enim aliter esset ius. Id si ab uno iusto et bono viro consequebantur, erant eo contenti; cum id minus contingeret, leges sunt inventae, quae cum omnibus semper una atque eadem voce loquerentur.' Cicero, *De officiis*, II.xii.41–2 (208 and 210/209 and 211).

87 *De civitate Dei* XIX.21.I; II.21.2–3, 6. See also the discussion in Kempshall, '*De Re Publica* I.39 in Medieval and Renaissance Political Thought,' 101–4.

88 'Populus est humanae multitudinis, iuris consensu et concordi communione sociatus,' Isidore of Seville, *Isidori Hispalensis episcopi Etymologiarvm sive originvm libri xx*, ed. Wallace M. Lindsay (Oxford: Clarendon Press, 1911), IX.iv.5; Isidore of Seville, *The Etymologies of Isidore of Seville*, trans. Stephen A. Barney, Wendy J. Lewis, Jennifer A. Beach and Oliver Berghof (Cambridge: Cambridge University Press, 2006), 203. See further Kempshall, '*De Re Publica* I.39 in Medieval and Renaissance Political Thought,' 104–5.

89 'Civitas est hominum multitudo societatis vinculo adunata, dicta a civibus, id est ab ipsis incolis urbis [pro eo quod plurimorum consciscat et contineat vitas],' Isidore of Seville, *Isidori Hispalensis episcopi Etymologiarvm*, XV.ii.1; Isidore of Seville, *The Etymologies of Isidore of Seville*, 305.

90 Aristotle, *Pol.* 1253a1–3. See also the discussions in Dominic O'Meara, 'Man as Political Animal: On the Relation between Plato and Aristotle,' in idem, *The Structure of Being and the Search for the Good: Essays on Ancient and Early Medieval Platonism* (Aldershot and Brookfield, VT: Ashgate, 1998), no. II [first published as 'Der Mensch als politisches Lebewesen: Zum Verhältnis zwischen Platon und Aristoteles,' in *Der Mensch – ein politisches Tier? Essays zur politischen Anthropologie*, ed. Otfried Höffe (Stuttgart: Reclam, 1992), 14–25]; Wolfgang Kullmann, 'Der Mensch als politisches Lebewesen bei Aristoteles,' *Hermes* 108 (1980): 419–43; rev. as idem, 'Man as a Political Animal in Aristotle,' in *A Companion to Aristotle's Politics*, ed. David Keyt and Fred D. Miller, Jr (Oxford and Cambridge, MA: B. Blackwell, 1991),

94–117; Richard G. Mulgan, 'Aristotle's Doctrine that Man is a Political Animal,' *Hermes* 102 (1974): 438–45.

91 'Sequitur quinta conclusio, quod est principatus duplex, vel auctoritas, scilicet paterna et politica. Politica duplex, scilicet in una persona vel in communitate.–Prima, scilicet paterna, iusta est, scilicet ex lege naturae, qua omnes filii tenentur parentibus obedire, nec ista per aliquam legem positivam, Mosaicam vel evangelicam, est revocata, sed magis confirmata.–Auctoritas vero politica, quae est supra extraneos, sive in una persona resideat sive in communitate, potest esse iusta ex communi consensu et electione ipsius communitatis. Et prima auctoritas respicit descensum naturalem, quamquam non cohabitantes civiliter. Secunda respicit cohabitantes quantumcumque nulla consanguinitate vel propinquitate sibi coniunctos, utpote si ad civitatem aliquam aedificandam vel inhabitandam concurrerunt extranei aliqui, videntes se non posse bene regi sine aliqua auctoritate, poterant concorditer consentire, ut vel uni personae vel communitati committerent illam communitatem; et uni personae vel pro se tantum–et successor eligeretur sicut ipse–vel pro se et tota sua posterioritate. Et ista auctoritas politica utraque iusta est, quia iuste potest quis se submittere uni personae vel communitati in his quae non sunt contra legem Dei, in quibus melius potest dirigi per illum cui se subicit vel submittit quam per seipsum. Ergo habemus complete quomodo poterat condi lex positiva iusta, quia ab habente prudentiam in se vel in consiliariis suis, et cum hoc habente auctoritatem iustam aliquo modo dictorum modorum in ista conlusione.' John Duns Scotus, *John Duns Scotus' Political and Economic Philosophy*, Latin text and Eng. trans. Allan B. Wolter (St Bonaventure, NY: Franciscan Institute, St Bonaventure University, 2001), 32 and 34 (Latin text)/33 and 35 (Eng. trans.). See also Luis A. De Boni, '*Legislator, lex, lex naturalis* und *dominium* bei Johannes Duns Scotus,' in *Lex und Ius: Beiträge zur Begründung des Rechts in der Philosophie des Mittelalters und der Frühen Neuzeit*, ed. Alexander Fidora et al. (Stuttgart and Bad Cannstatt: Frommann-Holzboog, 2010), 221–39; Roberto Lambertini, *La povertà pensata: Evoluzione storica della definizione dell'identità minoritica da Bonaventura ad Ockham* (Modena: Mucchi, 2000), 126–34; Jeannine Quillet, 'Community, Counsel and Representation,' in *The Cambridge History of Medieval Political Thought, c. 350–c. 1450*, ed. James H. Burns (Cambridge: Cambridge University Press, 1988), 520–72, at 536. For Scotus's political ideas in general, consult Luca Parisoli, *La philosophie normative de Jean Duns Scot: Droit et politique du droit* (Rome: Istituto Storico dei Cappuccini, 2001); Roberto Lambertini, 'Aspetti etico-politici del pensiero di Duns Scoto,' in *Etica e*

persona: Duns Scoto e suggestioni nel moderno, ed. Silvestro Casamenti (Bologna: Edizioni Francescane Bologna, 1994), 35–86.

92 Johannes Quidort von Paris, *Über königliche und päpstliche Gewalt (De regia potestate et papali)*, ed. and trans. Fritz Bleienstein (Stuttgart: Klein, 1969), 78; Arthur Monahan, *John of Paris on Royal and Papal Power: A Translation, with Introduction, of the De Potestate Regia et Papali of John of Paris* (New York and London: Columbia University Press, 1974), 9. On John of Paris's political ideas, see Francisco Bertelloni, 'Selbsterhaltungstrieb, *princeps, lex* and *ius* im Traktat *De potestate regia et papali* des Johannes Quidort,' in *Lex und Ius*, 175–94; Thomas [J.] Renna, 'Aristotle and the French Monarchy,' *Viator* 9 (1978): 309–24, esp. 319–24; idem, 'The Populus in John of Paris' Theory of Monarchy, 1260–1303,' *Tijdschrift voor Rechtsgeschiedenis* 42 (1974): 243–68; Adalbert Podlech, 'Die Herrschaftstheorie des Johannes von Paris,' *Der Staat* 16 (1977): 465–92.

93 'Nam cum homo sit animal naturaliter politicum seu civile ut dicitur *I Politicorum*, quod ostenditur secundum Philosophum ex victu, vestitu, defensione, in quibus sibi solus non sufficit, et etiam ex sermone qui est ad alterum.' Johannes Quidort von Paris, *Über königliche und päpstliche Gewalt*, 75–6; Monahan, *John of Paris on Royal and Papal Power*, 8.

94 'Ex quibus praedictis patet homini necessarium et utile in multitudine vivere et maxime in multitudine quae sufficere potest ad totam vitam, ut est civitas vel regio, et praecipue sub uno principante propter bonum commune qui rex dicitur. Et patet etiam quod hoc regimen derivatur a iure naturali, ex eo scilicet quod homo naturaliter est animal civile seu politicum et sociale in tantum, ut ante Belum et Ninum, qui primitus regnaverunt, homines non naturaliter nec ut homines, sed more bestiarum sine regimine vivebant, ut narrat quosdam dixisse Orosius primo libro suo *Contra Paganos*. Et Tullius consimilia dicit in principio *Veteris Rhetoricae*, et Philosophus dicit de talibus in *Politicis* quod non vivunt ut homines sed ut dii vel bestiae. [Et cum per verba communia ad vitam communem naturaliter eis convenientem, ut visum est, a vita bestiali non possent homines huiusmodi revocari, homines magis ratione utentes, eorum compatientes errori, ad vitam communem sub uno aliquo ordinatam rationalibus persuasoriis revocare conati sunt, ut dicit Tullius, et ita revocatos certis legibus ad vivendum communiter ligaverunt, quae quidem leges hic ius gentium dici possunt. Et sic patet quod huiusmodi regimen a iure naturali et gentium derivatur.]' Johannes Quidort von Paris, *Über königliche und päpstliche Gewalt*, 77–8; Monahan, *John of Paris on Royal and Papal Power*, 9.

95 Johannes Quidort von Paris, *Über königliche und päpstliche Gewalt*, 76; Monahan, *John of Paris on Royal and Papal Power*, 8.

96 'Primus itaque ortus regnorum et principatuum secundum hunc ordinem et modum naturae ab initio talis fuit, quod homines primae aetatis mundi quasi natura istingante et ratione ac experientia naturalis indigentiae compellente in locis et terminis securioribus, in quibus sub conformitate linguae et vitae ac morum simul in unum congregati cohabitabant, unum aliquem ex se magis vigentem ratione et intellectu ad ceteram multitudinem regendam, salvandam ac conservandam omnibus praeficiebant et ita sub pacto et vinculo subiectionis ad se regendos, salvandos et conservandos oboediebant et intendebant, sicut Tullius praeclare scribit in principio primae *Rhetoricae*.' Engelbert von Admont, *Vom Ursprung und Ende des Reiches und andere Schriften*, ed. Wilhelm Baum (Graz: Leykam, 1998), 16; Cary J. Nederman and Thomas M. Izbicki, trans., *Three Tracts on Empire: Engelbert of Admont, Aeneas Silvius Piccolomini, and Juan de Torquemada* (Bristol: Thoemmes Press, 2000), 39. See also Kempshall, '*De Re Publica* I.39 in Medieval and Renaissance Political Thought,' 108, 112–15. On Engelbert's political thought, consult Ubl, *Engelbert von Admont*.

97 Aristotle writes that in early times people lived in scattered families just like the Cyclopes as described by Homer. Compare Homer, *Odyssey*, 9.112–5, and Plato, *Laws*, 680D–E. On this, see also Carnes Lord, 'Aristotle's Anthropology,' in *Essays on the Foundations of Aristotelian Political Science*, ed. Carnes Lord and David K. O'Connor (Berkeley, CA: University of California Press, 1991), 49–73, 55–6.

98 Aegidius Romanus (Egidio Colonna), *De regimine principum libri III* (Rome, 1607; repr. Aalen: Scientia Verlag, 1967), 413–15; *The Governance of Kings and Princes: John Trevisa's Middle English Translation of the De Regimine Principum of Aegidius Romanus*, ed. David C. Fowler et al. (New York and London: Garland Pub., 1997), 295–7. See also the discussions in Eckhard Homann, *Totum posse, quod est in ecclesia, reservatur in summo pontifice: Studien zur politischen Theorie bei Aegidius Romanus* (Würzburg: Königshausen & Neumann, 2004), 43–51; Graham McAleer, 'Giles of Rome on Political Authority,' *Journal of the History of Ideas* 60 (1999): 21–36.

99 *Giles of Rome's On Ecclesiastical Power: A Medieval Theory of World Government*, ed. and trans. Robert W. Dyson (New York: Columbia University Press, 2004), 194–6 (Latin text); 195–7 (Eng. trans.). On this work, see Elmar Krüger, *Der Traktat "De ecclesiastica potestate" des Aegidius Romanus: Eine spätmittelalterliche Herrschaftskonzeption des päpstlichen Universalismus* (Cologne: Böhlau, 2007).

100 See, in general, the following studies by Cary J. Nederman: 'The Union of Wisdom and Eloquence before the Renaissance: The Ciceronian Orator in Medieval Political Thought,' *Journal of Medieval History* 18 (1992): 75–95;

idem, 'Nature, Sin and the Origins of Society: The Ciceronian Tradition in Medieval Political Thought,' *Journal of the History of Ideas* 49 (1988): 3–26 – both repr. in idem, *Medieval Aristotelianism and Its Limits*, nos. XII and XI, respectively.

101 *The Latin Rhetorical Commentaries by Thierry of Chartres*, ed. Karin M. Fredborg (Toronto: Pontifical Institute of Mediaeval Studies, 1988), 60–1.

102 On the civic function of rhetoric in the context of the Italian city states, see the works of Enrico Artifoni, such as 'Una forma declamatoria di eloquenza politica nelle città comunali (sec. XIII): la concione,' in *Papers on Rhetoric* 8: *Declamation*, ed. Lucia Calboli Montefusco (Rome: Herder, 2007), 1–27; 'Prudenza del consigliare. L'educazione del cittadino nel *Liber consolationis et consilii* di Albertano da Brescia (1246),' in *Consilium: Teorie e pratiche del consigliare nella cultura medievale*, ed. Carla Casagrande et al. (Florence: SISMEL edizioni del Galluzzo, 2004), 195–216; 'L'éloquence politique dans les cités communales (XIIIe siècle),' in *Cultures italiennes (XIIe–XVe siècle)*, ed. Isabelle Heullant-Donat (Paris: Cerf, 2000), 269–96; 'Gli uomini dell'assemblea. L'oratoria civile, i conciatori e i predicatori nella società comunale,' in *La predicazione dei Frati dalla metà del '200 alla fine del '300* (Spoleto: Centro Italiano di Studi sull'Alto Medioevo, 1995), 142–88; 'I podestà professionali e la fondazione retorica della politica comunale,' *Quaderni Storici* n. s. 63 (1986): 687–719. Also important are the studies by Peter von Moos, 'Die italienische *ars agregandi* des 13. Jahrhunderts als Schule der Kommunikation,' in *Wissensliteratur im Mittelalter und in der Frühen Neuzeit: Bedingungen, Typen, Publikum, Sprache*, ed. Horst Brunner und Norbert R. Wolf (Wiesbaden: Ludwig Reichert, 1993), 67–90 – rev. version in idem, *Rhetorik, Kommunikation und Medialität: Gesammelte Studien zum Mittelalter*, ed. Gert Melville (Münster: Lit, 2006), 127–52; Janet Coleman, 'Some Relations between the Study of Aristotle's *Rhetoric, Ethics* and *Politics* in Late Thirteenth- and Early Fourteenth-Century University Arts Courses and the Justification of Contemporary Civic Activities (Italy and France),' in *Political Thought and the Realities of Power in the Middle Ages*, 127–57; and, in general, Johannes Helmrath and Jörg Feuchter, 'Einleitung – Vormoderne Parlamentsoratorik,' in *Politische Redekultur in der Vormoderne: Die Oratorik europäischer Parlamente in Spätmittelalter und Früher Neuzeit*, ed. Jörg Feuchter and Johannes Helmrath (Frankfurt a. M.: Campus, 2008), 9–22.

103 See, in general, Virginia Cox and John O. Ward, *The Rhetoric of Cicero in Its Medieval and Early Renaissance Commentary Tradition* (Leiden and Boston: Brill, 2006). For a detailed discussion of Cicero's reception in medieval Italy, see Virginia Cox, 'Ciceronian Rhetoric in Late Medieval Italy: The

Latin and Vernacular Traditions,' ibid., 109–36; eadem, 'Ciceronian Rhetoric in Italy, 1260–1350,' *Rhetorica* 17 (1999): 239–88.

104 Ronald Witt, 'Rhetoric and Reform during the Eleventh and Twelfth Centuries,' in *Textual Cultures of Medieval Italy*, ed. William Robins (Toronto: University of Toronto Press, 2011), 53–79; idem, 'The Arts of Letter-Writing,' in *The Cambridge History of Literary Criticism* vol. 2: *The Middle Ages*, ed. Alastair Minnis and Ian Johnson (Cambridge: Cambridge University Press, 2005), 68–83; *The Waning of Medieval Ars Dictaminis*, ed. Martin Camargo [= *Rhetorica* 19:2 (2001)]; Martin Camargo, *Ars dictaminis, Ars Dictandi* (Turnhout: Brepols, 1991); Helene Wieruszowski, '*Ars dictaminis* in the Time of Dante,' *Medievalia et Humanistica* 1 (1943): 95–108 – repr. in eadem, *Politics and Culture in Medieval Spain and Italy* (Rome: Storia e Letteratura, 1971), 359–77.

105 Exemplars of this literature are: Raniero da Perugia, *Ars notaria* (ca. 1215); Tommaso da Capua, *Ars dictandi* (ca. 1230); Boncompagno da Signa, *Rhetorica novissima* (1235); Guido Faba, *Dictamina rhetorica* (1226–8), *Epistole* (1239–41), and *Parlamenti ed Epistole* (1242–43); Matteo de' Libri, *Arringhe* (ca. 1275); Giovanni da Vignano, *Flore de parlare* (ca. 1290); and Filippo Ceffi, *Dicerie* (ca. 1330). For further discussion and references, see Quentin Skinner, 'The Vocabulary of Renaissance Republicanism: A Cultural longue-durée?' in *Language and Images of Renaissance Italy*, ed. Alison Brown (Oxford: Clarendon Press, 1995) 87–110, at 88–9; Nicolai Rubinstein, 'Political Rhetoric in the Imperial Chancery during the Twelfth and Thirteenth Centuries,' *Medium aevum* 14 (1945): 21–43, at 22–5.

106 On the *podestà* manuals, see Albano Sorbelli, 'I teorici del Regimento comunale,' *Bullettino dell' Istituto Storico Italiano per il Medio Evo e Archivio Muratoriano* 59 (1944): 31–136; Fritz Hertter, *Die Podestàliteratur Italiens im 12. und 13. Jahrhundert* (Leipzig and Berlin: Teubner, 1910; repr. Hildesheim: Gerstenberg, 1973); Vittorio Franchini, 'Trattati *De regimine civitatum* (sec. XIII–XIV),' *Recueils de la Société Jean Bodin* 6 (1954): 319–40; idem, *Saggio di ricerche su l'instituto del Podestà nei comuni medievali* (Bologna: N. Zanichelli, 1912), ch. 'La letteratura del Podestà,' 223–64.

107 'Oculus pastoralis pascens officia et continens radium dulcibus pomis suis,' ed. Dora Franceschi, *Memorie dell'Accademia delle Scienze di Torino*, Classe di scienze morali, storiche e filologiche ser. 4, 11 (1966): 1–74; Terence O. Tunberg, trans., *Speeches from the Oculus pastoralis* (Toronto: Pontifical Institute of Mediaeval Studies, 1990); idem, '*Oculus pastoralis*' (Diss., University of Toronto, 1986), 131–252. On the *Oculus pastoralis*, see also Diego Quaglioni, 'Politica e diritto al tempo di Federico II: L'*Oculus pastoralis* (1222) e la 'sapienza civile,' in *Federico II e le nuove culture* (Spole-

to: Centro italiano di studi sull'alto Medioevo, 1995), 3–26; Tunberg, '*Oculus pastoralis*,' 1–130; Dora Franceschi, 'L'*Oculus pastoralis* e la fortuna,' *Atti dell'Accademia delle Scienze di Torino, Classe di scienze morali, storiche e filologiche* 99 (1964–5): 205–61.

108 Iohannis Viterbiensis, *Liber de regimine civitatum*, ed. Gaetano Salvemini. In *Bibliotheca Juridica Medii Aevi* (Bologna: Società Tipografica Azzoguidi, 1901), 3: 215–80; *Fürstenspiegel des frühen und hohen Mittelalters*, ed. Hans H. Anton (Darmstadt: Wissenschaftliche Buchgesellschaft, 2006), 231–83. For further discussion, see Gianfranco Folena, 'Parlamenti' podestarili di Giovanni da Viterbo,' *Lingua nostra* 20 (1959): 97–105; Gaetano Salvemini, 'Il *Liber de Regimine Civitatum* di Giovanni di Viterbo,' *Giornale storico della letteratura italiana* 41 (1903): 284–303 – repr. in idem, *Scritti di storia medievale*, vol. 2: *La dignità cavalleresca nel Comune di Firenze e altri scritti*, ed. Ernesto Sestan (Milan: Feltrinelli Editore, 1972), 358–70.

109 See also Paul O. Kristeller, *Studies in Renaissance Thought and Letters* (Rome: Storia e Letteratura, 1956; repr. 1969), 566–7.

110 Brunetto Latini, *Li Livres dou Tresor*, ed. Spurgeon Baldwin and Paul Barrette (Tempe, AZ: Arizona Center for Medieval and Renaissance Studies, 2003), III.1.2. (291); Brunetto Latini, *The Books of the Treasure (Li Livres dou Tresor)*, trans. Paul Barrette and Spurgeon Baldwin (New York and London: Garland Pub., 1993), 279. On Latini's political ideas, see Cary J. Nederman, 'Commercial Society and Republican Government in the Latin Middle Ages: The Economic Dimensions of Brunetto Latini's Republicanism,' *Political Theory* 31 (2003): 644–63; idem, *Lineages of European Political Thought: Explorations along the Medieval/Modern Divide from John of Salisbury to Hegel* (Washington, DC: Catholic University of America Press, 2009): 141–59. Latini's views on rhetoric are discussed in Ronald G. Witt, 'Brunetto Latini and the Italian Tradition of *Ars Dictaminis*,' *Stanford Italian Review* 2 (1983): 5–24 – repr. in idem, *Italian Humanism and Medieval Rhetoric* (Aldershot: Ashgate, 2001), no. V; Paola Sgrilli, 'Retorica e società: Tensioni anticlassiche nella *Rettorica* di Brunetto Latini,' *Medioevo Romanzo* 3 (1976): 380–93. See also Gian C. Alessio, 'Brunetto Latini e Cicerone (e i dettatori),' *Italia Medioevale e Umanistica* 22 (1979): 123–69; Guido Baldassarri, 'Ancora sulle 'fonti' della Rettorica: Brunetto Latini e Teodorico di Chartres,' *Studi e problemi di critica testuale* 19 (1979): 41–69; Helene Wieruszowski, 'Brunetto Latini als Lehrer Dantes und der Florentiner,' *Archivio Italiano per la Storia della Pietà* 2 (1957): 171–98 – repr. in eadem, *Politics and Culture in Medieval Spain and Italy*, 515–61.

111 Brunetto Latini, *Li Livres dou Tresor*, III.73.2 (363); *The Book of the Treasure*, 351.

112 Brunetto Latini, *Li Livres dou Tresor*, III.73.3 (363); *The Book of the Treasure*, 351.
113 Brunetto Latini, *Li Livres dou Tresor*, III.1.7 (292); *The Book of the Treasure*, 280.
114 Brunetto Latini, *Li Livres dou Tresor*, III.1.8 (292); *The Book of the Treasure*, 280. Amphion built the walls around Thebes, and was not the founder of Athens, as Latini writes. On this point, see Enrico Artifoni, 'Orfeo concionatore. Un passo di Tommaso d'Aquino e l'eloquenza politica nella città italiane nel secolo XIII,' in *La musica nel pensiero medievale*, ed. Letterio Mauro (Ravenna: Longo, 2001), 137–49, at 148.
115 Brunetto Latini, *Li Livres dou Tresor*, III.82.9 (375); *The Book of the Treasure*, 363.
116 *DP* I.iv.5.
117 *DP* I.xix.2.
118 *DP* I.iv.4.
119 *DP* I.iv.4.
120 Aristotle, *Eth. Nic.*1177a12ff.; *Pol.* 1324a25–b1. See also Gewirth, *Marsilius of Padua and Medieval Political Philosophy*, 63–4. On Aristotle's *eudaimonia* concept, see, e.g., Tilman Nagel, 'Aristotle on *Eudaimonia*,' *Phronesis* 17 (1972): 252–9; John L. Ackrill, 'Aristotle on *Eudaimonia*,' *Proceedings of the British Academy* 60 (1974): 339–59; Amélie Oksenberg Rorty, 'The Place of Contemplation in Aristotle's *Nicomachean Ethics*,' *Mind* 87 (1978): 343–58 – all three repr. in *Essays on Aristotle's Ethics*, ed. Amélie Oksenberg Rorty (Berkeley, CA: University of California Press, 1980), 7–14, 15–33, and 377–94, respectively.
121 Aristotle, *Pol.* 1333a37–b3. See further Maurice Defourny, 'The Aim of State: Peace,' in *Articles on Aristotle*, vol. 2: *Ethics and Politics*, ed. Jonathan Barnes et al. (London: Duckworth, 1977), 195–201. On Marsilius's concept of peace, see: Luciano Russi, 'L'idea di pace in Marsilio da Padova,' in *Prima di Machiavelli: Itinerari e linguaggi della politica tra il XIV e il XVI secolo*, ed. Gabriele Carletti (Pescara: Edizioni Scientifiche Abruzzesi, 2007), 87–106; Bernardo Bayona Aznar, 'La paz en la obra de Marsilio de Padua,' *Contrastes* 11 (2006): 44–63; Maurizio Merlo, 'Pace, guerra e identità della comunità politica in Marsilio da Padova,' in *Figure della guerra: la riflessione su pace, conflitto e giustizia tra Medioevo e prima età moderna*, ed. Merio Scattola (Milan: Franco Angeli, 2003), 111–44; Georg Wieland, 'Politik und Religion. Das Friedenskonzept des Marsilius von Padua,' in *Friedensethik im Spätmittelalter: Theologie im Ringen um die gottgegebene Ordnung*, ed. Gerhard Beestermöller and Heinz-Gerhard Justenhoven (Stuttgart: W. Kohlhammer, 1999), 79–94; Alessandro Ghisalberti, 'L'apirazione

alla pace come fondamento della politica in Marsilio da Padova,' in *Homo sapiens, homo humanus*, vol. 1: *La cultura italiana tra il passato ed il presente in un disegno di pace universale*, ed. Giovannangiola Tarugi (Florence: L.S. Olschki, 1990), 65–77; Andrea M. Moschetti, 'Il tema della pace in Marsilio da Padova, Petrarca e S. Caterina da Siena,' *Studia Patavina* 27 (1980): 280–5; Giovanna Cavallaro, *La 'pace' nella filosofia politica di Marsilio da Padova* (Ferrara: De Salvia, 1973); Horst Kusch, 'Friede als Ausgangspunkt der Staatstheorie des Marsilius von Padua: Zur Aristotelesrezeption im Mittelalter,' *Altertum* 1 (1955): 116–25. See also Piero Di Vona, *I principi del Defensor Pacis* (Naples: Morano, 1974), 51–9.

122 *DP* I.i.1, with reference to Cassiodorus's (AD 490–ca. 585) *Variae*, I.i. See also *DP* I.i.2. A reference to the same passage from Cassiodorus occurs in *De tranquillitate populorum* of Geremia da Montagnone's *Compendium moralium notabilium* (1295). See also Paolo Marangon, 'Marsilio tra preumanesimo e cultura delle arti. Ricerca sulle fonti padovane del I Discorso del *Defensor pacis*,' *Medioevo* 3 (1977): 89–119 – repr. in idem, *Ad cognitionem scientiae festinare. Gli studi nell'Università e nei Conventi di Padova nei secoli XIII e XIV*, ed. Tiziana Pesenti (Trieste: LINT, 1997), 380–410, at 382; Brett, *The Defender of the Peace*, 3.

123 Gewirth, *Marsilius of Padua and Medieval Political Philosophy*, 50–3, 65–6, 97–8.

124 Aristotle, *Pol.* 1318b6–27. On ancient views on Athenian democracy, see Josiah Ober, 'How to Criticize Democracy in Late Fifth- and Fourth-Century Athens,' in *Athenian Political Thought and the Reconstruction of American Democracy*, ed. J. Peter Euben et al. (Ithaca, NY: Cornell University Press, 1994), 149–71 – repr. in idem, *The Athenian Revolution: Essays on Ancient Greek Democracy and Political Theory* (Princeton, NJ: Princeton University Press, 1996), 140–60; Kurt A. Raaflaub, 'Contemporary Perceptions of Democracy in Fifth-Century Athens,' *Classica et mediaevalia* 40 (= *Aspects of Athenian Democracy*) (1990): 33–70; Robert K. Sinclair, *Democracy and Participation in Athens* (Cambridge: Cambridge University Press, 1988), 226–7; Delba Winthrop, 'Aristotle on Participatory Democracy,' *Polity* 11 (1978): 151–71; Mortimer Chambers, 'Aristotle's Forms of Democracy,' *Transactions of the American Philological Association* 92 (1961): 20–36; Jakob. A.O. Larsen, 'The Judgment of Antiquity on Democracy,' *Classical Philology* 49 (1954): 1–14; John S. Marshall, 'Aristotle and the Agrarians,' *Review of Politics* 9 (1947): 350–61.

125 Notaby in *De officiis* iii.1.1–4. See also Hans Baron, 'Cicero and the Roman Civic Spirit in the Middle Ages and Early Renaissance,' *Bulletin of the John Rylands Library* 22 (1938): 72–97, 74–5.

126 Compare Peter of Abano's ideas on corporeal symmetry as set out in his *Physiognomica* (*Compilatio physiognomiae*, 1295). For further discussion, see Graziella Federici Vescovini, 'La simmetria del corpo umano nella *Physiognomica* di Pietro d'Abano: un canone estetico,' in *Concordia discors: Studi su Niccolò Cusano e l'umanesimo europeo offerti a Giovanni Santinello*, ed. Gregorio Piaia (Padua: Antenore, 1993), 347–60.

127 'In has ergo miseri precipites feruntur tenebras propter discordiam seu litem ipsorum invicem, que velut animalis egritudo, sic prava civilis regiminis disposicio fore dignoscitur' (*DP* I.i.3); 'Debentes itaque describere tranquillitatem et suum oppositum, suscipiamus cum Aristotele primo et quinto Politice sue capitulis 2° et 3° civitatem esse velut animatam seu animalem naturam quandam. Nam sicuti animal bene dispositum secundum naturam componitur ex quibusdam proporcionatis partibus invicem ordinatis suaque opera [sibi] mutuo communicantibus et ad totum, sic civitas ex quibusdam talibus constituitur, cum bene disposita et instituta fuerit secundum racionem. Qualis est igitur comparacio animalis et suarum parcium ad sanitatem, talis videbitur civitatis sive regni et suarum parcium ad tranquillitatem. Huius vero illacionis fi dem accipere possumus ex eo, quod de ipsarum utraque comprehendunt omnes. Extimant enim sanitatem esse disposicionem animalis optimam secundum naturam, sic quoque tranquillitatem disposicionem optimam civitatis secundum racionem institute. Sanitas autem, ut aiunt periciores physicorum describentes ipsam, est bona disposicio animalis, qua potest unaqueque suarum parcium perfecte facere operaciones convenientes sue nature; secundum quam siquidem analogiam erit tranquillitas bona disposicio civitatis aut regni, qua poterit unaqueque suarum parcium facere perfecte operaciones convenientes sibi secundum racionem et suam institucionem. Et quia bene diffi niens contraria consignifi cat, erit intranquillitas prava disposicio civitatis aut regni, quemadmodum infi rmitas animalis, qua impediuntur omnes aut alique partes illius facere opera sibi conveniencia, simpliciter vel in complemento' (*DP* I.ii.3). See also Cesare Vasoli, 'Il carattere 'naturale' dello Stato e la sua 'patologia' nella tradizione politica aristotelica,' in *Aristotelismo politico e ragion di Stato*, ed. A. Enzo Baldini (Florence: L.S. Olschki, 1995), 53–65, 61–3; John M. Najemy, 'The Republic's Two Bodies: Body Metaphors in Italian Renaissance Political Thought,' in *Language and Images*, 237–62, at 245.

128 See also Elvio Ancona, *All'origine della sovranità: Sistema gerarchico e ordinamento giuridico nella disputa sui due poteri all'inizio del XIV secolo* (Turin: Giappichelli, 2004), 174–97; Miethke, 'Marsilius von Padua. Die politische Philosophie eines lateinischen Aristotelikers,' 56; Nederman, *Community*

and Consent, 53–5; Gewirth, *Marsilius of Padua and Medieval Political Philosophy*, 63, 65.

129 'Nihil enim prohibet, nobiliorem seu perfecciorem simpliciter habens accionem quantum ad aliquid dependere ab habente minus perfectam, et sic quantum ad quid esse imperfeccius. Corpus enim humanum, quod est perfeccius simpliciter omni corpore simplici aut mixto, generabili saltem, quantum ad aliquid potencia est et minus perfectum multis mixtis atque simplicibus. Est eciam hoc videre in partibus eiusdem tocius. Nam quamvis oculus sit membrum sive pars perfeccior manu vel pede, quoniam perfecciorem effi cit accionem, nil minus ab ipsis pendet et recipit aliquam accionem aut motum; e quoque converso hec ipsa dependent ab oculo, quoniam in fi nem, ad quem movent aut moventur, diriguntur per ipsum. Sic eciam dicebat apostolus 1a ad Corinthios 12°: *Non potest autem oculus dicere manui: opera tua non indigeo.* Quo siquidem igitur seu proporcionali modo principatus eciam dependent ac recipit aliqua per acciones aliquarum et inferiorum parcium civitatis, de quibus diximus 5° prime, quamvis non secundum iudicium coactivum; cum tamen ipse secundum aliquid melius et perfeccius a principatu dependeant, ut coactivum iudicium, ut ostensum est 15° prime. Sic ergo sacerdocium a principatu dependet ac recipit, et principatus a sacerdocio. Recipit enim sacerdocium a principatu iustifi cacionem suorum civilium actuum et custodiam ab iniuria, ne siquidem hanc inferat alteri nec illi ab altero inferatur in statu et pro statu presentis seculi; quoniam hoc est offi cium principantis et nullius alterius partis civitatis, quemadmodum demonstratum est 15° prime' (*DP* II.xxx.4). On Aristotle's notion of the hierarchy of ends, see Vernon Pratt, 'The Essence of Aristotle's Zoology,' *Phronesis* 29 (1984): 267–78. On the influence of this idea on Aristotle's political thinking, consult Andrew C. Bradley, 'Aristotle's Conception of the State,' in *Hellenica: A Collection of Essays on Greek Poetry, Philosophy, History and Religion*, ed. Evelyn Abbott (London: Rivingtons, 1880), 181–243 – repr. in *A Companion to Aristotle's Politics*, 13–56.

130 For a similar interpretation, see Miethke, 'Marsilius von Padua. Die politische Philosophie eines lateinischen Aristotelikers,' 56. On medieval views on the hierarchy of ends, see Gewirth, 'Philosophy and Political Thought in the Fourteenth Century,' 135–6.

131 Aristotle, *Pol.* 1301b10–26; 1307b1; 1275b35; 1292b18; 1296a6; 1301b6; 1302b34.

132 Aristotle, *Pol.* 1301b27–1302a113; 1304a12; 1306a37.

133 On Aristotle's theory of *stasis*, see Kostas Kalimtzis, *Aristotle on Political Enmity and Disease: An Inquiry into Stasis* (Albany, NY: State University of

New York Press, 2000); Ronald Polansky, 'Aristotle on Political Change,' in *A Companion to Aristotle's Politics*, 323–45; Andrew Lintott, *Violence, Civil Strife and Revolution in the Classical City, 750-330 BC* (Baltimore, MD: Johns Hopkins University Press, 1982), ch. 'The Philosophers and Civil Conflict – Aristotle's *Politics*,' 239–51; Ronald P. Legon, *Demos and Stasis: Studies in the Factional Politics of Classical Greece* (Diss., Cornell University, 1966); and, in general, Karen Piepenbrink, *Politische Ordnungskonzeptionen in der attischen Demokratie des vierten Jahrhunderts v. Chr. Eine vergleichende Untersuchung zum philosophischen und rhetorischen Diskurs* (Stuttgart: F. Steiner, 2001); Hans-Joachim Gehrke, *Stasis: Untersuchungen zu den inneren Kriegen in den griechischen Staaten des 5. und 4. Jahrhunderts v. Chr.* (Munich: Beck, 1985); Heinrich Ryffel, *ΜΕΤΑΒΟΛΗ ΠΟΛΙΤΕΙΩΝ: Der Wandel der Staatsverfassungen* (Bern: P. Haupt, 1949). The differences between *stasis* and *metavolē* are discussed in Marcus Wheeler's essay 'Aristotle's Analysis of the Nature of Political Struggle,' *The American Journal of Philology* 72 (1951): 145–61 – repr. in *Articles on Aristotle*, vol. 2: *Ethics and Politics*, 159–69. On the medical precedents of the *stasis* concept, see Kalimtzis, *Aristotle on Political Enmity and Disease*, xv, 5, 8, as well as Paul F. Mustacchio, *The Concept of 'Stasis' in Greek Political Theory* (Diss., New York University, 1972), ch. 'Social Pathology,' 36–68.

134 *De motu an.* 703a29–36.

135 Aristotle, *Pol.* 1290b21–39. See also James Day and Mortimer Chambers, *Aristotle's History of Athenian Democracy* (Berkeley, CA: University of California Press, 1962 – repr. Amsterdam: Hakkert, 1967), 41–2; Egon Braun, 'Die Ursache der Pluralität von Verfassungsformen nach Aristoteles,' *Wissenschaftliche Arbeiten aus dem Burgenland* 35 (1966): 57–65 – repr. in *Schriften zu den Politika des Aristoteles*, ed. Peter Steinmetz (Hildesheim and New York: G. Olms, 1973) 431–9.

136 Aristotle, *Pol.* 1302b35–38.

137 Aristotle, *Pol.* 1291b7–8. See also ibid., 1315a31–33; 1318a30–31. See, in general, Geoffrey E.M. de Ste. Croix, *The Class Struggle in the Ancient Greek World: From the Archaic Age to the Arab Conquests* (Ithaca, NY: Cornell University Press, 1981).

138 Aristotle, *Pol.* 1302b33. The other factors are 1) greed; 2) unjust distribution of honours; 3) insolence of the men in office; 4) fear of being punished or suffering wrongdoing; 5) excessive predominance of a particular segment of the body politic; and 6) contempt of the government (1302a23–34).

139 Aristotle, *Pol.* 1310a4–6.

140 Aristotle, *Pol.* 1296b35–1297a7.

141 Aristotle, *Pol.* 1296a7–22.

142 Aristotle differentiates in the *Pol.* 1291b30–2a38 five forms of democracy. For further discussion, see C. I. Papageorgiou, 'Four or Five Types of Democracy in Aristotle?' *History of Political Thought* 11 (1990): 1–8.

143 Aristotle, *Pol.* 1320a17–b17.

144 Aristotle, *Pol.* 4. book, 11. ch.; 1302b38ff. See also Stephen G. Salkever, *Finding the Mean: Theory and Practice in Aristotelian Political Philosophy* (Princeton, NJ: Princeton University Press, 1990); Day and Chambers, *Aristotle's History of Athenian Democracy*, 25.

145 Aristotle, *Pol.* Book 4, ch. 11. See Blythe, *Ideal Government*, 194. On the Aristotelian idea of the mixed constitution, see Gerhard J.D. Aalders, *Die Theorie der gemischten Verfassung im Altertum* (Amsterdam: A.M. Hakkert, 1968); idem, 'Die Mischverfassung und ihre historische Dokumentation in den *Politica* des Aristoteles,' in *La 'Politique' d'Aristote: Sept exposés et discussions* (Vandœuvres-Geneva: Fondation Hardt, 1964), 201–44; Egon Braun, 'Die Theorie der Mischverfassung bei Aristoteles,' *Wiener Studien* 80, N.F. 1 (1967): 79–89. On the classical background of the idea of the mixed constitution, see Kurt von Fritz, *The Theory of the Mixed Constitution in Antiquity* (New York: Columbia University Press, 1954; repr. 1975); Paula Zillig, *Die Theorie von der gemischten Verfassung in ihrer literarischen Entwickelung im Altertum und ihr Verhältnis zur Lehre Lockes und Montesquieus über Verfassung* (Diss., University of Würzburg, 1916).

146 *DP* I.i.3; I.i.7; I.xix.3, 4, 12, 13; II.xxvi.19; III.1. See also the discussions in John P. Gibbons, 'How a Liberal Picks a Fight: Marsilius of Padua and the Singular Cause of Strife,' in *Educating the Prince*, ed. Mark Blitz and William Kristol (Lanham, MD: Rowman & Littlefield, 2000), 18–29; Floriano J. Cesar, '*Causa singularis discordie* e situação italiana no *Defensor pacis* de Marsílio de Pádua' *Patristica et Mediaevalia* 18 (1997): 20–8; Nederman, *Community and Consent*, 15–16; Gewirth, *Marsilius of Padua and Medieval Political Philosophy*, 30.

147 See the following studies by Joseph R. Berrigan: 'Benzo d'Alessandria and the Cities of Northern Italy,' *Studies in Medieval and Renaissance History* 4 (1967): 125–92; idem, 'Prehumanist Views of Domestic Violence in the Early Trecento,' *Studies in Medieval Culture* 5 (1975): 159–63; idem, 'The Prehumanism of Benzo d'Alessandria,' *Traditio* 25 (1969): 249–63. See, in general, Antony Black, 'Harmony and Strife in Political Thought c. 1300–1500,' in *Sozialer Wandel im Mittelalter: Wahrnehmungsformen, Erklärungsmuster, Regelungsmechanismen*, ed. Jürgen Miethke and Klaus Schreiner (Sigmaringen: Thorbecke, 1994), 355–63 – repr. in idem, *Church, State and Community*, no. XV.

148 On the history of the *signoria*, see Trevor Dean, 'The Rise of the *signori*,' in *Italy in the Central Middle Ages: 1000–1300*, ed. David Abulafia (Oxford: Oxford University Press, 2004), 104–24; idem, 'The Rise of the *signori*,' in *The New Cambridge Medieval History*, vol. 5: *c. 1198–c. 1300*, ed. David Abulafia (Cambridge: Cambridge University Press, 1999), 458–78; Philip J. Jones, *The Italian City-State: From Commune to Signoria* (Oxford: Oxford University Press, 1997); Ovidio Capitani, 'Dal Comune alla Signoria,' in *Comuni e Signorie: Istituzioni, società e lotte per l'egemonia* (= *Storia d'Italia*; 4), ed. Ovidio Capitani, Raoul Manselli, Giovanni Cherubini, Antonio Ivan Pini and Giorgio Ghittolini (Turin: UTET, 1981), 135–75; Lauro Martines, *Power and Imagination: City-States in Renaissance Italy* (New York: A.A. Knopf, 1979), ch. 'Despotism: Signories,' 94–110; Ernesto Sestan, 'Le origini delle signorie cittadine: un problema storico esaurito?' *Bullettino dell'Istituto Storico Italiano per il Medio Evo e Archivio Muratoriano* 73 (1961): 41–69 – repr. in *La crisi degli ordinamenti comunali e le origini dello stato del Rinascimento*, ed. Giorgio Chittolini (Bologna: Il Mulino, 1979), 53–75 – German trans. by Lilo de Negri, 'Die Anfänge der städtischen Signorien: ein erschöpfend behandeltes historisches Problem?' in *Altständisches Bürgertum*, vol 1: *Herrschaft und Gemeinverfassung*, ed. Heinz Stoob (Darmstadt: Wissenschaftliche Buchgesellschaft, 1978), 346–79; Francesco Ercole, *Dal comune al principato: saggi sulla storia del diritto pubblico del rinascimento italiano* (Florence: Vallecchi, 1929); Maude V. Clarke, *The Medieval City State: An Essay on Tyranny and Federation in the Later Middle Ages* (London, Methuen & Co, 1926; repr. Cambridge/New York: Speculum Historiale/Barnes & Noble, 1966), ch. 'The Rise of Tyranny in Italy,' 99–146; Ernst Salzer, *Ueber die Anfaenge der Signorie in Italien: Ein Beitrag zur italienischen Verfassungsgeschichte* (Berlin: Ebering, 1900; repr. Vaduz: Kraus Repr., 1965). A useful examination on the role of the *popolo* in the political life of the Italian city states can be found in Guy Fourquin, *The Anatomy of Popular Rebellion in the Middle Ages*, trans. Anne Chesters (Amsterdam/New York: North Holland Pub. Co./New York: Elsevier North-Holland, 1978).

149 For further discussion, see Stephan R. Epstein, 'The Rise and Fall of Italian City-States,' in *A Comparative Study of Thirty City-State Cultures: An Investigation*, ed. Mogens H. Hansen (Copenhagen: Kongelige Danske Videnskabernes Selskab, 2000), 277–93; John K. Hyde, 'Contemporary Views on Faction and Civil Strife in Thirteenth- and Fourteenth-Century Italy,' in *Violence and Civil Disorder in Italian Cities, 1200–1500*, ed. Lauro Martines (Berkeley, CA: University of California Press, 1972), 273–307 – repr. in idem, *Literacy and Its Uses*, 58–86; Ephraim Emerton, ed. and trans., *Humanism and Tyranny: Studies in the Italian Trecento* (Cambridge,

MA: Harvard University Press, 1925; repr. Gloucester, MA: P. Smith, 1964). The Italian chroniclers' views on the crisis of communal government are surveyed in Maria C. de Matteis, 'La coscienza della crisi comunale nei cronisti del' 300,' in *Storici e storiografia del medioevo italiano: antologia di saggi*, ed. Gabriele Zanella (Bologna: Pàtron, 1984), 255–74. A synthesis of research on the history of the Italian communes can be found in Edward Coleman, 'The Italian Communes. Recent Work and Current Trends,' *Journal of Medieval History* 25 (1999): 373–97.

150 John K. Hyde, 'Italian Social Chronicles in the Middle Ages,' *Bulletin of the John Rylands Library* 49 (1966): 107–32 – repr. in idem, *Literacy and Its Uses: Studies on Late Medieval Italy* (Manchester/New York: Manchester University Press, 1993), 33–57, at 35–43; Giovanni Fabris, *Cronache e cronisti padovani* (Padua: Rebellato, 1977), ch. 'La cronaca di Giovanni da Nono,' 33–168 [first published in *Bollettino del Museo Civico di Padova* 25 (1932): 1–33; 26 (1933): 167–200; 27/28 (1934–9): 1–30]; Nicolai Rubinstein, 'Marsilius of Padua and the Italian Political Thought of His Time,' in *Europe in the Late Middle Ages*, ed. John R. Hale, John R.L. Highfield and Beryl Smalley (Evanston, IL: Northwestern University Press, 1965), 44–75, 58–9 – repr. in idem, *Studies in Italian History in the Middle Ages and the Renaissance*, vol. 1: *Political Thought and the Language of Politics: Art and Politics*, ed. Giovanni Ciappelli (Rome: Storia e letteratura, 2004), 99–130. Compare *DP* I.i.2; xiv.3.

151 Heremias de Montagnone, *Epytoma sapientie* (Venice, 1505), fols. 52r–54v. Geremia makes ample use of quotations from classical authors, including Plato, Isocrates, Cicero, Seneca, and Aristotle, Berthold L. Ullman, 'Hieremias de Montagnone and His Citations from Catullus,' *Classical Philology* 5 (1910): 66–82 – revised and enlarged version in idem, *Studies in the Italian Renaissance* (Rome: Storia e letteratura, 1955), 81–115; Roberto Weiss, *Il primo secolo dell' umanesimo: Studi e testi* (Rome: Storia e letteratura, 1949), ch. 'Geremia da Montagnone,' 13–50. A critical edition and analysis of the *Epytoma sapientie* remain crucial desiderata. On Geremia's work, see also Tiziano Dorandi, 'La versio latina antiqua di Diogene Laerzio e la sua ricezione nel Medioevo occidentale: Il *Compendim moralium notabilium* di Geremia da Montagnone e il *Liber de vita et moribus philosophorum* dello ps. Burleo,' *Documenti e studi sulla tradizione filosofica medievale* 10 (1999): 371–96. A comparison of Geremias's and Marsilius's political ideas appears in Marangon, *Ad cognitionem scientiae festinare* (1997), 380–410. For preliminary reflections on the transmission of Aristotle's political ideas in late medieval Italy, see Nicolai Rubinstein, 'Political Theories in the Renaissance,' in *The Renaissance: Essays in Interpretation*, ed. André Chastel

(London and New York: Methuen, 1982), 153–200, at 153–67; as well as Dagmar Schmidt, "'Regimen politicum" – Republikanisches Denken in den Stadtstaaten Italiens. Die Rezeption der aristotelischen Staatsformenlehre im frühen Trecento,' *Jahrbuch für Philosophie des Forschungsinstituts für Philosophie Hannover* 8 (1997): 44–67. On the reception of Aristotelian science in medieval Padua, see Paolo Marangon, *Alle origini dell'Aristotelismo Padovano (sec. XII–XIII)* (Padua: Antenore, 1977); Antonino Poppi, *Introduzione all'aristotelismo padovano* (Padua: Antenore, 1970); Bruno Nardi, *Saggi sull'aristotelismo padovano dal secolo XIV al XVI* (Florence: G.C. Sansoni 1958).

152 Moschetti, 'Il *De lite inter Naturam et Fortunam* e il *Contra causos fortuitos* di Albertino Mussato,' 592. For further discussion, see Ulrich Meier, '*Molte rivoluzioni, molte novità*. Gesellschaftlicher Wandel im Spiegel der politischen Philosophie und im Urteil von städtischen Chronisten des späten Mittelalters,' in *Sozialer Wandel im Mittelalter*, 119–76, at 146–8; Rubinstein, 'Some Ideas on Municipal Progress and Decline in the Italy of the Communes,' in *Fritz Saxl (1890–1948): A Volume of Memorial Essays from His Friends in England*, ed. James D. Gordon, (London and New York: T. Nelson, 1957), 165–83 – repr. in idem, *Political Thought and the Language of Politics*, 43–60; idem, 'Marsilius of Padua and the Italian Political Thought of His Time,' 44–75; Hyde, 'Contemporary Views on Faction and Civil Strife.'

153 On Sallust's views concerning the moral aspects of Roman decline, see Donald C. Earl, *The Political Thought of Sallust* (Cambridge: Cambridge University Press, 1961; repr. Chicago, IL: Argonaut, 1969), ch. 'The Moral Crisis in Sallust's View,' 41–59. Sallust's medieval and Renaissance reception is surveyed in Patricia J. Osmond, '*Princeps Historiae Romanae*: Sallust in Renaissance Political Thought,' *Memoirs of the American Academy in Rome* 40 (1995): 101–43; and Beryl Smalley, 'Sallust in the Middle Ages,' in *Classical Influences on European Culture A.D. 500–1500*, ed. Robert R. Bolgar (Cambridge: Cambridge University Press, 1971), 165–75.

154 *DP* I.xv.10. Aristotle traces the rise of the fourth form of democracy back to the growth of the population and the increase of revenues. Citizens participate in government due to the (numerical) superiority of the multitude and actually have a share in it and exercise their citizenship because even the poor are entitled to leisure by receiving remuneration. In this kind of democratic constitution, the multitude enjoys a great deal of leisure, as they are not hampered by the care of their private affairs, but the rich are and often take no part in the assembly or in the process of judging lawsuits. As a result, the multitude of the poor becomes sovereign over the government, instead of the laws – Aristotle, *Pol.* 1292b41–1293a10.

155 Hyde, 'Contemporary Views on Faction and Civil Strife,' 285; Brendan Cassidy, 'Laughing with Giotto at Sinners in Hell,' *Viator* 35 (2004): 355–86, at 369–71; Antonio Rigon, *Clero e città: Fratalea cappellanorum,' parroci, cura d'anime in Padova dal XII al XV secolo* (Padua: Istituto per la Storia Ecclesiastica Padovana, 1988); Maria C. Ganguzza Billanovich, 'Due statuti comunali dell' anno 1300: aspetti del rapporto tra potere civile ed ecclesiastico in Padova agli inizi del XIV secolo,' *Atti e Memorie dell'Accademia Patavina di Scienze, Lettere ed Arti* 87 (1974/5): 131–40; Luigi A. Botteghi, 'Clero e comune in Padova nel secolo XIII,' *Nuovo archivio veneto*, n. s., 9 (1905): 215–72. For a general survey of the role of religion in the political life of the Italian city states, see Augustine Thompson, *Cities of God: The Religion of the Italian Communes, 1125–1325* (University Park, PA: Pennsylvania State University Press, 2005).

156 Gewirth, *Marsilius of Padua and Medieval Political Philosophy*, 26–9. On the conflicts between the *magnati* and *pololani*, see, in general, Giovanni Cherubini, ed., *Magnati e popolani nell'Italia comunale* (Pistoia: Centro italiano di studi di storia e d'arte, 1997).

157 *DP* II.xxiii.11.

158 Aristotle, *Pol.* 1261a25–29. See also the discussions in Richard F. Stalley, 'Plato and Aristotle on Political Unity,' in *La Repubblica di Platone nella tradizione antica*, ed. Mario Vegetti and Michele Abbate (Naples: Bibliopolis, 1999), 29–48; idem, 'Aristotle's Criticism of Plato's Republic,' in *A Companion to Aristotle's Politics*, 182–99. For a fuller treatment of Aristotle's critique of Plato's political philosophy, see Robert Mayhew, *Aristotle's Criticism of Plato's Republic* (Lanham, MD: Rowman & Littlefield, 1997).

159 Aristotle, *Pol.* 1274b38–40.

160 Aristotle, *Pol.* 1295a40–b1.

161 Aristotle, *Metaph.* 1041b4ff.; 1023a32–35; 1033a13–17; 1033b20f.; 1041a26–33; 1043a13–16; 1043b5–7; 1070b28–30.

162 Aristotle, *Pol.* 1276b1–15.

163 *DP* I.xvii.11; 12; I.xix.2.

164 *DP* I.xvii.2.

165 *DP* I.xvii.1.

166 *DP* I.xvii.2.

167 *DP* I xvii.2. Compare Peter of Abano's discussion of the question whether a patient should be treated by a single physician or multiple physicians simultaneously: Peter argues that a patient can be treated by more than one physician given that there are an infinite number of sicknesses and the knowledge and skills of a single physician are inadequate. Peter recommends, however, the appointment of a *protomedicus*, i.e., a principal

physician, with the task of directing and coordinating the others; otherwise, there might occur differences of opinion which could result in the death of the patient. In support of his argument, Peter invokes the analogy between the human body and the political community to establish the necessity of a supreme leader in a regime with multiple rulers and governing officials (Peter of Abano, *Conciliaror*, fol. 10r–v). See also Marangon, *Ad cognitionem scientiae festinare*, 394–5.

168 Aristotle, *Eth. Nic.* 1167a22ff. On Aristotle's concept of political unity, see Jill Frank, *A Democracy of Distinction: Aristotle and the Work of Politics* (Chicago, IL, and London: University of Chicago Press, 2005), 138–80; Richard J. Klonoski, '*Homonoia* in Aristotle's Ethics and Politics,' *History of Political Thought* 17 (1996): 313–25; Gianfrancesco Zanetti, *La nozione di giustizia in Aristotele: Un percorso interpretativo* (Bologna: Il Mulino, 1993), 103–6; Athanasios Moulakis, *Homonoia: Eintracht und die Entwicklung eines politischen Bewußtseins* (Munich: List, 1973).

169 For a similar point, see Nederman, *Community and Consent*, 30, 53.

170 *DP* l.xvii.9; Aristotle, *Metaph.* 1076a3.

171 *DP* I.xvii.3.

172 *DP* I.xvii.4; I.xvii.6.

173 *DP* I.xvii.7.

174 'Adhuc, sicut in composito animali primum precipiens et movens ipsum, motu eo qui secundum locum, est unum, ut in eo libro qui De Motibus Animalium apparet, quoniam pluribus existentibus hiis principiis et contraria vel diversa simul precipientibus, necesse foret animal aut in contraria ferri vel omnino quiescere et hiis carere, que per motum sibi necessaria queruntur et commoda; sicque in civitate convenienter ordinata, quam animali bene formato secundum naturam proporcionaliter habere diximus 15° huius. Ideoque velut in animali talium principiorum ociosa, quinimo nociva foret pluralitas, eodem modo in civitate fi rmiter opinandum. Idem autem videre est, intendere volendi de primo alterante in animali, quemadmodum de movente secundum locum, et in toto similiter ordine movencium et motorum. Hec autem pretermittantur, quoniam ad naturale pertinent negocium magis; quantum autem suffi ciens est, de ipsis diximus ad presentem consideracionem' (*DP* I.xvii.8). Compare *MA* 702a21–22.

175 *DP* I.xvii.7.

176 *DP* I.v.4–6; II.xxii.4.

177 *DP* I.v.4, v.7.

178 *DP* I.v.4, x.1, 2.

179 *DP* I.v.7.

180 *DP* I.v.11.

181 *DP* II.ii.4.

182 *DP* II.viii.3.

183 *DP* I.v.7.

184 *DP* I.v.11.

185 See also Gewirth, *Marsilius of Padua and Medieval Political Philosophy*, 62; Moses I. Finley, 'Aristotle and Economic Analysis,' *Past and Present* 47 (1970): 3–25 – repr. in *Articles on Aristotle*, vol. 2: *Ethics and Politics*, 140–58; *Studies in Ancient Society*, ed. Moses I. Finley (London and Boston: Routledge and Kegan Paul, 1974), 26–52; Arnaldo Biscardi, 'Quod Graeci synallagma vocant,' *Labeo* 29 (1983): 127–39.

186 Aristotle, *Eth. Nic.* 1103b14–16; 1131b25–6. See also ibid., 1131b32–3; 1178a12.

187 Aristotle, *Eth. Nic.* 1131a1–5. For further discussion, see Max Hamburger, *Morals and Law: The Growth of Aristotle's Legal Theory* (New Haven, CT: Yale University Press, 1951), 14–32.

188 Aristotle, *Rh.* 1368b10–11. See also William M.A. Grimaldi, *Aristotle, Rhetoric: A Commentary* (New York: Fordham University Press, 1980), 1: 227–8.

189 Aristotle, *Eth. Nic.* 1111a23–24. See further Charles H. Kahn, 'Discovering the Will: From Aristotle to Augustine,' in *The Question of 'Eclecticism': Studies in Later Greek Philosophy*, ed. John M. Dillon and Anthony A. Long (Berkeley, CA: University of California Press, 1988), 234–59, at 238–44.

190 Gewirth, *Marsilius of Padua and Medieval Political Philosophy*, 62. For futher references, see Roberto Busa, ed., *Index Thomisticus: Sancti Thomae Aquinatis operum omnium indices et concordantiae* (Stuttgart: F. Frommann Verlag, 1974), s. vv. maneo (13: 381–405), permanentia (16: 1147–8), pertranseo (17: 177–82), transitivus (22: 355); Ludwig Schütz, *Thomas-Lexikon. Sammlung, Übersetzung und Erklärung der in sämtlichen Werken des h. Thomas von Aquin vorkommenden Kunstausdrücke und wissenschaftlichen Aussprüche* (Paderborn: F. Schöningh, 1895; repr. Stuttgart-Bad Cannstatt: Frommann-Holzboog, 1983), s. vv. manens (467), permanens (591), pertransiens (594), transiens (816), transitivus (816).

191 Gewirth, *Marsilius of Padua and Medieval Political Philosophy*, 103. See further Paul E. Sigmund, 'Law and Politics,' in *The Cambridge Companion to Aquinas*, ed. Norman Kretzmann and Eleonore Stump (Cambridge: Cambridge University Press, 1993), 217–31; Wolfgang Kluxen, *Philosophische Ethik bei Thomas von Aquin* (Darmstadt: Wissenschaftliche Buchgesellschaft, 3rd ed. 1998), 197–205.

192 On the following, see Gewirth, 'John of Jandun and the *Defensor pacis*,' 268–9.

193 Flüeler, *Rezeption und Interpretation der aristotelischen Politica*, 172–3.

194 *Quaestiones in duodecim libros metaphysicae*, fol. 14r. See also Gewirth, 'John of Jandun and the *Defensor pacis*,' 268–9.

195 Thomas Aquinas, *Summa Theologiae*, II.I. q. 100 a. 2. Resp. Compare *Summa Theologiae*, II.I. q. 100 a. 9. Resp.

196 Gewirth, *Marsilius of Padua and Medieval Political Philosophy*, 109–10.

197 For a fuller treatment of possible links between Marsilius's and Maimonides' political ideas, see Vasileios Syros, 'Did the Physician from Padua Meet the Rabbi from Cordoba? Marsilius of Padua and Moses Maimonides on the Political Utility of Religion,' *Revue des Études Juives* 170 (2011): 51–71.

198 On the fate of the *Guide of the Perplexed* in the medieval West, see especially Görge K. Hasselhoff, *Dicit Rabbi Moyses: Studien zum Bild von Moses Maimonides im lateinischen Westen vom 13. bis 15. Jahrhundert* (Würzburg: Königshausen & Neumann, 2004; 2nd extended ed., 2005), 88–93, 122–7; Mauro Zonta, 'Traduzioni e commenti alla *Guida dei perplessi* nell'Europa del secolo XIII: a proposito di alcuni studi recenti,' in *Maimonide e il suo tempo*, ed. Geri Cerchiai and Giovanni Rota (Milan: Franco Angeli, 2007), 51–60.

199 Hasselhoff, *Dicit Rabbi Moyses*, 122–9.

200 Hasselhoff, *Dicit Rabbi Moyses*, 54, 291, and 294–5. On Maimonidean influences on Peter's *Lucidator*, see *Il 'Lucidator dubitabilium astronomiae' di Pietro d'Abano: [e altre opere]; opere scientifiche inedite*, ed. and trans. Graziella Federici Vescovini (Padua: Programma e 1+1 Ed., 1988), 96, 167, 197–9, 202, 204, 209, 238, 275, 344, and 400. On the reception of Maimonides' medical works in the medieval West, see, e.g., Lola Ferre, 'Dissemination of Maimonides' Medical Writings in the Middle Ages,' *Traditions of Maimonideanism*, ed. Carlos Fraenkel (Leiden and Boston: Brill, 2009), 17–31; Görge K. Hasselhoff, 'The Translations and the Reception of the Medical Doctor Maimonides in the Christian Medicine of the 14th and 15th Century,' in *The Trias of Maimonides: Jewish, Arabic, and Ancient Culture of Knowledge*, ed. Georges Tamer (Berlin and New York: W. de Gruyter, 2005), 395–410.

201 References to the *Dux neutrorum* are to the following edition: *Rabi Mossei Aegyptii Dux seu Director dubitantium aut perplexorum* (Paris, 1520; repr. Frankfurt a. M.: Minerva, 1964), part II, ch. 41, fol. 66r. I have also consulted the following English translation: Moses Maimonides, *The Guide of the Perplexed*, trans. Shlomo Pines (Chicago, IL: Chicago University Press, 1963).

202 *Dux seu Director dubitantium aut perplexorum*, fols. 94v–95r: 'Notum est

quod praecepta dividuntur in duas partes. Una est prohibitionum et transgressionum quae sunt inter hominem et proximum suum. Altera est illorum que sunt inter hominem et Deum. Quae sunt inter hominem et proximum de partibus numeratis sunt quinta, sexta, septima, et pars quaedam tertiae partis. Aliae vero partes praeter istas sunt inter hominem et Creatorem suum.' Compare Moses Maimonides, *The Guide of the Perplexed*, 535–8.

203 *Dux seu Director dubitantium aut perplexorum*, fol. 97r; Maimonides, *The Guide of the Perplexed*, 536, 550.

204 *Dux seu Director dubitantium aut perplexorum*, fols. 97v–98r; Maimonides, *The Guide of the Perplexed*, 536.

205 *Dux seu Director dubitantium aut perplexorum*, fol. 98r–v; Maimonides, *The Guide of the Perplexed*, 536, 555.

206 *Dux seu Director dubitantium aut perplexorum*, fols. 98v–100v; Maimonides, *The Guide of the Perplexed*, 536, 558.

207 *Dux seu Director dubitantium aut perplexorum*, fols. 98v–100v; Maimonides, *The Guide of the Perplexed*, 536, 568.

208 *Dux seu Director dubitantium aut perplexorum*, fol. 95r; Maimonides, *The Guide of the Perplexed*, 538.

209 For Maimonides, see Menachem Lorberbaum, *Politics and the Limits of Law: Secularizing the Political in Medieval Jewish Thought* (Stanford, CA: Stanford University Press, 2001), 30–4.

210 *DP* I.vi.4, 7, 8; x.3; II.ix.3, 6, 9–12.

211 *DP* I.vi.4; II.ix.10.

212 *DP* II.ix.11; xv.1, 2.

213 *DP* II.v.4, 5.

214 *DP* II.viii.5; xii.3, 4.

215 *DP* I.x.4; II.viii.4, 5, 6.

216 *DP* II.xii.9. See also ibid., II.v.4, 5, 7; xxvi.13; xxx.4 as well as *Defensor minor* VIII.3; xiii.6; xv.3, 4.

217 *DP* I.v.5.

218 *DP* I.v.5.

219 *DP* I.v.6.

220 *DP* I.v.7, 10, 11.

221 Plato, *Politeia* 436A–437D.

222 Plato, *Politeia* 368D8–369A3; 428E; 433A; 434D6–E; 435B; 449A; 543C–D; 577C.

223 Calcidio, *Commentario al 'Timeo' di Platone: Testo latino a fronte*, ed. Claudio Moreschini (Milan: Bompiani, 2003), 17C–18A; Latin text, 8 and 10/

Ital. trans. 9 an 11; and Chalcidios's comments 498/499; *Timaeus a Calcidio translatus commentarioque instructus*, ed. Jan H. Waszink (London/Leiden: Warburg Institute/E.J. Brill, 1962), 8, as well as 246–7. On Chalcidios's translation and commentary, see Claudio Moreschini, 'Saggio introduttivo,' in Calcidio, *Commentario al 'Timeo' di Platone*, vii–lxxxvi; Jan H. Waszink, *Studien des Timaioskommentar des Calcidius* (Leiden: E.J. Brill, 1962). On Plato's doctrine of the tripartition of the human soul as expounded in the *Timaios*, see James M. Robinson, 'The Tripartite Soul in the *Timaeus*,' *Phronesis* 35 (1990): 103–10. *Timaios*'s medieval reception is discussed in Udo R. Jeck, 'Platons Götter im lateinischen Mittelalter: Ein Beitrag zur Rezeption des platonischen *Timaios* bei Augustin, Calcidius und Albertus Magnus,' *Bochumer Philosophisches Jahrbuch für Antike und Mittelalter* 14 (2009–11): 157–90; Nancy Van Deusen, 'The *Timaeus latinus* and Cusanus,' in *Mind Matters*, ed. Cary J. Nederman, Nancy Van Deusen and E. Ann Matter (Turnhout: Brepols, 2009), 217–31; Perfetti, 'Immagini della *Repubblica* nei commenti medievali alla *Politica*,' 89–93; Thomas Leinkauf and Carlos Steel, eds., *Platons Timaios als Grundtext der Kosmologie in Spätantike, Mittelalter und Renaissance* (Leuven: Leuven University Press, 2005); Paul E. Dutton, 'Medieval Approaches to Calcidius,' in *Plato's Timaeus as Cultural Icon*, ed. Gretchen J. Reydams-Schils (Notre Dame, IN: Notre Dame University Press, 2003), 183–205; idem, 'Material Remains of the Study of the *Timaeus* in the Later Middle Ages,' in *L'enseignement de la philosophie au XIIIe siècle: Autour du Guide de l'étudiant du ms. Ripoll 109*, ed. Claude Lafleur (Turnhout: Brepols, 1997), 203–30; idem, '*Illustre ciuitatis et populi exemplum*: Plato's *Timaeus* and the Transmission from Calcidius to the End of the Twelfth Century of a Tripartite Scheme of Society,' *Mediaeval Studies* 45 (1983): 79–119; Anna Somfai, 'The Transmission and Reception of Plato's *Timaeus* and Calcidius's *Commentary* during the Carolingian Renaissance' (Diss., University of Cambridge, 1998); Raymond Klibansky, *The Continuity of the Platonic Tradition during the Middle Ages* (London: Warburg Institute, 1939; repr. Millwood, NY: Kraus International Publications, 1984), 21–31.

224 *DP* I.iii.4.

225 *DP* I.xv.10.

226 *DP* I.xv.8.

227 See also Black, *The West and Islam*, 156–7.

228 Avicenna, *The Metaphysics of The Healing*, a parallel English-Arabic text translated, introduced, and annotated by Michael E. Marmura (Provo, UT: Brigham Young University Press, 2005), 370; Avicenna (Ibn Sīnā),

Metafisica: La scienza delle cose divine (al-Ilāhiyyāt) dal Libro della Guarigione (Kitāb al-Šifā'), trans. Olga Lizzini (Milan: Bompiani, 2002), 1028 (Arab text)/1029 (Italian trans.). On the reception of Avicenna's *Metaphysics* in the Arabic, Jewish, and Latin traditions, see Dag N. Hasse and Amos Bertolacci, eds., *The Arabic, Hebrew and Latin Reception of Avicenna's Metaphysics* (Berlin and Boston: W. de Gruyter, 2012).

229 *Averroes' Commentary on Plato's Republic*, ed. and trans. Erwin I.J. Rosenthal (Cambridge: Cambridge University Press, 1966), 23 (Hebrew text)/115 (Eng. trans.).

230 *Averroes' Commentary on Plato's Republic*, 50–1/160–1.

231 Giles Constable, *Three Studies in Medieval Religious and Social Thought* (Cambridge: Cambridge University Press, 1995), ch. 'The Orders of Society,' 251–360; Georges Duby, *The Three Orders: Feudal Society Imagined*, trans. Arthur Goldhammer (Chicago, IL and London: University of Chicago Press, 1980); Otto Gerhard Oexle, 'Die funktionale Dreiteilung als Deutungsschema der sozialen Wirklichkeit in der ständischen Gesellschaft des Mittelalters,' in *Ständische Gesellschaft und soziale Mobilität*, ed. Winfried Schulze (Munich: R. Oldenbourg, 1988), 19–51; idem, 'Tria genera hominum. Zur Geschichte eines Deutungsschemas der sozialen Wirklichkeit in Antike und Mittelalter,' in *Institutionen, Kultur und Gesellschaft im Mittelalter*, ed. Lutz Fenske et al. (Sigmaringen: J. Thorbecke, 1984), 483–500; Ottavia Niccoli, *I sacerdoti, i guerrieri, i contadini: Storia di un' immagine della società* (Turin: G. Einaudi, 1979); Ruth Mohl, *The Three Estates in Medieval and Renaissance Literature* (New York: Columbia University Press, 1933; repr. New York: F. Ungar, 1962). For a critical assessment of Duby's analysis of medieval ideas on the three orders, see especially Elizabeth A.R. Brown, 'Georges Duby and the Three Orders,' *Viator* 17 (1986): 51–64; Otto Gerhard Oexle, 'Die 'Wirklichkeit' und das 'Wissen.' Ein Blick auf das sozialgeschichtliche Œuvre von Georges Duby,' *Historische Zeitschrift* 232 (1981): 61–91. Their reception in medieval Jewish political writing is surveyed in Abraham Melamed, *The Philosopher-King in Medieval and Renaissance Jewish Thought* (Albany, NY: State University of New York Press, 2003), ch. 'The Class System,' 61–74.

232 For Avicenna's influence on medieval Latin political writing, see also the comments by Cranz, 'Aristotelianism in Medieval Political Theory,' 16–20. For Avicenna's Latin reception in general, consult Marie-Thérèse d'Alverny, *Avicenne en Occident* (Paris: J. Vrin, 1993).

233 'Oportet autem, ut in instituendo legem haec sit prima intentio, scilicet ordinare civitatem in tres partes: dispositores et ministros et legisperitos. Et unoquoque ordine istorum ordinetur aliquis praelatus; post quem

ordinentur alii praelati inferiores eo conseqenter; et post hos iterum ordinentur alii consequenter, quousque perveniatur ad paucos, ad hoc ut nullus sit in civitate inutilis, qui non habeat statum aliquem laudabilem, sed ut ab unoquoque perveniat utilitas civitati; et ideo prohibeat otiositatem et vacationem ita, ut nullus praetermittatur, qui secundum quod sibi competit non habet aliquem supra se, nec sit aliquis, qui non oboediat alicui.' Dominicus Gundissalinus, *De divisione philosophiae (Über die Einteilung der Philosophie): Lateinisch-Deutsch*, trans. Alexander Fidora and Dorothée Werner (Freiburg i. Br.: Herder, 2007), 256 and 258 (Latin text)/257 and 259 (German trans.). See also the discussions in Alexander Fidora, 'A tripartição da filosofia prática na obra *De divisione philosophiae* de Domingos Gundisalvo,' in *Idade Média: Tempo do mundo, tempo dos homens, tempo de Deus*, ed. José Antônio de C.R. de Souza (Porto Alegre: Ed. Est, 2006), 417–28; idem, *Die Wissenschaftstheorie des Dominicus Gundissalinus: Voraussetzungen und Konsequenzen des zweiten Anfangs der aristotelischen Philosophie im 12. Jahrhundert* (Berlin: Akademie-Verl., 2003), 167–79; Alessandro Levi, 'La partizione della filosofia pratica in un trattato medioevale,' *Atti del Reale Istituto di Scienze, Lettere ed Arti* 67 (1907/08): 1225–50; Dominicus Gundissalinus, *De divisione philosophiae*, ed. Ludwig Baur (Münster: Aschendorff, 1903), 308–14. For the reception of the *De divisione philosophiae* in the Parisian milieu, consult ibid., 40–9. The Avicennean background of Gundissalinus's classification of sciences is discussed in Henri Hugonnard-Roche, 'La classification des sciences de Gundissalinus et l'influence d'Avicenne,' in *Études sur Avicenne*, ed. Jean Jolivet and Roshdi Rashed (Paris: Les Belles Lettres, 1984), 41–75; Cranz, 'Aristotelianism in Medieval Political Theory,' 30–1. On Gundissalinus as purveyor of Arabic learning in Latin Europe, see the essays collected in Fuat Sezgin, Mazen Amawi, Carl Ehrig-Eggert and Eckhard Neubauer, eds., *Dominicus Gundissalinus (12th c.) and the Transmission of Arabic Philosophical Thought to the West: Texts and Studies* (Frankfurt a. M.: Institute for the History of Arabic-Islamic Science, Johann Wolfgang Goethe University, 2000). John of Jandun draws on Gundissalinus in his Questions on Book VI of the *Metaphysics* – on this see Mario Grignaschi, 'Le *De divisione philosophie* de Dominicus Gundissalinus et les *Questiones II–V in Sextum Metaphysicorum* de Jean de Jandun,' in *Knowledge and the Sciences in Medieval Philosophy*, ed. Simo Knuuttila et al. (Helsinki: Yliopistopaino, 1990), 2: 53–61.

234 For fuller accounts of Bacon's political and moral ideas, see Jeremiah Hackett, 'Mirrors of Princes, Errors of Philosophers: Roger Bacon and Giles of Rome (Aegidius Romanus) on the Education of the Government (the Prince),' in *Ireland, England and the Continent in the Middle Ages and*

Beyond, ed. Howard B. Clarke and J.R.S. Phillips (Dublin: University College Dublin Press, 2006), 105–27; Georg Wieland, 'Ethik und Metaphysik. Bemerkungen zur Moralphilosophie Roger Bacons,' in *Virtus Politica*, ed. Joseph Möller et al. (Stuttgart-Bad Cannstatt: Friedrich Fromann, 1974), 147–73.

235 'Secunda pars descendit ad leges et statuta hominum inter se. [. . .] Deinde dantur leges secundum quas ordinantur subditi ad praelatos et principes, et e converso, et servi ad dominos, secundum omne genus dominii et servitii, et secundum quas paterfamilias debet vivere in regimine prolis et familiae, et magister ad discipulos. Deinde statuuntur doctores et artifices in singulis scientiis et artibus; et eliguntur ex iuvenibus instruendis ad huiusmodi studia et officia exercenda aptiores iuxta consilium sapientum, et reliqui ad officium militare deputantur pro iustitia exequenda et malefactoribus compescendis. Et »oportet, ut dicit Avicenna, ut instituendo legem sit haec prima intentio, scilicet ordinare civitatem in tres partes, scilicet dispositores et ministros et legis peritos, et quod in unoquoque eorum ordinetur aliquis praelatus; post quem ordinentur alii praelati inferiores eo, et post hos iterum alii ordinentur, quousque perveniant ad paucos; ad hoc ut nullus sit in civitate inutilis, quin habeat aliquem statum laudabilem, sed ut ab unoquoque proveniat utilitas civitati«. Unde apud Platonem illa civitas iustissime ordinata traditur, in qua quisque proprios nescit affectus; et ideo, ut Avicenna dicit, prohibere debet princeps civitatis »otiositatem et vacationem«.' Roger Bacon, *Opus maius: Eine moralphilosophische Auswahl: Lateinisch-Deutsch*, trans. Pia A. Antolic-Piper (Freiburg i. Br.: Herder, 2008), 108 and 110 (Latin text)/109 and 111 (German trans.); Eng. trans. in *Medieval Political Philosophy: A Sourcebook*, 364–5. Compare Avicenna latinus, *Liber de philosophia sive scientia divina*, vol: 5/10, ed. Simone van Riet (Leiden: Brill, 1980), 542–4.

236 George T. Dennis, ed. and trans., *Three Byzantine Military Treatises* (Washington, DC: Dumbarton Oaks Research Library and Collection, 1985; repr. 2008), 10 (Greek text)/11 (Eng. trans.). See also Constable, *Three Studies in Medieval Religious and Social Thought*, 269. Although Constable's study is quite helpful for early Byzantine views on social organization, it does not cover late Byzantine writers, such as Thomas Magister and Plethon.

237 Ernest Barker, *Social and Political Thought in Byzantium: From Justinian I to the Last Palaeologus. Passages from Byzantine Writers and Documents* (Oxford: Clarendon Press, 1957), 168–9; Christos P. Baloglou, 'Economic Thought in the Last Byzantine Period,' in *Ancient and Medieval Economic Ideas and Concepts of Social Justice*, ed. S. Todd Lowry and Barry Gordon (Leiden: Brill, 1998), 405–38, 420.

238 *Advice to the Despot Theodore Concerning the Affairs of the Peloponnese* – Spyridon P. Lampros, *Palaiologeia kai Peloponnēsiaka* (Athens: V.N. Gregoriades, 1972), 4: 114–35 – partial English trans. in Barker, *Social and Political Thought in Byzantium*, 206–12.

239 *Georgios Gemistos to Manuel Palaeologus Concerning the Affairs of the Peloponnese* – Spyridon P. Lampros, *Palaiologeia kai Peloponnēsiaka* (Athens: V.N. Gregoriades, 1972), 3: 246–65 – partial English trans. in Barker, *Social and Political Thought in Byzantium: From Justinian I to the Last Palaeologus*, 198–206. For recent discussions of Pletho's memoranda, see Niketas Siniossoglou, *Radical Platonism in Byzantium: Illumination and Utopia in Gemistos Plethon* (Cambridge: Cambridge University Press, 2011), part III 'Mistra versus Athos,' 327–92; Peter Garnsey, 'Gemistus Plethon and Platonic Political Philosophy,' in *Transformations of Late Antiquity*, ed. Philip Rousseau and Manolis Papoutsakis (Farnham and Burlington, VT: Ashgate, 2009), 327–40, esp. 334–8.

240 Lampros, *Palaiologeia kai Peloponnēsiaka*, 4: 132.

241 Lampros, *Palaiologeia kai Peloponnēsiaka*, 4: 119. For further discussion, see Christos P. Baloglou, 'Die Einteilung des Volkes in drei Stande bei Georgios Gemistos im Vergleich zu Hippodamos von Milet und den Physiokraten,' *Jahrbuch der Österreichischen Byzantinistik* 46 (1996): 311–24.

242 On the 'circle of justice,' see the following studies by Linda T. Darling, 'Do Justice, Do Justice, for That Is Paradise': Middle Eastern Advice for Indian Muslim Rulers?' *Comparative Studies on South Asia, Africa, and the Middle East* 22 (2002): 3–19; eadem, 'Islamic Empires, the Ottoman Empire and the Circle of Justice,' in *Constitutional Politics in the Middle East: With Special Reference to Turkey, Iraq, Iran and Afghanistan*, ed. Saïd Amir Arjomand (Oxford and Portland, OR: Hart Pub., 2008), 11–32; as well as Jennifer A. London, 'The Circle of Justice,' *History of Political Thought* 32 (2011): 425–47; Ann K.S. Lambton, 'Justice in the Medieval Persian Theory of Kingship,' *Studia Islamica* 17 (1962): 91–119 – repr. in eadem, *Theory and Practice in Medieval Persian Government* (London: Variorum Reprints, 1980), no. IV; Black, *The West and Islam*, 58, 104–5; idem, *The History of Islamic Political Thought: From the Prophet to the Present* (New York: Routledge, 2001), 53–4, 111.

243 *'Ahd Ardashīr*, ed. Iḥsān 'Abbās (Beirut: Dār al-Ṣādir, 1967), 98; Mario Grignaschi, 'Quelques spécimens de la littérature sassanide conservés dans les bibliothèques d'Istanbul,' *Journal Asiatique* 254 (1966): 1–142, 46–90. For a set of maxims on rulership under the title *Ā'īn-i Ardashīr* and was ascribed to Ardashīr, see Grignaschi, 'Quelques spécimens de la littérature sassanide,' 91–133.

244 Josef Horovitz, 'Ibn Quteiba's 'Uyun al-Akhbar,' *Islamic Culture* 4 (1930): 171–98, at 190–1.

245 Angeliki E. Laiou, 'Economic Thought and Ideology,' in *The Economic History of Byzantium: From the Seventh through the Fifteenth Century*, ed. Angeliki E. Laiou (Washington, DC: Dumbarton Oaks Research Library and Collection, 2002), 1123–44, at 1140, makes a similar point, but does not provide any textual evidence.

246 *The Taktika of Leo VI*, ed. and trans. George T. Dennis (Washington, DC: Dumbarton Oaks, 2010), 610 and 612 (Greek text)/611 and 613 (Eng. trans.).

247 *The Taktika of Leo VI*, 12/13.

248 *The Taktika of Leo VI*, 46/47.

249 *The Taktika of Leo VI*, 90/91.

250 *The Taktika of Leo VI*, 196/197.

251 *The Taktika of Leo VI*, 158/159.

252 'Car tout ainsi comme le corps humain n'est mie entier, mais deffectueulx et diffourmé quant il lui fault aucun de ses membres, semblablement ne peut le corps de policie estre parfait, entier ne sain se tous les estas dont nous traictons ne sont en bonne conjonction et union ensemble, si qu'ilz puissent secourir et aidier l'un a l'autre, chascun excercitant l'office de quoy il doit servir, lesquelz divers offices ne sont a tout considerer establis et ne doivent servir ne mes pour la conservacion de tout ensemble, tout ainsi comme les membres de corps humain aident a gouverner et nourrir tout le corps. Et si tost comme l'un d'eulx deffault, couvient dire la maniere comment ces derrenieres parties du dit corps seront maintenues en santé et bonne convalessence, car il me semble que il sont les sousteneurs et ont la charge de tout le seurplus du dit corps, par quoy ont mestier d'avoir force et puissance de porter la pesanteur des autres parties, pour laquelle chose, commes nous avons devant dit de l'amour et cure que le bon prince doit avoir vers ses subgiez et peuple, et aussi de l'office des nobles, lesquelz sont etablis pour la garde et deffence du dit peuple, dire nous couvient de l'amour, reverence et obeissance que bon peuple doit avoir envers prince. Si dirons universelement a tous en tant que touche ceste matiere, comme tous estas doient au prince une meisme amour, reverence et obeissance.' Christine de Pizan, *Le livre du corps de policie*, ed. Angus J. Kennedy (Paris: H. Champion, 1998), 91; Christine de Pizan, *The Book of the Body Politic*, trans. Kate Langdon Forhan (Cambridge: Cambridge University Press, 1994), 90–1. On de Pizan's use of medical metaphors, see Cary J. Nederman, 'The Living Body Politic: The Diversification of Organic Metaphors in Nicole Oresme and Christine de

Pizan,' in *Healing the Body Politic: The Political Thought of Christine de Pizan*, ed. Karen Green and Constant J. Mews (Turnhout: Brepols, 2005), 19–33; idem, 'The Expanding Body Politic: Christine de Pizan and Medieval Political Economy,' in *Au Champ des écritures*, ed. Eric Hicks (Paris: Honoré Champion Éditeur, 2000), 383–97; Jean-Louis G. Picherit, 'Les références pathologiques et thérapeutiques dans l'œuvre de Christine de Pizan,' in *Une femme de Lettres au Moyen Age: Études autour de Christine de Pizan*, ed. Liliane Dulac and Bernard Ribémont (Orléans: Paradigme, 1995), 233–44; idem, *La Métaphore pathologique et thérapeutique à la fin du Moyen Age* (Tübingen: M. Niemeyer, 1994).

253 'Et en ce nous avons enseignement qu'en la chose publique bien gouvernee doivent certains hommes estre ordonnez en tous estas, chascun selon ce quoy il se doit mesler, si que devant est touchié, c'est a savoir ou fait de la chevalerie les gens d'armes et ceulx qui y sont propres, et aussi de clergié, [l]es estudians tant es sciences speculatives, en philosophie, es ars liberaux comme en autres, selon ce que dit Tulles. Et en ce le bon prince doit avoir grant entente, car l'onneur et la gloire du royame, ou de la terre ou pais, acroist moult par habondance et grant pluralité de clers et de saiges hommes, car part eulx, si comme j'ay dit, peut estre bien conseillé.' Christine de Pizan, *Le livre du corps de policie*, 40; Christine de Pizan, *The Book of the Body Politic*, 41.

254 Compare Plato, *Politeia* 351A; 443B–D; 444B; *The Laws* 716A; *Gorgias* 470B.

255 For a similar point, see Alfredo Sabetti, *Marsilio da Padova e la filosofia politica del secolo XIV* (Naples: Liguori, 1964), 105–6.

256 Anthony J. Parel, *The Machiavellian Cosmos* (New Haven: Yale University Press, 1992), 102.

257 For further references and discussion, see Otto Gerhard Oexle, 'Die Entstehung politischer Stände im Spätmittelalter – Wirklichkeit und Wissen,' in *Institutionen und Ereignis: Über historische Praktiken und Vorstellungen gesellschaftlichen Ordnens*, ed. Reinhard Blänkner and Bernhard Jussen (Göttingen: Vandenhoeck & Ruprecht, 1998), 137–62, at 151–4.

258 For a similar interpretation, see Parel, *The Machiavellian Cosmos*, 102.

259 'Lasciando, adunque, indrieto le cose circa uno principe imaginate, e discorrendo quelle che sono vere.' Machiavelli, *Il Principe*, chap. 15.

260 The following section is based on Parel, *The Machiavellian Cosmos*, 106–7. Machiavelli's use of medical motifs is discussed in Laurent Gerbier, 'Constitution mixte et complexion civile chez Machiavel (*Discorsi*, I, 2–9),' in *Le Gouvernement mixte*, 57–69; Eyal Chowers, 'The Physiology of the Citizen: The Present-Centered Body and Its Political Exile,' *Political Theory*

30 (2002): 649–76, esp. 656–9; Jean-Claude Zancarini, 'Gli umori del corpo politico. '"Popolo" e "plebe" nelle opere di Machiavelli,' in *La lingua e le lingue di Machiavelli*, ed. Alessandro Pontremoli (Florence: L.S. Olschki, 2001), 61–70.

261 'E però non abbiamo a cercare di uno governo immaginato e che sia più facile a apparire in su' libri che in pratica, come fu forse la republica di Platone; ma considerato la natura, la qualità, le condizioni, la inclinazione, e per stringere tutte queste cose in una parola, gli umori della città e de' cittadini, cercare di uno governo che non siamo sanza speranza che pure si potessi persuadere ed introducere, e che introdotto, si potessi secondo el gusto nostro comportare e conservare, seguitando in questo lo esempio de' medici che, se bene sono più liberi che non siamo noi, perché agli infermi possono dare tutte le medicine che pare loro, non gli danno però tutte quelle che in sé sono buone e lodate, ma quelle che lo infermo secondo la complessione sua ed altri accidenti è attto a sopportare.' Francesco Guicciardini, *Dialogo e discorsi del reggimento di Firenze*, ed. Roberto Palmarocchi (Bari: G. Laterza, 1932), 99; Eng. trans. *Dialogue on the Government of Florence*, ed. and trans. Alison Brown (Cambridge: Cambridge University Press, 1994), 96–7.

262 Giuseppe Cambiano, 'Patologia e metafora politica. Alcmeone, Platone, *Corpus Hippocraticum*,' *Elenchos* 3 (1982): 219–36.

263 Plato, *Timaios* 87C–D.

264 On Aristotle's idea of the mean, see Ioannis D. Evrigenis, 'The Doctrine of the Mean in Aristotle's Ethical and Political Theory,' *History of Political Thought* 20 (1999): 393–416; Richard Bosley, Roger A. Shiner and Janet D. Sisson, eds., *Aristotle, Virtue and the Mean* (Edmonton: Academic Printing & Publishing, 1995); James O. Urmson, 'Aristotle's Doctrine of the Mean,' in *Essays on Aristotle's Ethics*, 157–70; William F.R. Hardie, 'Aristotle's Doctrine that Virtue is a "Mean,"' *Proceedings of the Aristotelian Society* 65 (1964/65): 183–204 – repr. in *Articles on Aristotle*, vol. 2: *Ethics and Politics*, 33–46; Jan van der Meulen, *Aristoteles: Die Mitte in seinem Denken* (Meisenheim am Glan: Anton Hain, 1951). The medical and biological associations of the ancient doctrine of the mean are discussed in Wilfried Fiedler, *Analogiemodelle bei Aristoteles: Untersuchungen zu den Vergleichen zwischen den einzelnen Wissenschaften und Künsten* (Amsterdam: B.R. Grüner, 1978), 211–29; Geoffrey E.R. Lloyd, *Science, Folklore and Ideology: Studies in the Life of Sciences in Ancient Greece* (Cambridge: Cambridge University Press, 1983); idem, 'The Role of Medical and Biological Analogies in Aristotle's Ethics,' *Phronesis* 13 (1968): 68–83; Theodore J. Tracy, *Physiological Theory and the Doctrine of the Mean in Plato and Aristotle* (The Hague: Mouton,

1969); Helen North, *Sophrosyne: Self-Knowledge and Self-Restraint in Greek Literature* (Ithaca, NY: Cornell University Press, 1966), 199–200; Werner Jaeger, 'Aristotle's Use of Medicine as Model in his Ethics,' *The Journal of Hellenic Studies* 77 (1957): 54–61 – repr. in idem, *Scripta minora* (Rome: Storia e letteratura, 1960), 2: 491–509.

265 The medieval reception of Aristotle's idea of the mean merits detailed study. Useful comments can be found in Cary J. Nederman, 'The Aristotelian Doctrine of the Mean and John of Salisbury's Concept of Liberty,' *Vivarium* 24 (1986): 128–41 – repr. in idem, *Medieval Aristotelianism and Its Limits*, no. VIII.

266 Avicenna, *The Metaphysics of The Healing*, 377. On the following, see also Syros, 'Did the Physician from Padua Concur with the Rabbi from Cordoba?' 70–1.

267 Compare *Guide of the Perplexed*, II, 39. For further discussion, see David Bakan, Dan Merkur and David S. Weiss, *Maimonides' Cure of Souls: Medieval Precursor of Psychoanalysis* (Albany, NY: SUNY Press, 2009), 14–17; Marvin Fox, 'The Doctrine of the Mean in Aristotle and Maimonides: A Comparative Study,' in *Studies in Jewish Religious and Intellectual History: Presented to Alexander Altmann on the Occasion of His Seventieth Birthday*, ed. Siegfried Stein and Raphael Loewe (Tuscaloosa, AL: University of Alabama Press, 1979), 93–120 – repr. in idem, *Interpreting Maimonides: Studies in Methodology, Metaphysics, and Moral Philosophy* (Chicago, IL: University of Chicago Press, 1990), 93–123, and 117; Herbert A. Davidson, 'The Middle Way in Maimonides' Ethics,' *Proceedings of the American Academy for Jewish Research*, 54 (1987): 31–72; David Shatz, 'Maimonides' Moral Theory' and Haim Kreisel, 'Maimonides' Political Philosophy,' both in *The Cambridge Companion to Maimonides*, ed. Kenneth Seeskin (Cambridge: Cambridge University Press, 2005), 167–92 (esp. 171–83) and 193–220 (esp. 194, 199), respectively.

268 Shem Tob ben Joseph ibn Falaquera, *Falaquera's Book of the Seeker (Sefer Ha-Mebaqqesh)*, ed. M. Herschel Levine (New York: Yeshiva University Press, 1976), xvii.

269 Ibid., 60.

270 Ibid., 54–5.

271 Aristotle, *Pol.* 1290b39–1291a10; 1291a22–28; 1291a33–1291b2; 1328b33–1329a39. The third and most extensive exposition of the organization of the model *polis* occurs in the fourth book of the *Politics*. Aristotle lists three kinds of offices. First, there are six indispensable offices (superintendents of the market, superintendents of streets and buildings, superintendents of farms, revenue officers, archivists, officers in charge of

the execution of punishments). In addition to these absolutely necessary offices, Aristotle mentions four offices that are less necessary, but higher in dignity because they require a good deal of experience and trustworthiness: military officers, auditors, the council, and religious officials. Aristotle also refers to the following offices which exist in communities that allow for more leisure, exhibit a higher degree of prosperity, and pay more attention to public order: superintendents of women and children, custodians of the laws, preliminary councillors, and the council (Aristotle, *Pol.* 1321b4–1323a3). For further discussion, see John J. Navone, 'The Division of Parts in Society According to Plato and Aristotle,' *Philosophical Studies* 6 (1956): 113–22.

272 Aristotle, *Pol.* 1291b2–6.

273 Aristotle, *Pol.* 1328b2–23.

274 *DP* I.v.5; Aristotle, *Pol.* 1319a19–20.

275 *DP* I.v.6. Marsilius's characterization of medicine as an architectonic art can be construed as an allusion to the hierarchy of qualifications as expounded in Aristotle's *Pol.* 1282a1–10: at the top stands 'architectonic' competence, which approaches the overall view of a scientific branch as well as the knowledge of the specific causes and ends of human actions. At the second level is located the 'demiurgical' qualification that is concerned with performance of concrete tasks. At the bottom stand those who are educated in medicine, but lack expertise and are thus incapable of providing a correct diagnosis. The definition of medicine as practical art harks back to Al-Fārābī, Averroes, Hugo of St Victor (1096–1141), and Dominicus Gundissalinus. For further references and comments, see Nancy G. Siraisi, *Medicine and the Italian Universities, 1250–1600* (Leiden: Brill, 2001), 194; Lucia Miccoli, *'Le "arti meccaniche" nelle classificazioni delle scienze di Ugo di San Vittore e Domenico Gundisalvi,' Annali della Facoltà di Lettere e Filosofia* (Bari) 24 (1981): 73–101; and, on the mechanical arts in the Middle Ages, see, in general, Elspeth Whitney, *Paradise Restored: The Mechanical Arts from Antiquity through the Thirteenth Century* (Philadelphia, PA: American Philosophical Society, 1990); Ria Jansen-Sieben, ed., *Artes mechanicae en Europe médiévale* (Brussels: Archives et bibliothèques de Belgique, 1989); George Ovitt, Jr, *The Restoration of Perfection: Labor and Technology in Medieval Culture* (New Brunswick, NJ, and London: Rutgers University Press, 1987).

276 *DP* I.v.7.

277 *DP* I.v.8; xiv.8.

278 *DP* I.v.9.

279 *DP* I.v.10.

280 For medieval attitudes toward Pythagoras's teachings, see Manegold of Lautenbach, *Liber contra Wolfelmum*, trans. Robert Ziomkowski (Paris: Peeters, 2002), 70–1.

281 *DP* I.v.11.

282 A comprehensive study of the use of pagan examples in medieval Islamic and Jewish discussions on the political aspects of religion remains a desideratum. For stimulating reflections on the topic, see Gotthard Strohmaier, 'Das Bild und die Funktion vorchristlicher griechischer Religion bei arabischen Autoren des Mittelalters,' in *Reflections on Reflections: Near Eastern Writers Reading Literature*, ed. Angelika Neuwirth and Andreas C. Islebe (Wiesbaden: Reichert Verlag, 2006), 181–90.

283 Thérèse-Anne Druart, 'Le Sommaire du Livre des *Lois* de Platon (*Ǧawāmi' Kitāb al-Nawāmīs li-Aflāṭūn*) par Abū Nasr al-Fārābī, édition critique et introduction,' *Bulletin d'Études Orientales* 50 (1998): 109–55, at 130; *Medieval Political Philosophy: A Sourcebook*, 91. See also the discussion in Steven Harvey, 'Can a Tenth-Century Islamic Aristotelian Help Us Understand Plato's *Laws?*' in *Plato's Laws: From Theory into Practice*, ed. Samuel Scolnicov and Luc Brisson (St. Augustin: Academia-Verlag, 2003), 320–30, at 328.

284 *Averroes' Tahafut al-Tahafut (The Incoherence of the Incoherence)*, trans. from the Arabic with intro. and notes Simon van den Bergh (London: Luzac, 1954), 1: 359–60. See also Richard C. Taylor, 'Averroes: God and the Noble Lie,' in *Laudemus viros gloriosos*, ed. Rollen E. Houser (Notre Dame, IN: University of Notre Dame Press 2007), 38–59, at 50–1.

285 *Dux dubitantium*, part III, ch. 30, fol. 91r. The following section on Maimonides's views on the Sabians builds on Syros, 'Did the Physician from Padua Concur with the Rabbi from Cordoba?' 67–8.

286 *Dux dubitantium*, part III, ch. 30, fol. 90v.

287 *Dux dubitantium*, part III, ch. 31, fol. 92r.

288 *Dux dubitantium*, part III, ch. 31, fol. 92r.

289 *Dux dubitantium*, part III, ch. 31, fol. 92r.

290 *Dux dubitantium*, part III, ch. 38, fol. 96v.

291 *DP* I.v.11.

292 *DP* I.v.11.

293 *DP* I.x.3.

294 *Conciliator controversiarum*, fols. 13v–14r. Consider also Friedrich von Bezold, 'Astrologische Geschichtskonstruktion im Mittelalter,' *Deutsche Zeitschrift für Geschichtswissenschaft* 8 (1892): 29–72, 47–9 – repr in. idem, *Aus Mittelalter und Renaissance: Kulturgeschichtliche Studien* (Munich and Berlin: R. Oldenbourg, 1918), 165–95; John M. Headley, *Tommaso Campanella and the Transformation of the World* (Princeton, NJ: Princeton

University Press, 1997), 185–6. For Peter of Abano's ideas on astrology, see the following studies by Graziella Federici Vescovini: 'Il sole e la luna nelle citazioni di Pietro d'Abano dei segreti di Albumasar, di Sadan,' *Micrologus* 12 (2004): 185–94; 'Gli astronomi arabi e il *Lucidator dubitabilium astronomiae* di Pietro d'Abano (1303–1310),' in *Filosofia e scienza classica, arabo-latina medievale e l'età moderna*, ed. Graziella Federici Vescovini (Louvain-la-Neuve: Fédération internationale des instituts d'études médiévales, 1999), 29–42; '« Albumasar in Sadan » e Pietro d'Abano,' in *La diffusione delle scienze islamiche nel Medio Evo europeo*, ed. Biancamaria Scarcia Amoretti (Rome: Accademia nazionale dei Lincei, 1987), 29–55. Medieval views on the nexus between astrology and history are surveyed in Krzystof Pomian, 'Astrology as a Naturalistic Theology of History' and John D. North, 'Celestial Influence – the Major Premiss of Astrology,' both in *'Astrologi hallucinati': Stars and the End of the World in Luther's Time*, ed. Paola Zambelli (Berlin and New York: W. de Gruyter, 1986), 29–43 and 45–100, respectively [North's paper has been reprinted in his *Stars, Minds and Fate: Essays in Ancient and Medieval Cosmology* (London and Ronceverte, WV: Hambledon Press, 1989), 243–98]; Peter Biller, 'Words and the Medieval Notion of "Religion,"' *Journal of Ecclesiastical History* 36 (1985): 351–69.

295 *Abū Ma'šar on Historical Astrology, The Book of Religions and Dynasties (On the Great Conjunctions)*, ed. and trans. into English Keiji Yamamoto and Charles Burnett (Leiden: Brill, 2000), 1: 10–13, 106–11; 2: 8–10, 70–3. On Abū Ma'shar's reception in the medieval West, consult David Pingree, 'The Sayings of Abū Ma'shar in Arabic, Greek, and Latin,' in *Ratio et superstitio*, ed. Giancarlo Marchetti et al. (Louvain-la-Neuve: Fédération internationale des instituts d'études médiévales, 2003), 41–57; Graziella Federici Vescovini, 'L'influenza dell'opera di Albumasar nel pensiero latino del XIV secolo: la dottrina astrologica di Biagio Pelacani da Parma,' in *Actas del V Congreso Internacional de filosofia medieval* (Madrid: Ed. Nacional, 1979), 2: 715–29; Richard Lemay, *Abu Ma ' shar and Latin Aristotelianism in the Twelfth Century: The Recovery of Aristotle's Natural Philosophy through Arabic Astrology* (Beirut: American University of Beirut, 1962).

296 Godefroid de Callataÿ, *Annus Platonicus: A Study of World Cycles in Greek, Latin and Arabic Sources* (Louvain-la Neuve: Université Catholique de Louvain/Institut Orientaliste, 1996), 138–9. See also Yves Marquet, 'La détermination astrale de l'évolution selon les Frères de la Pureté,' *Bulletin d'Etudes Orientales* 44 (1992): 127–46; idem, *La philosophie des Ikwān al-Ṣafā'* (Algiers: Société nationale d'édition et de diffusion, 1973), 139–47.

297 On the following, see Martin L. Pine, *Pietro Pomponazzi: Radical Philosopher*

of the Renaissance (Padua: Antenore, 1986), 268–71; Miguel A. Granada, *Cosmología, religión y política en el Renacimiento: Ficino, Savonarola, Pomponazzi, Maquiavelo* (Barcelona: Anthropos Editorial del Hombre, 1988), 196–217.

298 Pietro Pomponazzi, *Abhandlung über die Unsterblichkeit der Seele: Lateinisch-Deutsch*, trans. Burkhard Mojsisch (Hamburg: F. Meiner, 1990), 197 and 198 (Latin text)/199 (German trans.); Eng. trans. in Petrus Pomponatius, *Tractatus de immortalitate animae*, trans. William Henry Hay II (Haverford, PA: Haverford College, 1938), 50.

299 Of specific interest to the line of argumentation pursued here are the studies by David Wootton, *Paolo Sarpi: Between Renaissance and Enlightenment* (Cambridge: Cambridge University Press, 1983), 22; Pietro Pomponazzi, *Trattato sull'immortalità dell'anima*, ed. Vittoria Perrone Compagni (Florence: L.S. Olschki, 1999), 100; Vittorio Frajese, 'Maimonide, il desiderio di immortalità e l'immagine di Dio: problemi di interpretazzione dell' insegnamento esoterico di Sarpi,' in *Ripensando Paolo Sarpi*, ed. Corrado Pin (Venice: Ateneo Veneto, 2006), 153–81.

300 Wootton, *Paolo Sarpi*, 20. A copy of the *Defensor pacis* was included in the list of books ordered for Sarpi; on this see Paul F. Grendler, 'Books for Sarpi,' in *Essays Presented to Myron P. Gilmore*, ed. Sergio Bertelli and Gloria Ramakus (Florence: La Nuova Italia, 1978), 1: 105–14. Tommaso Campanella (1568–1639), in his *Monarchia Messiae* (1605/6) and *Antiveneti* (1606), points to Marsilius as a source of Sarpi. For further discussion, see Gregorio Piaia, 'La 'presenza' di Marsilio da Padova in Tommaso Campanella,' in *Logica e semantica ed altri saggi*, ed. Carlo Giacon (Padua: Antenore, 1975), 183–98.

301 Paolo Sarpi, *Pensieri naturali, metafisici e matematici*, ed. Luisa Cozzi and Libero Sosio (Milan: R. Ricciardi, 1996), no. 403 (306–7). On this and the following, see also Wootton, *Paolo Sarpi*, 20; Vittorio Frajese, *Sarpi scettico: Stato e Chiesa a Venezia tra Cinque e Seicento* (Bologna: Il Mulino, 1994).

302 Sarpi, *Pensieri naturali, metafisici e matematici*, no. 405 (307–8).

303 Aristotle, *Metaph.* 1074b3–5; 997b10; 1000a9–25. See further ibid., 983b27ff.; 1071b27–28; 1075b26–27; 1091a3ff.; Aristotle, *Pol.* 1330a12–13; 1329a32–34, as well as Werner Jaeger, *The Theology of the Early Greek Philosophers*, trans. Edward S. Robinson (Oxford: Clarendon Press, 1948; repr. Westport, CT: Greenwood Press, 1980), 5–6. A general survey of medieval and early modern views on the political implications of religious belief appears in Mark Silk, 'Numa Pompilius and the Idea of Civil Religion in the West,' *Journal of the American Academy of Religion* 72 (2004): 863–96.

304 Muhsin Mahdi, ed., *Alfarabi's 'Book of Religion' and Related Texts* (Beirut:

Dār al-Mashriq, 1968), 43; Eng. trans. Oliver Leaman, *An Introduction to Classical Islamic Philosophy* (Cambridge: Cambridge University Press, 2nd ed. 2002), 169.

305 *Averroes' Tahafut al-tahafut (The Incoherence of the Incoherence)*, 360. See also the discussion in Emilio Tornero, 'La función sociopolítica de la religión según Averroes,' *Anales del Seminario de Historia de la Filosofía* 4 (1984): 75–82.

306 Aristotle, *Pol.* 1314b38–1315a4; 1322b18–22;1328b11–13. See further Susan M. Babbitt, '*Praeter Politicos Principatus Ponendum*: Priests as Magistrates and Citizens in Medieval Texts Using Aristotle's *Politics*,' in *Popes, Teachers and Canon Law in the Middle Ages*, ed. James Ross Sweeney and Stanley Chodorow (Ithaca, NY: Cornell University Press, 1989), 145–59, at 146–8; Jeannine Quillet, 'L'organisation de la société humaine selon le Defensor pacis de Marsile de Padoue,' in *Beiträge zum Berufsbewußtsein des mittelalterlichen Menschen*, ed. Paul Wilpert (Berlin: W. de Gruyter, 1964), 185–203, at 188.

307 *DP* I.v.12.

308 *DP* I.v.13.

309 For further discussion, see Christiane Sourvinou-Inwood, 'Further Aspects of *Polis* Religion,' in *Oxford Readings in Greek Religion*, ed. Richard Buxton (Oxford: Oxford University Press, 2000), 38–55; eadem, 'What Is *Polis* Religion?' in *The Greek City: From Homer to Alexander*, ed. Oswyn Murray and Simon Price (Oxford: Clarendon Press, 1990), 295–322 – repr. in *Oxford Readings in Greek Religion*, 13–37; Robert Parker, *Athenian Religion: A History* (Oxford: Clarendon Press, 1996).

310 Aristotle, *Pol.* 1329a28–34; 1329a14–16. Consider also the remarks by Mary P. Nichols, *Citizens and Statesmen: A Study of Aristotle's Politics* (Savage, MD: Rowman & Littlefield Publishers, 1992), 147–8.

311 *DP* I.v.1; Aristotle, *Pol.* 1328b2–23.

312 Brett, *The Defender of the Peace*, 76; Gewirth, *Marsilius of Padua and Medieval Political Philosophy*, 180, 198–9; Guggenheim, 'Marsilius von Padua und die Staatslehre des Aristoteles,' 355. Consider also Blythe, *Ideal Government and the Mixed Constitution*, 18.

313 See *A Greek-English Lexicon*, ed. Henry George Liddell and Robert Scott, s.v. *τίμημα*, as well as Plato, *Politeia*, 550C–D; Aristotle, *Pol.* 1278a15–24; 1294b3–6.

314 Aristotle, *Pol.* 1328b16–23; 1329a15–27; 1329a35–39. See also Gewirth, *Marsilius of Padua and Medieval Political Philosophy*, 192.

315 *DP* II.xxx.4.

316 On Plato's, Aristotle's, and Xenophon's ideas on manual labour, see Xenophon, *Oeconomicus: A Social and Historical Commentary*, trans. Sarah B. Pomeroy (Oxford: Clarendon Press, 1994), 235–6; Richard Kraut, *Socrates and the State* (Princeton, NJ: Princeton University Press, 1984), 200. Compare Aristotle, *Pol.* 1294a37–b1, 1297a17ff., 1298b18–19. For a useful discussion of the numbers of Athenian citizens attending the *ecclesia*, see Mogens H. Hansen, 'How Many Athenians Attended the *Ecclesia*?' *Greek, Roman and Byzantine Studies* 17 (1976): 115–34 – repr. in idem, *The Athenian Ecclesia: A Collection of Articles 1976–1983* (Copenhagen: Museum Tusculanum Press, 1983), 1–20 (addenda 21–3). Aristotle regards representation as a form of oligarchy. See Aristotle, *Pol.* 1298a40–b2, as well as Jakob A.O. Larsen, *Representative Government in Greek and Roman History* (Berkeley, CA: University of California Press, 1955), 18–19; idem, 'Aristotle on the Electors of Mantinea and Representative Government,' *Classical Philology* 45 (1950): 180–3.

317 E.g. Plato, *Laws* 846D.

318 Aristotle, *Pol.* 1278a7ff.

319 Aristotle, *Pol.* 1277a37–1277b3; 1278a11–13; *Eth. Nic.* 1095b20–21; 1260a36–1260b2; *Rh.* 1367a28–32.

320 Aristotle, *Pol.* 1342a21–23; 1337b11–15; 1328b34–1329a2. On this, see also Jason L.A. West, 'Distorted Souls: The Role of Banausics in Aristotle's *Politics*,' *Polis* 13 (1994): 77–95.

321 Scholarly treatments of Aristotle's ideas on leisure include Paul Demont, 'Le loisir (*skholē*) dans la *Politique* d'Aristote,' in *Aristote politique: Etudes sur la Politique d'Aristote*, ed. Pierre Aubenque and Alonso Tordesillas (Paris: Presses Universitaires de France, 1993), 209–30; Lucio Bertelli, 'La *scholé* aristotelica tra norma e prassi empirica,' in *Atti del Colloquio su poetica e politica fra Platone e Aristotele* (Rome: Edizioni dell'Ateneo, 1988), 97–129; Elisabeth C. Welskopf, *Probleme der Musse im alten Hellas* (Berlin: Rütten & Loening, 1962), 209–77; Eino Mikkola, '"Schole" bei Aristoteles,' *Arctos* n.s. 2 (1958): 68–87; Friedrich Solmsen, 'Leisure and Play in Aristotle's Ideal State,' *Rheinisches Museum für Philologie* 107 (1964): 193–220 – repr. in idem, *Kleine Schriften* (Hildesheim: G. Olms, 1968), 2: 1–28; John L. Stocks, 'ΣΧΟΛΗ,' *The Classical Quarterly* 30 (1936): 177–87.

322 Aristotle, *Pol.* 1275a22–23. See further 1283b42–1284a1; 1275a21; 1275b19–20; 1277b15–16 1332b26–7; 1333a1–2.

323 Aristotle, *Pol.* 1275a23–26.

324 Aristotle, *Pol.* 1275a33–35.

325 Aristotle, *Pol.* 1275b18–20.

326 'Civem autem dico, secundum Aristotelem book III *Politice*, chapters 1, 3 et 7, eum qui participat in communitate civili, principatu aut consiliativo vel iudicativo secundum gradum suum.' *DP* I.viii.3.

327 *DP* I.xii.4.

328 *DP* I.v.1. See also Gewirth, *Marsilius of Padua and Medieval Political Philosophy*, 176.

329 *Statuti del comune di Padova dal secolo XII all'anno 1285*, ed. Andrea Gloria (Padua: F. Sacchetto, 1873) [hereafter *Statuti (1873)*], no. 412.II (133); *Statuti del Comune di Padova*, trans. Guido Beltrame, Guerrino Citton and Daniela Mazzon (Cittadella: Biblos, 2000) [hereafter *Statuti (2000)*], 628–45; Hyde, *Padua in the Age of Dante*, 238.

330 'Aliquis qui non sit civis nacione Padue vel Paduani districtus ipse, vel pater eius, vel mater, et continus (*continuus*) habitator civitatis Padue et suburbiorum, et non solverit dacyam ad minus pro libris vigintiquinque comuni, et aliquis qui sit clericus vel habeat partem in aliqua prebenda, non possit venire ad brevia offi cialium. Et pro qualibet dacya non possit venire nisi unus ad brevia offi cialium. Nec aliquis qui non habeat annos decem et octo. Et si quis venerit acceptum brevia officialium contra formam statutorum, solvat pro banno solidos centum comuni, et electio eius non valeat. Cuius banni medietas sit comunis et altera accusantis.' *Statuti (1873)*, no. 248 (85); *Statuti (2000)*, 114–15. 'Si quis receperit officium gastaldie pro aliqua fratalia, de aliqua alia fratalia gastaldio esse non possit. Et nisi solverit daciam pro libris vigintiquinque, non possit aliquis esse gastaldio alicuius fratalie, et nisi sit nacione et origine Paduanus.' *Statuti (1873)*, no. 403 (130); *Statuti (2000)*, 167; 'Ad quorum ancianorum electionem non veniant naute, ortolani, terrarum laboratores, bovarii, artifi ces vel laboratores artis mecanice, familea alicuius, piscatores, ystriones qui per se non habitent, massariciam non teneant aut vestes recipiant ab aliquo novas vel veteres aut pannum pro vestibus, minores annis XVIII qui non sint in dacia pro libris C, et qui non sint origine Paduani. Et qui contra predictos modos et formam venerit ad electionem ancianorum condempnetur in libris XXV pro quolibet et qualibet vice. Et quilibet possit accusare et habeat medietatem banni. Quas penas potestas teneatur exigere et infra triduum a die electionis in antea de his solempniter examinare et inquirere. Que si non fecerit perdat de suo salario libras C. et de his debeat syndicari.' *Statuti (1873)*, no. 412.II (133); *Statuti (2000)*, 171. See also Hagen Keller, 'Wahlformen und Gemeinschaftsverständnis in den italienischen Stadtkommunen (12./14. Jahrhundert),' in *Wahlen und Wählen im Mittelalter*, ed. Reinhard Schneider and Herbert Zimmermann (Sigmaringen: J. Thorbecke, 1990), 345–74, at 340–9; Hyde, *Padua in the Age of Dante*, 216–17; Quillet, *La philosophie politique*, 23. General surveys

of citizenship in the late medieval Italian city states include: Pietro Costa, *Civitas: storia della cittadinanza in Europa*, vol. 1: *Dalla civiltà comunale al Settecento* (Rome: Laterza, 1999); Diego Quaglioni, 'The Legal Definition of Citizenship in the Late Middle Ages,' in *City States in Classical Antiquity and Medieval Italy*, ed. Anthony Molho et al. (Ann Arbor, MI: University of Michigan Press, 1991), 155–67; Hagen Keller, '"Kommune": Städtische Selbstregierung und mittelalterliche "Volksherrschaft" im Spiegel italienischer Wahlverfahren des 12.–14. Jahrhunderts,' in *Person und Gemeinschaft im Mittelalter*, ed. Gerd Althoff, Dieter Geuenich, Otto Gerhard Oexle, and Joachim Wollasch (Sigmaringen: J. Thorbecke, 1988), 573–616; Peter Riesenberg, 'Citizenship at Law in Late Medieval Italy,' *Viator* 5 (1974): 333–46; idem, 'Citizenship and Equality in Late Medieval Italy,' *Studia Gratiana* 15 (1972): 425–39; Dina Bizzarri, 'Ricerche sul diritto di *cittadinanza* nella costituzione comunale,' *Studi Senesi* 32 (1916): 19–136 – repr. in eadem, *Studi di storia del diritto italiano*, ed. Federico Patetta and Mario Chiaudano (Turin: S. Lattes, 1937), 62–158.

331 However, it is not clear to what extent the partisans of communal organization saw the Italian city states as the historical realization of classical democracy. For a similar position, see Quentin Skinner, 'The Italian City-Republics,' in *Democracy: The Unfinished Journey, 508 BC to AD 1993*, ed. John Dunn (Oxford: Oxford University Press, 1992), 57–69, at 59.

332 Antony Black, 'The Commune in Political Theory in the Late Middle Ages,' in *Theorien kommunaler Ordnung in Europa*, ed. Peter Blickle (Munich: Oldenbourg, 1996), 99–112, at 107 – repr. in idem, *Church, State and Community*, no. XIII; idem, *Guilds and Civil Society in European Political Thought from the Twelfth Century to the Present* (Ithaca, NY: Cornell University Press, 1984), 83. On Albert, see also the discussion in Marcella T. McCann, 'Political Ideas of Some Thirteenth Century Commentators on Aristotle's *Ethics* and *Politics*' (MA thesis, University of Wisconsin-Madison, 1962), 51–4. A detailed survey of Renaissance attitudes towards Athenian democracy can be found in Jennifer T. Roberts, *Athens on Trial: The Antidemocratic Tradition in Western Thought* (Princeton, NJ: Princeton University Press, 1994), 119–36.

333 *DP* I.xv.10.

334 *DP* I.xiv.8.

335 *Defensor minor* II.7.

4 Marsilius's Legal Theory

1 *DP* I.x.3. *Ius* and *lex* are used by Marsilius interchangeably. On this, see also Alessandro Ghisalberti, 'Sulla legge naturale in Ockham e in Marsilio,'

in *MPCI*, 303–15, at 310. An extended discussion of Marsilius's notion of law can be found in Di Vona, *I principi del Defensor Pacis*, 59–103.

2 *DP* I.x.3.
3 *DP* I.x.3.
4 *DP* I.x.3; Aristotle, *Metaph.* 995a4.
5 *DP* I.x.3; Aristotle, *Metaph.* 1074b3.
6 *DP* I.x.4.
7 On Marsilius's use of the term *iudex*, see also Di Vona, *I principi del Defensor Pacis*, 135–48.
8 *DP* II.ii.8.
9 *DP* II.ii.8.
10 Aristotle, *Rh.* 1354b6–11.
11 *DP* II.xi.8.
12 The following section on Marsilius's views on the ideal ruler is partly based on my 'Marsilius of Padua on Princely Virtues and Aristotle's Absolute Ruler,' *Archiv für mittelalterliche Philosophie und Kultur* 13 (2007): 212–29.
13 On medieval views on the relationship between the ruler and the law, see Kenneth Pennington, *The Prince and the Law, 1200–1600: Sovereignty and Rights in the Western Legal Tradition* (Berkeley, CA: University of California Press, 1993); Pietro Costa, *Iurisdictio. Semantica del potere politico nella pubblicistica medievale, 1100–1433* (Milan: A. Giuffrè, 1969; repr. 2002); Dieter Wyduckel, *Princeps legibus solutus: Eine Untersuchung zur frühmodernen Rechts- und Staatslehre* (Berlin: Duncker & Humblot, 1979); Fritz Kern, 'Recht und Verfassung im Mittelalter,' *Historische Zeitschrift* 120 (1919): 1–79 – repr. as *Recht und Verfassung im Mittelalter* (Tübingen: Wissenschaftliche Buchgesellschaft, 1952; repr. 1992).
14 *DP* I.iv.4.
15 *DP* I.xiv.9.
16 *DP* II.viii.6; *Eth. Nic.* 1132a21–22: The judge ought to be the 'animate justice.' See also *Defensor pacis* I.iv.4; I.xviii.2. On ancient and medieval variants of the *lex animata* concept, see Laurent Mayali, '*Lex animata*. Rationalisation du pouvoir politique et science juridique. (XIIème–XIVème siècles),' in *Renaissance du pouvoir législatif et genèse de l'État*, ed. André Gouron and Albert Rigaudière (Montpellier: Société d'Histoire du Droit et des Institutions des Anciens Pays de Droit Écrit, 1988), 131–64; Gerhard J. D. Aalders, 'ΝΟΜΟΣ ΕΜΨΥΧΟΣ,' in *Politeia und Res Publica*, 315–29; Artur Steinwerter, 'ΝΟΜΟΣ ΕΜΨΥΧΟΣ: Zur Geschichte einer politischen Theorie,' *Abhandlungen der Akademie Wien, phil.-hist. Klasse* 83 (1936): 250–68.
17 *DP* I.iv.4, I.viii.6. See also ibid., I.xviii.1.

18 *DP* I.x.4; Aristotle, *Eth. Nic.* 1180a21–22. For further discussion, see also Kay Waechter, 'Der Gesetzesbegriff bei Marsilius von Padua: Positivismus mit naturgarantierter Rückversicherung,' in *Transformation des Gesetzesbegriffs im Übergang zur Moderne? Von Thomas von Aquin zu Francisco Suárez*, ed. Manfred Walther et al. (Stuttgart: F. Steiner, 2008), 93–102; Miethke, 'Marsilius von Padua. Die politische Philosophie eines lateinischen Aristotelikers,' 58–9. Aristotle's views on the coercive aspects of the law are treated in greater detail in Albrecht Dihle, 'Der Begriff des Nomos in der griechischen Philosophie,' in *Nomos und Gesetz: Ursprünge und Wirkungen des griechischen Gesetzesdenkens*, ed. Okko Behrends and Wolfgang Sellert (Göttingen: Vandenhoeck & Ruprecht, 1995), 117–34, esp. 126–7.

19 See also Jürgen Miethke, 'Die Frage der Legitimität rechtlicher Normierung in der politischen Theorie des 14. Jahrhunderts,' in *Die Begründung des Rechts als historisches Problem*, ed. Dietmar Willoweit (Munich: R. Oldenbourg, 2000), 171–202, esp. 194–5.

20 *DP* I.x.6.

21 *DP* I.x.5.

22 *DP* I.xii.6.

23 Aristotle, *Rh.* 1373b2–9; 1374a20ff. On the ancient concept of the unwritten law, see Francesco Flumene, *La 'legge non scritta' nella storia e nella dottrina etico-giuridica della Grecia classica* (Sassari: Stamperia de la L.I.S, 1925); Rudolf Hirzel, *Agraphos nomos* (Leipzig: B.G. Teubner, 1900; repr. Hildesheim: Gerstenberg, 1977). Martin Ostwald, 'Was There a Concept *agraphos nomos* in Classical Greece?' in *Exegesis and Argument: Studies in Greek Philosophy Presented to Gregory Vlastos*, ed. by Edward N. Lee, Alexander P.D. Mourelatos and Richard M. Rorty (New York: Humanities Press, 1973), 70–104, is also germane.

24 Aristotle, *Rh.* 1375b5–8. Aristotle concurs with Plato and the Stoics that the genuinely virtuous man ought to orientate his conduct toward the unwritten laws. On this see Erwin R. Goodenough, 'The Political Philosophy of Hellenistic Kingship,' *Yale Classical Studies* 1 (1928): 55–102, at 62. Consider also Plato, *Laws*, 793.

25 Aristotle, *Pol.* 1319b40–1320a2. See further ibid., 1310a14–18; 1337a14–17.

26 *DP* I.iii.4.

27 Aristotle, *Eth. Nic.* 1130b31–33. For further discussion, see David Keyt, 'Aristotle's Theory of Distributive Justice,' in *A Companion to Aristotle's Politics*, 238–78. On Aristotle's theory of justice, see Max Salomon, *Der Begriff der Gerechtigkeit bei Aristoteles: nebst einem Anhang über den Begriff des Tauschgeschäfts* (Leiden: A.W. Sijthoff, 1937); Walter Siegfried, *Der Rechtsgedanke bei Aristoteles* (Zurich: Schulthess, 1947); Peter Trude, *Der Begriff der*

Gerechtigkeit in der aristotelischen Rechts– und Staatsphilosophie (Berlin: W. de Gruyter, 1955).

28 Aristotle, *Eth. Nic.* 1131a15ff.

29 Aristotle, *Eth. Nic.* 1131a22–24.

30 See also Rudolf Hirzel, *Themis, Dike und Verwandtes: Ein Beitrag zur Geschichte der Rechtsidee bei den Griechen* (Leipzig: S. Hirzel, 1907 – repr. Hildesheim: Olms, 1966), 162–3.

31 Aristotle, *Eth. Nic.* 1131a1ff.

32 Aristotle, *Eth. Nic.* 1131b33–1132a19.

33 Aristotle, *Eth. Nic.* 1152b32–33; 1154a29–31; 1104b16–18; 1220a34–37.

34 *Eth. Nic.* 1180a5–9; 1179b10; 1113b21.

35 Aristotle, *Eth. Nic.* 1155a22ff. On Aristotle's views on the civic value of friendship, see, e.g., Anthony W. Price, 'Friendship and Politics,' in *The Legacy of Aristotle's Political Thought*, ed. Carlos Steel (Brussels: Brussel Palais der Academiën, 1999), 101–20; idem, *Love and Friendship in Plato and Aristotle* (Oxford/New York: Clarendon Press/Oxford University Press, 1989), ch. 'The City,' 179–205; John M. Cooper, 'Political Animals and Civic Friendship,' in *Aristoteles' 'Politik,'* ed. Günther Patzig (Göttingen: Vandenhoeck & Ruprecht, 1990), 220–41 – repr. in *Aristotle's Politics: Critical Essays*, ed. Richard Kraut and Steven Skultety (Lanham, MD: Rowman & Littlefield, 2005), 65–89; idem, 'Aristotle on the Forms of Friendship,' *Review of Metaphysics* 30 (1976/77): 619–48. See, in general, also Jean-Claude Fraisse, *Philia: La notion d'amitié dans la philosophie antique: Essai sur un problème perdu et retrouvé* (Paris: J. Vrin, 1974) (on Aristotle, 189–286).

36 *DP* II.xii.12.

37 Aristotle, *Pol.* 1282b8–13.

38 See also Gewirth, *Marsilius of Padua and Medieval Political Philosophy*, 106; idem, *Marsilius of Padua, The Defender of Peace*, lxxxiv; Brett, *The Defender of the Peace*, 26.

39 *DP* II.viii.5.

40 *DP* I.xv.6; I.iv.4; II.xii.12.

41 *DP* I.v.7; I.xvi.8; I.xix.12; II.viii.7.

42 *DP* I.v.7. See also ibid., II.ix.13.

43 *DP* I.xv.11.

44 *DP* I.xv.11.

45 *DP* II.viii.7.

46 *DP* I.xi.1.

47 *DP* I.xi.1.

48 Aristotle, *Rh.* book I.3.

49 *Rh.* 1354b10–11. For further discussion, see Friederike Rese, *Praxis und*

Logos bei Aristoteles: Handlung, Vernunft und Rede in Nikomachischer Ethik, Rhetorik und Politik (Tübingen: Mohr Siebeck, 2003), 282, 304, 308–9; Markus H. Wörner, *Das Ethische in der Rhetorik des Aristoteles* (Freiburg i.Br. and Munich: K. Alber, 1990), 110–11.

50 Aristotle, *Pol.* 1284a3–17; 1288a15–19. For further discussion on Aristotle's notion of absolute kingship (*pamvasileia*), see Pierre Carlier, 'La notion de *pambasileia* dans la pensée politique d'Aristote,' in *Aristote et Athènes*, ed. Marcel Piérart (Fribourg: Séminaire d'histoire ancienne de l'Université de Fribourg, 1993), 103–18; Richard G. Mulgan, 'A Note on Aristotle's Absolute Ruler,' *Phronesis* 19 (1974): 66–9; idem, 'Aristotle and Absolute Rule.' *Antichthon* 8 (1974): 21–8.

51 *DP* I.xi.1.

52 *DP* I.xi.1. See Aristotle, *Pol.* 1286a18–20.

53 *DP* I.xi.1

54 *DP* I.xi.3; Aristotle, *Metaph.* 993b2–4. On Marsilius's views on the nexus between *experiencia* and the evolution of social life, see *DP* I.iii.5. Marsilius's ideas on history are discussed in David R. Carr, 'Marsilius of Padua: The Use and Image of History in *Defensor pacis*,' in *Altro Polo: A Volume of Italian Renaissance Studies*, ed. Conal Condren and Roslyn Pesman Cooper (Sydney: Frederick May Foundation for Italian Studies, University of Sydney, 1982), 13–28.

55 Aristotle, *Pol.* 1282b14ff., 1288b10ff., 1331b37ff., 1341b7ff.; *Metaphysics* 981a1; *Rhetoric* 1362b25.

56 *DP* I.xi.3.

57 *DP* I.xi.3.

58 Aristotle, *Pol.* 1269a18–25; 1287a34–35.

59 Aristotle, *Eth. Nic.* 1098a24.

60 On ancient theories of progress, see, e.g., Eric R. Dodds, *The Ancient Concept of Progress and Other Essays on Greek Literature and Belief* (Oxford: Clarendon Press, 1973); idem, s.v. 'Progress in Classical Antiquity,' in *Dictionary of the History of Ideas: Studies of Selected Pivotal Ideas*, ed. Philip P. Wiener (New York: Charles Scribner's Sons, 1973), 3: 623–33; Walter Burkert, 'Impact and Limits of the Idea of Progress in Antiquity,' in *The Idea of Progress*, ed. Arnold Burgen et al. (Berlin and New York: W. de Gruyter, 1997), 19–46 (on Aristotle 30–4); Robert A. Nisbet, *History of the Idea of Progress* (New York: Basic Books, 1980; repr. New Brunswick, NJ: Transaction Pub., 1994); Ludwig Edelstein, *The Idea of Progress in Classical Antiquity* (Baltimore, MD: Johns Hopkins Press, 1967); idem, 'The Greco-Roman Concept of Scientific Progress,' in *ITHACA: Actes du Xème Congrès International d'Histoire des Sciences* (Paris: Hermann, 1965), 47–59 – repr. in

Selected Philosophical Papers by Ludwig Edelstein, ed. Leonardo Tarán (New York and London: Garland Publishing, 1987), no. 2. Consider also Woldemar Uxkull-Gyllenband, *Griechische Kultur-Entstehungslehren* (Berlin: Simion, 1924); John B. Bury, *The Idea of Progress: An Inquiry into Its Origin and Growth* (New York: Macmillan Company, 1932), 11. On the ancient inventor concept, see the following articles in the *Reallexikon für Antike und Christentum*: Karl Jax and Klaus Thraede, 'Erfinder I (historisch)' (5: 1179–91); Klaus Thraede, 'Erfinder II (geistesgeschichtlich)' (5: 1191–1278); idem, 'Fortschritt' (8: 141–82); and Adolf Kleingünther, *ΠΡΩΤΟΣ ΕΥΡΕΤΗΣ: Untersuchungen zur Geschichte einer Fragestellung* (Leipzig: Dieterich, 1933). Aristotle's ideas on the linkage between prudence and experience are discussed in Ralf Elm, *Klugheit und Erfahrung bei Aristoteles* (Paderborn: F. Schöningh, 1996).

61 *DP* I.xiii.6.

62 *DP* I.xiii.7.

63 *DP* I.xiii.7.

64 *DP* I.xiii.7.

65 *DP* I.xi.3. Compare *Aristotelis opera cum Averrois commentariis*, vol. 8: *Aristotelis Metaphysicorum libri XIIII cum Averrois Cordubensis in eosdem commentariis, et epitome, Theophrasti Metaphysicorum Liber* (= editio Juntina secunda) (Venice, 1562; repr. Frankfurt a. M.: Minerva, 1962), fol. 28v.

66 Averroes, *On the Harmony of Religion and Philosophy*, a translation, with introduction and notes, of Ibn Rushd's *Kitāb faṣl al-maqāl*, with its appendix (*Ḍamīma*) and an extract from *Kitāb al-kashf 'an manāhij al-adilla* by George F. Hourani (London: Luzac, 1967), 47–8, 88. For further references, see Vasileios Syros, 'The Principle of the Sovereignty of the Multitude in the Works of Marsilius of Padua, Peter of Auvergne and Some Other Aristotelian Commentators,' in *The World of Marsilius of Padua*, 227–48, at 245–7.

67 Joachim Ritter, s.v. 'Fortschritt,' in *Historisches Wörterbuch der Philosophie*, ed. Joachim Ritter (Basel and Stuttgart: Schwabe, 1972), 2: 1032–59, esp. 1035–7; and, in general, Giorgos Steiris, 'The Formation of the Notion of Progress in the Philosophy of History from Augustine to Bodin,' *Epistēmonikē Epetēris tēs Philosophikēs Scholēs tou Panepistēmiou Athēnōn* 26 (2006): 195–212 [in Greek]; Andrew G. Molland, 'Medieval Ideas of Scientific Progress,' *Journal of the History of Ideas* 39 (1978): 561–77; Johannes Spörl, 'Das Alte und das Neue im Mittelalter. Studien zum Problem des mittelalterlichen Fortschrittsbewußtseins,' *Historisches Jahrbuch* 50 (1930): 297–341, 498–524; Walter Freund, *Modernus und andere Zeitbegriffe des Mittelalters* (Cologne and Graz: Böhlau, 1957); Marie-Dominique Chenu, *La théologie au douzième siècle* (Paris: J. Vrin, 1957), 386–92; idem, 'Notes de lex-

icographie philosophique médiévale. Antiqui, moderni,' *Revue des sciences philosophiques et théologiques* 17 (1928): 82–94 – repr. in idem, *Studi di lessicografia filosofica medievale*, ed. Giacinta Spinosa (Florence: L.S. Olschki, 2001), 69–81.

68 For a comparative discussion of Marsilius's and Abravanel's political ideas, see Vasileios Syros, 'Marsilius of Padua and Isaac Abravanel on Kingship: The Medieval Precedents of Modern Republicanism Revisited,' *Medieval Encounters* (forthcoming). See also in general Abraham Melamed, 'Isaac Abravanel and Aristotle's *Politics*: A Drama of Errors,' *Jewish Political Studies Review* 5 (1993): 55–75; idem, 'Jethro's Advice in Medieval and Early Modern Jewish and Christian Political Thought,' *Jewish Political Studies Review* 2 (1990): 3–41.

69 'Cum igitur lex sit oculus ex multis oculis, id est comprehensio examinata ex multis comprehensoribus ad errorem evitandum circa civilia iudicia et recte iudicandum, tucius est ea ferri secundum legem, quam secundum iudicantis arbitrium' (*DP* I.xi.3). See also Aristotle, *Pol.* 1283b38; 1286a22.

70 *DP* I.xi.3; Aristotle, *Pol.* 1287b26–29.

71 Aristotle, *Pol.* 1287b30–35.

72 See also Barker, *The Political Thought of Plato and Aristotle*, 514; Gewirth, *Marsilius of Padua and Medieval Political Philosophy*, 173–74; idem, *Marsilius of Padua, The Defender of Peace*, lxxxvi–lxxxvii; and, in general, Michael Gagarin, *Early Greek Law* (Berkeley, CA: University of California Press, 1986); George P. Nakos, *Forms of Ancient Greek Legislation* (Thessaloniki: University Studio Press, 1986) [in Greek].

73 Aristotle, *Pol.* 1273b27–1274b26; *Eth. Nic.* 1102a7–12. On Solon, see Josine H. Blok and André P.M.H. Lardinois, eds., *Solon of Athens: New Historical and Philological Approaches* (Leiden and Boston: Brill, 2006), 276–89; Eberhard Ruschenbusch, 'Πάτριος πολιτεία. Theseus, Drakon, Solon und Kleisthenes in Publizistik und Geschichtsschreibung des 5. und 4. Jahrhunderts v. Chr.,' *Historia* 7 (1958): 398–424; John J. Keaney, 'Aristotle's *Politics* 2.12 1274a22b–a28,' *American Journal of Ancient History* 6 (1981): 97–100. On Solon and the beginnings of Athenian democracy, see Claude Mossé, 'Comment s'élabore un mythe politique: Solon, "Père fondateur" de la démocratie athénienne,' *Annales* 34 (1979): 425–37, and, in general, Blok and Lardinois, eds., *Solon of Athens: New Historical and Philological Approaches*.

74 Mainly in Book 10. Consider also Aristotle, *Pol.* 1286a21–24; 1333a37.

75 Ann K.S. Lambton, *State and Government in Medieval Islam: An Introduction to the Study of Islamic Political Theory: The Jurists* (Oxford: Oxford University Press, 1985; repr. 1991), 71–3, 316–25.

76 For further references and discussion, see Kummerer, *Der Fürst als Gesetzgeber*, 49–52; Lambertini, 'Zur Frage der Rolle des Averroes.'

77 Kummerer, *Der Fürst als Gesetzgeber*, 63–4. See, in general, also Pedro Roche Arnas, 'El gobernante y el gobierno recto en la *Exposición de la República de Platón* de Averroes,' in *Averroes y los averroísmos*, 241–9; Erwin I.J. Rosenthal, 'The Place of Politics in the Philosophy of Ibn Rushd,' *Bulletin of the School of Oriental and African Studies* 15 (1953): 246–78 – repr. in idem, *Studia Semitica*, vol. 2: *Islamic Themes*, 60–92.

78 *DP* I.xi.5. Compare Aristotle, *Pol.* 1273b21; 1286b2, 1296a7–8, 1296a6–11; 1302a10.

79 Aristotle, *Pol.* 1312b38–1313a5; 'Regnum enim, inquit Aristoteles, ab extrinsecis quidem minime corrumpitur, ex seipso autem plurime corrupciones accidunt. Corrumpitur autem secundum duos modos: uno quidem sedicionem facientibus hiis, qui participant regno; alio autem modo magis tyrampnice temptantibus gubernare, quando exegerint esse domini plurium et preter legem. Non fiunt autem adhuc regna nunc, sed si fi ant monarchie et tyrampnides magis' (*DP* I.xi.5).

80 Compare Aristotle's idea that the less power the ruler has, the longer his rule is likely to last, for he will act in a less despotic or arbitrary manner and, hence, he will be less envied by his subjects (Aristotle, *Pol.* 1313a19–21).

81 'Nos autem dicamus secundum veritatem atque consilium Aristotelis 3o Politice, capitulo 6o, legislatorem seu causam legis effectivam primam et propriam esse populum seu civium universitatem aut eius valenciorem partem, per suam eleccionem seu voluntatem in generali civium congregacione per sermonem expressam precipientem seu determinantem aliquid fieri vel omitti circa civiles actus humanos sub pena vel supplicio temporali: valenciorem inquam partem, considerata quantitate personarum et qualitate in communitate illa super quam lex fertur, sive id fecerit universitas predicta civium aut eius pars valencior per seipsam immediate, sive id alicui vel aliquibus commiserit faciendum, qui legislator simpliciter non sunt nec esse possunt, sed solum ad aliquid et quandoque, ac secundum primi legislatoris auctoritatem' (*DP* I.xii.3).

82 *DP* I.xii.2.

83 For further discussion of the various interpretations of the *valencior pars* concept, see *Marsilio da Padova*, ed. Elvio Ancona and Franco Todescan (Padua: CEDAM, 2007), 57–61.

84 *DP* II.xxii.15.

85 *DP* I.xiii.2.

86 *DP* I.xiii.2.

87 Aristotle, *Pol.* 1296b16–17. Consider also ibid.,1332b30–32.
88 Aristotle, *Pol.* 1307a17–18. See also ibid., 1309b14–18; 1315a35–39.
89 *DP* I.xiii.2.
90 *DP* I.xiii.2.
91 For a similar interpretation, see Gewirth, *Marsilius of Padua and Medieval Political Philosophy*, 185–90; Blythe, *Ideal Government*, 197–8.
92 See also Black, *Guilds and Civil Society in European Political Thought*, 93; Alessandro Passerin d'Entrèves, *The Medieval Contribution to Political Thought, Thomas Aquinas, Marsilius of Padua, Richard Hooker* (Oxford: Oxford University Press, 1939; repr. New York: Humanities Press, 1959), 56–7.
93 Consider also Conal Condren, 'Democracy and the *Defensor pacis*: On the English Language Tradition of Marsilian Interpretation,' *Il Pensiero Politico* 8 (1980): 301–16. For scholarly attempts to portray Marsilius as an apologist for 'democratic' ideas, see, e.g., Mary E. Sullivan, 'Democracy and the *Defensor Pacis* Revisited: Marsiglio of Padua's Democratic Arguments,' *Viator* 41 (2010): 257–69; Gilles Lebreton, 'Le problème de la démocratie dans le *Defensor pacis*. Essai sur la philosophie politique de Marsile de Padoue' (Diss., Université de Paris IV, 1987); Richard Scholz, 'Marsilius von Padua und die Idee der Demokratie,' *Zeitschrift für Politik* 1 (1907): 61–94. See also the discussion in Donato Del Prete, 'Il pensiero politico ed ecclesiologico di Marsilio da Padova,' *Annali di Storia* (Lecce) 1 (1980): 17–124 , esp. 19–68.
94 As in Florence, for example. For further discussion, see Gaetano Salvemini, *Magnati e popolani a Firenze dal 1280 al 1295* (Milan: Feltrinelli, 1966); Marvin B. Becker, 'A Study in Political Failure: The Fiorentine Magnates (1280–1343),' *Medieval Studies* 27 (1965): 246–308 – repr. in *Florentine Essays: Selected Writings of Marvin B. Becker*, ed. James Banker and Carol Lansing (Ann Arbor, MI: University of Michigan Press, 2002), 94–159; Nicolai Rubinstein, *La lotta contro i magnati a Firenze. II – La prima legge sul 'sodamento'* (Florence: L.S. Olschiki, 1939). Consider, in general, Giovanni Tabacco, *The Struggle for Power in Medieval Italy: Structures of Political Rule*, trans. Rosalind Brown Jensen (Cambridge: Cambridge University Press, 1989); Gina Fasoli, 'Ricerche sulla legislazione antimagnatizia nei comuni dell'alta e media Italia,' *Rivista di storia del diritto italiano* 12 (1939): 86–133, 240–309.
95 Marangon, *Ad cognitionem scientiae festinare*, 385; idem, 'Principi di teoria politica nella Marca Trevigiana. Clero e comune a Padova al tempo di Marsilio,' in *MPCI*, 317–36 – repr. in idem, *Ad cognitionem scientiae festinare*, 411–30; Witt, '*In the Footsteps of the Ancients*,' 146ff.
96 See, e.g., *Statuti (1873)*, nos. 85, 457–8, 461, 595, 628–45; *Statuti (2000)*, 58,

188–9, 190–1; 237–8, 251–61; Maria A. Zorzi, 'L'ordinamento Comunale Padovano nella seconda metà del secolo XIII. – Studio storico con Documenti inediti,' *Miscellanea di Storia Veneta* s. 4, 5 (1931): 1–248, at 48–84; Hyde, *Padua in the Age of Dante*, 217–18, 238–9.

97 *DP* I.x.3.

98 Aristotle, *Pol.* 1318a3–10. See also the discussion in Richard G. Mulgan, 'Aristotle and the Democratic Conception of Freedom,' in *Auckland Classical Essays Presented to E.M. Blaiklock*, ed. Bruce F. Harris (Auckland: Aukland University Press, 1970), 95–111.

99 Aristotle, *Pol.* 1296b17–24. See also James H. Burns, 'Majorities: An Exploration,' *History of Political Thought* 24 (2003): 66–85, at 67–9.

100 Aristotle, *Pol.* 1282a15–16; 1281a40–42. Major studies devoted to Aristotle's doctrine of collective prudence include: Jeremy Waldron, 'The Wisdom of the Multitude: Some Reflections on Book 3, Chapter 11 of Aristotle's *Politics*,' *Political Theory* 23 (1995): 563–84 – repr. in *Aristotle's Politics: Critical Essays*, 145–65; J.T. Bookman, 'The Wisdom of the Many: An Analysis of the Arguments of Book III and IV of Aristotle's *Politics*,' *History of Political Thought* 13 (1992): 1–12; Egon Braun, 'Die Summierungstheorie des Aristoteles,' *Jahreshefte des österreichischen archeologischen Instituts* 44 (1959): 157–84 – repr. in *Schriften zu den Politika des Aristoteles*, 396–423; idem, *Das dritte Buch der aristotelischen Politik: Interpretation* (Vienna: Böhlaus Nachf., Kommissionsverlag der Österreichischen Akademie der Wissenschaften, 1965); Tommaso Mirabella, *Il concetto di sovranità nella Politica di Aristotele* (Palermo: Libreria Agate, 1941); Antoine Leandri, 'L'aporie de la souveraineté,' in *Aristote politique*, 315–29; Richard S. Pianka, 'The Sovereignty of the plêthos in Aristotle's *Politics*,' in *Aristotelian Political Philosophy*, ed. Konstantinos I. Boudouris (Athens: International Center for Greek Philosophy and Culture, 1995), 2: 116–24; Ioannes S. Tulumakos, *Die theoretische Begründung der Demokratie in der klassischen Zeit Griechenlands: die demokratische Argumentation in der Politik des Aristoteles* (Athens: Papazisis, 1985); Hanns-Dieter Voigtländer, *Der Philosoph und die Vielen: die Bedeutung des Gegensatzes der unphilosophischen Menge zu den Philosophen (und das Problem des argumentum e consensu omnium) im philosophischen Denken der Griechen bis auf Aristoteles* (Wiesbaden: Steiner, 1980), esp. 573–9.

101 Aristotle, *Pol.* 1281b4–7. For a similar notion of the city as the replica of a large man, see Plato, *Politeia* 368D–369A; 434D–435D; 462C; 543D.

102 Aristotle, *Pol.* 1281b7–10.

103 Aristotle, *Rh.* 1354a6–15.

104 Aristotle, *Rh.* 1354b23–31.

105 Aristotle, *Pol.* 1286a32–b1.

106 On Aristotle's use of the *plēthos* concept, see Édith Parmentier-Morin, 'Recherches sur le vocabulaire politique d'Aristote: demos et plethos dans la Constitution d'Athènes et dans le livre III de la Politique,' *Ktèma* 29 (2004): 95–108.

107 Aristotle, *Pol.* 1273b35–1274a7.

108 Aristotle, *Pol.* 1282a14–17.

109 Aristotle, *Pol.* 1281b15–21.

110 Aristotle, *Pol.* 1281b21–24; 1286a36–37.

111 Aristotle, *Pol.* 1254b16–23.

112 Aristotle, *Eth. Nic.* 1134b18–24; 1137b28ff.; 1141b27–28; 1151b15–16.

113 Aristotle, *Eth. Nic.* 1137b13.

114 Aristotle, *Pol.* 1292a18–37. Compare *Eth. Nic.* 1152a20–23. See also Martin Ostwald, *From Popular Sovereignty to the Sovereignty of Law: Law, Society, and Politics in Fifth-Century Athens* (Berkeley, CA: University of California Press, 1986); Graham Maddox, 'Constitution,' in *Political Innovation and Conceptual Change*, ed. Terence Ball, James Farr and Russell L. Hanson (Cambridge: Cambridge University Press, 1989), 50–67, at 53–4; Barry S. Strauss, 'On Aristotle's Critique of Athenian Democracy,' in *Essays on the Foundations of Aristotelian Political Science*, ed. Carnes Lord and David K. O'Connor (Berkeley, CA: University of California Press, 1991), 212–33; David Cohen, 'The Rule of Law and Democratic Ideology in Classical Athens,' in *Die athenische Demokratie im 4. Jahrhundert v. Chr.: Vollendung oder Verfall einer Verfašungsform?*, ed. Walter Eder (Stuttgart: F. Steiner, 1995), 227–47; Mogens H. Hansen, '*Nomos* and *Psephisma* in Fourth-Century Athens,' *Greek, Roman and Byzantine Studies* 19 (1978): 315–30 – repr. in idem, *The Athenian Ecclesia: A Collection of Articles 1976–1983* (Copenhagen: Museum Tusculanum Press, 1983), 161–76 (addenda 177); Friedemann Quaß, *Nomos und Psephisma: Untersuchung zum griechischen Staatsrecht* (Munich: Beck, 1971); Arnold H.M. Jones, *Athenian Democracy* (Baltimore, MD: Johns Hopkins University Press, 1957), 41–72.

115 *DP* I.xiii.3.

116 *DP* I.xii.3.

117 *Discorsi*, I.LVIII,22. On this point, see also Domenico Taranto, *Le virtù della politica: Civismo e prudenza tra Machiavelli e gli antichi* (Naples: Bibliopolis, 2003), 113–14.

118 See also Annabel Brett, 'Issues in Translating the *Defensor Pacis*,' in *The World of Marsilius of Padua*, 91–108, at 105; Marsilius of Padua, *Defensor pacis*, trans. Gewirth, lxxxviii–lxxxix; Andrew Lockyer, 'Aristotle: *The Politics*,' in *A Guide to the Political Classics: Plato to Rousseau*, ed. Murray

Forsyth and Maurice Keens-Soper (Oxford: Oxford University Press, 1988), 46; Richard G. Mulgan, 'Aristotle's Sovereign,' *Political Studies* 18 (1970): 518–22; idem, *Aristotle's Political Theory: An Introduction for Students of Political Theory* (Oxford: Clarendon Press, 1977), 59–60; and, in general, *Donatella Marocco Stuardi, 'Sovrano* e *governo* nel pensiero di *Marsilio* da Padova,' in *Studi politici in onore di Luigi Firpo*, ed. Silvia Rota Ghibaudi and Franco Barcia (Milan: Franco Angeli, 1990), 1: 15–48. On medieval and Renaissance ideas on sovereignty, see now Robert S. Sturges, ed., *Law and Sovereignty in the Middle Ages and the Renaissance* (Turnhout: Brepols, 2011).

119 *DP* I.xii.5 and xiii.2. On Marsilius's use of the part-whole principle, consult Luigi Olivieri, 'Il tutto e la parte nel *Defensor pacis* di Marsilio da Padova' *Rivista critica di storia della filosofia* 37 (1982): 65–74; Di Vona, *I principi del Defensor Pacis*, ch. 'Il tutto e la parte,' 273–340; Gewirth, *Marsilius of Padua and Medieval Political Philosophy*, 212–19.

120 *DP* I.xiii.4.

121 *DP* I.xiii.3. See also ibid., I.xi.3.

122 *DP* I.xiii.4; Aristotle, *Pol.* 1282a38–41.

123 *DP* I.xiii.4.

124 *DP* I.xiii.1, 3; Aristotle, *Pol.* 1282a15ff.

125 *DP* I.xiii.3. See also Antonio Toscano, *Marsilio da Padova e Niccolò Machiavelli* (Ravenna: Longo, 1981), 98–9; and, in general, Conal Condren, 'Marsilius and Machiavelli,' in *Comparing Political Thinkers*, ed. Ross Fitzgerald (Sydney: Pergamon Press, 1980), 94–115.

126 *DP* I.xiii.2; Aristotle, *Pol.* 1296b14–16.

127 *DP* I.xiii.2.

128 Along with Albert the Great, Peter considers pygmies, for example, to be human beings that are bereft of rational capacities. See Theodor W. Köhler, *Homo animal nobilissimum: Konturen des spezifisch Menschlichen in der naturphilosophischen Aristoteleskommentierung des dreizehnten Jahrhunderts* (Leiden and Boston: Brill, 2008), 420–43; Joseph Koch 'Sind die Pygmäen Menschen? Ein Kapitel aus der philosophischen Anthropologie der mittelalterlichen Scholastik,' *Archiv für Geschichte der Philosophie* 40 (1931): 194–213.

129 On the following, see Syros, 'The Principle of the Sovereignty of the Multitude,' 2315; Dunbabin, 'The Reception and Interpretation of Aristotle's *Politics*,' 726–7, 732–7. See also Peter of Auvergne, 'Commentary and Questions on Book III of Aristotle's Politics (Selections),' in *The Cambridge Translations of Medieval Philosophical Texts*, vol. 2: *Ethics and Political Philosophy*, ed. Arthur S. McGrade, John Kilcullen and Matthew Kempshall

(Cambridge: Cambridge University Press, 2001), 216–56, esp. 249–51. On Peter's political ideas as set out in his *Quaestiones*, see Marco Toste, 'Nobiles, optimi viri, philosophi. The Role of the Philosopher in the Political Community at the Faculty of Arts in Paris in Late Thirteenth Century,' in *Itinéraires de la raison*, ed. José F. Meirinhos (Louvain-La-Neuve: F.I.D.E.M., 2005), 269–308; Roberto Lambertini, 'La monarchia prima della *Monarchia*: Le ragioni del *regnum* nella ricezione medioevale di Aristotele,' in *Pour Dante: Dante et l'Apocalypse; Lectures humanistes de Dante*, ed. Bruno Pichard (Paris: Champion, 2001), 39–75, at 52 and 55–7; Christoph Flüeler, 'Ontologie und Politik: Quod racio principantis et subiecti sumitur ex racione actus et potencie,' *Freiburger Zeitschrift für Philosophie und Theologie* 41 (1994): 445–62; Gianfranco Fioravanti, 'Servi, rustici, barbari: interpretazioni medievali dela *Politica* aristotelica,' *Annali della Scuola Normale Superiore di Pisa, Classe di Lettere e Filosofia* 11 (1981): 399–429; Mario Grignaschi, 'La definition du civis dans la Scholastique,' *Ancien Pays et Assemblées d'Etats* 36 (1966): 71–88; Cranz, 'Aristotelianism in Medieval Political Theory: A Study of the Reception of the Politics,' 153–60, 282–300. For a comparison of Peter of Auvergne's and Thomas Aquinas's political ideas, consult Aldo Vendemiati, 'Le inclinazioni naturali e il bene. Letture parallele della *Politica* di Aristotele da parte di Tommaso d'Aquino e Pietro d'Alvernia,' *Rivista di Filosofia Neo-Scolastica* 89 (1997): 299–316.

130 [John Buridan], *Quaestiones super octo libros politicorum Aristotelis* (Paris, 1513; repr. Frankfurt a. M.: Minerva, 1969), fols. 33v–34r; 40v. On the authorship of the treatise, see Flüeler, *Rezeption und Interpretation der aristotelischen Politica*, 1: 132–68; William J. Courtenay, 'A Note on Nicolaus Girardi de Waudemonte, pseudo-Johannes Buridanus,' *Bulletin de philosophie médiévale* 46 (2004): 163–8. On the content of the *Quaestiones*, see Mario Grignaschi, 'Un commentaire nominaliste de la *Politique* d'Aristote: Jean Buridan,' *Anciens Pays et Assemblées d'Etats* 19 (1960): 125–42.

131 *DP* I.xii.7 and 8.

132 *DP* I.xii.8; xiii.5.

133 *DP* I.xiii.2. See also Gewirth, *Marsilius of Padua and Medieval Political Philosophy*, 56–63, 213–14; idem, *Marsilius of Padua, The Defender of Peace*, 435–8.

134 Laws must be the best laws possible for the specific configuration of the city or the best laws absolutely (Aristotle, *Pol.* 1294a3–9). On the ancient concept of *eunomia*, see Martin Ostwald, *Nomos and the Beginnings of the Athenian Democracy* (Oxford: Clarendon Press, 1969), 62–85; Antony Andrewes, 'Eunomia,' *Classical Quarterly* 32 (1938): 89–102; Victor Ehrenberg,

'Eunomia,' in *Charisteria: Alois Rzach zum achtzigsten Geburstag dargebracht* (Reichenberg: Gebrüder Stiepel, 1930), 16–29 – repr. in idem, *Polis und Imperium: Beiträge zur alten Geschichte*, ed. Karl F. Stroheker and Alexander J. Graham (Zurich: Artemis Verlag, 1965), 139–58; Eng. trans. in idem, *Aspects of the Ancient World: Essays and Reviews* (Oxford: B. Blackwell, 1946), 70–93.

135 *Eth. Nic.* 1152a19–24.

136 *DP* I.xii.6.

137 *DP* I.xii.6.

138 *DP* I.xii.6.

139 *DP* I.xviii.6. Compare Aristotle, *Pol.* 1269a20–22; Aegidius Romanus, *De regimine principum libri III*, 318v–320v.

140 Aristotle, *Pol.* 1307b32–39.

5 Marsilius's Theory of Government

1 *DP* I.viii.3. On Aristotle's *politeuma* concept, see Edmond Lévy, '*Politeia* et *politeuma* chez Aristote,' in *Aristote et Athènes*, ed. Marcel Piérart (Fribourg: Séminaire d'histoire ancienne de l'Université de Fribourg, 1993), 65–90, and, in general, Mogens H. Hansen, 'Polis, politeuma and politeia: A Note on Arist. *Pol.* 1278b6–14,' in *From Political Architecture to Stephanus Byzantius: Sources for the Ancient Greek Polis*, ed. David Whitehead (Wiesbaden: F. Steiner, 1994), 91–8; Walter Ruppel, 'Politeuma. Bedeutungsgeschichte eines staatsrechtlichen Terminus,' *Philologus* 82 (1927): 268–312, 433–54.

2 Aristotle, *Eth. Nic.* 1160a31–36.

3 Aristotle, *Pol.* 1279a17–21.

4 Aristotle, *Pol.* 1307b30–31. See Gewirth, *Marsilius of Padua, The Defender of Peace*, lxxxv.

5 Compare *DP* I.ii.2. Marsilius concurs with Aristotle on the view that constitutional transformation occurs due to the disproportionate growth of a part of the body politic: just as the body is composed of various parts and organs, one of which often grows without its being noticed, so too is the case with the number of poor in the models of democracy and polity (*politeia*) – see Aristotle, *Pol.* 1302b33–36. This idea derives from Aristotle's biology, in which *krasis* is used to denote a symmetry according to the Aristotelian principle that all natural or artificial products rest on a proportional relationship. *Gen. an.*, 767a16–17.

6 *DP* I.viii.2.

7 *DP* I.viii.3.

8 *DP* I.ix.1, 3, 4, 5.
9 *DP* I.ix.4; Aristotle, *Pol.* 1285a15ff., 1285b20ff.
10 Aristotle, *Pol.* 1285a27–28; 1313a14–17.
11 Aristotle, *Pol.* 1285a27–28; 1313a14–17.
12 Aristotle, *Pol.* 1285b2–3. See also the discussion in Frank E. Romer, 'The *Aisymnēteia*: A Problem in Aristotle's Historical Method,' *The American Journal of Philology* 103 (1982): 25–46.
13 Aristotle, *Pol.* 1285b3–19.
14 Tyranny comes into being through the violation of the existing constitution when the traditional rules and mores are changed. For further discussion, see Karen Blomqvist, *The Tyrant in Aristotle's Politics: Theoretical Assumptions and Historical Background* (Stockholm: Almqvist & Wiksell International, 1998); Andreas Kamp, 'Die aristotelische Theorie der Tyrannis,' *Philosophisches Jahrbuch* 92 (1985): 17–34.
15 Gewirth, *Marsilius of Padua and Medieval Political Philosophy*, 240. Marsilius adopts both criteria from Aristotle, but adopts the former not from Aristotle's discussion of constitutional forms but from his account of the five variations and sub-types of royal government.
16 *DP* I.ix.5.
17 *DP* I.viii.2. See also Gewirth, *Marsilius of Padua, The Defender of Peace*, lxxxi.
18 *DP* I.ix.4; Aristotle, *Pol.* 1285a1–1286a7, 1285b20ff.
19 Aristotle notes in the *Politics* that the first type of kingship amounts to a lifelong generalship that can be hereditary or elective (1285a3ff.) and describes Spartan kingship as a hereditary generalship for life (1285b27). He concedes, however, that command of the army for life can be found as an office in all forms of constitution and as such it cannot be counted as a distinct type of kingship (*Pol.* 1286a2ff.). On Mycenaean kingship, see Pedro Barceló, *Basileia, Monarchia, Tyrannis: Untersuchungen zu Entwicklung und Beurteilung von Alleinherrschaft im vorhellenistischen Griechenland* (Stuttgart: F. Steiner Verlag, 1993), 24–35.
20 *DP* I.ix.5.
21 *DP* I.ix.4. The *constabulus* (*Connétable de France*), one of the highest offices of the French monarchy, was the supreme commander of the army. On this, see Salzer, *Ueber die Anfaenge der Signorie in Oberitalien*, 187–222.
22 *DP* I.ix.4.
23 *DP* I.ix.4. On medieval views on oriental despotism, see Patricia Springborg, *Western Republicanism and the Oriental Prince* (Cambridge: Polity Press, 1992), 284–5; and, in general, Franco Venturi, 'Oriental Despotism,' *Journal of the History of Ideas* 24 (1963): 133–42.
24 *De regimine principum* III.xxii (64) and IV.viii (76).

25 Aristotle, *Eth. Nic.* 1144b3–6.
26 Aristotle, *Pol.* 1327b23–29.
27 Siraisi, 'The *Expositio Problematum Aristotelis* of Peter of Abano,' 332–3.
28 *DP* I.ix.4.
29 Aristotle, *Pol.* 1284b4–5.
30 *DP* I.ix.4.
31 Lynn Thorndike, *A History of Magic and Experimental Science*, vols. 3 and 4: *Fourteenth and Fifteenth Centuries* (New York: Macmillan, 1923), 260.
32 Consult the following studies by Graziella Federici Vescovini: 'La place privilégiée de l'astronomie-astrologie dans l'encyclopédie des sciences théoriques de Pierre d'Abano,' in *Knowledge and the Sciences in Medieval Philosophy*, ed. Reijo Työrinoja, Anja I. Lehtinen, and Dagfinn Føllesdal (Helsinki: Yliopistopaino, 1990), 3: 42–51 – repr. in *Historia philosophiae Medii Aevi: Studien zur Geschichte der Philosophie des Mittelalters*, ed. Burkhard Mojsisch and Olaf Pluta (Amsterdam and Philadelphia, PA: B.R. Grüner, 1991), 1: 259–69; 'Pietro d'Abano e gli affreschi astrologici del Palazzo della Ragione di Padova,' *Labyrinthos* 9 (1986): 50–75; 'Pietro d'Abano e l'astrologia-astronomia,' *Bollettino del Centro Internazionale di Storia dello Spazio e del Tempo* 5 (1986): 9–28. In general, see also Roger French, 'Astrology in Medical Practice,' in *Practical Medicine from Salerno to the Black Death*, ed. Luis García Ballester, Roger French, Jon Arrizabalaga and Andrew Cunningham (Cambridge: Cambridge University Press, 1994), 30–59, at 55–9.
33 See, in general, Bernhard Schmeidler, *Italienische Geschichtsschreiber des XII. und XIII. Jahrhunderts: Ein Beitrag zur Kulturgeschichte* (Leipzig: Quelle, 1909), 48–9.
34 On the status of astrology in *Trecento* Padua, see Enrico Berti, 'Astronomia e astrologia da Pietro d'Abano a Giovanni Dondi dell'Orologio,' in *Padova carrarese*, 175–84; idem, 'Filosofia, astrologia e vita quotidiana nella Padova del Trecento,' in *I Dondi dell'Orologio e la Padova dei Carraresi: Padua sidus preclarum*, ed. Nicola Mazzonetto ([Brugine]: Edizioni 1 + 1, 1989), 17–28 – repr. in *Il Palazzo della Ragione a Padova: Dalle Pitture di Giotto agli affreschi del '400*, ed. Centro Internazionale di Storia della nozione e della misura dello Spazio e del Tempo (Rome: Istituto Poligrafico e Zecca dello Stato, 1992), 3: 97–108. Mussato's use of astrological motifs is discussed in Siraisi, *Arts and Sciences at Padua*, 89–90; Witt, '*In the Footsteps of the Ancients*,' 148–9, 151.
35 "Ora potrà dire chi questo capitolo leggerà, che utole porta di sapere questa strolomia al presente trattato? Rispondiamo che a chi fia discreto e proveduto, e vorrà investigare delle mutazioni che sono state per li tempi adietro in questo nostro paese e altrove, leggendo questa cronica assai

potrà comprendere per comparazione di quelle sono passate pronosticare delle future, aconsentiente Idio, che questa congiunzione in questa tripicità de' segni dell'aere fu e cominciò a questi nostri presenti tempi gli anni MCCV nel segno della Libra; e poi gli anni MCCCXXV nel segno del Gemini [...] E in DCCCCLX overo DCCCCLIII anni fornite XLVII congiunzioni, e tornando alla prima, ch'è la più ponderosa di tutte, se cerhi adietro troverrai il cominciamento del calo della potenza del romano imperio alla venuta de' Gotti e di Vandali inn-Italia, e molte turbazioni a santa Chiesa etc.' *Giovanni Villani* (Rome: Istituto Poligrafico e Zecca dello Stato, 2002), bk. XIII, ch. xli (958). For further discussion, see Paula Clarke, 'The Villani Chronicles,' in *Chronicling History: Chroniclers and Historians in Medieval and Renaissance Italy*, ed. Sharon Dale, Alison Williams Lewin and Duane J. Osheim (University Park, PA: Pennsylvania State University Press, 2007), 113–43, at 122–3; Louis Green, *Chronicle into History: An Essay on the Interpretation of History in Florentine Fourteenth-Century Chronicles* (Cambridge: Cambridge University Press, 1972), 26, 29–37; Ernst. Mehl, *Die Weltanschauung des Giovanni Villani: Ein Beitrag zur Geistesgeschichte Italiens im Zeitalter Dantes* (Leipzig: B.G. Teubner, 1927), 39–47, 162–79.

36 'Questa congiunzione co' suoi aspetti delli altri pianeti e segni, secondo il detto e scritto de' libri degli antichi grandi maestri di strolomia, significa, Idio consentiente, grandi cose al mondo, e battaglie, e micidi, e grandi commutazioni di regni e di popoli, e morte di re, e tralazione di signorie e di sette, e aparimento d'alcuno profeta e di nuovi errori a fede, e nuova venuta di signori e di nuove genti, e carestia e mortalità apresso in quelli crimanti, regni, paesi e cittadi, la cui infruenza de' detti segni e pianeti è atribuita.' *Giovanni Villani*, bk. XIII, ch. xli (957); Clarke, 'The Villani Chronicles,' 133–4.

37 *DP* I.ix.7.

38 *DP* I.ix.5.

39 *DP* I.ix.5.

40 *DP* I.ix.6.

41 *DP* I.ix.5.

42 *DP* I.ix.7.

43 *DP* I.xvi.11.

44 *DP* I.xv.2; II.xxx.8.

45 *DP* I.xv.2.

46 *DP* I.xv.3.

47 Aristotle, *Ph.* 194a22–25. For further discussion of Marsilius's application of the 'ars imitatur naturam' principle, see Arne Moritz, 'Politik als künstliche Vollendung der menschlichen Natur. Aristoteles, Marsilius von

Padua und Nikolaus von Kues über die artifizielle Kompensation der Defizite in der Naturausstattung des Menschen,' in *Ars imitatur naturam: Transformationen eines Paradigmas menschlicher Kreativität im Übergang vom Mittelalter zur Neuzeit*, ed. Arne Moritz (Münster: Aschendorff, 2010), 229–49, esp. 230–40; and Francis Cheneval, '"Ars imitatur naturam" als methodisches Prinzip der politischen Philosophie und seine Anwendung im *Defensor pacis* des Marsilius von Padua,' *Archives d'histoire doctrinale et littéraire du moyen âge* 60 (1993): 133–45.

48 *DP* I.xv.3. See also Didier Ottaviani, 'Le peuple en puissance: Marsile de Padoue,' in *De la puissance du peuple*, vol. 1: *La démocratie de Platon à Rawls*, ed. Yves Vargas (Pantin: Le Temps des Cerises, 2000), 43–55.

49 *DP* I.xiv.9.

50 *DP* I.xv.4; *DP* I.xii.3.

51 For further references, see Cristina D'Ancona and Richard C. Taylor, s.v. '*Liber de causis*,' *Dictionnaire des philosophes antiques. Supplément*, ed. Richard Goulet et al. (Paris: CNRS Éditions, 2003), 599–64. For the Arabic versions, see Abdurrahman Badawi, 'Procli: Liber (Pseudo-Aristotelis) de expositione bonitatis purae,' in *Neoplatonici apud Arabes* (Cairo: n.p., 1957), 1–33; *Die pseudo-aristotelische Schrift Ueber das reine Gute bekannt unter dem Namen Liber de causis*, ed. Otto Bardenhewer (Freiburg i.Br.: Herder, 1882; repr. Frankfurt a. M.: Minerva, 1957), 58–118.

52 The critical edition of the Latin translation can be found in Adrian Pattin, 'Le *Liber de causis* – Édition établie à l'aide de 90 manuscrits avec introduction et notes,' *Tijdschrift voor Filosofie* 28 (1966): 90–203, whereas a number of amendments were recommended by Richard C. Taylor, 'Remarks on the Latin Text and the Translator of the *Kalâm fi mahd al-khair/Liber de causis*,' *Bulletin de Philosophie Medievale* 31 (1989): 75–102. For a parallel Latin-German translation and commentary of the text based on Pattin's edition and Taylor's revisions, see *Liber de causis = Das Buch von den Ursachen*, trans. Andreas Schönfeld (Hamburg: F. Meiner, 2003). Eng. trans. Thomas Aquinas, *The Book of Causes*, trans. Dennis J. Brand (Milwaukee: Marquette University Press, 1984); French trans. Pierre Magnard et al., *La demeure de l'être. Autour d'un anonyme. Étude et traduction du Liber de Causis* (Paris: Vrin, 1990). On the Latin reception of the *Liber de causis*, see Alexander Fidora and Andreas Niederberger, *Von Bagdad nach Toledo: das 'Buch der Ursachen' und seine Rezeption im Mittelalter; lateinisch – deutscher Text, Kommentar und Wirkungsgeschichte des Liber de causis* (Mainz: Dieterich, 2001); Thomas Aquinas, *Commentary on the Book of Causes [Super Librum De Causis Expositio]*, trans. Vincent A. Guagliardo et al. (Washington, DC: Catholic University of America Press, 1996), 'Introduction,' ix–xxxii; Cristina D'Ancona

Costa, *Recherches sur le Liber de Causis* (Paris: J. Vrin, 1995); Charles H. Lohr, 'The Pseudo-Aristotelian *Liber de causis* and Latin Theories of Science in the Twelfth and Thirteenth Centuries,' in *Pseudo-Aristotle in the Middle Ages: The Theology and Other Texts*, ed. Jill Kraye et al. (London: Warburg Institute, University of London, 1986), 53–62. For the Hebrew translations, see Jean-Pierre Rothschild, 'Les traductions du *Livre des causes* et leurs copies,' *Revue d'Histoire des Textes* 24 (1994): 393–484; idem, 'Les traductions hébraïques du *Liber de causis* latin' (Thèse de doctorat, Université Paris III, 1985). Extant commentaries before 1500 are indicated in Richard C. Taylor, 'The *Liber de causis*: A Preliminary List of Extant mss,' *Bulletin de Philosophie Medievale* 25 (1983): 63–84.

53 Clemens Vansteenkiste, 'Procli Elementatio theologica translata a Guilelmo de Moerbeke (textus ineditus),' *Tijdschrift voor Filosofie* 13 (1951): 263–302, 491–531; Helmut Boese, *Wilhelm von Moerbeke als Übersetzer der Stoicheiosis theologike des Proclus: Untersuchungen und Texte zur Überlieferung der Elementatio theologica* (Heidelberg: Bitsch, 1985); and, in general, *On Proclus and His Influence in Medieval Philosophy*, ed. Egbert P. Bos and Pieter A. Meijer (Leiden: E.J. Brill, 1992). It is possible that Moerbeke identified the text and as a consequence translated Proclos and that he studied the *Liber de causis* in Latin in his formation in philosophy. I owe this remark to Richard Taylor.

54 *Sancti Thomae de Aquino super Librum de causis expositio*, ed. Henri D. Saffrey (Fribourg and Leuven: Société Philosophique/Éditions E. Nauwelaerts, 1954); Eng. Trans. Thomas Aquinas, *The Book of Causes*, 3–163. On Aquinas and *De Liber de causis*, see Werner Beierwaltes, 'Der Kommentar zum *Liber de causis* als neuplatonisches Element in der Philosophie des Thomas von Aquin,' *Philosophische Rundschau* 11 (1964): 192–215; Clemens Vansteenkiste, 'Il *Liber de Causis* negli scritti di San Tommaso,' *Angelicum* 35 (1958): 325–74. For Neoplatonic influences on Aquinas, see Kathryn Tanner, *God and Creation in Christian Theology: Tyranny or Empowerment?* (Oxford: B. Blackwell, 1988), 91–2; Klaus Kremer, *Die neuplatonische Seinsphilosophie und ihre Wirkung auf Thomas von Aquin* (Leiden: E.J. Brill, 1966).

55 Albert the Great, *De causis et processu universitatis a prima causa*, ed. Winfried Fauser (= Alberti Magni Opera Omnia; vol. 12, 2) (Münster: Aschendorff, 1993). See also Andreas Bächli, *Monotheismus und neuplatonische Philosophie. Eine Untersuchung zum pseudo-aristotelischen Liber de causis und dessen Rezeption durch Albert den Großen* (St. Augustin: Academia-Verlag, 2004).

56 Roger Bacon, 'Quaestiones supra Librum de causis,' in *Opera hactenus inedita Roberti Baconi*, Fasc. 12, ed. Robert Steele (Oxford: Clarendon Press,

1935). See also Cristina D'Ancona, '"Philosophus in libro De Causis." La recezione del *Liber de Causis* come opera aristotelica nei commenti di Ruggero Bacone, dello ps. Enrico di Gand e dello ps. Adamo di Bocfeld,' *Documenti e studi sulla tradizione filosofica medievale* 3 (1992): 611–49, esp. 622–33 – French trans. as '"Philosophus in libro *De Causis*." Le *Liber de Causis* comme ouvrage aristotélicien dans les commentaires de Roger Bacon, du ps. Henri de Gand et du ps. Adam di Bocfeld,' in eadem, *Recherches sur le Liber de Causis*, 195–228.

57 *Les Quaestiones in Librum de causis attribueés à Henri de Gand*, ed. John P. Zwaenepoel (Louvain-la-Neuve: Publications universitaires, 1974).

58 Siger of Brabant, *Les Quaestiones super Librum de Causis de Siger de Brabant*, ed. Antonio Marlasca (Louvain-la-Neuve: Publications universitaires, 1972).

59 Aegidius Romanus, *Fundatissimi Aegidii Romani Archiepiscopi Bituricensis Doctorem praecipue Ordinis Eremitarum Sancti Augustine, Opus super Authorem de Causis Alpharabium* (Venice, 1550; repr. Frankfurt a. M.: Minerva, 1968).

60 [Pseudo-Adam of Bocfeld], *Scriptum super Librum de causis*. The text has not yet been edited.

61 The text can be found in Elizabeth A.R. Brown, '*Cessante Causa* and the Taxes of the Last Capetians: The Political Applications of a Philosophical Maxim,' *Studia Gratiana* 15 (1972): 567–87 – repr. in eadem, *Politics and Institutions in Capetian France* (Aldershot and Brookfield, VT: Variorum; Gower, 1991), no. II. See also the discussion in Cary J. Nederman, 'Aristotle as Authority: Alternative Aristotelian Sources of Late Medieval Political Theory,' *History of European Ideas* 8 (1987): 31–44, at 33 – repr. in idem, *Medieval Aristotelianism and Its Limits*, no. XV.

62 Francisco Bertelloni, 'Die Anwendung von Kausalitätstheorien im politischen Denken von Thomas von Aquin und Aegidius Romanus,' in *Politische Reflexion in der Welt des späten Mittelalters*, 85–108; idem, 'Los fundamentos teóricos de la caducidad del orden jurídico en el *De ecclesiastica potestate* de Egidio Romano,' *Patristica et Mediaevalia* 22 (2001): 17–29. On the relationship between Giles's hierocratic theory and the Pseudo-Dionysian notion of hierarchy, see David E. Luscombe, 'Hierarchy in the Late Middle Ages: Criticism and Change,' in *Political Thought and the Realities of Power in the Middle Ages*, 113–26, at 116–17; Elvio Ancona, 'Mediazione e immediatezza nella disputa sui due poteri all'inizio del XIV secolo,' *Medioevo* 22 (1996): 491–502.

63 For further discussion, see Alexander Aichele, 'Heart and Soul of the State: Some Remarks Concerning Aristotelian Ontology and Medieval Theory of

Medicine in Marsilius of Padua's *Defensor pacis*,' in *The World of Marsilius of Padua*, 163–86. On the use of the heart and soul metaphor in late medieval political writing, consult Roberto Lambertini, 'Il cuore e l'anima della città: Osservazioni a margine sull'uso di metafore organistiche in testi politici bassomedievali,' in *Anima e corpo nella cultura medievale*, 289–303.

64 'Fuit autem in hoc humana sollicitudo convenienter imitata naturam. Quia enim civitas et ipsius partes secundum racionem institute analogiam habent animali et suis partibus, perfecte formatis secundum naturam, ut apparet ex Aristotele 1° et 5° Politice, 2is capitulis. Qualis igitur est nature accio in animali perfecte formando, proporcionata fuit ea que humane mentis ad civitatem et ipsius partes instituendas convenienter. Ad quam siquidem describendam proporcionem, ex qua patebit amplius effi ciencia et determinacio parcium civitatis, suscipiemus cum Aristotele in 16° De Animalibus, et a Galieno in suo quodam libro, quem vocavit De Zogonia, cum reliquis quoque magis expertis posteriorum, a principio quodam seu causa movente aliqua, sit illud forma materie aut separata vel alterum quiddam virtutem habens generativam animalis et parcium eius, formari primum tempore atque natura partem quandam organicam animalis ipsius, et *in* ipsa virtutem seu potenciam naturalem cum calore aliquo, tamquam activo principio, virtutem inquam et calorem universales activa causalitate ad formandum et distinguendum unamquamque reliquarum parcium animalis. Et est pars ista primum formata cor aut cordi proporcionalis aliqua, sicut dixit Aristoteles ubi supra, et reliqui philosophorum periciores, quibus credere oportet propter ipsorum experienciam in hoc, et absque probacione nunc supponere, quoniam id demonstrare non est presentis inquisicionis. Hec siquidem pars formata primum nobilior est et perfeccior in suis qualitatibus et disposicionibus ceteris partibus animalis. Statuit enim in ea natura generans virtutem et instrumentum, per que partes animalis relique formantur ex convenienti materia, separantur, distiguunter, invicem ordinantur, in suis disposicionibus conservantur et a nocumento, quantum natura patitur, preservantur per ipsam; lapse vero a sui natura propter egritudinem aut alterum impedimentum, huius partis virtute reparantur' (*DP* I.xv.5). See also *Gen. an.*, 740b29–37.

65 'Hiis autem proporcionaliter contemplandum in civitate convenienter instituta secundum racionem. Nam ab anima universitatis civium aut eius valencioris partis formatur aut formari debet in ea pars una primum proporcionata cordi, in qua siquidem virtutem quandam seu formam statuit cum activa potencia seu auctoritate instituendi partes reliquas civitatis. Hec autem pars est principatus, cuius quidem virtus causalitate universalis lex est, et cuius activa potencia est auctoritas iudicandi, precipiendi

et exequendi sentencias conferencium et iustorum civilium, propter quod dixit Aristoteles 7° Politice, cap. 6°, partem hanc esse *omnium* aliarum *necessariissimam* in civitate. Causa vero eius est, quoniam suffi ciencia que habetur per reliquas partes seu officia civitatis, si non inexisterent, posset aliunde suffi cienter haberi, licet non sic faciliter, ut per navigium et reliqua vectigalia. Sed sine principatus inexistencia civilis communitas manere aut diu manere non potest, quoniam *necesse est ut scandala veniant*, ut dicitur in Mattheo. Hee autem sunt contenciones atque iniurie hominum invicem, que non vindicate aut mensurate per iustorum regulam, legem videlicet, et per principantem, cuius est secundum illam talia mensurare, contingeret inde congregatorum hominum pugna et separacio, et demum corrupcio civitatis et privacio suffi cientis vite' (*DP* I.xv.6).

66 *DP* I.xv.12, 13.

67 *DP* I.xv.7. Compare Aristotle, *Pol.* 1332b16–23.

68 Aristotle, *Gen. corr.* 336a13.

69 Aristotle, *De an.* 418b11.

70 'Debet eciam pars hec in civitate nobilior atque perfeccior esse in suis disposicionibus, prudencia scilicet atque virtute moris, ceteris partibus civitatis. Unde 7° Politice, cap. 12° dixit Aristoteles: 'Si tantum fuerint differentes alteri ab alteris, quantum deos et heroes extimamus ab hominibus differre, confestim primo secundum corpus multam habentes excellenciam, deinde secundum animam, ut indubitata et manifesta sit excellencia principancium respectu subiectorum, palam quidem, quia melius per eosdem, hos quidem principari, hos autem subici secundum semel, id est secundum vitam. Statuit eciam principium factivum civitatis, anima videlicet univesitatis, in hac prima parte virtutem quandam causalitate universalem, legem scilicet, auctoritatem quoque seu potestatem agendi secundum illam iudicia civilia, precipiendi et exequendi de hiis, non aliter. Quoniam sicut caliditas innata ipsius cordis tamquam subiecti, per quam cor seu forma eius omnes acciones complet, dirigitur et mensuratur in agendo per cordis formam seu virtutem, nec aliter ageret ad debitum fi nem; adhuc eciam sicut calor, quem spiritum dicunt, tamquam instrumentum ad complendas acciones, per totum corpus ab eadem virtute regitur, nec aliter horum calorum alteruter ageret ad debitum fi nem, quoniam deterius agit *i*gnis quam organa, ut in 2° Perigeneseos et De Anima: sic quoque auctoritas principandi alicui hominum data, caliditati cordis tamquam subiecti proporcionata. Sic eciam ipsius armata seu coactiva potestas *instrumentalis*, calori, quem spiritus diximus, proporcionalis, debet regulari per legem in iudicando, precipiendo et exequendo de iustis et conferentibus civilibus; aliter enim non ageret principans ad debitum finem, conservacionem scili-

cet civitatis, quemadmodum demonstratum est 11° huius' (*DP* I.xv.7); 'Nos autem dicamus, quod principans per suam accionem secundum legem et sibi datam auctoritatem regula est atque mensura cuiuslibet civilis actus, quemadmodum cor in animali, ut satis ostensum est 15° huius. Quod si pricipans aliam formam non reciperet preter legem, auctoritatem et desiderium agendi secundum illam, *numquam* minus debitam aut corrigibilem seu mensurabilem ab alio faceret accionem. Et ideo tam ipse, quam eius accio sic esset mensura cuiuslibet civilis actus aliorum a se, quod nequaquam ab aliis mensuratus; quemadmodum cor bene formatum in animali, quod quidem, quoniam formam non recipit, per quam inclinetur ad accionem contrariam accioni, que provenire habet a virtute sua et calore naturali, semper convenientem agit accionem naturaliter, contrariam vero minime; propter quod sic regulat et mensurat per suam infl uenciam seu accionem reliquas parcium animalis, quod ab ipsis nullatenus regulatur nec ipsarum influenciam recipit aliquam' (*DP* I.xviii.2).

71 The *De partibus animalium* was translated into Latin from Arabic by Michael Scotus. For its reception in the medieval West, see Theodor W. Köhler, 'Die wissenschaftstheoretische und inhaltliche Bedeutung der Rezeption von *De animalibus* für den philosophisch–anthropologischen Diskurs im 13. Jahrhundert,' in *Aristotle's Animals in the Middle Ages and Renaissance*, ed. Carlos Steel, Guy Guldentops and Pieter Beullens. (Leuven: Leuven University Press, 2000), 249–74; Luciano Cova, 'Il Corpus zoologico di Aristotele nei dibattiti fra gli *artisti* parigini alle soglie del XIV secolo,' in *L'enseignement des disciplines à la Faculté des arts*, 281–302.

72 *DP* I.xv.5.

73 Galen, *Über die Ausformung der Keimlinge*, ed. and trans. Diethard Nickel (Berlin: Akademie Verlag, 2001), 38–9. On Galen's Latin reception, see Gerhard Baader, 'Galen im mittelalterlichen Abendland,' in *Galen: Problems and Prospects*, ed. Vivian Nutton (London: Wellcome Institute for the History of Medicine, 1981), 213–28. For the Arabic reception, consult Fuat Sezgin, Mazin Amawi, Carl Ehrig-Eggert and Eckhard Neubauer, eds., *Galen in the Arabic Philosophical Tradition: Texts and Studies* (Frankfurt a. M.: Institute for the History of Arabic-Islamic Science, Johann Wolfgang Goethe University, 2000).

74 Galen, *Über die Ausformung der Keimlinge*, 674.12–675.21, 78 (Greek text)/79 (German trans). Consider also Brett, *The Defender of the Peace*, 91; *The Defensor Pacis of Marsilius of Padua*, ed. Previté-Orton, 69. On Galen's embryology, see Véronique Boudon-Millot, 'La naissance de la vie dans la théorie médicale et philosophique de Galien,' and Ann Ellis Hanson, 'The Gradualist View of Fetal Development,' both in Luc Brisson, Marie-Hélène

Congourdeau, and Jean-Luc Solère, eds., *L'embryon: Formation et animation. Antiquité grecque et latine tradition hébraïque, chrétienne et islamique* (Paris: J. Vrin, 2008), 79–94 and 95–108, respectively; Diethard Nickel, *Untersuchungen zur Embryologie Galens* (Berlin: Akademie-Verlag, 1989); Rudoph E. Siegel, *Galen's System of Physiology and Medicine: An Analysis of his Doctrines and Observations on Blood Flow, Respiration, Tumors and Internal Diseases* (Basel and New York: Karger, 1968). On Galen's critique of the Stoics, see especially Diethard Nickel, 'Stoa und Stoiker in Galens Schrift *De foetuum formatione*,' in *Galen und das hellenistische Erbe*, ed. Jutta Kollesch and Diethard Nickel (Stuttgart: F. Steiner, 1993), 79–86. Medieval theories of embryology and generation are surveyed in Marie-Hélène Congourdeau, *L'embryon et son âme dans les sources grecques (VIe siècle av. J.-C.-Ve siècle apr. J.-C.)* (Paris: Association des Amis du Centre d'Histoire et Civilisation de Byzance, 2007); Romana Martorelli Vico, *Medicina e filosofia: per una storia dell'embriologia medievale nel XIII e XIV secolo* (Milan: Guerini e associati, 2002) (for Peter of Abano, 93–100); Gordon R. Dunstan, ed., *The Human Embryo: Aristotle and the Arabic and European Traditions* (Exeter: University of Exeter Press, 1990).

75 Michael Walzer, Menachem Lorberbaum, Noam J. Zohar, and Yair Lorberbaum, eds., *The Jewish Political Tradition*, vol. 1: *Authority* (New Haven, CT and London: Yale University Press, 2000), 151. See also Abraham Melamed, 'The Organic Theory of the State in Medieval and Renaissance Jewish Political Thought,' in *Ideal Constitutions in the Renaissance*, ed. Heinrich C. Kuhn and Diana Stanciu (Frankfurt a. M.: P. Lang, 2009), 113–44.

76 *Claudii Galeni opera omnia*, ed. Carl G. Kühn (Leipzig: K. Knobloch, 1822; repr. Hildesheim: G. Olms, 1964), 4: 663; Galen, *Selected Works*, trans. Peter N. Singer (Oxford: Oxford University Press, 1997), 182.

77 On the *De spermate* and its medieval reception, see Outi Merisalo, 'In *Horis Sanguinis*: Physiology and Generation in the Pseudo-Galenic *De Spermate*,' in *Pūrvāparaprajñābhinandanam: East and West, Past and Present*, ed. Bertil Tikkanen and Albion M. Butters (Helsinki: Finnish Oriental Society, 2011), 231–42; eadem, 'Les voies de diffusion des textes médicaux au Moyen Âge: L'exemple du *De spermate* pseudo-galénien, XIIe–XVe siècle,' *Gazette du livre médiéval* 52–53 (2008): 45–50; eadem and Päivi Pahta, 'Tracing the Trail of Transmission: The Pseudo-Galenic *De spermate* in Latin,' in *Science Translated: Latin and Vernacular Translations of Scientific Treatises in Medieval Europe*, ed. Michèle Goyens et al. (Leuven: Leuven University Press, 2008), 91–104; Päivi Pahta, 'Medieval Andrology and the Pseudo-Galenic *De spermate*,' *Medicina nei Secoli* 13 (2001): 509–21; eadem, *Medieval Embryology in the Vernacular: The Case of De spermate* (Helsinki: Société Néophilologique,

1998). Consider also Anthony Preus, 'Galen's Criticism of Aristotle's Conception Theory,' *Journal of the History of Biology* 10 (1977): 65–85. The *De spermate* was included among the Galenic and pseudo-Galenic treatises that were translated by Niccolò da Reggio (ca. 1280–1350) from the Greek into Latin in the first half of the fourteenth century – for further details, consult Michael R. McVaugh, 'Niccolò da Reggio's Translations of Galen and Their Reception in France,' *Early Science and Medicine* 11 (2006): 275–301.

78 De Leemans, 'Was Peter of Abano the Translator of pseudo-Aristotle's *Problemata physica*?' 108.

79 On Peter of Abano's translations of Galen's works, see Stefania Fortuna, 'Pietro d'Abano e le traduzioni latine di Galeno,' *Medicina nei Secoli* 20 (2008): 447–63; Marie-Thérèse d'Alverny, 'Pietro d'Abano, traducteur de Galien,' *Medioevo* 11 (1985): 19–64 – repr. in eadem, *La transmission des textes philosophiques et scientifiques au Moyen Age*, ed. Charles Burnett (Aldershot and Brookfield, VT: Variorum, 1994), no. XIII.

80 Ioannis Philoponi, *In Aristotelis libros De generatione et corruptione commentaria*, ed. Girolamo Vitelli (Berlin: Reimer, 1897), 289.

81 Frans A.J. de Haas, '"Introduction,"' to Johannes Philoponus, *Commentaria in libros De generatione et corruptione Aristotelis*, trans. Hieronymus Bagolinus (Venice, 1558; repr.) Stuttgart-Bad Cannstatt: Frommann-Holzboog, 2004), v–xiv, at x–xi.

82 For the medieval reception of the *De generatione et corruptione*, see *Lire Aristote au Moyen Âge et à la Renaissance: Réception du traité Sur la génération et la corruption*, ed. Joëlle Ducos and Violaine Giacomotto-Charra (Paris: H. Champion 2011); Marwan Rashed, *Die Überlieferungsgeschichte der aristotelischen Schrift De generatione et corruptione* (Wiesbaden: L. Reichert, 2001). On ancient and medieval commentaries on that work, consult the articles assembled in Johannes M.M.H. Thijssen and Henk A.G. Braakhuis, eds., *The Commentary Tradition on Aristotle's De generatione et corruptione: Ancient, Medieval, and Early Modern* (Turnhout: Brepols, 1999).

83 *Averrois Cordubensis Commentarium medium in Aristotelis De generatione et corruptione libros*, ed. Francis H. Fobes (Cambridge, MA: Mediaeval Academy of America, 1956), 145; Eng. trans. *Averroes on Aristotle's De Generatione et Corruptione: Middle Commentary and Epitome*, trans. Samuel Kurland (Cambridge, MA: Medieval Academy of America, 1958), 100. Compare Averroes (Abū l-Walīd Ibn Rušd), *Mittlerer Kommentar zu Aristoteles' De generatione et corruptione*, ed. and comm. Heidrun Eichner (Paderborn: Verlag F. Schöningh, 2005), [edition of the Arabic text] 130; [German commentary] 390. For Averroes's commentary on the *De generatione et corruptione*,

see Pieter De Leemans, '*Alia translatio planior*: Les traductions latines du *De generatione et corruptione* et les commentateurs médiévaux,' in *Lire Aristote au Moyen Âge et à la Renaissance*, 27–53, at 36–8.

84 *Aegidius Aurelianensis, Quaestiones super De Generatione et corruptione*, ed. Zdzislaw Kuksewicz) (Amsterdam and Philadelphia, PA: B.R. Grüner, 1993), 200. On this work, see Pieter De Leemans, '*Alia translatio planior*,' 48–53.

85 'Preter hos autem dictos habitus et disposiciones necessarium est principanti extrinsecum organum quoddam, armatorum videlicet numerus certus, quo suas civiles sentencias in rebelles et inobedientes per coactivam potenciam exequi posit' (*DP* I.xiv.8).

86 *DP* I.xiv.1–7, 9–10.

87 Aristotle, *Pol.* 1286b27–37.

88 *DP* I.xiv.8.

89 *DP* I.xiv.8.

90 *DP* I.xiv.8.

91 On the following, see Blythe, *Ideal Government and the Mixed Constitution in the Middle Ages*, 80, 84; Dunbabin, 'The Reception and Interpretation of Aristotle's *Politics*,' in *The Cambridge History of Later Medieval Philosophy*, ed. Norman Kretzmann et al. (Cambridge: Cambridge University Press, 1982), 723–37, at 726–8.

92 Marsilius differs from Aristotle in that he does not see laws as a means to promote the education or edification of the citizens or implant and nurture virtue in them. On Aristotle's views on the educative function of the laws, see Aristotle, *Pol.* 1287a32; 1286a11ff. and Book. For a comprehensive study of the role of education in Aristotle's political theory, see Carnes Lord, *Education and Culture in the Political Thought of Aristotle* (Ithaca, NY: Cornell University Press, 1982).

93 'Et propterea numquam debet accio principantis in civitate cessare, quemadmodum nec accio cordis in animali' (*DP* I.xv.13); 'Quo modo conservabit in esse debito unamquamque parcium civitatis, et a nocumentis ac iniuriis preservabit' (*DP* I.xv.11).

94 *DP* I.xv.11

95 *DP* I.xv.12.

96 Eugenio Garin, *Astrology in the Renaissance: The Zodiac of Life*, trans. Carolyn Jackson and June Allen (London and Boston: Routledge & Kegan Paul, 1983), 11–12. See further Quillet, *La philosophie politique*, 66; Graziella Federici Vescovini, 'The Place of the Sun in Medieval Arabo-Latin Astronomy: The *Lucidator dubitabilium astronomiae* (1303–10) of Peter of Padua,' *Journal for the History of Astronomy* 29 (1998): 151–5. On the medieval usage on the

king-sun analogy, see Jean-Patrice Boudet, 'Le roi–soleil dans la France médiévale,' *Micrologus* 12 (2004): 455–78.

97 *Ioannis Saresberiensis episcopi Carnotensis Policratici sive De nvgis cvrialivm et vestigiis philosophorvm libri VIII*, ed. Clemens C.J. Webb (Oxford: Clarendon Press, 1909), 1: 282–3; John of Salisbury, *Policraticus: Of the Frivolities of Courtiers and the Footprints of Philosophers*, ed. and trans. Cary J. Nederman (Cambridge: Cambridge University Press, 1990), 66–7. John of Salisbury's use of medical metaphors is the subject of the following studies by Cary J. Nederman: 'Social Bodies and the Non-Christian "Other" in the Twelfth Century: John of Salisbury and Peter of Celle,' in *Meeting the Foreign in the Middle Ages*, ed. Albrecht Classen (New York and London: Routledge, 2002), 192–201, at 193–7; idem, 'The Physiological Significance of the Organic Metaphor in John of Salisbury's *Policraticus*,' *History of Political Thought* 8 (1987): 211–23 – repr. in idem, *Medieval Aristotelianism and Its Limits*, no. VI.

98 Marsilius notes in the *Defensor pacis* (I.ix.5) that kingship is perhaps the most perfect form of government.

Conclusion

1 An interesting precedent has been set by Cary Nederman, who distinguishes five principal modes of cross-cultural dialogue in the Middle Ages; see his 'Varieties of Dialogue: Dialogical Models of Intercultural Communication in Medieval Inter-religious Writings,' in *Western Political Thought in Dialogue with Asia*, ed. Takashi Shogimen and Cary J. Nederman (Lanham, MD: Lexington Books, 2009), 45–64.

2 A salutary step in this direction has been taken by Paul A. Rahe in his study *Against Throne and Altar: Machiavelli and Political Theory under the English Republic* (Cambridge: Cambridge University Press, 2008), esp. 59–83.

Selected Bibliography

Primary Sources

Abū Ma'šar on Historical Astrology, The Book of Religions and Dynasties (On the Great Conjunctions). Edited and translated by Keiji Yamamoto and Charles Burnett. Leiden: Brill, 2000.

Aegidius Romanus (Egidio Colonna). *De regimine principum libri III*. Rome, 1607. Repr. Aalen: Scientia Verlag, 1967.

– *Fundatissimi Aegidii Romani Archiepiscopi Bituricensis Doctorem praecipue Ordinis Eremitarum Sancti Augustine, Opus super Authorem de Causis Alpharabium*. Venice, 1550. Repr. Frankfurt a. M.: Minerva, 1968.

– *Aegidius Aurelianensis, Quaestiones super De Generatione et corruptione*. Edited by ZdzislawKuksewicz. Amsterdam and Philadelphia, PA: B.R. Grüner, 1993.

– *The Governance of Kings and Princes: John Trevisa's Middle English Translation of the De Regimine Principum of Aegidius Romanus*. Edited by David C. Fowler, Charles F. Briggs, and Paul G. Remley. New York and London: Garland Pub., 1997.

– *Giles of Rome's On Ecclesiastical Power: A Medieval Theory of World Government*. Edited and and translated by Robert W. Dyson. New York: Columbia University Press, 2004.

'Ahd Ardashīr. Edited by Iḥsān 'Abbās. Beirut: Dār al-Ṣādir, 1967.

Albert the Great. *De causis et processu universitatis a prima causa*. Edited by Winfried Fauser (= Alberti Magni Opera Omnia; vol. 12, 2). Münster: Aschendorff, 1993.

Al-Bīrūnī. Takī ed Dīn al-Hilālī. *Die Einleitung zu Al-Bīrūnī's Steinbuch*. Leipzig: O. Harrassowitz, 1941.

Al-Fārābī. *Alfarabi's 'Book of Religion' and Related Texts*. Edited by Muhsin Mahdi. Beirut: Dār al-Mashriq, 1968.

– Thérèse-Anne Druart, 'Le Sommaire du Livre des *Lois* de Platon (*Ǧawāmi' Kitāb al-Nawāmīs li-Aflāṭūn*) par Abū Nasr al-Fārābī, édition critique et introduction.' *Bulletin d'Études Orientales* 50 (1998): 109–55.

[Anonymous]. 'Oculus pastoralis pascens officia et continens radium dulcibus pomis suis.' Edited by Dora Franceschi. *Memorie dell'Accademia delle Scienze di Torino, Classe di scienze morali, storiche e filologiche* ser. 4, 11 (1966): 1–74.

[Anonymous]. *Oculus pastoralis*. Terence O. Tunberg, '*Oculus pastoralis*.' Diss., University of Toronto, 1986.

[Anonymous]. Terence O. Tunberg, trans. *Speeches from the Oculus pastoralis*. Toronto: Pontifical Institute of Mediaeval Studies, 1990.

[Anonymous]. 'Recommentatio civitatis Parisiensis = Éloge de la cité de Paris.' In Le Roux de Lincy and Tisserand, *Paris et ses historiens aux XIV e et XVe siècles*, 22–9.

Aquinas, Thomas. '*De regno*,' in *S. Thomae Aquinatis Opuscula omnia necnon opera minora*, vol. 1: *Opuscula philosophica*, 221–426. Edited by Jean Perrier. Paris: P. Lethielleux, 1949.

– *Sancti Thomae de Aquino super Librum de causis expositio*. Edited by Henri D. Saffrey. Fribourg and Leuven: Société Philosophique/Éditions E. Nauwelaerts, 1954.

– 'De regno ad regem Cypri.' In *Sancti Thomae de Aquino opera omnia* (= Editio Leonina; 42). Edited by Antoine Dondaine, 417–71. Rome: Editori di San Tommaso, 1979.

– *Commentary on the Book of Causes [Super Librum De Causis Expositio]*. Translated by Vincent A. Guagliardo, Charles R. Hess and Richard C. Taylor Washington, DC: Catholic University of America Press, 1996.

The Arabic Version of the Nicomachean Ethics, *with an Introduction and Annotated Translation by Douglas M. Dunlop*. Edited by Anna A. Akasoy and Alexander Fidora. Leiden and Boston: Brill, 2005.

Aristotelis opera cum Averrois commentariis, vol. 8: *Aristotelis Metaphysicorum libri XIIII cum Averrois Cordubensis in eosdem commentariis, et epitome, Theophrasti Metaphysicorum Liber* (= editio Juntina secunda). Venice, 1562. Repr. Frankfurt a. M.: Minerva, 1962.

Aristotelis Politicorum libri octo; cum vetusta translatione Guilelmi de Moerbeka. Edited by Franz Susemihl. Leipzig: B.G. Teubner, 1972.

Averroes (Abū l-Walīd Ibn Rušd). *Francisci Philelphi De morali disciplina libri quinque. Averrois paraphrasis in libros de Republica Platonis. Francisci Robortelli in Libros Politicos Aristotelis disputatio*. Venice, 1552.

– *Averroes' Tahafut al-Tahafut (The Incoherence of the Incoherence)*. Translated from the Arabic with intro. and notes by Simon van den Bergh. London: Luzac, 1954.

– *Averrois Cordubensis Commentarium medium in Aristotelis De generatione et corruptione libros*. Edited by Francis H. Fobes. Cambridge, MA: Mediaeval Academy of America, 1956.
– *Averroes on Aristotle's De Generatione et Corruptione: Middle Commentary and Epitome*. Translated by Samuel Kurland. Cambridge, MA: Mediaeval Academy of America, 1958.
– *Averroes' Commentary on Plato's Republic*. Edited and translated by Erwin I.J. Rosenthal. Cambridge: Cambridge University Press, 1966.
– *On the Harmony of Religion and Philosophy*, a translation, with introduction and notes, of Ibn Rushd's *Kitāb faṣl al-maqāl*, with its appendix (*Ḍamīma*) and an extract from *Kitāb al-kashf 'an manāhij al-adilla* by George F. Hourani. London: Luzac, 1967.
– Averroè, *Parafrasi della 'Repubblica' nella traduzione latina di Elia del Medigo*. Edited by Annalisa Coviello and Paolo E. Fornaciari. Florence: L.S. Olschki, 1992.
– *Mittlerer Kommentar zu Aristoteles' De generatione et corruptione*. Edited and commented by Heidrun Eichner. Paderborn: Verlag F. Schöningh, 2005.
Avicenna. Avicenna latinus, *Liber de philosophia sive scientia divina*, vol: 5/10. Edited by Simone van Riet. Leiden: Brill, 1980.
– *Metafisica: La scienza delle cose divine (al-Ilāhiyyāt) dal Libro della Guarigione (Kitāb al-Šifā')*. Translated into Italian Olga Lizzini. Milan: Bompiani, 2002.
– *The Metaphysics of The Healing*, a parallel English-Arabic text translated, introduced, and annotated by Michael E. Marmura. Provo, UT: Brigham Young University Press, 2005.
Bacon, Roger. 'Quaestiones supra Librum de causis.' In *Opera hactenus inedita Roberti Baconi*, Fasc. 12. Edited by Robert Steele. Oxford: Clarendon Press, 1935.
– *Opus maius: Eine moralphilosophische Auswahl: Lateinisch-Deutsch*. Translated into German Pia A. Antolic-Piper. Freiburg i. Br.: Herder, 2008.
Barker, Ernest. *Social and Political Thought in Byzantium: From Justinian I to the Last Palaeologus. Passages from Byzantine Writers and Documents*. Oxford: Clarendon Press, 1957.
[Buridan John], *Quaestiones super octo libros politicorum Aristotelis*. Paris, 1513. Repr. Frankfurt a. M.: Minerva, 1969.
Calcidios. *Timaeus a Calcidio translatus commentarioque instructus*. Edited by Jan H. Waszink. London/Leiden: Warburg Institute/E.J. Brill, 1962.
– *Commentario al 'Timeo' di Platone: Testo latino a fronte*. Edited by Claudio Moreschini. Milan: Bompiani, 2003.
Chartularium Universitatis Parisiensis sub auspiciis consilii generalis facultatum Parisiensum. Ex diversis bibliothecis tabulariisque collegit cum authenticis chartis

contulit, notisque illustravit, vol. 2: *Ab anno MCCLXXXVI usque ad annum MCCCL*. Edited by Heinrich Denifle and Emile Châtelain. Paris: Ex typis fratrum Delalain, 1891. Repr. Brussels: Culture et Civilisation, 1964.

Christine de Pizan. *The Book of the Body Politic*. Translated by Kate Langdon Forhan. Cambridge: Cambridge University Press, 1994.

– *Le livre du corps de policie*. Edited by Angus J. Kennedy. Paris: H. Champion, 1998.

Cicero. *De officiis*. Translated by Walter Miller. Cambridge, MA/London: W. Heinemann/Macmillan 1921.

– *De inventione; De optimo genere oratorum; Topica*. Translated by Harry M. Hubbell. Cambridge, MA/London: Heinemann/Harvard University Press, 1949.

– *The Speeches: Pro Sestio and In Vatinium*. Translated by Robert Gardner. London/Cambridge, MA: Heinemann/Harvard University Press, 1958.

Contarini, Gasparo. *De Magistratibus et Republica Venetorum*. Venice, 1589.

– *The Commonwealth and Government of Venice*. Translated by Lewes Lewkenor Esquire. London, 1599. Repr. Theatrum Orbis Terrarum/Da Capo Press, 1969.

– *La Republica e i Magistrati di Vinegia*. Edited by Vittorio Conti. Florence: Centro editoriale toscano, 2003.

Dales, Richard C., and Omar Argerami, eds. *Medieval Latin Texts on the Eternity of the World*. Leiden: E.J. Brill, 1991.

Dennis, George T., ed. and trans. *Three Byzantine Military Treatises*. Washington, DC: Dumbarton Oaks Research Library and Collection, 1985. Repr. 2008.

Denzinger, Heinrich. *Enchiridion symbolorum definitionum et declarationum de rebus fidei et morum*. Edited by Helmut Hoping and Peter Hünermann. Freiburg i. Br.: Herder, 43rd ed. 2010.

Duns Scotus, John. *John Duns Scotus' Political and Economic Philosophy*. Latin text and English translation by Allan B. Wolter. St Bonaventure, NY: Franciscan Institute, St Bonaventure University, 2001.

Emerton, Ephraim, ed. and trans. *Humanism and Tyranny: Studies in the Italian Trecento*. Cambridge, MA: Harvard University Press, 1925. Repr. Gloucester, MA: P. Smith, 1964.

Engelbert of Admont. *Vom Ursprung und Ende des Reiches und andere Schriften*. Edited by Wilhelm Baum. Graz: Leykam, 1998.

Fürstenspiegel des frühen und hohen Mittelalters. Edited by Hans H. Anton. Darmstadt: Wissenschaftliche Buchgesellschaft, 2006.

Galen. *Claudii Galeni opera omnia*. Edited by Carl G. Kühn, vol. 4. Leipzig: K. Knobloch, 1822. Repr. Hildesheim: G. Olms, 1964.

– *Selected Works*. Translated by Peter N. Singer. Oxford: Oxford University Press, 1997.
– *Über die Ausformung der Keimlinge*. Edited and translated by Diethard Nickel. Berlin: Akademie Verlag, 2001.
Gemistos Plethon, George. 'Advice to the Despot Theodore Concerning the Affairs of the Peloponnese.' In Lampros, *Palaiologeia kai Peloponnēsiaka*, 4: 114–35.
– 'Georgios Gemistos to Manuel Palaeologus Concerning the Affairs of the Peloponnese.' In Lampros, *Palaiologeia kai Peloponnēsiaka*, 3: 246–65.
George of Trebizond. *Collectanea Trapezuntiana: Texts, Documents and Bibliographies of George of Trebizond*. Edited by John Monfasani. Binghamton, NY: Medieval & Renaissance Texts & Studies, 1984.
– 'Preface to His Translation of Plato's *Laws*.' Translated by John Monfasani. In *Cambridge Translations of Renaissance Philosophical Texts* 2: *Political Philosophy*, edited by Jill Kraye, 128–33. Cambridge: Cambridge University Press, 1997.
Giannotti, Donato. *Della Repubblica de' Viniziani*. In idem, *Opere politiche*, edited by Furio Diaz, 1:27–151. Milan: Marzorati, 1974.
– *Republica fiorentina*. Edited by Giovanni Silvano. Geneva: Droz, 1990.
– *Die Republik Florenz (1534)*. Edited by Alois Riklin. Translated by Daniel Höchli. Munich: Fink, 1997.
Giovanni Villani. Rome: Istituto Poligrafico e Zecca dello Stato, 2002.
Guicciardini, Francesco. *Dialogo e discorsi del reggimento di Firenze*. Edited by Roberto Palmarocchi. Bari: G. Laterza, 1932.
– *Dialogue on the Government of Florence*. Edited and translated by Alison Brown. Cambridge: Cambridge University Press, 1994.
Gundissalinus, Dominicus. *De divisione philosophiae (Über die Einteilung der Philosophie): Lateinisch-Deutsch*. Translated by Alexander Fidora and Dorothée Werner. Freiburg i. Br.: Herder, 2007.
Heremias de Montagnone. *Epytoma sapientie*. Venice, 1505.
Ibn Qutaybah. Josef Horovitz, 'Ibn Quteiba's "Uyun al-Akhbar."' *Islamic Culture* 4 (1930): 171–98.
Isidore of Seville. *Isidori Hispalensis episcopi Etymologiarvm sive originvm libri xx*. Edited by Wallace M. Lindsay. Oxford: Clarendon Press, 1911.
– *The Etymologies of Isidore of Seville*. Translated by Stephen A. Barney, Wendy J. Lewis, Jennifer A. Beach, and Oliver Berghof. Cambridge: Cambridge University Press, 2006.
John of Jandun. *Quaestiones super octos libros physicorum Aristotelis*. Venice, 1551. Repr. Frankfurt a. M.: Minerva, 1969.
– *Ioannis de Ianduno In libros Aristotelis De coelo et mundo quaestiones subtilissimae*. Venice, 1552.

– *Quaestiones in duodecim libros metaphysicae*. Venice, 1553. Repr. Frankfurt a. M.: Minerva, 1966.
– *Super libros Aristotelis De anima*. Venice, 1587. Repr. Frankfurt a. M.: Minerva, 1966.
– 'Éloge de Paris, composé en 1323 par un habitant de Senlis, Jean de Jandun.' Edited by Nicolas R. Taranne and Antoine J.V. Le Roux de Lincy, *Bulletin du Comité de la langue, de l'histoire et des arts de la France* 3 (1855/6): 505–40.
– 'Tractatus de laudibus Parisius = Traité des louanges de Paris.' In Le Roux de Lincy and Tisserand, *Paris et ses historiens aux XIV e et XVe siècles*, 32–79.
– Roberto Lambertini and Andrea Tabarroni, 'Le *Quaestiones super Metaphysicam* attribuite a Giovanni di Jandun. Osservazioni e problemi.' *Medioevo* 10 (1984): 41–106.
– 'Les questions de Jean de Jandun au sujet du sens agent.' In Adrian Pattin, *Pour l'histoire du sens agent: La controverse entre Barthélemy de Bruges et Jean de Jandun, ses antécédents et son évolution*, 111–234. Leuven: Leuven University Press, 1988.
– 'A Treatise of the Praises of Paris,' In *In Old Paris: An Anthology of Source Descriptions, 1323–1790*, edited by Robert W. Berger, 7–17. New York: Italica Press, 2002.
John of Paris (Quidort). Johannes Quidort von Paris, *Über königliche und päpstliche Gewalt (De regia potestate et papali)*. Edited and translated by Fritz Bleienstein. Stuttgart: Klein, 1969.
– Arthur Monahan. *John of Paris on Royal and Papal Power: A Translation, with Introduction, of the De Potestate Regia et Papali of John of Paris*. New York and London: Columbia University Press, 1974.
John of Salisbury. *Ioannis Saresberiensis episcopi Carnotensis Policratici sive De nvgis cvrialivm et vestigiis philosophorvm libri VIII*. Edited by Clemens C.J. Webb. Oxford: Clarendon Press, 1909.
– *Policraticus: Of the Frivolities of Courtiers and the Footprints of Philosophers*. Edited and translated by Cary J. Nederman. Cambridge: Cambridge University Press, 1990.
John of Viterbo [Iohannis Viterbiensis] *Liber de regimine civitatum*. Edited by Gaetano Salvemini. In *Bibliotheca Juridica Medii Aevi*. Bologna: Società Tipografica Azzoguidi, 1901, 3: 215–80.
Lampros, Spyridon P. *Palaiologeia kai Peloponnēsiaka*. Athens: V.N. Gregoriades, 1972.
Latini, Brunetto. *The Book of the Treasure (Li Livres dou Tresor)*. Translated by Paul Barrette and Spurgeon Baldwin. New York and London: Garland Pub., 1993.

– *Li Livres dou Tresor*. Edited by Spurgeon Baldwin and Paul Barrette. Tempe, AZ: Arizona Center for Medieval and Renaissance Studies, 2003.

Leo VI. *The Taktika of Leo VI*. Edited and translated by George T. Dennis. Washington, DC: Dumbarton Oaks, 2010.

Lerner, Ralph, and Muhsin Mahdi, eds. *Medieval Political Philosophy: A Sourcebook*. New York: Free Press of Glencoe, 1963.

Le Roux de Lincy, Antoine J.V., and Lazare M. Tisserand, eds. *Paris et ses historiens aux XIV et XVe siècles*. Paris: Imprimerie impériale, 1867.

Liber de causis, Liber de causis = Das Buch von den Ursachen. Translated by Andreas Schönfeld. Hamburg: F. Meiner, 2003.

– Abdurrahman Badawi. 'Procli: Liber (Pseudo-Aristotelis) de expositione bonitatis purae.' In *Neoplatonici apud Arabes*, 1–33. Cairo: n.p., 1957.

– *Die pseudo-aristotelische Schrift Ueber das reine Gute bekannt unter dem Namen Liber de causis*. Edited by Otto Bardenhewer. Freiburg i.Br.: Herder, 1882. Repr. Frankfurt a. M.: Minerva, 1957.

– Adrian Pattin. 'Le *Liber de causis* – Édition établie à l'aide de 90 manuscrits avec introduction et notes.' *Tijdschrift voor Filosofie* 28 (1966): 90–203.

– *The Book of Causes*. Translated by Dennis J. Brand. Milwaukee: Marquette University Press, 1984.

– Pierre Magnard. *La demeure de l'être. Autour d'un anonyme. Étude et traduction du Liber de Causis*. Paris: J. Vrin, 1990.

– Alexander Fidora and Andreas Niederberger. *Von Bagdad nach Toledo: das 'Buch der Ursachen' und seine Rezeption im Mittelalter; lateinisch – deutscher Text, Kommentar und Wirkungsgeschichte des Liber de causis*. Mainz: Dieterich, 2001.

Lovati, Lovato. *Lupati de Lupatis, Bovetini de Bovetinis, Albertini Mussati necnon et Iamboni Andreae de Favafuschis carmina quaedam ex codice veneto nunc primum edita*. Edited by Luigi Padrin. Padua: Tip. del Seminario, 1887.

Machiavelli, Niccolò. *The Prince*. Edited by Quentin Skinner and Russell Price. Cambridge: Cambridge University Press, 1988.

– *Discourses on Livy*. Translated by Harvey C. Mansfield and Nathan Tarcov. Chicago, IL, and London: University of Chicago Press, 1996.

– *Opere*. Ed. Corrado Vivanti. Turin: Einaudi-Gallimard, 1997.

– *The Prince*. Translated by Harvey C. Mansfield. Chicago, IL, and London: University of Chicago Press, 2nd ed. 1998.

Maimonides, Moses. *The Guide of the Perplexed*. Translated by Shlomo Pines. Chicago, IL: Chicago University Press, 1963.

– *Rabi Mossei Aegyptii Dux seu Director dubitantium aut perplexorum*. Paris 1520. Repr. Frankfurt a. M.: Minerva, 1964.

Manegold of Lautenbach. *Liber contra Wolfelmum*. Translated by Robert Ziomkowski. Paris: Peeters, 2002.

Marsilius of Padua. *The defence of peace: lately translated out of laten in to englysshe, with the kynges moste gracyous privilege.* Translated by William Marshall. London, 1535.
– *The Defensor Minor of Marsilius of Padua.* Edited by C. Kenneth Brampton. Birmingham: Cornish Brothers, 1922.
– *The Defensor Pacis of Marsilius of Padua.* Edited by Charles W. Previté-Orton Cambridge: Cambridge University Press, 1928.
– *Defensor pacis.* Edited by Richard Scholz (= Fontes iuris Germanici antiqui in usum scholarum ex Monumentis Germaniae Historicis separatim editi; 7). Hanover: Hahn, 1932/3.
– Marsilius of Padua. *The Defender of Peace,* vol. 2: *The Defensor pacis.* Translated by Alain Gewirth. New York: Columbia University Press, 1956. Repr. 2001.
– *Der Verteidiger des Friedens.* Translated by Horst Kusch. 2 vols. Berlin: Rütten & Loening, 1958.
– *Il difensore della pace.* Translated by Cesare Vasoli. Turin: UTET, 1960; rev. ed. 1975.
– *Le Défenseur de la paix.* Translated by Jeannine Quillet. Paris: J. Vrin, 1968.
– *Il Difensore minore.* Translated by Cesare Vasoli. Naples: Guida, 1975.
– Marsile de Padoue. *Œuvres mineures: Defensor minor, De translatione imperii.* Edited and translated by Colette Jeudy and Jeannine Quillet. Paris: Éditions du Centre national de la recherche scientifique, 1979.
– 'Marsílio de Pádua, *Sobre a jurisdição do imperador em questões matrimoniais,*' [trans. José Antônio de C.R. de Souza]. In *Estudos Sobre Filosofia Medieval,* edited by José Lourenço da Araujo and José Antônio de C.R. de Souza, 175–87. São Paulo: Loyola, 1984.
– *El defensor de la paz.* Translated by Luis Martínez Gómez. Madrid: Tecnos, 1989.
– *O Defensor menor.* Translated by José Antônio C.R. de Souza. In *Marsílio de Pádua e Jerônimo Savonarola – Escritos,* 115–66. Petrópolis: Vozes, 1991.
– *Writings on the Empire: Defensor minor and De translatione Imperii.* Translated by Cary J. Nederman. Cambridge: Cambridge University Press, 1993.
– *O defensor da paz.* Translated by José Antônio C.R. de Souza. Petrópolis: Vozes, 1997.
– José Antônio C.R. de Souza, 'Marsílio de Pádua, *Sobre a Translação do Império.*' *Veritas* 43 (1998): 703–23. Repr. in *A ciência e a organização dos saberes na Idade Média,* edlted by Luis A. de Boni, 299–313. Porto Alegre: EDIPUCRS, 2000.
– *Il difensore della pace.* Translated by Mario Conetti, Claudio Fiocchi, Stefano Radice, and Stefano Simonetta. 2 vols. Milan: Rizzoli, 2001.

– *The Defender of the Peace*. Edited and translated by Annabel Brett. Cambridge: Cambridge University Press, 2005.
– *Sobre el poder del imperio y del Papa: El defensor menor; La transferencia del imperio*. Translated by Bernardo Bayona and Pedro Roche Arnas. Madrid: Biblioteca Nueva, 2005.
Mussato, Albertino. *Écérinide, Épîtres métriques sur la poésie, Songe*. Edited by Jean-Frédéric Chevalier. Paris: Les Belles Lettres, 2000.
– Andrea M. Moschetti. 'Il *De lite inter Naturam et Fortunam* e il *Contra causos fortuitos* di Albertino Mussato.' In *Miscellanea di studi critici in onore di Vincenzo Crescini*, 567–99. Cividale: Tipografia Fratelli Stagni, 1927. Repr. Milan: Erasmo, [1957?].
– *Sette libri inediti del 'De gestis italicorum post Henricum VII' di Albertino Mussato*. Edited by Luigi Padrin. Venice: Società Veneta di Storia Patria, 1903.
– 'Albertini Mussati Ludovicus Bavarus.' In *Geschichtsquellen Deutschlands* vol. 1: *Johannes Victoriensis und andere Geschichtsquellen Deutschlands im vierzehnten Jahrhundert*, edited by Johannes F. Boehmer, 170–89. Stuttgart: Cotta, 1843. Repr. Aalen: Scientia Verlag, 1969.
– Walter Friedensburg. 'Des Albertinus Mussatus Kaisergeschichte oder Geschichte Kaiser Heinrichs VII.' In *Das Leben Kaiser Heinrichs VII. Berichte der Zeitgenossen über ihn*, 71–334. Leipzig: Dyk, 1882; new ed. Roland Pauler. Neuried: Ars Una, 1999.
– 'Albertini Mussati Ludovicus Bavarus ad Filium.' In *Rerum Italicarum Scriptores*, 10: cols. 769–84.
– 'Albertini Mušati Paduani Historiographi et Tragœdi de gestis Heinrici VII Cæsaris *Historia Augusta*.' In *Rerum Italicarum Scriptores*, 10: cols. 9–568.
– 'Albertini Mussati Historici Patavini de gestis Italicorum post mortem Henrici VII. Cæsaris *Historia*.' In *Rerum Italicarum Scriptores*, 10: cols. 571–768.
Nederman, Cary J., and Thomas M. Izbicki, trans. *Three Tracts on Empire: Engelbert of Admont, Aeneas Silvius Piccolomini, and Juan de Torquemada*. Bristol: Thoemmes Press, 2000.
Nemesios of Emesa. *De natura hominis; traduction de Burgundio de Pise*. Edited by Gérard Verbeke and J.R. Moncho. Leiden: E.J. Brill, 1975.
– Nemesio di Emesa. *La natura dell'uomo*. Translated by Moreno Morani. Salerno: Grafiche Moriniello, 1982.
– *Nemesii Emeseni De natura hominis*. Edited by Moreno Morani. Leipzig: Teubner, 1987.
– *On the Nature of Man*. Translated by Robert W. Sharples and Philip van der Eijk. Liverpool: Liverpool University Press, 2008.
Origen. *Contra Celsum*. Translated by Henry Chadwick. Cambridge: Cambridge University Press, 1953.

Peter of Abano. *Conciliator controversiarum, quae inter philosophos et medicos versantur*. Venice, 1565; Facsimile. Edited by Ezio Riondato and Luigi Olivieri. Padua: Antenore 1985.

– *Il 'Lucidator dubitabilium astronomiae' di Pietro d'Abano; opere scientifiche inedite*. Edited by Graziella Federici Vescovini. Padua: Programma e 1+1 Ed., 1988.

Peter of Auvergne. 'Commentary and Questions on Book III of Aristotle's Politics (Selections).' In *The Cambridge Translations of Medieval Philosophical Texts*, vol. 2: *Ethics and Political Philosophy*. Edited by Arthur S. McGrade, John Kilcullen, and Matthew Kempshall, 216–56.Cambridge: Cambridge University Press, 2001.

Philoponus, John. (Ioannis Philoponi.) *In Aristotelis libros De generatione et corruptione commentaria*. Edited by Girolamo Vitelli. Berlin: Reimer, 1897.

Pomponazzi, Pietro. *Tractatus de immortalitate animae*. Translated by William Henry Hay II. Haverford, PA: Haverford College, 1938.

– *Abhandlung über die Unsterblichkeit der Seele: Lateinisch-Deutsch*. Translated by Burkhard Mojsisch. Hamburg: F. Meiner, 1990.

– *Trattato sull'immortalità dell'anima*. Edited by Vittoria Perrone Compagni. Florence: L.S. Olschki, 1999.

Pseudo-Henry of Ghent. *Les Quaestiones in Librum de causis attribueés à Henri de Gand*. Edited by John P. Zwaenepoel. Louvain-la-Neuve: Publications universitaires, 1974.

Ptolemy of Lucca. *On the Government of Rulers = De Regimine Principum; with portions attributed to Thomas Aquinas*. Translated by James M. Blythe. Philadelphia, PA: University of Pennsylvania Press, 1997.

Rerum Italicarum Scriptores. Edited by Lodovico A. Muratori. Milan: Societas Palatina, 1727.

Riezler Sigmund. *Vatikanische Akten zur deutschen Geschichte in der Zeit Kaiser Ludwigs des Bayern*. Innsbruck: Wagner, 1891. Repr. Aalen: Scientia Verlag, 1973.

Rolandino [da Padova]. *Rolandini Patavini Cronica in factis et circa facta Marchie Trivixane*. Edited by Antonio Bonardi. In *Rerum Italicarum Scriptores* 2nd series VIII/1: 5–174. Città di Castello: Lapi, 1905.

– *The Chronicles of the Trevisan March*. Translated by Joseph R. Berrigan. Lawrence, KS: Coronado Press, 1980.

– *Vita e morte di Ezzelino da Romano (Cronaca)*. Edited by Flavio Fiorese. Rome and Milan: Fondazione Lorenzo Valla / A. Mondadori, 2004.

Sarpi, Paolo. *Pensieri naturali, metafisici e matematici*. Edited by Luisa Cozzi and Libero Sosio. Milan: R. Ricciardi, 1996.

Shem-Ṭov ben Joseph ibn Falaquera. *Falaquera's Book of the Seeker (Sefer Ha-*

Mebaqqesh). Edited by M. Herschel Levine. New York: Yeshiva University Press, 1976.

Siger of Brabant. *Les Quaestiones super Librum de Causis de Siger de Brabant.* Edited by Antonio Marlasca. Louvain-la-Neuve: Publications universitaires, 1972.

Statuti del Comune di Padova. Translated into Italian Guido Beltrame, Guerrino Citton and Daniela Mazzon. Cittadella: Biblos, 2000.

Statuti del comune di Padova dal secolo XII all'anno1285. Edited by Andrea Gloria. Padua: F. Sacchetto, 1873.

Themistios. Irfan Shahid. *Themistii Orationes ex codice medioelanensi.* Edited by Wilhelm Dindorf. Leipzig: K. Knobloch, 1832. Repr. Hildesheim: G. Olms, 1961.

– *Die 34. Rede des Themistios (Peri tēs archēs).* Edited by Hugo Schneider. Winterthur: P.G. Keller, 1966.

– 'Epistula de re publica gerenda.' In *Themistii orationes quae supersunt*, edited by Heinrich Schenkl, 3: 73–119. Leipzig: Teubner, 1974.

Thierry of Chartres. *The Latin Rhetorical Commentaries by Thierry of Chartres.* Edited by Karin M. Fredborg. Toronto: Pontifical Institute of Mediaeval Studies, 1988.

Walzer, Michael,Menachem Lorberbaum, Noam J. Zohar, and Yair Lorberbaum, eds. *The Jewish Political Tradition*, vol. 1: *Authority*. New Haven, CT and London: Yale University Press, 2000.

Xenophon. *Oeconomicus: A Social and Historical Commentary.* Translated by Sarah B. Pomeroy. Oxford: Clarendon Press, 1994.

Secondary Sources

Aalders, Gerhard J.D. 'Die Mischverfassung und ihre historische Dokumentation in den *Politica* des Aristoteles.' In *La 'Politique' d'Aristote: Sept exposés et discussions*, 201–44. Vandœuvres-Geneva: Fondation Hardt, 1964.

– *Die Theorie der gemischten Verfassung im Altertum.* Amsterdam: A.M. Hakkert, 1968.

– 'ΝΟΜΟΣ ΕΜΨΥΧΟΣ.' In Steinmetz, *Politeia und res publica*, 315–29.

Ackrill, John L. 'Aristotle on *Eudaimonia*.' *Proceedings of the British Academy* 60 (1974): 339–59. Repr. in Oksenberg Rorty, *Essays on Aristotle's Ethics*, 15–33.

Aertsen, Jan A., and Andreas Speer, eds. *Was ist Philosophie im Mittelalter?* Berlin and New York: W. de Gruyter, 1998.

Agrimi Jole, and Chiara Crisciani. *Edocere medicos: Medicina scolastica nei secoli XIII–XV.* Naples: Guerini e associati, 1988.

Aichele, Alexander. 'Heart and Soul of the State: Some Remarks Concerning Aristotelian Ontology and Medieval Theory of Medicine in Marsilius of Padua's *Defensor pacis*.' In Moreno-Riaño, *The World of Marsilius of Padua*, 163–86.

Alessio, Franco. 'Filosofia e scienza. Pietro da Abano.' In Folena, *Storia della cultura veneta*, vol. 2: *Il Trecento*, 171–206.

Alessio, Gian Carlo. 'Brunetto Latini e Cicerone (e i dettatori).' *Italia Medioevale e Umanistica* 22 (1979): 123–69.

Ancona, Elvio. *All'origine della sovranità: Sistema gerarchico e ordinamento giuridico nella disputa sui due poteri all'inizio del XIV secolo*. Turin: Giappichelli, 2004.

Ancona, Elvio, and Franco Todescan, eds. *Marsilio da Padova*. Padua: CEDAM, 2007.

Andrewes, Antony. 'Eunomia.' *Classical Quarterly* 32 (1938): 89–102.

Andrews, Frances. 'Albertano of Brescia, Rolandino of Padua and the Rhetoric of Legitimation.' In *Building Legitimacy: Political Discourses and Forms of Legitimacy in Medieval Societies*, edited by Isabel Alfonso, Hugh Kennedy and Julio Escalona, 319–40. Leiden and Boston: Brill, 2004.

Annas, Julia. 'Cicero on Stoic Moral Philosophy and Private Property.' In *Philosophia togata: Essays on Philosophy and Roman Society*, edited by Miriam Griffin and Jonathan Barnes, 151–73. Oxford: Clarendon Press, 1989.

Arnaldi, Girolamo. *Studi sui cronisti della Marca Trevigiana nell'età di Ezzelino da Romano*. Rome: Istituto storico italiano per il Medio Evo, 1963.

– 'Il mito di Ezzelino da Rolandino al Mussato.' In *La rinascita della tragedia nell'Italia dell'umanesimo*, 85–97. Viterbo: Agnesotti, 1980.

Arnaldi, Girolamo, and Lidia Capo. 'I Cronisti di Venezia e della Marca Trevigiana dalle origini alla fine del secolo XIII.' In Folena, *Storia della cultura veneta*, vol. 1: *Dalle origini al Trecento*, 387–423.

Artifoni, Enrico. 'I podestà professionali e la fondazione retorica della politica comunale.' *Quaderni Storici* n.s. 63 (1986): 687–719.

– 'Gli uomini dell'assemblea. L'oratoria civile, i conciatori e i predicatori nella società comunale.' In *La predicazione dei Frati dalla metà del '200 alla fine del '300*, 141–88. Spoleto: Centro Italiano di Studi sull'Alto Medioevo, 1995.

– 'L'éloquence politique dans le cités communales (XIIIe siècle).' In *Cultures italiennes (XIIe–XVe siècle)*, edited by Isabelle Heullant-Donat, 269–96. Paris: Cerf, 2000.

– 'Orfeo concionatore. Un passo di Tommaso d'Aquino e l'eloquenza politica nella città italiane nel secolo XIII.' In *La musica nel pensiero medievale*, edited by Letterio Mauro, 137–49. Ravenna: Longo, 2001.

– 'Prudenza del consigliare. L'educazione del cittadino nel *Liber consolationis et consilii* di Albertano da Brescia (1246).' In *Consilium: Teorie e pratiche del consigliare nella cultura medievale*, edited by Carla Casagrande et al., 195–216. Florence: SISMEL edizioni del Galluzzo, 2004.

– 'Una forma declamatoria di eloquenza politica nelle città comunali (sec. XIII): la concione.' In *Papers on Rhetoric* 8: *Declamation*, edited by Lucia Calboli Montefusco, 1–27. Rome: Herder, 2007.

Atger, Frédéric. *Essai sur l'histoire des doctrines du contrat social.* Paris: F. Alcan, 1906.

Aubenque, Pierre. *La prudence chez Aristote.* Paris: Presses Universitaires de France, 1963.

Aubenque, Pierre, and Alonso Tordesillas, eds. *Aristote politique: Etudes sur la Politique d'Aristote.* Paris: Presses Universitaires de France, 1993.

Averroismo e aristotelismo padovano. Padua: CEDAM, 1939.

Baader, Gerhard. 'Galen im mittelalterlichen Abendland.' In *Galen: Problems and Prospects*, edited by Vivian Nutton, 213–28. London: Wellcome Institute for the History of Medicine, 1981.

Babbitt, Susan M. '*Praeter Politicos Principatus Ponendum*: Priests as Magistrates and Citizens in Medieval Texts Using Aristotle's *Politics*.' In *Popes, Teachers and Canon Law in the Middle Ages*, edited by James Ross Sweeney and Stanley Chodorow, 145–59. Ithaca, NY: Cornell University Press, 1989.

Bächli, Andreas. *Monotheismus und neuplatonische Philosophie. Eine Untersuchung zum pseudo-aristotelischen Liber de causis und dessen Rezeption durch Albert den Großen*. St. Augustin: Academia-Verlag, 2004.

Bakan, David, Dan Merkur, and David S. Weiss. *Maimonides' Cure of Souls: Medieval Precursor of Psychoanalysis*. Albany, NY: SUNY Press, 2009.

Baldassarri, Guido. 'Ancora sulle "fonti" della Rettorica: Brunetto Latini e Teodorico di Chartres.' *Studi e problemi di critica testuale* 19 (1979): 41–69.

Baloglou, Christos P. 'Die Einteilung des Volkes in drei Stande bei Georgios Gemistos im Vergleich zu Hippodamos von Milet und den Physiokraten.' *Jahrbuch der Österreichischen Byzantinistik* 46 (1996): 311–24.

– 'Economic Thought in the Last Byzantine Period.' In *Ancient and Medieval Economic Ideas and Concepts of Social Justice*, edited by S. Todd Lowry and Barry Gordon, 405–38. Leiden: Brill, 1998.

Barcaro, Francesco A. *Tre grandi Europei del Trecento: Pietro d'Abano, Jacopo e Giovanni de'Dondi dall'Orologio*. Padua: Panda, 1991.

Barceló, Pedro. *Basileia, Monarchia, Tyrannis: Untersuchungen zu Entwicklung und Beurteilung von Alleinherrschaft im vorhellenistischen Griechenland*. Stuttgart: F. Steiner Verlag, 1993.

Barker, Ernest. *The Political Thought of Plato and Aristotle.* London: Methuen, 1906. Repr. New York: Dover Publications, 1959.

Barnes, Harry E. 'Theories of the Origin of the State in Classical Political Philosophy.' *The Monist* 34 (1924): 15–62.

Barnes, Jonathan, Malcolm Schofield, and Richard Sorabji, eds. *Articles on Aristotle*, vol. 2: *Ethics and Politics*. London: Duckworth, 1977.

Baron, Hans. 'Cicero and the Roman Civic Spirit in the Middle Ages and Early Renaissance.' *Bulletin of the John Rylands Library* 22 (1938): 72–97.

Battaglia, Felice. 'La dottrina dello stato misto nei politici fiorentini del Rinascimento.' *Rivista internazionale di filosofia del diritto* 7 (1927): 286–304.

– *Marsilio da Padova e la filosofia politica del medio evo*. Florence: F. Le Monnier, 1928.

Bayona Aznar, Bernardo. 'La paz en la obra de Marsilio de Padua.' *Contrastes* 11 (2006): 44–63.

– 'La incongruencia de la denominación "averroísmo político".' In *Maimónides y el pensamiento medieval: VIII Centenario de la muerte de Maimónides*, edited by José Luis Cantón Alonso, 329–40. Cordoba: Servicio de Publicaciones, Universidad de Córdoba, 2007.

– *Religión y poder: Marsilio de Padua: ¿La primera teoría laica del Estado?* Madrid: Biblioteca Nueva, 2007.

Bazzana, André, Nicole Bériou, and Pierre Guichard, eds. *Averroès et l'averroïsme (XIIe–XVe siècle): Un itinéraire historique du Haut Atlas à Paris et à Padoue*. Lyon: Presses Universitaires de Lyon, 2005.

Becker, Marvin B. 'A Study in Political Failure: The Fiorentine Magnates (1280–1343).' *Medieval Studies* 27 (1965): 246–308. Repr. in *Florentine Essays: Selected Writings of Marvin B. Becker*, edited by James Banker and Carol Lansing, 94–159. Ann Arbor, MI: University of Michigan Press, 2002.

Behler, Ernst. *Die Ewigkeit der Welt: Problemgeschichtliche Untersuchungen zu den Kontroversen um Weltanfang und Weltunendlichkeit im Mittelalter*, vol. 1: *Die Problemstellung in der arabischen und jüdischen Philosophie des Mittelalters*. Munich: Schöningh, 1965.

Beierwaltes, Werner. 'Der Kommentar zum *Liber de causis* als neuplatonisches Element in der Philosophie des Thomas von Aquin.' *Philosophische Rundschau* 11 (1964): 192–215.

Berg, Martin. 'Der Italienzug Ludwigs des Bayern. Das Itinerar der Jahre 1327–1330.' *Quellen und Forschungen aus italienischen Archiven und Bibliotheken* 67 (1987): 142–97.

Berman, Lawrence V. 'Greek into Hebrew: Samuel ben Judah of Marseilles, Fourteenth-Century Philosopher and Translator.' In *Jewish Medieval and Renaissance Studies*, edited by Alexander Altmann, 289–320. Cambridge, MA: Harvard University, 1967.

Berns, Thomas. 'Construire un idéal vénitien de la constitution mixte à la Renaissance: L'enseignement de Platon par Trébizonde.' In *Le Gouvernement mixte: De l'idéal politique au monstre constitutionnel en Europe (XIIIe–XVIIe siècle)*, edited by Marie Gaille-Nikodimov, 25–38. Saint-Etienne: Publications de l'Université de Saint-Étienne, 2005.

Berrigan, Joseph R. 'Benzo d'Alessandria and the Cities of Northern Italy.' *Studies in Medieval and Renaissance History* 4 (1967): 125–92.

– 'The *Ecerinis*: A Prehumanist View of Tyranny.' *Delta Epsilon Sigma Bulletin* 12 (1967): 71–86.

– 'The Prehumanism of Benzo d'Alessandria.' *Traditio* 25 (1969): 249–63.

– 'Prehumanist Views of Domestic Violence in the Early Trecento.' *Studies in Medieval Culture* 5 (1975): 159–63.

Bertelli, Lucio. 'La *scholé* aristotelica tra norma e prassi empirica.' In *Atti del Colloquio su poetica e politica fra Platone e Aristotele*, 97–129. Rome: Edizioni dell'Ateneo, 1988.

Bertelloni, Francisco. 'Presupuestos de la recepción de la *Política* de Aristóteles.' In *Aristotelica et Lulliana*, edited by Fernando Domínguez, Ruedi Imbach, Theodor Pindl, and Peter Walter, 35–54. Steenbrugge/The Hague: In Abbatia S. Petri/M. Nijhoff International, 1995.

– 'Zur Rekonstruktion des politischen Aristotelismus im Mittelalter (Die Entwicklung der dreigliedrigen *philosophia practica* vor der Rezeption der aristotelischen *libri morales*).' In Aertsen and Speer, *Was ist Philosophie im Mittelalter?*, 999–1011.

– 'Los fundamentos teóricos de la caducidad del orden jurídico en el *De ecclesiastica potestate* de Egidio Romano.' *Patristica et Mediaevalia* 22 (2001): 17–29.

– 'Die Anwendung von Kausalitätstheorien im politischen Denken von Thomas von Aquin und Aegidius Romanus.' In Kaufhold, *Politische Reflexion in der Welt des späten Mittelalters*, 85–108.

– 'Nähe und Distanz zu Aristoteles: Die neue Bedeutung von *civitas* im politischen Denken zwischen Thomas von Aquin und Nikolaus von Kues.' In *University, Council, City: Intellectual Culture on the Rhine (1300–1550)*, edited by Laurent Cesalli, Nadja Germann, and Maarten J.F.M. Hoenen, 323–47. Turnhout: Brepols, 2007.

– 'Selbsterhaltungstrieb, *princeps*, *lex* and *ius* im Traktat *De potestate regia et papali* des Johannes Quidort.' In Fidora, Lutz-Bachmann, and Wagner, *Lex und Ius*, 175–94.

Berti, Enrico. 'Filosofia, astrologia e vita quotidiana nella Padova del Trecento.' In *I Dondi dell'Orologio e la Padova dei Carraresi: Padua sidus preclarum*, edited by Nicola Mazzonetto, 17–28 . [Brugine]: Edizioni 1 + 1, 1989. Repr. in *Il Palazzo della Ragione a Padova: Dalle Pitture di Giotto agli affreschi del '400*, edited by Centro Internazionale di Storia della nozione e della misura dello Spazio e del Tempo, 3: 97–108. Rome: Istituto Poligrafico e Zecca dello Stato, 1992.

– 'Astronomia e astrologia da Pietro d'Abano a Giovanni Dondi dell'Orologio.' In Longo, *Padova carrarese*, 175–84.

Bezold, Friedrich von. 'Astrologische Geschichtskonstruktion im Mittelalter.' *Deutsche Zeitschrift für Geschichtswissenschaft* 8 (1892): 29–72. Repr in. idem, *Aus Mittelalter und Renaissance: Kulturgeschichtliche Studien*, 165–95. Munich and Berlin: R. Oldenbourg, 1918.

Bianchi, Luca. 'Filosofi, uomini e bruti. Note per la storia di un'antropologia averroista.' *Rinascimento* 32 (1992): 185–201.

Billanovich, Giuseppe. *I primi umanisti e le tradizioni dei classici latini*. Freiburg i.d.S.: Edizioni Universitarie, 1953.

– 'Il Livio di Pomposa e i primi umanisti padovani.' *La bibliofilia* 85 (1983): 125–48.

– *Petrarca e il primo umanesimo*. Padua: Antenore, 1996.

Billanovich, Guido. 'Vetera vestigia vatum nei carmi dei preumanisti padovani.' *Italia Medioevale e Umanistica* 1 (1958): 155–243.

– 'Il preumanesimo padovano.' In Folena, *Storia della cultura veneta*, vol. 2: *Il Trecento*, 19–110.

– 'Il Seneca tragico di Pomposa e i primi umanisti padovani.' *La Bibliofilia* 85 (1983): 149–69.

Biller, Peter. 'Words and the Medieval Notion of "Religion."' *Journal of Ecclesiastical History* 36 (1985): 351–69.

Birkenmajer, Alexandre [Aleksander]. 'Le rôle joué par les médecins et les naturalistes dans la réception d'Aristote au XII-e et XIII-e siècles.' In *La Pologne au VI-e Congrès International des Sciences Historiques, Oslo 1928*. Warsaw and Lviv: Société Polonaise d'Histoire, 1930, 1–15. Repr. in idem, *Études d'histoire des Sciences et de la Philosophie du Moyen Âge*, 73–87. Wroclaw: Zakład Narodowy im. Ossolińskich, 1970.

Biscardi, Arnaldo. 'Quod Graeci synallagma vocant.' *Labeo* 29 (1983): 127–39.

Bizzarri, Dina. 'Ricerche sul diritto di *cittadinanza* nella costituzione comunale.' *Studi Senesi* 32 (1916): 19–136. Repr. in eadem, *Studi di storia del diritto italiano*, edited by Federico Patetta and Mario Chiaudano, 62–158. Turin: S. Lattes, 1937.

Black, Antony. *Guilds and Civil Society in European Political Thought from the Twelfth Century to the Present*. Ithaca, NJ: Cornell University Press, 1984.

– 'Political Languages in Later Medieval Europe.' In *The Church and Sovereignty c. 590–1918*, edited by Diana Wood, 313–28. Oxford and Cambridge, MA: B. Blackwell, 1991. Repr. in idem, *Church, State and Community*, no. XI.

– *Political Thought in Europe, 1250–1450*. Cambridge: Cambridge University Press, 1992.

– 'The Commune in Political Theory in the Late Middle Ages.' In *Theorien kommunaler Ordnung in Europa*, edited by Peter Blickle, 99–112. Munich: Oldenbourg, 1996. Repr. in idem, *Church, State and Community*, no. XIII.
– *The History of Islamic Political Thought: From the Prophet to the Present*. New York: Routledge, 2001.
– *Church, State and Community: Historical and Comparative Perspectives*, no. XIII. Aldershot: Ashgate, 2003.
– 'Harmony and Strife in Political Thought c. 1300–1500.' In Miethke and Schreiner, *Sozialer Wandel im Mittelalter*, 355–63. Repr. in idem, *Church, State and Community*, no. XV.
– *The West and Islam: Religion and Political Thought in World History*. Oxford: Oxford University Press, 2008.
Blackstein, Erdmann. 'Der venezianische Staatsgedanke im 16. Jahrhundert und das zeitgenössische Venedig-Bild in der Staatstheorie des republikanischen Florenz.' Diss., University of Frankfurt a. M., 1973.
Blair, Ann. 'The Problemata as a Natural Philosophical Genre.' In *Natural Particulars*, 171–204.
Blok, Josine H., and André P.M.H. Lardinois, eds. *Solon of Athens: New Historical and Philological Approaches*. Leiden and Boston: Brill, 2006.
Blomqvist, Karen. *The Tyrant in Aristotle's Politics: Theoretical Assumptions and Historical Background*. Stockholm: Almqvist & Wiksell International, 1998.
Blundell, Sue. *The Origins of Civilization in Greek and Roman Thought*. London and Sydney: C. Helm, 1986.
Blythe, James M. 'Family, Government, and the Medieval Aristotelians.' *History of Political Thought* 10 (1989): 1–16.
– *Ideal Government and the Mixed Constitution in the Middle Ages*. Princeton, NJ: Princeton University Press, 1992.
– 'Aristotle's Politics and Ptolemy of Luca.' *Vivarium* 40 (2002): 103–36.
– *The Life and Works of Tolomeo Fiadoni (Ptolemy of Lucca)*. Turnhout: Brepols, 2009.
– *The Worldview and Thought of Tolomeo Fiadoni (Ptolemy of Lucca)*. Brepols: Turnhout, 2009.
Boas, George. *Primitivism and Related Ideas in the Middle Ages*. Baltimore, MD: Johns Hopkins University Press, 1948. Repr. 1997.
Boas, Marie. 'The Establishment of the Mechanical Philosophy.' *Osiris* 10 (1952): 412–541.
Boese, Helmut. *Wilhelm von Moerbeke als Übersetzer der Stoicheiosis theologike des Proclus: Untersuchungen und Texte zur Überlieferung der Elementatio theologica*. Heidelberg: Bitsch, 1985.
Bookman, J.T. 'The Wisdom of the Many: An Analysis of the Arguments of

Book III and IV of Aristotle's Politics.' *History of Political Thought* 13 (1992): 1–12.

Bortolami, Sante. 'Albertino Mussato: un nuovo autografo e precisazioni biografiche.' *Italia Medioevale e Umanistica* 25 (1985): 189–208.

– 'Da Rolandino al Mussato: tensioni ideali e senso della storia nella storiografi a padovana di tradizione "repubblicana."' In *Il senso della storia nella cultura medievale italiana (1100–1350)*, 53–86. Pistoia: Centro Italiano di Studi di Storia e d'Arte, 1995.

Bos, Egbert P., and Pieter A. Meijer, eds. *On Proclus and His Influence in Medieval Philosophy*. Leiden: E.J. Brill, 1992.

Bosl, Karl. 'Die "Geistliche Hofakademie" Kaiser Ludwigs des Bayern im alten Franziskanerkloster zu München.' In *Der Mönch im Wappen: Aus Geschichte und Gegenwart des katholischen München*, 97–129. Munich: Schnell & Steiner, 1960.

Bosley, Richard, Roger A. Shiner, and Janet D. Sisson, eds. *Aristotle, Virtue and the Mean*. Edmonton: Academic Printing & Publishing, 1995.

Botteghi, Luigi A. 'Clero e comune in Padova nel secolo XIII.' *Nuovo archivio veneto*, n.s., 9 (1905): 215–72.

Boudet, Jean-Patrice. 'Le roi-soleil dans la France médiévale.' *Micrologus* 12 (2004): 455–78.

Boudon-Millot, Véronique. 'La naissance de la vie dans la théorie médicale et philosophique de Galien.' In Brisson, Congourdeau and Solère, *L'embryon: Formation et animation*, 79– 94.

Bouyges, Maurice. 'Notes sur les traductions arabes d'auteurs grecs.' *Archives de philosophie* 2, 3 (1924): 1–23.

Bowsky, William M. *Henry VII in Italy: The Conflict of Empire and City-State, 1310–1313*. Lincoln, NE: University of Nebraska Press, 1960.

Braden, Gordon. *Renaissance Tragedy and the Senecan Tradition: Anger's Privilege*. New Haven, CT: Yale University Press, 1985.

Bradley, Andrew C. 'Aristotle's Conception of the State.' In *Hellenica: A Collection of Essays on Greek Poetry, Philosophy, History and Religion*, edited by Evelyn Abbott, 181–243. London: Rivingtons, 1880. Repr. in Keyt and Miller, *A Companion to Aristotle's Politics*, 13–56.

Brampton, C. Kenneth. 'Marsiglio of Padua.' *English Historical Review* 37 (1922): 501–15.

Braun, Egon. 'Die Summierungstheorie des Aristoteles.' *Jahreshefte des österreichischen archeologischen Instituts* 44 (1959): 157–84. Repr. in Steinmetz, *Schriften zu den Politika des Aristoteles*, 396–423.

– *Das dritte Buch der aristotelischen Politik: Interpretation*. Vienna: Böhlaus Nachf., Kommissionsverlag der Österreichischen Akademie der Wissenschaften, 1965.

– 'Die Ursache der Pluralität von Verfassungsformen nach Aristoteles.' *Wissenschaftliche Arbeiten aus dem Burgenland* 35 (1966): 57–65. Repr. in Steinmetz, *Schriften zu den Politika des Aristoteles*, 431–9.

– 'Die Theorie der Mischverfassung bei Aristoteles.' *Wiener Studien* 80, N.F. 1 (1967): 79–89.

Brenet, Jean-Baptiste. *Transferts du sujet: La noétique d'Averroès selon Jean de Jandun*. Paris: Vrin, 2003.

Brenet, Jean-Baptiste, ed. *Averroès et les averroïsmes juif et latin*. Turnhout: Brepols, 2007.

Brett, Annabel. 'Issues in Translating the *Defensor Pacis*.' In Moreno-Riaño, *The World of Marsilius of Padua*, 91–108.

Briguglia, Gianluca. *Il corpo vivente dello Stato: Una metafora politica*. Milan: B. Mondadori, 2006.

– 'Il diletto del linguaggio. La scelta della lingua come spazio politico in alcuni testi politici e letterari della seconda metà del Duecento.' In *Thinking Politics in the Vernacular: From the Midlle Ages to the Renaissance*, edited by Gianluca Briguglia and Thomas Ricklin, 43–56. Fribourg: Fribourg Academic Press, 2011.

– 'The Minor Marsilius: The Other Works of Marsilius of Padua.' In Moreno-Riaño and Nederman, *A Companion to Marsilius of Padua*, 265–303.

Brisson, Luc, Marie-Hélène Congourdeau, and Jean-Luc Solère, eds. *L'embryon: Formation et animation. Antiquité grecque et latine tradition hébraïque, chrétienne et islamique*. Paris: J. Vrin, 2008.

Brown, Elizabeth A.R. '*Cessante Causa* and the Taxes of the Last Capetians: The Political Applications of a Philosophical Maxim.' *Studia Gratiana* 15 (1972): 567–87. Repr. in eadem, *Politics and Institutions in Capetian France*. no. II.

– 'Reform and Resistance to Royal Authority in Fourteenth-Century France: The Leagues of 1314–1315.' *Parliaments, Estates and Representation* 1 (1981): 109–37. Repr. in eadem, *Politics and Institutions in Capetian France*, no. V.

– 'Georges Duby and the Three Orders.' *Viator* 17 (1986): 51–64.

– *Politics and Institutions in Capetian France*. Aldershot and Brookfield, VT: Variorum; Gower, 1991.

Brückle, Wolfgang. *Civitas terrena: Staatsrepräsentation und politischer Aristotelismus in der französischen Kunst, 1270–1380*. Munich and Berlin: Deutscher Kunstverlag, 2005.

Brunschwig, Jacques. 'The Aristotelian Theory of Equity.' In *Rationality in Greek Thought*, edited by Michael Frede and Gisela Striker, 115–55. Oxford: Clarendon, 1996.

Burkert, Walter. 'Impact and Limits of the Idea of Progress in Antiquity.' In *The Idea of Progress*, edited by Arnold Burgen, Peter McLaughlin, and Jürgen Mittelstrass, 19–46. Berlin and New York: W. de Gruyter, 1997.

Burns, James H. 'Majorities: An Exploration.' *History of Political Thought* 24 (2003): 66–85.

Bury, John B. *The Idea of Progress: An Inquiry into Its Origin and Growth*. New York: Macmillan Company, 1932.

Busa, Roberto, ed. *Index Thomisticus: Sancti Thomae Aquinatis operum omnium indices et concordantiae*. Stuttgart: F. Frommann Verlag, 1974.

Butterfield, Herbert. *The Origins of Modern Science, 1300–1800*. London: G. Bell, 1950.

Butterworth, Charles E. 'What Is Political Averroism?' In Niewöhner and Sturlese, *Averroismus im Mittelalter und in der Renaissance*, 239–50.

– 'The Political Teaching of Avicenna.' *Topoi* 19 (2000): 35–44.

Butts, Mary A. 'The Political Doctrines of Augustine of Hippo and Marsilius of Padua: A Comparison.' Diss., University of Toronto, 1974.

Buxton, Richard, ed. *Oxford Readings in Greek Religion*. Oxford: Oxford University Press, 2000.

Cadili, Alberto. 'Marsilio da Padova amministratore della Chiesa ambrosiana.' *Pensiero Politico Medievale* 3–4 (2005/6): 193–225.

Cadoni, Giorgio. *L'utopia repubblicana di Donato Giannotti*. Milan: Giuffrè, 1978.

– *Crisi della mediazione politica e conflitti sociali: Niccolò Machiavelli, Francesco Guicciardini e Donato Giannotti di fronte al tramonto della Florentina Libertas*. Rome: Jouvence, 1994.

Callataÿ, Godefroid de. *Annus Platonicus: A Study of World Cycles in Greek, Latin and Arabic Sources*. Louvain-la Neuve: Université Catholique de Louvain/ Institut Orientaliste, 1996.

Calma, Dragos. 'La polysémie du terme averroïsme.' *Freiburger Zeitschrift für Philosophie und Theologie* 57 (2010): 189–98.

Camargo, Martin, ed. *The Waning of Medieval Ars Dictaminis* [= *Rhetorica* 19:2 (2001)].

Camargo, Martin. *Ars dictaminis, Ars Dictandi*. Turnhout: Brepols, 1991.

Cambiano, Giuseppe. 'Patologia e metafora politica. Alcmeone, Platone, *Corpus Hippocraticum*.' *Elenchos* 3 (1982): 219–36.

Canning, Joseph, and Otto Gerhard Oexle, eds. *Political Thought and the Realities of Power in the Middle Ages*. Göttingen: Vandenhoeck & Ruprecht, 1998.

Capitani, Ovidio. 'Dal Comune alla Signoria.' In *Comuni e Signorie: Istituzioni, società e lotte per l'egemonia* (= *Storia d'Italia*; 4), edited by Ovidio Capitani, Raoul Manselli, Giovanni Cherubini, Antonio Ivan Pini, and Giorgio Ghittolini, 135–75. Turin: UTET, 1981.

Cardelle de Hartmann, Carmen. *Lateinische Dialoge 1200–1400: Literaturhistorische Studie und Repertorium*. Leiden: Brill, 2007.

Carile, Antonio. 'Le origini di Venezia nella tradizione storiografica.' In Folena, *Storia della cultura veneta*, vol. 1: *Dalle origini al Trecento*, 134–66.

Carlier, Pierre. 'La notion de *pambasileia* dans la pensée politique d'Aristote.' In *Aristote et Athènes*, edited by Marcel Piérart, 103–18. Fribourg: Séminaire d'histoire ancienne de l'Université de Fribourg, 1993.

Carr, David R. 'Marsilius of Padua: The Use and Image of History in *Defensor Pacis*.' In *Altro Polo: A Volume of Italian Renaissance Studies*, edited by Conal Condren and Roslyn Pesman Cooper, 13–28. Sydney: Frederick May Foundation for Italian Studies, University of Sydney, 1982.

Casagrande, Carla, and Silvana Vecchio, eds. *Anima e corpo nella cultura medievale*. Tavarnuzze: SISMEL–Edizioni del Galluzzo, 1999.

Cassidy, Brendan. 'Laughing with Giotto at Sinners in Hell.' *Viator* 35 (2004): 355–86.

Castello Dubra, Julio A. 'Nota sobre el aristotelismo y el averroísmo político de Marsilio de Padua,' *Veritas* 42 (1997): 671–77.

Cavallaro, Giovanna. *La 'pace' nella filosofia politica di Marsilio da Padova*. Ferrara: De Salvia, 1973.

Cecchini, Enzo. 'Le epistole metriche del Mussato sulla poesia.' In *Tradizione classica e letteratura umanistica. Per Alessandro Perosa*, edited by Roberto Cardini, 1: 95–119. Rome: Bulzoni, 1985.

Cesar, Floriano. '*Causa singularis discordie* e situação italiana no *Defensor pacis* de Marsílio de Pádua.' *Patristica et Mediaevalia* 18 (1997): 20–8.

Chambers, Mortimer. 'Aristotle's Forms of Democracy.' *Transactions of the American Philological Association* 92 (1961): 20–36.

Checchini, Aldo, and Norberto Bobbio, eds. *Marsilio da Padova: Studi raccolti nel VI centenario della morte*. Padua: CEDAM, 1942.

Cheneval, Francis. '"Ars imitatur naturam" als methodisches Prinzip der politischen Philosophie und seine Anwendung im *Defensor pacis* des Marsilius von Padua.' *Archives d'histoire doctrinale et littéraire du moyen âge* 60 (1993): 133–45.

Chenu, Marie-Dominique. 'Notes de lexicographie philosophique médiévale. Antiqui, moderni.' *Revue des sciences philosophiques et théologiques* 17 (1928): 82–94. Repr. in idem, *Studi di lessicografia filosofica medievale*, edited by Giacinta Spinosa, 69–81. Florence: L.S. Olschki, 2001.

– *La théologie au douzième siècle*. Paris: J. Vrin, 1957.

Chowers, Eyal. 'The Physiology of the Citizen: The Present-Centered Body and Its Political Exile.' *Political Theory* 30 (2002): 649–76.

Chroust, Anton-Hermann. 'The Origin and Meaning of the Social Compact Doctrine.' *Ethics* 57 (1946): 38–56.

– 'The Corporate Idea and the Body Politic in the Middle Ages.' *Review of Politics* 9 (1947): 423–52.

Chuska, Jeff. *Aristotle's Best Regime: A Reading of Aristotle's Politics VII. 1–10.* Lanham, MD: University Press of America, 2000.

Clarke, Maude V. *The Medieval City State: An Essay on Tyranny and Federation in the Later Middle Ages.* London, Methuen & Co, 1926. Repr. Cambridge/New York: Speculum Historiale/Barnes & Noble, 1966.

Clarke, Paula. 'The Villani Chronicles.' In *Chronicling History: Chroniclers and Historians in Medieval and Renaissance Italy*, edited by Sharon Dale, Alison Williams Lewin, and Duane J. Osheim, 113–43. University Park, PA: Pennsylvania State University Press, 2007.

Classen, Carl J. *Die Stadt im Spiegel der Descriptiones und Laudes urbium in der antiken und mittelalterlichen Literatur bis zum Ende des zwölften Jahrhunderts.* Hildesheim and New York: Olms, 1980.

Coby, Patrick J. *Thomas Cromwell: Machiavellian Statecraft and the English Reformation.* Lanham, MD: Lexington Books, 2009.

Coccia, Emanuele. *La trasparenza delle immagini: Averroè e l'averroismo.* Milan: B. Mondadori, 2005.

Cochrane, Eric. *Historians and Historiography in the Italian Renaissance.* Chicago, IL: University of Chicago Press, 1981.

Cohen, David. 'The Rule of Law and Democratic Ideology in Classical Athens.' In *Die athenische Demokratie im 4. Jahrhundert v. Chr.: Vollendung oder Verfall einer Verfašungsform?*, edited by Walter Eder, 227–47. Stuttgart: F. Steiner, 1995.

Cole, Thomas. *Democritus and the Sources of Greek Anthropology.* Atlanta: Scholars Press, 1990.

Coleman, Edward. 'The Italian Communes. Recent Work and Current Trends.' *Journal of Medieval History* 25 (1999): 373–97.

Coleman, Janet. 'Some Relations between the Study of Aristotle's *Rhetoric, Ethics* and *Politics* in Late Thirteenth- and Early Fourteenth-Century University Arts Courses and the Justification of Contemporary Civic Activities (Italy and France).' In Canning and Oexle, *Political Thought and the Realities of Power in the Middle Ages*, 127–57.

– *A History of Political Thought*, vol. 2: *From the Middle Ages to the Renaissance.* Oxford and Malden, MA: Blackwell, 2000.

Colish, Marcia L. *The Stoic Tradition from Antiquity to the Early Middle Ages.* 2 vols. Leiden: E.J. Brill, 1985/90.

Collodo, Silvana. *Una società in transformazione: Padova tra XI e XV secolo.* Padua: Antenore, 1990.

– 'Marsilio da Padova e la polemica sul Papato nella testimonianza di Albertino Mussato.' In *Chiesa, vita religiosa. società nel Medioevo italiano*, edited by Mariaclara Rossi and Gian Maria Varanini, 237–51. Rome: Herder, 2005.

Colmo, Christopher. 'On the Prudence of Founders.' *Review of Politics* 60 (1998): 719–41.

Comentarios a la 'Política' de Aristóteles en la Europa Medieval y Moderna (siglos XIII al XVII): La historia de un equilibrio inestable. Madrid: Fundación Ignacio Larramendi, 2008.

Condren, Conal. 'Democracy and the *Defensor pacis*: On the English Language Tradition of Marsilian Interpretation.' *Il Pensiero Politico* 8 (1980): 301–16.

– 'Marsilius and Machiavelli.' In *Comparing Political Thinkers*, edited by Ross Fitzgerald, 94–115. Sydney: Pergamon Press, 1980.

Congourdeau, Marie-Hélène. 'On Interpreting Marsilius' Use of St. Augustine.' *Augustiniana* 25 (1975): 217–22.

– *L'embryon et son âme dans les sources grecques (VIe siècle av. J.-C.-Ve siècle apr. J.-C.).* Paris: Association des Amis du Centre d'Histoire et Civilisation de Byzance, 2007.

Constable, Giles. *Three Studies in Medieval Religious and Social Thought.* Cambridge: Cambridge University Press, 1995.

Conti, Vittorio. 'The Mechanization of Virtue: Republican Rituals in Italian Political Thought in the Sixteenth and Seventeenth Centuries.' In *Republicanism: A Shared European Heritage*, vol. 2: *The Values of Republicanism in Early Modern Europe*, edited by Martin van Gelderen and Quentin Skinner, 73–83. Cambridge: Cambridge University Press 2002.

Cooper, John M. 'Aristotle on the Forms of Friendship.' *Review of Metaphysics* 30 (1976/7): 619–48.

– 'Political Animals and Civic Friendship.' In *Aristoteles' 'Politik,'* Edited by Günther Patzig, 220–41. Göttingen: Vandenhoeck & Ruprecht, 1990. Repr. in Kraut and Skultety, *Aristotle's Politics: Critical Essays*, 65–89.

Costa, Pietro. *Iurisdictio. Semantica del potere politico nella pubblicistica medievale, 1100–1433.* Milan: A. Giuffrè, 1969. Repr. 2002.

– *Civitas: storia della cittadinanza in Europa*, vol. 1: *Dalla civiltà comunale al Settecento.* Rome: Laterza, 1999.

Coucke, Gijs. 'The Needle in the Haystack. In Search of the Model of Peter of Abano's *Expositio problematum*.' *Revue d'Histoire des Textes* n.s. 4 (2009): 179–214.

Coucke, Gijs, and Tine Swaenepoel. 'The Relation between Bartholomew of Messina's Translation of the *Problemata* and Peter of Abano's *Expositio Problematum*.' In *The Aristoteles Latinus: Past, Present, Future*, edited by Pieter De Leemans and Carlos Steel, 85–114. Brussels: The Royal Flemish Academy of Belgium for Science and the Arts, 1999.

Courtenay, William J. 'A Note on Nicolaus Girardi de Waudemonte, pseudo-Johannes Buridanus.' *Bulletin de philosophie médiévale* 46 (2004): 163–8.

– 'University Masters and Political Power: The Parisian Years of Marsilius of Padua.' In Kaufhold, *Politische Reflexion in der Welt des späten Mittelalters*, 209–23.

– 'Marsilius of Padua at Paris.' In Moreno-Riaño and Nederman, *A Companion to Marsilius of Padua*, 57–70.

Cova, Luciano. 'Il Corpus zoologico di Aristotele nei dibattiti fra gli *artisti* parigini alle soglie del XIV secolo.' In Weijers and Holtz, *L'enseignement des disciplines à la Faculté des arts (Paris et Oxford, XIIIe–XVe siècles)*, 281–302.

Cox, Virginia. 'Ciceronian Rhetoric in Italy, 1260–1350.' *Rhetorica* 17 (1999): 239–88.

– 'Ciceronian Rhetoric in Late Medieval Italy: The Latin and Vernacular Traditions.' In Cox and Ward, *The Rhetoric of Cicero in Its Medieval and Early Renaissance Commentary Tradition*, 109–36.

Cox, Virginia, and John O. Ward, eds. *The Rhetoric of Cicero in Its Medieval and Early Renaissance Commentary Tradition*. Leiden and Boston: Brill, 2006.

Cracco, Giorgio. *Nato sul mezzogiorno: La storia di Ezzelino.* Vicenza: N. Pozza, 1995.

Cranz, F. Edward. 'Aristotelianism in Medieval Political Theory: A Study of the Reception of the *Politics*.' Diss., Harvard University, 1938.

Croissant, Jeanne. 'Un nouveau Discours de Thémistius.' *Serta Leodiensia* 44 (1930): 7–30.

Cusimano, Richard C. 'Albertino Mussato and the Politics of Early *Trecento* Padua: A Prehumanist in the Transition from Commune to *Signoria*.' Diss., University of Georgia, 1970.

D'Addio, Mario. *L'idea del contratto sociale dai Sofisti alla riforma e il 'De principatu' di Mario Salamonio.* Milan: Giuffrè, 1954.

Dagron, Gilbert. 'L'Empire romain d'Orient au IVe siècle et les traditions politiques de l'hellénisme: le témoignage de Thémistios.' *Travaux et Mémoires du Centre de Recherche d'Histoire et Civilisation byzantines* 3 (1968): 1–242.

Dales, Richard C. *Medieval Discussions of the Eternity of the World*. Leiden and New York: E.J. Brill, 1990.

D'Alverny, Marie-Thérèse. 'Pietro d'Abano et les "naturalistes" à l'époque de Dante.' In *Dante e la cultura veneta*, ed. Vittore Branca and Giorgio Padoan, 207–19. Florence: L.S. Olschki, 1966.

– 'Pietro d'Abano, traducteur de Galien.' *Medioevo* 11 (1985): 19–64. Repr. in eadem, *La transmission des textes philosophiques et scientifiques au Moyen Age*, no. XIII, edited by Charles Burnett. Aldershot and Brookfield, VT: Variorum, 1994.

– *Avicenne en Occident*. Paris: J. Vrin, 1993.

Daly, Lowrie J. 'Medieval and Renaissance Commentaries on the *Politics* of Aristotle.' *Duquesne Review* 13 (1968): 41–55.

D'Ancona, Alessandro. 'La poesia politica italiana ai tempi di Lodovico il Bavaro.' In idem, *Varietà storiche e letterarie*, 1: 75–113. Milan: Fratelli Treves, 1885.

D'Ancona, Cristina, and Richard C. Taylor, s.v. '*Liber de causis*.' In *Dictionnaire des philosophes antiques. Supplément*, edited by Richard Goulet, Jean-Marie Flamand and Maroun Aouad, 599–647. Paris: CNRS Éditions, 2003.

D'Ancona [Costa], Cristina. '"Philosophus in libro De Causis." La recezione del *Liber de Causis* come opera aristotelica nei commenti di Ruggero Bacone, dello ps. Enrico di Gand e dello ps. Adamo di Bocfeld.' *Documenti e studi sulla tradizione filosofica medievale* 3 (1992): 611–49.

– *Recherches sur le Liber de Causis*. Paris: J. Vrin, 1995.

Darling, Linda T. '"Do Justice, Do Justice, for That is Paradise": Middle Eastern Advice for Indian Muslim Rulers?' *Comparative Studies on South Asia, Africa, and the Middle East* 22 (2002): 3–19.

– 'Islamic Empires, the Ottoman Empire and the Circle of Justice.' In *Constitutional Politics in the Middle East: with Special Reference to Turkey, Iraq, Iran and Afghanistan*, edited by Saïd Amir Arjomand, 11–32. Oxford and Portland, OR, Hart Pub., 2008.

Davidson, Herbert A. 'The Middle Way in Maimonides' Ethics.' *Proceedings of the American Academy for Jewish Research* 54 (1987): 31–72.

– *Proofs for Eternity, Creation and the Existence of God in Medieval Islamic and Jewish Philosophy*. Oxford: Oxford University Press, 1987.

Davis, Charles T. 'Tolomeus of Lucca and the Roman Republic.' *Proceedings of the American Philosophical Society* 118 (1974): 30–50. Repr. in *Renaissance Thought: A Reader*, edited by Robert Black, 254–89. London and New York: Routledge, 2001.

Dazzi, Manlio T. 'Intorno alla nascita di Albertino Mussato.' *Archivio Muratoriano* 16 (1915): 263–72.

– 'Il Mussato storico.' *Archivio Veneto*, ser. 5, 6 (1929): 357–471.

– *Intorno alla nascita di Albertino Mussato*. Venice: La R. Deputazione Editrice, 1930.

– *Il Mussato preumanista (1261–1329): L'ambiente e l'opera*. Vicenza: Neri Pozza, 1964.

Day, James, and Mortimer Chambers. *Aristotle's History of Athenian Democracy*. Berkeley, CA: University of California Press, 1962. Repr. Amsterdam: Hakkert, 1967.

Dean, Trevor. 'The Rise of the *signori*.' In *The New Cambridge Medieval History*, vol. 5: *c. 1198–c. 1300*, edited by David Abulafia, 458–78. Cambridge: Cambridge University Press, 1999.

– 'The Rise of the *signori*.' In *Italy in the Central Middle Ages: 1000–1300*, edited by David Abulafia. 104–24. Oxford: Oxford University Press, 2004.

De Boni, Luis A. '*Legislator, lex, lex naturalis* und *dominium* bei Johannes Duns Scotus.' In Fidora, Lutz-Bachmann, and Wagner, *Lex und Ius*, 221–39.

Defourny, Maurice. 'The Aim of State: Peace.' In Barnes, Schofield and Sorabji, *Articles on Aristotle*, vol. 2: *Ethics and Politics*, 195–201.

De Haas, Frans A.J. '"Introduction" to Johannes Philoponus. *Commentaria in libros De generatione et corruptione Aristotelis*. Translated by Hieronymus Bagolinus, v–xiv. Venice, 1558. Repr. Stuttgart-Bad Cannstatt: Frommann-Holzboog, 2004.

De Lagarde, Georges. 'Une adaptation de la politique d'Aristote au XIVe siècle.' *Revue Historique de Droit Français et Étranger* ser. 4, 11 (1932): 227–69.

De Leemans, Pieter. '*Alia translatio planior*: Les traductions latines du *De generatione et corruptione* et les commentateurs médiévaux.' In Ducos and Giacomotto-Charra, *Lire Aristote au Moyen Âge et à la Renaissance: Réception du traité Sur la génération et la corruption*, 27–53.

– 'Was Peter of Abano the Translator of pseudo-Aristotle's *Problemata physica*?' *Bulletin de Philosophie Médiévale* 49 (2007): 103–18.

De Leemans, Pieter, and Michèle Goyens, eds. *Aristotle's Problemata in Different Times and Tongues*. Leuven: Leuven University Press, 2006.

Del Prete, Donato. 'Il pensiero politico ed ecclesiologico di Marsilio da Padova.' *Annali di Storia* (Lecce) 1 (1980): 17–124.

– 'La confutazione nel *Defensor pacis* di Marsilio da Padova da Siberto da Beek, Guglielmo Amidani e Pietro da Lutra a Giovanni XXII.' *Annali del Dipartimento di Scienze Storiche e Sociali dell'Università degli Studi di Lecce* 1 (1983): 213–83.

De Matteis, Maria C. 'La coscienza della crisi comunale nei cronisti del' 300.' In *Storici e storiografia del medioevo italiano: antologia di saggi*, edited by Gabriele Zanella, 255–74. Bologna: Pàtron, 1984.

Demont, Paul. 'Le loisir (*skholē*) dans la *Politique* d'Aristote.' In Aubenque and Tordesillas, *Aristote politique*, 209–30.

De Ste. Croix, Geoffrey E.M. *The Class Struggle in the Ancient Greek World: From the Archaic Age to the Arab Conquests*. Ithaca, NY: Cornell University Press, 1981.

Dihle, Albrecht. 'Der Begriff des Nomos in der griechischen Philosophie.' In *Nomos und Gesetz: Ursprünge und Wirkungen des griechischen Gesetzesdenkens*, edited by Okko Behrends and Wolfgang Sellert, 117–34. Göttingen: Vandenhoeck & Ruprecht, 1995.

Dijksterhuis, Eduard J. *The Mechanization of the World Picture*. Translated by C. Dikshoorn. Oxford: Clarendon Press, 1961.

Di Salvo. Andrea. 'L'affermazione della signoria cittadina nella percezione dei contemporanei: L'esempio dei Carraresi a Padova nella prima metà del Trecento.' Tesi di dottorato, Università Ca' Foscari Venezia, 1997.

Di Vona, Piero. *I principi del Defensor Pacis*. Naples: Morano, 1974.

– 'L'ontologia di Marsilio da Padova nelle *Quaestiones I–II super IV librum Metaphysicae*.' *Atti dell'Accademia di Scienze Morali e Politiche* (Napoli) 89 (1978): 251–81.

Dobler, Emil. *Zwei syrische Quellen der theologischen Summa des Thomas von Aquin: Nemesios von Emesa und Johannes von Damaskus: Ihr Einfluss auf die anthropologischen Grundlagen der Moraltheologie (S. Th. I-II, qq 6–17; 22–48)*. Fribourg: Universitätsverlag, 2000.

Dodds, Eric R. *The Ancient Concept of Progress and Other Essays on Greek Literature and Belief*. Oxford: Clarendon Press, 1973.

– s.v. 'Progress in Classical Antiquity.' In *Dictionary of the History of Ideas: Studies of Selected Pivotal Ideas*, edited by Philip P. Wiener, 3: 623–33. New York: Charles Scribner's Sons, 1973.

Dolcini, Carlo. 'Osservazioni sul *Defensor Minor* di Marsilio da Padova.' *Atti della Accademia delle Scienze dell'Istituto di Bologna. Classe di Scienze Morali* 64 (1975/6): 87–102. Repr. in idem, *Crisi di poteri e politologia in crisi: Da Sinibaldo Fieschi a Guglielmo d'Ockham*, 251–67.

– 'Marsilio contro Ockham. Intorno a una recente edizione del *Defensor minor*.' *Rubiconia Accademia dei Filopatridi* Quaderno 12 (1979): 251–68. Repr. in idem, *Crisi di poteri e politologia in crisi: Da Sinibaldo Fieschi a Guglielmo d'Ockham*, 269–89.

– *Crisi di poteri e politologia in crisi: Da Sinibaldo Fieschi a Guglielmo d'Ockham*. Bologna: Pàtron, 1988.

– *Introduzione a Marsilio da Padova*. Rome and Bari: Laterza, 1995.

Dorandi, Tiziano. 'La versio latina antiqua di Diogene Laerzio e la sua ricezione nel Medioevo occidentale: Il *Compendim moralium notabilium* di Geremia da Montagnone e il *Liber de vita et moribus philosophorum* dello ps. Burleo.' *Documenti e studi sulla tradizione filosofica medievale* 10 (1999): 371–96.

Downey, Glanville. 'Aristotle as an Expert on Urban Problems.' *Talanta* 3 (1971): 56–73.

Duby, Georges. *The Three Orders: Feudal Society Imagined*. Translated by Arthur Goldhammer. Chicago, IL and London: University of Chicago Press, 1980.

Ducos, Joëlle, and Violaine Giacomotto-Charra, eds. *Lire Aristote au Moyen Âge et à la Renaissance: Réception du traité Sur la génération et la corruption*. Paris: H. Champion 2011.

Dunbabin, Jean. 'Aristotle in the Schools.' In Smalley, *Trends in Medieval Political Thought*, 65–85.

– 'The Reception and Interpretation of Aristotle's *Politics*.' In *The Cambridge History of Later Medieval Philosophy*, edited by Norman Kretzmann, 723–37. Cambridge: Cambridge University Press, 1982.

Dunstan , Gordon R., ed. *The Human Embryo: Aristotle and the Arabic and European Traditions*. Exeter: University of Exeter Press, 1990.

Dutton, Paul E. '*Illustre ciuitatis et populi exemplum*: Plato's *Timaeus* and the Transmission from Calcidius to the End of the Twelfth Century of a Tripartite Scheme of Society.' *Mediaeval Studies* 45 (1983): 79–119.

– 'Material Remains of the Study of the *Timaeus* in the Later Middle Ages.' In *L'enseignement de la philosophie au XIIIe siècle: Autour du Guide de l'étudiant du ms. Ripoll 109*, edited by Claude Lafleur, 203–30. Turnhout: Brepols, 1997.

– 'Medieval Approaches to Calcidius.' In *Plato's Timaeus as Cultural Icon*, edited by Gretchen J. Reydams-Schils, 183–205. Notre Dame, IN: Notre Dame University Press, 2003.

Dvornik, Francis. 'The Emperor Julian's 'Reactionary' Ideas on Kingship.' In *Late Classical and Mediaeval Studies in Honor of Albert Mathias Friend, Jr.*, edited by Kurt Weitzmann, 71–81. Princeton, NJ: Princeton University Press, 1955.

– *Early Christian and Byzantine Political Philosophy: Origins and Background* vol. 2. Washington, DC: Dumbarton Oaks Center for Byzantine Studies, 1966.

Earl, Donald C. *The Political Thought of Sallust*. Cambridge: Cambridge University Press, 1961. Repr. Chicago, IL: Argonaut, 1969.

Edelstein, Ludwig. 'The Greco-Roman Concept of Scientific Progress.' In *ITHACA: Actes du Xème Congrès International d'Histoire des Sciences*, 47–59. Paris: Hermann, 1965. Repr. in *Selected Philosophical Papers by Ludwig Edelstein*, edited by Leonardo Tarán. New York and London: Garland Publishing, 1987, no. 2.

– *The Idea of Progress in Classical Antiquity.* Baltimore, MD: Johns Hopkins Press, 1967.

Ehrenberg, Victor. 'Eunomia.' In *Charisteria: Alois Rzach zum achtzigsten Geburstag dargebracht*. Reichenberg: Gebrüder Stiepel, 1930, 16–29. Repr. in idem, *Polis und Imperium: Beiträge zur alten Geschichte*, edited by Karl Friedrich Stroheker and Alexander J. Graham, 139–58. Zurich: Artemis Verlag, 1965; Eng. trans. in idem, *Aspects of the Ancient World: Essays and Reviews*, 70–93, Oxford: B. Blackwell, 1946.

Elm, Ralf. *Klugheit und Erfahrung bei Aristoteles.* Paderborn: F. Schöningh, 1996.

Emerton, Ephraim. *The Defensor pacis of Marsiglio of Padua: A Critical Study*. Cambridge, MA: Harvard University Press, 1920. Repr. 1951.

Engberg-Pedersen, Troels. *The Stoic Theory of Oikeiosis: Moral Development and Social Interaction in Early Stoic Philosophy*. Aarhus: Aarhus University Press, 1990.

Epstein, Stephan R. 'The Rise and Fall of Italian City-States.' In *A Comparative Study of Thirty City-State Cultures: An Investigation*, edited by Mogens H. Hansen, 277–93. Copenhagen: Kongelige Danske Videnskabernes Selskab, 2000.

Ercole, Francesco. *Dal comune al principato: saggi sulla storia del diritto pubblico del rinascimento italiano*. Florence: Vallecchi, 1929.

Ermatinger, Charles J. 'John of Jandun in His Relations with Arts Masters and Theologians.' In *Arts libéraux et philosophie au Moyen Age*, 1173–84. Montreal/Paris: Institut d'études médiévales/J. Vrin, 1969.

Evans, Gillian R. 'The Use of Mathematical Method in Medieval Political Science: Dante's *Monarchia* and the *Defensor Pacis* of Marsilius of Padua.' *Archives Internationales d'Histoire des Sciences* 32 (1982): 78–94.

Evrigenis, Ioannis D. 'The Doctrine of the Mean in Aristotle's Ethical and Political Theory.' *History of Political Thought* 20 (1999): 393–416.

Fabris, Giovanni. *Cronache e cronisti padovani*. Padua: Rebellato, 1977.

Fasoli, Gina. 'Ricerche sulla legislazione antimagnatizia nei comuni dell'alta e media Italia.' *Rivista di storia del diritto italiano* 12 (1939): 86–133, 240–309.

– 'Nascita di un mito.' In *Studi storici in onore di Gioacchino Volpe per il suo 80 compleanno*, 1: 445–79. Florence: Sansoni, 1958.

– 'Un cronista e un tiranno: Rolandino da Padova e Ezzelino da Romano.' *Atti della Accademia delle Scienze dell'Istituto di Bologna, Scienze Morali, Rendiconti* 72 (1984/5): 25–48.

– 'Ezzelino da Romano, fra tradizione chronachistica e revisione storiografica.' In *Storia e cultura a Padova nell'età di Sant'Antonio*, 85–101.

Federici Vescovini, Graziella. 'L'influenza dell'opera di Albumasar nel pensiero latino del XIV secolo: la dottrina astrologica di Biagio Pelacani da Parma.' In *Actas del V Congreso Internacional de filosofia medieval*, 2: 715–29. Madrid: Ed. Nacional, 1979.

– 'Pietro d'Abano e le fonti astronomiche greco-arabo-latine (a proposito del *Lucidator dubitabilium astronomiae o astrologiae*).' *Medioevo* 11 (1985): 65–96.

– 'Pietro d'Abano e gli affreschi astrologici del Palazzo della Ragione di Padova.' *Labyrinthos* 9 (1986): 50–75.

– 'Pietro d'Abano e l'astrologia-astronomia.' *Bollettino del Centro Internazionale di Storia dello Spazio e del Tempo* 5 (1986): 9–28.

– '«Albumasar in Sadan» e Pietro d'Abano.' In *La diffusione delle scienze islamiche nel Medio Evo europeo*, edited by Biancamaria Scarcia Amoretti, 29–55. Rome: Accademia nazionale dei Lincei, 1987.
– 'Peter of Abano and Astrology.' In *Astrology, Science and Society: Historical Essays*, edited by Patrick Curry, 19–39. Woodbridge: Boydell Press, 1987.
– 'La place privilégiée de l'astronomie-astrologie dans l'encyclopédie des sciences théoriques de Pierre d'Abano.' In *Knowledge and the Sciences in Medieval Philosophy*, edited by Reijo Työrinoja, Anja I. Lehtinen, and Dagfinn Føllesdal, 3: 42–51. Helsinki: Yliopistopaino, 1990. Repr. in *Historia philosophiae Medii Aevi: Studien zur Geschichte der Philosophie des Mittelalters*, edited by Burkhard Mojsisch and Olaf Pluta, 1: 259–69. Amsterdam and Philadelphia, PA: B.R. Grüner, 1991.
– 'La simmetria del corpo umano nella *Physiognomica* di Pietro d'Abano: un canone estetico.' In *Concordia discors: Studi su Niccolò Cusano e l'umanesimo europeo offerti a Giovanni Santinello*, edited by Gregorio Piaia, 347–60. Padua: Antenore, 1993.
– 'The Place of the Sun in Medieval Arabo-Latin Astronomy: The *Lucidator dubitabilium astronomiae* (1303–10) of Peter of Padua.' *Journal for the History of Astronomy* 29 (1998): 151–5.
– 'Gli astronomi arabi e il *Lucidator dubitabilium astronomiae* di Pietro d'Abano (1303–1310).' In *Filosofia e scienza classica, arabo-latina medievale e l'età moderna*, edited by Graziella Federici Vescovini, 29–42. Louvain-la-Neuve: Fédération internationale des instituts d'études médiévales, 1999.
– 'Il sole e la luna nelle citazioni di Pietro d'Abano dei segreti di Albumasar, di Sadan.' *Micrologus* 12 (2004): 185–94.
Feldman, Noah [R.]. 'Reading the *Nicomachean Ethics* with Ibn Rushd.' Diss., University of Oxford, 1994.
– 'The Translators of Ibn Rushd's Commentary on the Nicomachean Ethics.' *Turjumān* 8 (1999): 69–85.
Felsberg, Otto. 'Beiträge zur Geschichte des Römerzuges Heinrichs VII.: Innere- und Finanzpolitik Heinrichs VII. in Italien.' Diss., University of Freiburg, 1886.
Ferre, Lola. 'Dissemination of Maimonides' Medical Writings in the Middle Ages.' In *Traditions of Maimonideanism*, edited by Carlos Fraenkel, 17–31. Leiden and Boston: Brill, 2009.
Fidora, Alexander. *Die Wissenschaftstheorie des Dominicus Gundissalinus: Voraussetzungen und Konsequenzen des zweiten Anfangs der aristotelischen Philosophie im 12. Jahrhundert*. Berlin: Akademie-Verl., 2003.
– 'A tripartição da filosofia prática na obra *De divisione philosophiae* de Domingos Gundisalvo.' In *Idade Média: Tempo do mundo, tempo dos homens, tempo*

de Deus, edited by José Antônio de C.R. de Souza, 417–28. Porto Alegre: Ed. Est, 2006.

Fidora, Alexander, Johannes Fried, Matthias Lutz-Bachmann, and Luise Schorn-Schütte, eds. *Politischer Aristotelismus und Religion in Mittelalter und Früher Neuzeit*. Berlin: Akademie, 2007.

Fidora, Alexander, Matthias Lutz-Bachmann, and Andreas Wagner, eds. *Lex und Ius: Beiträge zur Begründung des Rechts in der Philosophie des Mittelalters und der Frühen Neuzeit*. Stuttgart and Bad Cannstatt: Frommann-Holzboog, 2010.

Fiedler, Wilfried. *Analogiemodelle bei Aristoteles: Untersuchungen zu den Vergleichen zwischen den einzelnen Wissenschaften und Künsten*. Amsterdam: B.R. Grüner, 1978.

Finley, Moses I. 'Aristotle and Economic Analysis.' *Past and Present* 47 (1970): 3–25. Repr. in Barnes, Schofield, and Sorabji, *Articles on Aristotle*, vol. 2: *Ethics and Politics*, 140–58, and *Studies in Ancient Society*, edited by Moses I. Finley, 26–52. London and Boston: Routledge and Kegan Paul, 1974.

Finley, Robert. 'The Immortal Republic: The Myth of Venice during the Italian Wars (1494–1530).' *Sixteenth Century Journal* 30 (1999): 931–44.

Fiocchi, Claudio. *Dispotismo e libertà nel pensiero politico medievale: Riflessioni all'ombra di Aristotele (sec. XIII–XIV)*. Bergamo: Lubrina, 2007.

Fioravanti, Gianfranco. 'Servi, rustici, barbari: interpretazioni medievali dela *Politica* aristotelica.' *Annali della Scuola Normale Superiore di Pisa, Classe di Lettere e Filosofia* 11 (1981): 399–429.

– 'La *Politica* aristotelica nel Medioevo: linee di una ricezione.' *Rivista di storia della filosofia* n.s. 52 (1997): 17–29.

– 'La réception de la *Politique* d'Aristote au Moyen Âge tardif.' In *Aspects de la pensée médiévale dans la philosophie politique moderne*, edited by Yves Zarka, 9–24. Paris: Presses Universitaires de France, 1999.

Flüeler, Christoph. *Rezeption und Interpretation der aristotelischen Politica im späten Mittelalter*. 2 vols. Amsterdam and Philadelphia, PA: B.R. Grüner, 1992.

– 'Ontologie und Politik: Quod racio principantis et subiecti sumitur ex racione actus et potencie.' *Freiburger Zeitschrift für Philosophie und Theologie* 41 (1994): 445–62.

– 'Politischer Aristotelismus im Mittelalter. Einleitung.' *Vivarium* 40 (2002): 1–13.

– 'Der Einfluß der aristotelischen *Politica* auf die philosophische Begründung von politischer Herrschaft.' In *Gewalt und ihre Legitimation im Mittelalter*, edited by Günther Mensching, 65–78. Würzburg: Königshausen & Neumann, 2003.

Flumene, Francesco. *La 'legge non scritta' nella storia e nella dottrina etico-giuridica della Grecia classica.* Sassari: Stamperia de la L.I.S, 1925.

Folena, Gianfranco. 'Parlamenti podestarili di Giovanni da Viterbo.' *Lingua nostra* 20 (1959): 97–105.

– ed. *Storia della cultura veneta*, vol. 1: *Dalle origini al Trecento.* Vicenza: Neri Pozza, 1976.

– ed. *Storia della cultura veneta*, vol. 2: *Il Trecento.* Vicenza: Neri Pozza, 1976.

Foligno, Cesare. 'Epistole inedite di Lovato de' Lovati e d'altri a lui.' *Studi Medievali* 2 (1906–07): 37–58.

Fornaro, Pierpaolo. 'Tragedia e *argumenta* senecani in Albertino Mussato.' In *Hommages à Carl Deroux*, vol. 5: *Christianisme et Moyen Âge, Néo-latin et survivance de la latinité*, edited by Pol Defosse, 396–407. Brussels: Latomus, 2003.

Foronda, François, ed. *Avant le contrat social. Le contrat politique dans l'Occident médiéval XIII*[e]*–XV*[e] *siècle.* Paris: Publications de la Sorbonne, 2011.

Fortuna, Stefania. 'Pietro d'Abano e le traduzioni latine di Galeno.' *Medicina nei Secoli* 20 (2008): 447–63.

Fortuna, Stefania, and Anna M. Urso. 'La tradizione latina dell'*ars medica* di Galeno: la *translatio antiqua* e il completamento di Burgundio.' In *Sulla tradizione indiretta dei testi medici greci: Le traduzioni*, edited by Ivan Garofalo, Stefania Fortuna, Alessandro Lami, and Amneris Roselli, 137–68. Pisa: F. Serra, 2010.

Fourquin, Guy. *The Anatomy of Popular Rebellion in the Middle Ages.* Translated by Anne Chesters. Amsterdam/New York: North Holland Pub. Co.; New York: Elsevier North-Holland, 1978.

Fox, Marvin. 'The Doctrine of the Mean in Aristotle and Maimonides: A Comparative Study.' In *Studies in Jewish Religious and Intellectual History: Presented to Alexander Altmann on the Occasion of His Seventieth Birthday*, edited by Siegfried Stein and Raphael Loewe, 93–120. Tuscaloosa, AL: University of Alabama Press, 1979. Repr. in idem, *Interpreting Maimonides: Studies in Methodology, Metaphysics, and Moral Philosophy*, 93–123. Chicago, IL: University of Chicago Press, 1990.

Frajese, Vittorio. *Sarpi scettico: Stato e Chiesa a Venezia tra Cinque e Seicento.* Bologna: Il Mulino, 1994.

– 'Maimonide, il desiderio di immortalità e l'immagine di Dio: problemi di interpretazzione dell' insegnamento esoterico di Sarpi.' In *Ripensando Paolo Sarpi*, edited by Corrado Pin, 153–81. Venice: Ateneo veneto, 2006.

Franceschi, Dora. 'L'*Oculus pastoralis* e la fortuna.' *Atti dell'Accademia delle*

Scienze di Torino, Classe di scienze morali, storiche e filologiche 99 (1964–65): 205–61.

Franchini, Vittorio. *Saggio di ricerche su l'instituto del Podestà nei comuni medievali*. Bologna: N. Zanichelli, 1912.

– 'Trattati *De regimine civitatum* (sec. XIII–XIV).' *Recueils de la Société Jean Bodin* 6 (1954): 319–40.

Fragnito, Gigliola. *Gasparo Contarini. Un magistrato veneziano al servizio della Cristianità*. Florence: L.S. Olschki, 1988.

Fraisse, Jean-Claude. *Philia: La notion d'amitié dans la philosophie antique: Essai sur un problème perdu et retrouvé*. Paris: J. Vrin, 1974.

Frank, Daniel H. 'Aristotle on Freedom in the *Politics*.' *Prudentia* 15 (1983): 109–16.

Frank, Jill. *A Democracy of Distinction: Aristotle and the Work of Politics*. Chicago, IL and London: University of Chicago Press, 2005.

Franke, Maria E. *Kaiser Heinrich VII. im Spiegel der Historiographie: Eine faktenkritische und quellenkundliche Untersuchung ausgewählter Geschichtsschreiber der ersten Hälfte des 14. Jahrhunderts*. Cologne: Böhlau, 1992.

Frede, Dorothea. 'Constitution and Citizenship: Peripatetic Influence on Cicero's Political Conceptions in the *De re publica*.' In *Cicero's Knowledge of the Peripatos*, edited by William W. Fortenbaugh and Peter Steinmetz, 4: 77–100. New Brunswick, NJ and London: Transaction Pub., 1989.

French, Roger. 'Astrology in Medical Practice.' In *Practical Medicine from Salerno to the Black Death*, edited by Luis García Ballester, Roger French, Jon Arrizabalaga, and Andrew Cunningham, 30–59. Cambridge: Cambridge University Press, 1994.

Freund, Walter. *Modernus und andere Zeitbegriffe des Mittelalters*. Cologne and Graz: Böhlau, 1957.

Gaeta, Franco. 'Alcune considerazioni sul mito di Venezia.' *Bibliothèque d'Humanisme et Renaissance* 23 (1961): 58–75.

– 'Giorgio da Trebisonda, le *Leggi* di Platone e la costituzione di Venezia.' *Bullettino dell'Istituto storico italiano per il medio evo e Archivio Muratoriano* 82 (1970): 479–501.

– '*Storiografia*, coscienza nazionale e politica culturale nella Venezia del Rinascimento.' In *Storia della cultura veneta* 3/I: *Dal primo Quattrocento al Concilio di Trento*, edited by Girolamo Arnaldi and Manlio Pastore Stocchi, 1–91. Vicenza: N. Pozza, 1980.

Gagarin, Michael. *Early Greek Law*. Berkeley, CA: University of California Press, 1986.

Gaille-Nikodimov, Marie, ed. *Le Gouvernement mixte: De l'idéal politique au monstre constitutionnel en Europe (XIIIe–XVIIe siècle)*. Saint-Etienne: Publications de l'Université de Saint-Étienne, 2005.

– 'L'ideale del governo misto tra Venezia e Firenze. Un aristotelismo politico a doppia faccia.' *Filosofia Politica* 19 (2005): 63–76.

Gallo, Donato. 'L'epoca delle signorie: Scaligeri e Carraresi (1317–1405).' In *Monselice: Storia, cultura e arte di un centro 'minore' del Veneto*, edited by Antonio Rigon, 173–89. Treviso: Canova, 1994.

Galston, Miriam. 'Realism and Idealism in Avicenna's Political Philosophy.' *The Review of Politics* 41 (1979): 561–77.

Ganguzza Billanovich, Maria C. 'Due statuti comunali dell' anno 1300: aspetti del rapporto tra potere civile ed ecclesiastico in Padova agli inizi del XIV secolo,' *Atti e Memorie dell'Accademia Patavina di Scienze, Lettere ed Arti* 87 (1974/75): 131–40.

Garfagnini, Gian Carlo. 'Platone politico, ovvero il sogno di uno stato "divino."' In Vegetti and Pissavino, *I Decembrio e la tradizione della Repubblica di Platone tra Medioevo e Umanesimo*, 99–125.

Garin, Eugenio. *Astrology in the Renaissance: The Zodiac of Life* Translated by Carolyn Jackson and June Allen. London and Boston: Routledge & Kegan Paul, 1983.

Garnsey, Peter. 'Gemistus Plethon and Platonic Political Philosophy.' In *Transformations of Late Antiquity*, edited by Philip Rousseau and Manolis Papoutsakis, 327–40. Farnham and Burlington, VT: Ashgate, 2009.

Gehrke, Hans-Joachim. *Stasis: Untersuchungen zu den inneren Kriegen in den griechischen Staaten des 5. und 4. Jahrhunderts v. Chr.* Munich: Beck, 1985.

Gerbier, Laurent. 'Constitution mixte et complexion civile chez Machiavel (*Discorsi*, I, 2–9).' In Gaille-Nikodimov, *Le Gouvernement mixte*, 57–69.

Gewirth, Alan. 'John of Jandun and the *Defensor pacis*.' *Speculum* 23 (1948): 267–72.

– *Marsilius of Padua, The Defender of Peace*, vol. 1: *Marsilius of Padua and Medieval Political Philosophy*. New York and London: Columbia University Press, 1951.

– 'Philosophy and Political Thought in the Fourteenth Century.' In *The Forward Movement of the Fourteenth Century*, edited by Francis L. Utley, 125–64. Columbus, OH: Ohio State University Press, 1961.

– 'Republicanism and Absolutism in the Thought of Marsilius of Padua.' In *MPCI*, 23–48.

Ghisalberti, Alessandro. 'Sulla legge naturale in Ockham e in Marsilio.' In *MPCI*, 303–15.

– 'L'apirazione alla pace come fondamento della politica in Marsilio da Padova.' In *Homo sapiens, homo humanus*, vol. 1: *La cultura italiana tra il passato ed il presente in un disegno di pace universale*, edited by Giovannangiola Tarugi, 65–77. Florence: L.S. Olschki, 1990.

Gianola, Giovanna M. 'Tra Padova e Verona: il Cangrande di Mussato (e quello di Dante).' In *Gli Scaligeri: 1277–1387*, edited by Gian Maria Varanini, 51–60. Verona: Mondadori, 1988.

– 'L'*Ecerinis* di Albertino Mussato tra Ezzelino e Cangrande.' In *Nuovi Studi Ezzeliniani*, edited by Giorgio Cracco, 2: 537–74. Rome: Istituto storico italiano per il Medio Evo, 1992.

Gibbons, John P. 'Marsilius of Padua's Defense of the Peace.' Diss., Harvard University, 1981.

– 'How a Liberal Picks a Fight: Marsilius of Padua and the Singular Cause of Strife.' In *Educating the Prince*, edited by Mark Blitz and William Kristol, 18–29. Lanham, MD: Rowman & Littlefield, 2000.

Gierke, Otto von. *Political Theories of the Middle Ages*. Translated by Frederic W. Maitland. Cambridge: Cambridge University Press, 1958.

– *The Development of Political Theory*. Translated by Bernard Freyd. New York: H. Fertig, 1966.

Gilbert, Felix. 'The Venetian Constitution in Florentine Political Thought.' In *Florentine Studies: Politics and Society in Renaissance Florence*, edited by Nicolai Rubinstein, 463–500. Evanston, IL: Northwestern University Press, 1968.

Gilbert, Neal W. *Renaissance Concepts of Method*. New York: Columbia University Press, 1960.

Giuriati, Paolo. 'Marsilio da Padova e il *Defensor pacis* al vaglio di una sociologia della conocenza.' *Studia Patavina* 27 (1980) [= *Marsilio, ieri e oggi*, ed. Gregorio Piaia]: 268–80.

Gleason, Elisabeth G. *Gasparo Contarini: Venice, Rome, and Reform*. Berkeley, CA: University of California Press, 1993.

Godthardt, Frank. 'The Life of Marsilius of Padua' [trans. from the German Cornelia Oefelein]. In Moreno-Riaño and Nederman, *A Companion to Marsilius of Padua*, 13–55.

Goodenough, Erwin R. 'The Political Philosophy of Hellenistic Kingship.' *Yale Classical Studies* 1 (1928): 55–102.

Gorochov, Nathalie. *Le Collège de Navarre, de sa fondation (1305) au début du XV e siècle (1418): histoire de l'institution, de sa vie intellectuelle et de son recrutement*. Paris: H. Champion, 1997.

Gough, John W. *The Social Contract: A Critical Study of Its Development*. Oxford: Clarendon Press, 1936.

Grabmann, Martin. 'Die mittelalterlichen Kommentare zur *Politik* des Aristoteles.' *Sitzungsberichte der Bayerischen Akademie der Wissenschaften zu München, Philos.-hist. Abt.* 1941, II: 4–78. Repr. in idem *Gesammelte Akademieabhandlun-*

gen, edited by Grabmann-Institut der Univerität München, 2: 1725–1800. Paderborn: F. Schöningh, 1979.

Grafton, Anthony, and Nancy Siraisi, eds. *Natural Particulars: Nature and the Disciplines in Renaissance Europe*. Cambridge, MA, and London: MIT Press, 1999.

Granada, Miguel A. *Cosmología, religión y política en el Renacimiento: Ficino, Savonarola, Pomponazzi, Maquiavelo*. Barcelona: Anthropos Editorial del Hombre, 1988.

Green, Louis. *Chronicle into History: An Essay on the Interpretation of History in Florentine Fourteenth-Century Chronicles*. Cambridge: Cambridge University Press, 1972.

– 'The Image of Tyranny in Early Fourteenth-Century Italian Historical Writing.' *Renaissance Studies* 7 (1993): 335–51.

Grendler, Paul F. 'Books for Sarpi.' In *Essays Presented to Myron P. Gilmore*, edited by Sergio Bertelli and Gloria Ramakus, 1: 105–14. Florence: La Nuova Italia, 1978.

Grignaschi, Mario. 'Il matrimonio di Margarete Maultasch e il *Tractatus de matrimonio* di Marsilio di Padova.' *Rivista di storia del diritto italiano* 25 (1952): 195–204.

– 'Le rôle de l'aristotélisme dans le *Defensor Pacis* de Marsile de Padoue.' *Revue d'Histoire et de Philosophie Religieuses* 35 (1955): 301–40.

– 'Il pensiero politico e religioso di Giovanni di Jandun.' *Bullettino dell'Istituto Storico Italiano per il Medioevo e Archivio Muratoriano* 70 (1958): 425–96.

– 'Un commentaire nominaliste de la *Politique* d'Aristote: Jean Buridan.' *Anciens Pays et Assemblées d'Etats* 19 (1960): 125–42.

– 'Le problème du contrat social et l'origine de la 'civitas' dans la scolastique.' *Anciens Pays et Assemblées d'Etats* 22 (1961): 67–85.

– 'La definition du civis dans la Scholastique.' *Ancien Pays et Assemblées d'Etats* 36 (1966): 71–88.

– 'Quelques spécimens de la littérature sassanide conservés dans les bibliothèques d'Istanbul.' *Journal Asiatique* 254 (1966): 1–142.

– 'L'ideologia marsiliana si spiega con l'adesione dell'autore all'uno o all'altro dei grandi sistemi filosofi ci dell'inizio del Trecento?' In *MPCI*, 201–22.

– 'Indagine sui passi del "commento" suscettibili di avere promosso la formazione di un averroismo politico.' In *L'Averroismo in Italia*, 237–78. Repr. in *Il pensiero politico del basso Medioevo: Antologia di saggi*, edited by Carlo Dolcini, 273–312. Bologna: Pàtron, 1983.

– 'Réflexions suggérées par une dernière lecture du *Defensor Pacis* de Marsile de Padoue.' In *Papers in Comparative Political Science – Estudios de Ciencia Politica Comparada*, edited by Manuel J. Peláez, 4507–28. Barcelona: [Cátedra de Historia del Derecho y de las Instituciones, Facultad de Derecho, Universidad de Málaga], 1990.

Grimaldi, William M.A. *Aristotle, Rhetoric: A Commentary*. Vol. 1. New York: Fordham University Press, 1980.

Guggenheim, Max. 'Marsilius von Padua und die Staatslehre des Aristoteles.' *Historische Vierteljahresschrift* 7 (1904): 343–62.

Guthrie, William K.C. *In the Beginning: Some Greek Views on the Origins of Life and the Early State of Man*. Ithaca, NY: Cornell University Press, 1957. Repr. Westport, CT: Greenwood Press, 1986.

Hackert, Hermann. *Die Staatsschrift Gasparo Contarinis und die politischen Verhältnisse Venedigs im sechzehnten Jahrhundert*. Heidelberg: Winter, 1940.

Hackett, Jeremiah. 'Mirrors of Princes, Errors of Philosophers: Roger Bacon and Giles of Rome (Aegidius Romanus) on the Education of the Government (the Prince).' In *Ireland, England and the Continent in the Middle Ages and Beyond*, edited by Howard B. Clarke and J.R.S. Phillips, 105–27. Dublin: University College Dublin Press, 2006.

Hallberg, Peter, and Björn Wittrock. 'From *koinonìa politikè* to *societas civilis*: Birth, Disappearance and First Renaissance of the Concept.' In *The Languages of Civil Society*, edited by Peter Wagner, 28–51. New York and Oxford: Berghahn Books, 2006.

Haller, Johannes. 'Zur Lebensgeschichte des Marsilius von Padua.' *Zeitschrift für Kirchengeschichte* 48 (1929): 166–97. Repr. in idem *Abhandlungen zur Geschichte des Mittelalters*, 335–68. Stuttgart: Cotta, 1944.

Hamburger, Max. *Morals and Law: The Growth of Aristotle's Legal Theory*. New Haven, CT: Yale University Press, 1951.

Hanauer, Gustav. 'Das Berufspodestat im dreizehnten Jahrhundert.' *Mitt[h] eilungen des Instituts fur Österreichische Geschichtsforschung* 23 (1902): 377–426.

Hankins, James. *Plato in the Italian Renaissance*. 2 vols. Leiden and New York: Brill, 1991.

Hansen, Mogens H. 'How Many Athenians Attended the *Ecclesia?' Greek, Roman and Byzantine Studies* 17 (1976): 115–34. Repr. in idem, *The Athenian Ecclesia: A Collection of Articles 1976– 1983*, 1–20 (addenda 21–3). Copenhagen: Museum Tusculanum Press, 1983.

– '*Nomos* and *Psephisma* in Fourth-Century Athens.' *Greek, Roman and Byzantine Studies* 19 (1978): 315–30. Repr. in idem, *The Athenian Ecclesia: A Collection of Articles 1976–1983*, 161–76 (addenda 177). Copenhagen: Museum Tusculanum Press, 1983.

– 'Initiative and Decision: The Separation of Powers in Fourth-Century Athens.' *Greek, Roman and Byzantine Studies* 22 (1981): 345–70.

– 'Polis, politeuma and politeia: A Note on Arist. *Pol.* 1278b6–14.' In *From*

Political Architecture to Stephanus Byzantius: Sources for the Ancient Greek Polis, edited by David Whitehead, 91–8. Wiesbaden: F. Steiner, 1994.

Hanson, Ann Ellis. 'The Gradualist View of Fetal Development.' In Brisson, Congourdeau, and Solère, *L'embryon: Formation et animation*, 95–108.

Hardie, William F. R. 'Aristotle's Doctrine that Virtue Is a "Mean."' *Proceedings of the Aristotelian Society* 65 (1964/65): 183–204. Repr. in Barnes, Schofield, and Sorabji, *Articles on Aristotle*, vol. 2: *Ethics and Politics*, 33–46.

Harvey, Steven. 'Can a Tenth-Century Islamic Aristotelian Help Us Understand Plato's *Laws*?' in *Plato's Laws: From Theory into Practice*, edited by Samuel Scolnicov and Luc Brisson, 320–30. St. Augustin: Academia-Verlag, 2003.

Hasse, Dag N., and Amos Bertolacci, eds. *The Arabic, Hebrew and Latin Reception of Avicenna's Metaphysics*. Berlin and Boston: W. de Gruyter, 2012.

Hasselhoff, Görge K. *Dicit Rabbi Moyses: Studien zum Bild von Moses Maimonides im lateinischen Westen vom 13. bis 15. Jahrhundert*. Würzburg: Königshausen & Neumann, 2004; 2nd extended ed., 2005.

– 'The Translations and the Reception of the Medical Doctor Maimonides in the Christian Medicine of the 14th and 15th Century.' In *The Trias of Maimonides: Jewish, Arabic, and Ancient Culture of Knowledge*, edited by Georges Tamer, 395–410. Berlin and New York: W. de Gruyter, 2005.

Headley, John M. *Herkunft und Ursprung: Historische und mythische Formen der Legitimation*, edited by Peter Wunderli. Sigmaringen: J. Thorbecke, 1994.

– *Tommaso Campanella and the Transformation of the World*. Princeton, NJ: Princeton University Press, 1997.

Heather, Peter. 'Themistius: A Political Philosopher.' In *The Propaganda of Power: The Role of Panegyric in Late Antiquity*, edited by Mary Whitby, 125–50. Leiden: Brill, 1998.

Heck, Paul L. *The Construction of Knowledge in Islamic Civilization: Qudāma b. Ja'far and his Kitāb al-Kharāj wa-ṣinā'at al-kitāba*. Leiden: Brill, 2002.

Heckel, Johannes. 'Marsilius von Padua und Martin Luther. Ein Vergleich ihrer Rechts- und Soziallehre.' *Zeitschrift der Savigny Stiftung für Rechtsgeschichte, Kanon. Abt.*, 44 (1958): 268–336. Repr. in idem, *Das blinde, undeutliche Wort 'Kirche": Gesammelte Aufsätze*, edited by Siegried Grundmann, 49–110. Cologne and Graz: Böhlau, 1964.

Helmrath, Johannes, and Jörg Feuchter. 'Einleitung – Vormoderne Parlamentsoratorik.' In *Politische Redekultur in der Vormoderne: Die Oratorik europäischer Parlamente in Spätmittelalter und Früher Neuzeit*, edited by Jörg Feuchter and Johannes Helmrath, 9–22. Frankfurt a. M.: Campus, 2008.

Hertter, Fritz, *Die Podestàliteratur Italiens im 12. und 13. Jahrhundert*. Leipzig and Berlin: Teubner, 1910. Repr. Hildesheim: Gerstenberg, 1973.

Hirzel, Rudolf. *Agraphos nomos*. Leipzig: B.G. Teubner, 1900. Repr. Hildesheim: Gerstenberg, 1977.

– *Themis, Dike und Verwandtes: Ein Beitrag zur Geschichte der Rechtsidee bei den Griechen*. Leipzig: S. Hirzel, 1907. Repr. Hildesheim: Olms, 1966.

Hödl, Ludwig. 'Über die averroistische Wende der lateinischen Philosophie des Mittelalters im 13. Jahrhundert.' *Recherches de théologie ancienne et médiévale* 39 (1972): 171–204.

Hollander, Robert. 'Dante's *Theologus-Poeta*.' *Dante Studies* 94 (1976): 91–136. Repr. in idem, *Studies in Dante*, 39–89. Ravenna: Longo, 1980.

Homann, Eckhard. *Totum posse, quod est in ecclesia, reservatur in summo pontifice: Studien zur politischen Theorie bei Aegidius Romanus*. Würzburg: Königshausen & Neumann, 2004.

Horn, Christoph, and Ada Neschke-Hentschke, eds. *Politischer Aristotelismus: Hauptstationen seiner Rezeption vom Hellenismus bis zum 19. Jahrhundert*. Stuttgart: Metzler, 2008.

Hübener, Wolfgang. 'Unvorgreifliche Überlegungen zum möglichen Sinn des Topos "politischer Averroismus."' In *Averroismus im Mittelalter und in der Renaissance*, 222–38.

Hugonnard-Roche, Henri. 'La classification des sciences de Gundissalinus et l'influence d'Avicenne.' In *Études sur Avicenne*, edited by Jean Jolivet and Rashed Roshdi, 41–75. Paris: Les Belles Lettres, 1984.

Hyde, John K. 'Italian Social Chronicles in the Middle Ages.' *Bulletin of the John Rylands Library* 49 (1966): 107–32. Repr. in idem, *Literacy and Its Uses*, 33–57.

– *Padua in the Age of Dante*. Manchester and New York: Manchester University Press/Barnes & Noble, 1966.

– 'Contemporary Views on Faction and Civil Strife in Thirteenth- and Fourteenth-Century Italy.' In *Violence and Civil Disorder in Italian Cities, 1200–1500*, edited by Lauro Martines, 273–307. Berkeley, CA: University of California Press, 1972. Repr. in idem, *Literacy and Its Uses*, 58–86.

– *Society and Politics in Medieval Italy: The Evolution of the Civil Life 1000–1350*. New York: St Martin's Press, 1973.

– 'La prima scuola di storici accademici, da Buoncompagno da Signa a Rolandino da Padova.' In *Storia e cultura a Padova nell'età di Sant'Antonio*, 305–23.

– *Literacy and Its Uses: Studies on Late Medieval Italy*. Edited by Daniel Waley. Manchester and New York: Manchester University Press, 1993.

Imbach, Ruedi. 'L'averroïsme latin du XIIIe siècle.' In *Gli studi di filosofia medievale fra otto e novecento, contributo a un bilancio storiografico*, edited by Ruedi Imbach and Alfonso Maierù, 191–208. Rome: Storia e Letteratura 1991. Repr. in idem, *Quodlibeta: Ausgewählte Artikel*, edited by Francis Cheneval, Thomas Ricklin, Claude Pottier, Silvia Maspoli, and Marianne Mösch, 45–62. Freiburg i. S.: Universitätsverlag Freiburg/Schweiz, 1996.

Inglis, Eric. 'Gothic Architecture and a Scholastic: Jean de Jandun's *Tractatus de laudibus Parisius.*' *Gesta* 42 (2003): 63–85.

Izbicki, Thomas M. 'The Reception of Marsilius.' In Moreno-Riaño and Nederman, *A Companion to Marsilius of Padua*, 305–33.

Jaeger, Werner. *The Theology of the Early Greek Philosophers*. Translated by Edward S. Robinson. Oxford: Clarendon Press, 1947. Repr. Westport, CT: Greenwood Press, 1980.

– 'Aristotle's Use of Medicine as Model in his Ethics.' *The Journal of Hellenic Studies* 77 (1957): 54–61. Repr. in idem, *Scripta minora*, 2: 491–509. Rome: Storia e letteratura, 1960.

Jansen-Sieben, Ria, ed. *Artes mechanicae en Europe médiévale*. Brussels: Archives et bibliothèques de Belgique, 1989.

Jeck, Udo R. 'Platons Götter im lateinischen Mittelalter: Ein Beitrag zur Rezeption des platonischen *Timaios* bei Augustin, Calcidius und Albertus Magnus.' *Bochumer Philosophisches Jahrbuch für Antike und Mittelalter* 14 (2009–2011): 157–90.

Jones, Arnold H.M. *Athenian Democracy*. Baltimore, MD: Johns Hopkins University Press, 1957.

Jones, Philip J. *The Italian City-State: From Commune to Signoria*. Oxford: Oxford University Press, 1997.

Joutsivuo, Timo. *Scholastic Tradition and Humanist Innovation: The Concept of Neutrum in Renaissance Medicine*. Helsinki: Academia Scientiarum Fennica, 1999.

Kahn, Charles H. 'Discovering the Will: From Aristotle to Augustine.' In *The Question of 'Eclecticism': Studies in Later Greek Philosophy*, edited by John M. Dillon and Anthony A. Long, 234–59. Berkeley, CA: University of California Press, 1988.

Kalimtzis, Kostas. *Aristotle on Political Enmity and Disease: An Inquiry into Stasis*. Albany, NY: State University of New York Press, 2000.

Kallendorf, Craig. *Virgil and the Myth of Venice: Books and Readers in the Italian Renaissance*. Oxford: Clarendon Press, 1999.

Kamp, Andreas. 'Die aristotelische Theorie der Tyrannis.' *Philosophisches Jahrbuch* 92 (1985): 17–34.

Kantorowicz, Ernst H. *The King's Two Bodies: A Study in Mediaeval Political Theology*. Princeton, NJ: Princeton University Press, 1957. Repr. 1997.

Kaufhold, Martin, ed. *Politische Reflexion in der Welt des späten Mittelalters*. Leiden and Boston: Brill, 2004.

Keaney, John J. 'Aristotle's *Politics* 2.12 1274a22b–a28.' *American Journal of Ancient History* 6 (1981): 97–100.

Keller, Hagen. '"Kommune": Städtische Selbstregierung und mittelalterliche "Volksherrschaft" im Spiegel italienischer Wahlverfahren des 12.–14. Jahrhunderts.' In *Person und Gemeinschaft im Mittelalter*, edited by Gerd Althoff, Dieter Geuenich, Otto Gerhard Oexle, and Joachim Wollasch, 573–616. Sigmaringen: J. Thorbecke, 1988.

– 'Wahlformen und Gemeinschaftsverständnis in den italienischen Stadtkommunen (12./14. Jahrhundert).' In *Wahlen und Wählen im Mittelalter*, edited by Reinhard Schneider and Herbert Zimmermann, 345–74. Sigmaringen: J. Thorbecke, 1990.

Kelly, Henry A. *Ideas and Forms of Tragedy from Aristotle to the Middle Ages.* Cambridge: Cambridge University Press, 1993.

Kempshall, Matthew. '*De Re Publica* I.39 in Medieval and Renaissance Political Thought.' In *Cicero's Republic* (= *Bulletin of the Institute of Classical Studies* Supplement 76), edited by Jonathan G.F. Powell and John A. North, 99–135. London: Institute of Classical Studies, School of Advanced Study, University of London, 2001.

Kern, Fritz. 'Recht und Verfassung im Mittelalter.' *Historische Zeitschrift* 120 (1919): 1–79. Repr. as *Recht und Verfassung im Mittelalter*. Tübingen: Wissenschaftliche Buchgesellschaft, 1952. Repr. 1992.

Keyt , David, and Fred D. Miller, Jr, eds. *A Companion to Aristotle's Politics*. Oxford and Cambridge, MA: B. Blackwell, 1991.

Kibre, Pearl. 'Logic and Medicine in Fourteenth Century Paris.' In *Studi sul XIV secolo in memoria di Anneliese Maier*, edited by Alfonso Maierù and Agostino Paravicini Bagliani, 416–20. Rome: Storia e letteratura, 1981.

Kleingünther, Adolf. *ΠΡΩΤΟΣ ΕΥΡΕΤΗΣ: Untersuchungen zur Geschichte einer Fragestellung*. Leipzig: Dieterich, 1933.

Klemm, Matthew. 'Medicine and Moral Virtue in the *Expositio Problematum Aristotelis* of Peter of Abano.' *Early Science and Medicine* 11 (2006): 302–35.

– 'Medical Anthropology in the Late Middle Ages: Body, Soul, and the Virtues According to Peter of Abano (d. 1316).' Diss., The Johns Hopkins University, 2007.

Klibansky, Raymond. *The Continuity of the Platonic Tradition during the Middle Ages.* London: Warburg Institute, 1939. Repr. Millwood, NY: Kraus International Publications, 1984.

Klonoski, Richard J. '*Homonoia* in Aristotle's Ethics and Politics.' *History of Political Thought* 17 (1996): 313–25.

Kluxen, Wolfgang. *Philosophische Ethik bei Thomas von Aquin.* Darmstadt: Wissenschaftliche Buchgesellschaft, 3rd ed. 1998.

Koch, Joseph. 'Sind die Pygmäen Menschen? Ein Kapitel aus der philosophischen Anthropologie der mittelalterlichen Scholastik.' *Archiv für Geschichte der Philosophie* 40 (1931): 194–213.

Koebner, Richard. 'Despot and Despotism: Vicissitudes of a Political Term.' *Journal of the Warburg and Courtauld Institutes* 14 (1951): 275–302.

Kohl, Benjamin G. *Padua under the Carrara, 1318–1405*. Baltimore, MD: Johns Hopkins University Press, 1998.

– 'Government and Society in Renaissance Padua.' *Journal of Medieval and Renaissance Studies* 2 (1972): 205–21. Repr. in idem, *Culture and Politics in Early Renaissance Padua*. Aldershot: Ashgate, 2001, no. XI.

Köhler, Theodor W. 'Die wissenschaftstheoretische und inhaltliche Bedeutung der Rezeption von *De animalibus* für den philosophisch–anthropologischen Diskurs im 13. Jahrhundert.' In *Aristotle's Animals in the Middle Ages and Renaissance*, edited by Carlos Steel, Guy Guldentops, and Pieter Beullens, 249–74. Leuven: Leuven University Press, 2000.

– *Homo animal nobilissimum: Konturen des spezifisch Menschlichen in der naturphilosophischen Aristoteleskommentierung des dreizehnten Jahrhunderts*. Leiden and Boston: Brill, 2008.

Korolec, Jerzy B. 'Le Commentaire d'Averroès sur l'*Ethique à Nicomaque*.' *Bulletin de philosophie médiévale* 27 (1985): 104–7.

– 'Averroès et son Commentaire Moyen sur l'Ethique à Nicomaque.' *Internationale de l'Imaginaire* 17–18 (1991) [= *Le choc Averroès. Comment les philosophes arabes ont fait l'Europe*]: 66–77.

– 'Mittlerer Kommentar von Averroes zur *Nikomachischen Ethik* des Aristoteles.' *Mediaevalia philosophica Polonorum* 31 (1992): 61–118.

Koyré, Alexandre. *From the Closed World to the Infinite Universe*. New York: Harper, 1968.

Krämer, Werner. *Konsens und Rezeption: Verfassungsprinzipien der Kirche im Basler Konziliarismus*. Münster: Aschendorff, 1980.

Kraut, Richard. *Socrates and the State*. Princeton, NJ: Princeton University Press, 1984.

Kraut, Richard, and Steven Skultety, eds. *Aristotle's Politics: Critical Essays*. Lanham, MD: Rowman & Littlefield, 2005.

Kraye, Jill, W.F. Ryan, and Charles B. Schmitt, eds. *Pseudo-Aristotle in the Middle Ages: The Theology and Other Texts*. London: Warburg Institute, University of London, 1986.

Kreisel, Haim [Kreisel, Howard T.]. *Maimonides' Political Thought: Studies in Ethics, Law, and the Human Ideal*. Albany, NY: State University of New York Press, 1999.

– 'Maimonides' Political Philosophy.' In Seeskin, *The Cambridge Companion to Maimonides*, 193–220.

Kremer, Klaus. *Die neuplatonische Seinsphilosophie und ihre Wirkung auf Thomas von Aquin*. Leiden: E.J. Brill, 1966.

Kristeller, Paul O. *Studies in Renaissance Thought and Letters*. Rome: Storia e Letteratura, 1956. Repr. 1969.

– 'Umanesimo e Scolastica a Padova fino al Petrarca.' *Medioevo* 11 (1985): 1–18.

Krüger, Elmar. *Der Traktat 'De ecclesiastica potestate' des Aegidius Romanus: Eine spätmittelalterliche Herrschaftskonzeption des päpstlichen Universalismus*. Cologne: Böhlau, 2007.

Krüger, Sabine. 'Bemerkungen zu einem Buch von Christoph Flüeler.' *Deutsches Archiv für Erforschung des Mittelalters* 50 (1994): 215–21.

Krynen, Jacques. 'Naturel. Essai sur l'argumentation de la nature dans la pensée politique française à la fin du moyen âge.' *Journal des Savants* (April–June 1982): 169–90.

Kühn, Wilfried. 'Zur Kritik des politischen Platonismus im Mittelalter. Marsilius von Padua gegen Aegidius Romanus.' *Freiburger Zeitschrift für Philosophie und Theologie* 55 (2008): 98–128.

Kuksewicz, Zdzislaw. *De Siger de Brabant à Jacques de Plaisance. La théorie de l'intellect chez les averroïstes latins des XIIIe et XIVe siécles*. Wrocław: Ossolineum, 1968.

– 'Les *Problemata* de Pietro d'Abano et leur 'rédaction' par Jean de Jandun.' *Medioevo* 11 (1985): 113–37.

– 'A Mediaeval Theory of Felicity.' *Dialectics and Humanism* 2–3 (1986): 229–35.

Kullmann, Wolfgang. 'Der Mensch als politisches Lebewesen bei Aristoteles.' *Hermes* 108 (1980), 419–43.

– 'Man as a Political Animal in Aristotle.' In Keyt and Miller, *A Companion to Aristotle's Politics*, 94–117.

Kummerer, Christoph. *Der Fürst als Gesetzgeber in den lateinischen Übersetzungen von Averroes*. Ebelsbach: Gremer, 1989.

Kusch, Horst. 'Friede als Ausgangspunkt der Staatstheorie des Marsilius von Padua: Zur Aristotelesrezeption im Mittelalter.' *Altertum* 1 (1955): 116–25.

Laiou, Angeliki E. 'Economic Thought and Ideology.' In *The Economic History of Byzantium: From the Seventh through the Fifteenth Century*, edited by Angeliki E. Laiou, 1123–44. Washington, DC: Dumbarton Oaks Research Library and Collection, 2002.

Lambertini, Roberto. 'Philosophus videtur tangere tres rationes. Egidio Romano lettore ed interprete della *Politica* nel terzo libro del *De regimine Principum*.' *Documenti e studi sulla tradizione filosofica medievale* 1 (1990): 277–325.

– 'The *Sophismata* attributed to Marsilius of Padua.' In *Sophisms in Medieval Logic and Grammar*, edited by Stephen Read, 86–102. Dordrecht and Boston: Kluwer, 1993.

– 'Aspetti etico-politici del pensiero di Duns Scoto.' In *Etica e persona: Duns*

Scoto e suggestioni nel moderno, edited by Silvestro Casamenti, 35–86. Bologna: Edizioni Francescane Bologna, 1994.

– '*Felicitas politica* und *speculatio*. Die Idee der Philosophie in ihrem Verhältnis zur Politik nach Johannes von Jandun.' In Aertsen and Speer, *Was ist Philosophie im Mittelalter*, 984–90.

– 'Il cuore e l'anima della città: Osservazioni a margine sull'uso di metafore organistiche in testi politici bassomedievali.' In Casagrande and Vecchio, *Anima e corpo nella cultura medievale*, 289–303.

– 'La diffusione della *Politica* e la definizione di un linguaggio politico aristotelico.' *Quaderni storici* n.s. 102 (1999): 677–704.

– *La povertà pensata: Evoluzione storica della definizione dell'identità minoritica da Bonaventura ad Ockham*. Modena: Mucchi, 2000.

– 'Lo studio e la recezione della *Politica* tra XIII e XIV secolo.' In *Il pensiero politico dell'età antica e medioevale: Dalla polis alla formazione degli Stati europei*, edited by Carlo Dolcini, 145–73. Turin: UTET, 2000.

– 'La monarchia prima della *Monarchia*: Le ragioni del *regnum* nella ricezione medioevale di Aristotele.' In *Pour Dante: Dante et l'Apocalypse; Lectures humanistes de Dante*, edited by Bruno Pichard, 39–75. Paris: Champion, 2001.

– 'Zur Frage der Rolle des Averroes in der praktischen Philosophie des Spätmittelalters: Vorbemerkung zur Rezeption seines Ethikkommentars.' In *Averroes (1126–1198) oder der Triumph des Rationalismus*, edited by Raif G. Khoury, 243–53. Heidelberg: C. Winter, 2002.

– 'Politische Fragen und politische Terminologie in mittelalterlichen Kommentaren zur *Ethica Nicomachea*.' In Kaufhold, *Politische Reflexion in der Welt des späten Mittelalters*, 109–27.

– 'Jenseits des politischen Augustinismus: Zur Rezeption Augustins in der politischen Theorie des Spätmittelalters.' In *Augustinus – Recht und Gewalt*, edited by Cornelius Mayer, 73–96. Würzburg: Augustinus bei Echter, 2010.

Lambton, Ann K.S. 'Justice in the Medieval Persian Theory of Kingship.' *Studia Islamica* 17 (1962): 91–119. Repr. in eadem. *Theory and Practice in Medieval Persian Government*. London: Variorum Reprints, 1980, no. IV.

– *State and Government in Medieval Islam: An Introduction to the Study of Islamic Political Theory: The Jurists*. Oxford: Oxford University Press, 1985. Repr. 1991.

Lammert, Friedrich. 'Hellenistische Medizin bei Ptolemaios und Nemesios. Ein Beitrag zur Geschichte der christlichen Anthropologie.' *Philologus* 94 (1940): 125–41.

Larsen, Jakob A.O. 'Aristotle on the Electors of Mantinea and Representative Government.' *Classical Philology* 45 (1950): 180–3.

– 'The Judgment of Antiquity on Democracy.' *Classical Philology* 49 (1954): 1–14.
– *Representative Government in Greek and Roman History*. Berkeley, CA: University of California Press, 1955.
L'Averroismo in Italia. Rome: Accademia Nazionale dei Lincei, 1979.
Lazzarini, Lino. *Paolo de Bernardo e i primordi dell'Umanesimo in Venezia*. Geneva: L.S. Olschki, 1930.
La Terra Bellina, Rosario. 'Albertino Mussato e Marsilio da Padova: un ricordo (*Ep*. XII, vv. 50–5).' *Pensiero Politico Medievale* 2 (2004): 189–94.
Leaman, Oliver. *An Introduction to Classical Islamic Philosophy*. Cambridge: Cambridge University Press, 2nd ed. 2002.
Leandri, Antoine. 'L'aporie de la souveraineté.' In Aubenque and Tordesillas, *Aristote politique*, 315–29.
Lebreton, Gilles. 'Le problème de la démocratie dans le *Defensor pacis*. Essai sur la philosophie politique de Marsile de Padoue.' Diss., Université de Paris IV, 1987.
Legon, Ronald P. *Demos and Stasis: Studies in the Factional Politics of Classical Greece*. Diss., Cornell University, 1966.
Leinkauf, Thomas, and Carlos Steel, eds. *Platons Timaios als Grundtext der Kosmologie in Spätantike, Mittelalter und Renaissance*. Leuven: Leuven University Press, 2005.
Lemay, Richard. *Abu Ma ' shar and Latin Aristotelianism in the Twelfth Century: The Recovery of Aristotle's Natural Philosophy through Arabic Astrology*. Beirut: American University of Beirut, 1962.
Lennox, James G. 'Nature Does Nothing in Vain.' In *Beiträge zur antiken Philosophie*, edited by Hans-Christian Günther and Antonios Rengakos, 199–214. Stuttgart: F. Steiner, 1997.
Leschhorn, Wolfgang. *'Gründer der Stadt': Studien zu einem politisch-religiösen Phänomen der griechischen Geschichte*. Stuttgart: F. Steiner, 1984.
Levi, Alessandro. 'La partizione della filosofia pratica in un trattato medioevale.' *Atti del Reale Istituto di Scienze, Lettere ed Arti* 67 (1907/08): 1225–50.
Lévy, Edmond. '*Politeia* et *politeuma* chez Aristote.' In *Aristote et Athènes*, edited by Marcel Piérart, 65–90. Fribourg: Séminaire d'histoire ancienne de l'Université de Fribourg, 1993.
Ley, Hermann. *Studie zur Geschichte des Materialismus im Mittelalter*. Berlin: Deutscher Verlag der Wissenschaften, 1957.
Lintott, Andrew. *Violence, Civil Strife and Revolution in the Classical City, 750–330 BC*. Baltimore, MD: Johns Hopkins University Press, 1982.
Llinarès, Armand. 'Un averroïste déclaré: Jean de Jandun.' *Anuario de estudios medievales* 4 (1967): 393–402.

Lloyd, Geoffrey E.R. 'The Role of Medical and Biological Analogies in Aristotle's Ethics.' *Phronesis* 13 (1968): 68–83.

– *Science, Folklore and Ideology: Studies in the Life of Sciences in Ancient Greece.* Cambridge: Cambridge University Press, 1983.

Locati, Silvia, *La rinascita del genere tragico nel Medioevo: l'Ecerinis di Albertino Mussato.* Florence: F. Cesati, 2006.

Lockwood, Shelley. 'Marsilius of Padua and the Case for the Royal Ecclesiastical Supremacy.' *Transactions of the Royal Historical Society* 6th Ser., 1 (1991): 89–119.

Lockyer, Andrew. 'Aristotle: *The Politics*.' In *A Guide to the Political Classics: Plato to Rousseau*, edited by Murray Forsyth and Maurice Keens-Soper. Oxford: Oxford University Press, 1988.

Lohr, Charles H. 'The Pseudo-Aristotelian *Liber de causis* and Latin Theories of Science in the Twelfth and Thirteenth Centuries.' In Kraye, Ryan and Schmitt, *Pseudo-Aristotle in the Middle Ages*, 53–62.

London, Jennifer A. 'The Circle of Justice.' *History of Political Thought* 32 (2011): 425–47.

Longo, Oddone, ed. *Padova carrarese*. Padua: Il Poligrafo, 2005.

Lorberbaum, Menachem. *Politics and the Limits of Law: Secularizing the Political in Medieval Jewish Thought*. Stanford, CA: Stanford University Press, 2001.

Lord, Carnes. *Education and Culture in the Political Thought of Aristotle.* Ithaca, NY: Cornell University Press, 1982.

– 'Aristotle's Anthropology.' In *Essays on the Foundations of Aristotelian Political Science*, edited by Carnes Lord and David K. O'Connor. Berkeley, CA: University of California Press, 1991, 49–73.

Lovejoy, Arthur O., and George Boas. *Primitivism and Related Ideas in Antiquity*. Baltimore, MD: John Hopkins Press, 1935. Repr. 1997.

Luscombe, David E. 'Commentaries on the *Politics*: Paris and Oxford, XIII–XVth Centuries.' In Weijers and Holtz, *L'enseignement des disciplines à la Faculté des arts (Paris et Oxford, XIIIe–XVe siècles)*, 313–27.

– 'Hierarchy in the Late Middle Ages: Criticism and Change.' In Canning and Oexle, *Political Thought and the Realities of Power in the Middle Ages*, 113–26.

MacClintock, Stuart. *Perversity and Error: Studies on the 'Averroist' John of Jandun*. Bloomington, IN: Indiana University Press, 1956.

MacGregor, Alexander. 'Mussato's Commentary on Seneca's Tragedies: 149 New Fragments.' *Illinois Classical Studies* 5 (1980): 149–62.

– 'L'Abbazia di Pomposa, centro originario della tradizione 'E' delle tragedie di Seneca.' *La Bibliofilia* 85 (1983): 171–85.

Maddox, Graham. 'Constitution.' In *Political Innovation and Conceptual Change*, edited by Terence Ball, James Farr, and Russell L. Hanson, 50–67. Cambridge: Cambridge University Press, 1989.

Maglio, Gianfranco. *L'idea costituzionale nel Medioevo: Dalla tradizione antica al 'costituzionalismo cristiano.'* Negarine di S. Pietro in Cariano [Verona]: Gabrielli Editori, 2006.

Magnati e popolani nell'Italia comunale, edited by Giovanni Cherubini. Pistoia: Centro italiano di studi di storia e d'arte, 1997.

Mahoney, Edward P. 'John of Jandun and Agostino Nifo on Human Felicity ("Status").' In *L'homme et son univers au moyen âge*, vol. 1: *Philosophes médievaux*, edited by Christian Wenin, 465–77. Louvain-la-Neuve: Éd. de l'Inst. Supérieur de Philosophie, 1986. Repr. in idem, *Two Aristotelians of the Italian Renaissance: Nicoletto Vernia and Agostino Nifo.* Aldershot and Burlington, VT: Ashgate, 2000, no. XII.

Maier, Anneliese. *Zwei Untersuchungen zur nachscholastischen Philosophie: Die Mechanisierung des Weltbilds im 17. Jahrhundert; Kants Qualitätskategorien.* Rome: Storia e letteratura, 2nd ed. 1968.

Makdisi, George, ed. *La notion de liberté au Moyen Age: Islam, Byzance, Occident.* Paris: Les Belles Lettres, 1985.

Malkin, Irad. *Religion and Colonization in Ancient Greece.* Leiden and New York: Brill, 1987.

Mandonnet, Pierre. *Siger de Brabant et l'averroïsme latin au XIIIme siécle.* 2 vols. Leuven: Institut supérieur de philosophie de l'Université, 2nd rev. ed. 1911.

Manselli, Raoul. 'Ezzelino da Romano nella politica italiana del sec. XIII.' In *Studi Ezzeliniani*, 35–79.

Marangon, Paolo. *Alle origini dell'Aristotelismo Padovano (sec. XII–XIII).* Padua: Antenore, 1977.

– 'Marsilio tra preumanesimo e cultura delle arti. Ricerca sulle fonti padovane del I Discorso del *Defensor pacis.*' *Medioevo* 3 (1977): 89–119. Repr. in idem, *Ad cognitionem scientiae festinare*, 380–410.

– 'Principi di teoria politica nella Marca Trevigiana. Clero e comune a Padova al tempo di Marsilio.' In *MPCI*, 317–36. Repr. in idem, *Ad cognitionem scientiae festinare*, 411–30.

– *Ad cognitionem scientiae festinare. Gli studi nell'Università e nei Conventi di Padova nei secoli XIII e XIV*. Edited by Tiziana Pesenti. Trieste: LINT, 1997.

Marchesi, Angelo. 'Stato democratico e programmazione urbanistica nel pensiero politico dell'Aquinate.' In *Les philosophies morales et politiques au Moyen Âge*, edited by B. Carlos Bazán, Eduardo Andújar, and Léonard G. Sbrocchi, 3: 1542–54. New York: LEGAS, 1995.

Marenbon, John. 'Peter Abelard and Platonic Politics.' In *The Political Identity of the West: Platonism in the Dialogue of Cultures*, edited by Marcel van Ackeren and Orrin Finn Summerell, 133–50. Frankfurt a. M.: P. Lang, 2007.

Marenghi, Gerardo. 'Un capitolo dell'Aristotele medievale: Bartolomeo da Messina traduttore dei Problemata physica.' *Aevum* 36 (1962): 268–83.

Marquet, Yves. *La philosophie des Iḫwān al-Ṣafā'*. Algiers: Société nationale d'édition et de diffusion, 1973.

– 'La détermination astrale de l'évolution selon les Frères de la Pureté.' *Bulletin d'Etudes Orientales* 44 (1992): 127–46.

Marshall, John S. 'Aristotle and the Agrarians.' *Review of Politics* 9 (1947): 350–61.

Martin, Conor. 'The Commentaries on the *Politics* of Aristotle in the Late Thirteenth and Early Fourteenth Century, with Reference to the Thought and Political Life of the Time.' Diss., University of Oxford, 1949.

– 'Some Medieval Commentaries on Aristotle's *Politics*.' *History* n.s. 36 (1951): 29–44.

Martines, Lauro. *Power and Imagination: City-States in Renaissance Italy*. New York: A.A. Knopf, 1979.

Martínez, Jorge M. Ayala, ed. *Averroes y los averroísmos*. Zaragoza: Sociedad de Filosofía Medieval, 1999.

Martínez Lorca, Andrés. 'El lenguaje filosófico de Aristóteles en las versiones greco-latina de Moerbeke y árabo-latina de Escoto.' In *A recepção do pensamento greco-romano, árabe e judaico pelo Ocidente Medieval*, edited by Luis A. De Boni and Roberto Hofmeister Pich, 39–53. Porto Alegre: Pontificia Universidade Católica do Rio Grande do Sul, 2004.

Martorelli Vico, Romana. 'Anima e corpo nell'embriologia medievale.' In Casagrande and Vecchio, *Anima e corpo nella cultura medievale*, 95–106.

– *Medicina e filosofia: per una storia dell'embriologia medievale nel XIII e XIV secolo*. Milan: Guerini e associati, 2002.

Mairey, Aude . 'Les langages politiques au Moyen Âge (XIIe–XVe siècle).' *Médiévales* 57 (2009) [= *Langages politiques, XIIe–XVe siècle*, edited by Alban Gautier and Aude Mairey]: 5–14.

Mayali, Laurent. '*Lex animata*. Rationalisation du pouvoir politique et science juridique. (XIIème–XIVème siècles).' In *Renaissance du pouvoir législatif et genèse de l'État*, edited by André Gouron and Albert Rigaudière, 131–64. Montpellier: Société d'Histoire du Droit et des Institutions des Anciens Pays de Droit Écrit, 1988.

Mayhew, Robert. *Aristotle's Criticism of Plato's Republic*. Lanham, MD: Rowman & Littlefield, 1997.

McAleer, Graham. 'Giles of Rome on Political Authority.' *Journal of the History of Ideas* 60 (1999): 21–36.

McCann, Marcella T. 'Political Ideas of Some Thirteenth Century Commentators on Aristotle's *Ethics* and *Politics*.' MA thesis, University of Wisconsin-Madison, 1962.

McVaugh, Michael R. 'Niccolò da Reggio's Translations of Galen and Their Reception in France.' *Early Science and Medicine* 11 (2006): 275–301.

Megas, Anastasios C. 'The Pre-humanistic Circle of Padua (Lovato Lovati–Albertino Mussato) and the Tragedies of L. A. Seneca.' Diss., Aristotle University of Thessalonike, 1967 [in Greek].

– *Albertini Mussati argumenta tragoediarum Senecae: Commentarii in L.A. Senecae tragoedias fragmenta nuper reperta*. Thessalonike: n.p., 1969.

Mehl, Ernst. *Die Weltanschauung des Giovanni Villani: Ein Beitrag zur Geistesgeschichte Italiens im Zeitalter Dantes*. Leipzig: B.G. Teubner, 1927.

Meier, Ulrich. '*Molte rivoluzioni, molte novità*. Gesellschaftlicher Wandel im Spiegel der politischen Philosophie und im Urteil von städtischen Chronisten des späten Mittelalters.' In Miethke and Schreiner, *Sozialer Wandel im Mittelalter*, 119–76.

Melamed, Abraham. 'Jethro's Advice in Medieval and Early Modern Jewish and Christian Political Thought.' *Jewish Political Studies Review* 2 (1990): 3–41.

– 'Isaac Abravanel and Aristotle's *Politics*: A Drama of Errors.' *Jewish Political Studies Review* 5 (1993): 55–75.

– 'Maimonides on the Political Nature of Man: Needs and Responsibilities.' In *Minah le-Sarah: Mekhqarim be-Filosofiyah Yehudit ve-Qabbalah* (= *Sarah Heller Wilensky Jubilee Volume*), edited by Mosheh Idel, Devorah Dimanṭ, and Shalom Rozenberg, 292–333. Jerusalem: Magnes Press, 1994.

– *The Philosopher-King in Medieval and Renaissance Jewish Thought*. Albany, NY: State University of New York Press, 2003.

– 'The Organic Theory of the State in Medieval and Renaissance Jewish Political Thought.' In *Ideal Constitutions in the Renaissance*, edited by Heinrich C. Kuhn and Diana Stanciu, 113–44. Frankfurt a. M.: P. Lang, 2009.

– 'Aristotle's *Politics* in Medieval and Renaissance Jewish Political Thought.' In *Well Begun Is Only Half Done: Tracing Aristotle's Political Ideas in Medieval Arabic, Syriac, Byzantine, and Jewish Sources*, edited by Vasileios Syros, 145–86. Tempe, AZ: Arizona Center for Medieval and Renaissance Studies, 2011.

Merisalo, Outi. 'Les voies de diffusion des textes médicaux au Moyen Âge: L'exemple du *De spermate* pseudo-galénien, XIIe-XVe siècle.' *Gazette du livre médiéval* 52–3 (2008): 45–50.

– 'In *Horis Sanguinis*: Physiology and Generation in the Pseudo-Galenic *De Spermate*.' In *Pūrvāparaprajñābhinandanam: East and West, Past and Present,* edited by Bertil Tikkanen and Albion M. Butters, 231–42. Helsinki: Finnish Oriental Society, 2011.

Merisalo, Outi, and Päivi Pahta. 'Tracing the Trail of Transmission: The Pseudo-Galenic *De spermate* in Latin.' In *Science Translated: Latin and Vernacular Translations of Scientific Treatises in Medieval Europe*, edited by Michèle Goyens et al., 91–104. Leuven: Leuven University Press, 2008.

Merlo, Maurizio. 'Pace, guerra e identità della comunità politica in Marsilio da Padova.' In *Figure della guerra: la riflessione su pace, conflitto e giustizia tra Medioevo e prima età moderna*, edited by Merio Scattola, 111–44. Milan: Franco Angeli, 2003.

– 'La sintassi del 'regimen bene commixtum' e del 'regimen politicum' fra Tommaso d'Aquino e Tolomeo da Lucca.' *Filosofia Politica* 19 (2005): 33–47.

Meulen, Jan van der. *Aristoteles: Die Mitte in seinem Denken*. Meisenheim am Glan: Anton Hain, 1951.

Miccoli, Lucia. 'Le "arti meccaniche" nelle classificazioni delle scienze di Ugo di San Vittore e Domenico Gundisalvi.' *Annali della Facoltà di Lettere e Filosofia* (Bari) 24 (1981): 73–101.

Miethke, Jürgen. 'Marsilius von Padua. Die politische Philosophie eines lateinischen Aristotelikers des 14. Jahrhunderts.' In *Lebenslehren und Weltentwürfe im Übergang vom Mittelalter zur Neuzeit: Politik-Naturkunde-Theologie*, edited by Hartmut Boockmann, Bernd Moeller, and Karl Stackmann, 52–76. Göttingen: Vandenhoeck & Ruprecht, 1989.

– 'Politische Theorie in der Krise der Zeit, Aspekte der Aristotelesrezeption im früheren 14. Jahrhundert.' In *Institutionen und Geschichte: Theoretische Aspekte und mittelalterliche Befunde*, edited by Gert Melville, 157–86. Cologne and Vienna: Böhlau, 1992.

– 'Wirkungen politischer Theorie auf die Praxis der Politik im Römischen Reich des 14. Jahrhunderts: Gelehrte Politikberatung am Hofe Ludwigs des Bayern.' In Canning and Oexle, *Political Thought and the Realities of Power in the Middle Ages*, 173–210.

– *De potestate papae: Die päpstliche Amtskompetenz im Widerstreit der politischen Theorie von Thomas von Aquin bis Wilhelm von Ockham*. Tübingen: Mohr Siebeck, 2000.

– 'Die Frage der Legitimität rechtlicher Normierung in der politischen Theorie des 14. Jahrhunderts.' In *Die Begründung des Rechts als historisches Problem*, edited by Dietmar Willoweit, 171–202. Munich: R. Oldenbourg, 2000.

– 'Der Kampf Ludwigs des Bayern mit Papst und avignonesischer Kurie in seiner Bedeutung für die deutsche Geschichte.' In Nehlsen and Hermann, *Kaiser Ludwig der Bayer*, 39–74.

– 'Die Eheaffäre der Margarete »Maultasch«, Gräfin von Tirol (1341/42). Ein Beispiel hochadliger Familienpolitik im Spätmittelalter.' In *Päpste, Pilger, Pönitentiarie*, edited by Andreas Meyer et al., 353–91. Tübingen: M. Niemeyer, 2004.

– 'Die Briefgedichte des Albertino Mussato.' *Pensiero Politico Medievale* 6 (2008): 49–65.

Miethke, Jürgen, and Klaus Schreiner. *Sozialer Wandel im Mittelalter: Wahrnehmungsformen, Erklärungsmuster, Regelungsmechanismen*. Sigmaringen: Thorbecke, 1994.

Mikkola, Eino. '"Schole" bei Aristoteles.' *Arctos* n.s. 2 (1958): 68–87.

Minecan, Ana María C. 'Introducción al debate historiográfico en torno a la noción de "averroísmo latino."' *Anales del Seminario de Historia de Filosofía* 27 (2010): 63–85.

Mirabella, Tommaso. *Il concetto di sovranità nella Politica di Aristotele*. Palermo: Libreria Agate, 1941.

Mittelstraß, Jürgen. *Neuzeit und Aufklärung: Studien zur Entstehung der neuzeitlichen Wissenschaft und Philosophie*. Berlin and New York: W. de Gruyter, 1970.

Mohl, Ruth. *The Three Estates in Medieval and Renaissance Literature*. New York: Columbia University Press, 1933. Repr. New York: F. Ungar, 1962.

Molland, Andrew G. 'Medieval Ideas of Scientific Progress.' *Journal of the History of Ideas* 39 (1978): 561–77.

Molnár, Péter. 'Une étape négligée de la réception d'Aristote en Occident: Averroès, le *Liber Nicomachie* et la science politique.' In Bazzana, Bériou, and Guichard, *Averroès et l'averroïsme*, 265–73.

Monahan, Arthur P. *Consent, Coercion, and Limit: The Medieval Origins of Parliamentary Democracy*. Kingston: McGill-Queen's University Press, 1987.

Monfasani, John. *George of Trebizond: A Biography and a Study of His Rhetoric and Logic*. Leiden: E.J. Brill, 1976.

– 'The Pseudo-Aristotelian Problemata and Aristotle's *De animalibus* in the Renaissance.' In Grafton and Siraisi, *Natural Particulars*, 205–47.

Montobbio, Luigi. *Splendore e utopia nella Padova dei Carraresi*. Venice: Corbo e Fiore, 1989.

Moos, Peter von. 'Die italienische *ars agregandi* des 13. Jahrhunderts als Schule der Kommunikation.' In *Wissensliteratur im Mittelalter und in der Frühen Neuzeit: Bedingungen, Typen, Publikum, Sprache*, edited by Horst Brunner und Norbert R. Wolf, 67–90. Wiesbaden: Ludwig Reichert, 1993. Rev. version in idem, *Rhetorik, Kommunikation und Medialität: Gesammelte Studien zum Mittelalter*, edited by Gert Melville, 127–52. Münster: Lit, 2006.

Morani, Moreno. *La tradizione manoscritta del 'De natura hominis' di Nemesio*. Milan: Vita e pensiero, 1981.

Moreno-Riaño, Gerson, ed. *The World of Marsilius of Padua*. Tunhout: Brepols, 2006.

Moreno-Riaño, Gerson, and Cary J. Nederman, eds. *A Companion to Marsilius of Padua*. Leiden and Boston: Brill, 2012.

Moreschini, Claudio. 'Saggio introduttivo.' In Calcidio, *Commentario al 'Timeo' di Platone*, vii–lxxxvi.

Moritz, Arne. 'Politik als künstliche Vollendung der menschlichen Natur. Aristoteles, Marsilius von Padua und Nikolaus von Kues über die artifizielle Kompensation der Defizite in der Naturausstattung des Menschen.' In *Ars imitatur naturam: Transformationen eines Paradigmas menschlicher Kreativität im Übergang vom Mittelalter zur Neuzeit*, edited by Arne Moritz, 229–49. Münster: Aschendorff, 2010.

Moschetti, Andrea M. 'Il tema della pace in Marsilio da Padova, Petrarca e S. Caterina da Siena.' *Studia Patavina* 27 (1980): 280–5.

Mossé, Claude. 'Comment s'élabore un mythe politique: Solon, "Père fondateur" de la démocratie athénienne.' *Annales* 34 (1979): 425–37.

Motta, Beatrice. *La mediazione estrema: L'antropologia di Nemesio di Emesa fra platonismo e aristotelismo*. Padua: Il Poligrafo, 2004.

Moulakis, Athanasios. *Homonoia: Eintracht und die Entwicklung eines politischen Bewußtseins*. Munich: List, 1973.

MPCI = *Marsilio da Padova: Convegno internazionale (Padova, 18-20 settembre 1980)* [= *Medioevo* 5–6 (1979/80].

Mugnai Carrara, Daniella. 'Epistemological Problems in Giovanni Mainardi's Commentary on Galen's *Ars parva*.' In *Natural Particulars*, 251–73.

Muir, Edward. *Civic Ritual in Renaissance Venice*. Princeton, NJ: Princeton University Press, 1981.

Mulcahy, Daniel G. 'The Hands of Augustine but the Voice of Marsilius.' *Augustiniana* 21 (1971): 457–66.

– 'Marsilius of Padua's Use of St. Augustine.' *Revue des Études Augustiniennes* 18 (1972): 180–90.

Mulgan, Richard G. 'Aristotle's Sovereign.' *Political Studies* 18 (1970): 518–22.

– 'Aristotle and the Democratic Conception of Freedom.' In *Auckland Classical Essays Presented to E.M. Blaiklock*, edited by Bruce F. Harris, 95–111. Auckland: Aukland University Press, 1970.

– 'Aristotle's Doctrine that Man Is a Political Animal.' *Hermes* 102 (1974): 438–45.

– 'Aristotle and Absolute Rule.' *Antichthon* 8 (1974): 21–8.

– 'A Note on Aristotle's Absolute Ruler.' *Phronesis* 19 (1974): 66–9.

– *Aristotle's Political Theory: An Introduction for Students of Political Theory*. Oxford: Clarendon Press, 1977.

Müller, Hubert. *Früher Humanismus in Oberitalien: Albertino Mussato, Ecerinis.* Frankfurt a. M.: P. Lang, 1987.

Muller, Robert. 'La logique de la liberté dans la *Politique*.' In Aubenque and Tordesillas, *Aristote politique*, 185–208.

Mustacchio, Paul F. *The Concept of 'Stasis' in Greek Political Theory*. Diss., New York University, 1972.

Nafissi, Massimo. *La nascita del kosmos: Studi sulla storia e la società di Sparta.* Naples: Edizioni Scientifiche Italiane, 1991.

Nagel, Tilman. 'Aristotle on *Eudaimonia*.' *Phronesis* 17 (1972): 252–9. Repr. in Oksenberg Rorty, *Essays on Aristotle's Ethics*, 7–14.

Nagle, D. Brendan. *The Household as the Foundation of Aristotle's Polis.* Cambridge: Cambridge University Press, 2006.

Najemy, John M. 'The Republic's Two Bodies: Body Metaphors in Italian Renaissance Political Thought.' In *Language and Images of Renaissance Italy*, edited by Alison Brown, 237–62. Oxford: Clarendon Press, 1995.

Nakos, George P. *Forms of Ancient Greek Legislation*.Thessaloniki: University Studio Press, 1986 [in Greek].

Nardi, Bruno. *Saggi sull'aristotelismo padovano dal secolo XIV al XVI.* Florence: G.C. Sansoni 1958.

Navone, John J. 'The Division of Parts in Society according to Plato and Aristotle.' *Philosophical Studies* 6 (1956): 113–22.

Nederman, Cary J. 'The Aristotelian Doctrine of the Mean and John of Salisbury's Concept of Liberty.' *Vivarium* 24 (1986): 128–41. Repr. in idem, *Medieval Aristotelianism and Its Limits*, no. VIII.

– 'Aristotle as Authority: Alternative Aristotelian Sources of Late Medieval Political Theory.' *History of European Ideas* 8 (1987): 31–44. Repr. in idem, *Medieval Aristotelianism and Its Limits*, no. XV.

– 'The Physiological Significance of the Organic Metaphor in John of Salisbury's *Policraticus*.' *History of Political Thought* 8 (1987): 211–23. Repr. in idem, *Medieval Aristotelianism and Its Limits*, no. VI.

– 'Nature, Sin and the Origins of Society: The Ciceronian Tradition in Medieval Political Thought.' *Journal of the History of Ideas* 49 (1988): 3–26. Repr. in idem, *Medieval Aristotelianism and Its Limits*, no. XI.

– Private Will, Public Justice: Household, Community and Consent in Marsiglio of Padua's *Defensor Pacis*.' *Western Political Quarterly* 43 (1990): 699–717.

– 'Aristotelianism and the Origins of "Political Science" in the Twelfth Century.' *Journal of History of Ideas* 52 (1991): 179–94. Repr. in idem, *Medieval Aristotelianism and Its Limits*, no. II.

– 'Character and Community in the *Defensor Pacis*: Marsiglio of Padua's Adaptation of Aristotelian Moral Psychology.' *History of Political Thought* 13 (1992): 377–90.
– 'The Union of Wisdom and Eloquence before the Renaissance: The Ciceronian Orator in Medieval Political Thought.' *Journal of Medieval History* 18 (1992): 75–95. Repr. in idem, *Medieval Aristotelianism and Its Limits*, no. XII.
– *Community and Consent: The Secular Political Theory of Marsiglio of Padua's Defensor pacis*. Lanham, MD: Rowman & Littlefield, 1995.
– 'From *Defensor pacis* to *Defensor minor*: The Problem of Empire in Marsiglio of Padua.' *History of Political Thought* 16 (1995): 313–29.
– 'The Meaning of "Aristotelianism" in Medieval Moral and Political Thought.' *Journal of the History of Ideas* 57 (1996): 563–85.
– *Medieval Aristotelianism and Its Limits: Classical Traditions in Moral and Political Philosophy, 12th–15th Centuries*. Aldershot and Brookfield, VT: Variorum, 1997.
– 'The Expanding Body Politic: Christine de Pizan and Medieval Political Economy.' In *Au Champ des écritures*, edited by Eric Hicks, 383–97. Paris: Honoré Champion Éditeur, 2000.
– 'Social Bodies and the Non-Christian "Other" in the Twelfth Century: John of Salisbury and Peter of Celle.' In *Meeting the Foreign in the Middle Ages*, edited by Albrecht Classen, 192–201. New York and London: Routledge, 2002.
– 'Commercial Society and Republican Government in the Latin Middle Ages: The Economic Dimensions of Brunetto Latini's Republicanism.' *Political Theory* 31 (2003): 644–63.
– 'Body Politics: The Diversification of Organic Metaphors in the Later Middle Ages.' *Pensiero Politico Medievale* 2 (2004): 59–87.
– 'The Living Body Politic: The Diversification of Organic Metaphors in Nicole Oresme and Christine de Pizan.' In *Healing the Body Politic: The Political Thought of Christine de Pizan*, edited by Karen Green and Constant J. Mews, 19–33. Turnhout: Brepols, 2005.
– *Lineages of European Political Thought: Explorations along the Medieval/Modern Divide from John of Salisbury to Hegel*. Washington, DC: Catholic University of America Press, 2009.
– 'Varieties of Dialogue: Dialogical Models of Intercultural Communication in Medieval Inter-religious Writings.' In *Western Political Thought in Dialogue with Asia*, edited by Takashi Shogimen and Cary J. Nederman, 45–64. Lanham, MD: Lexington Books, 2009.
Nederman, Cary J., and Mary E. Sullivan. 'Reading Aristotle through Rome:

History and Republicanism in Ptolemy of Lucca's *De regimine principum.' European Journal of Political Theory* 7 (2008), 223–40.

Nehlsen, Hermann, and Hans-Georg Hermann, eds. *Kaiser Ludwig der Bayer: Konflikte, Weichenstellungen und Wahrnehmung seiner Herrschaft*. Paderborn: Schöningh, 2002.

Nehlsen, Hermann. 'Die Rolle Ludwigs des Bayern und seiner Berater Marsilius von Padua und Wilhelm von Ockham im Tiroler Ehekonflikt.' In Nehlsen and Hermann, *Kaiser Ludwig der Bayer*, 285–328.

Niccoli, Ottavia. *I sacerdoti, i guerrieri, i contadini: Storia di un' immagine della società*. Turin: G. Einaudi, 1979.

Nichols, Mary P. *Citizens and Statesmen: A Study of Aristotle's Politics*. Savage, MD: Rowman & Littlefield Publishers, 1992.

Nickel, Diethard. 'Stoa und Stoiker in Galens Schrift *De foetuum formatione*.' In *Galen und das hellenistische Erbe*, edited by Jutta Kollesch and Diethard Nickel, 79–86. Stuttgart: F. Steiner, 1993.

– *Untersuchungen zur Embryologie Galens*. Berlin: Akademie-Verlag, 1989.

Niewöhner, Friedrich, and Loris Sturlese, eds. *Averroismus im Mittelalter und in der Renaissance*. Zürich: Spur-Verlag, 1994.

Nippel, Wilfried. *Mischverfassungstheorie und Verfassungsrealität in Antike und früher Neuzeit*. Stuttgart: Klett-Cotta, 1980.

– 'Ancient and Modern Republicanism: "Mixed Constitution" and "Ephors."' In *The Invention of the Modern Republic*, edited by Biancamaria Fontana, 6–26. Cambridge: Cambridge University Press, 1994.

Nisbet, Robert A. *History of the Idea of Progress*. New York: Basic Books, 1980. Repr. New Brunswick, NJ: Transaction Pub., 1994.

Nitschke, August. *Naturerkenntnis und politisches Handeln im Mittelalter: Körper-Bewegung-Raum*. Stuttgart: Klett, 1967.

Norpoth, Leo. 'Zur Bio-, Bibliographie und Wissenschaftslehre des Pietro d'Abano.' *Kyklos* 3 (1930): 292–353.

North, Helen. *Sophrosyne: Self-Knowledge and Self-Restraint in Greek Literature*. Ithaca, NY: Cornell University Press, 1966.

North, John D. 'Celestial Influence – the Major Premiss of Astrology.' In Zambelli, *'Astrologi hallucinati,'* 45–100.

– *Stars, Minds and Fate: Essays in Ancient and Medieval Cosmology*. London and Ronceverte, WV: Hambledon Press, 1989.

Ober, Josiah. 'How to Criticize Democracy in Late Fifth- and Fourth-Century Athens.' In *Athenian Political Thought and the Reconstruction of American Democracy*, edited by J. Peter Euben, John Wallach and Josiah Ober, 149–71. Ithaca, NY: Cornell University Press, 1994. Repr. in idem, *The Athenian Revo-*

lution: Essays on Ancient Greek Democracy and Political Theory, 140–60. Princeton, NJ: Princeton University Press, 1996.

O'Boyle, Cornelius. 'An Updated Survey of the Life and Works of Bartholomew of Bruges (†1356).' *Manuscripta* 40 (1996): 67–95.

– *The Art of Medicine: Medical Teaching at the University of Paris, 1250–1400*. Leiden: Brill, 1998.

Oexle, Otto Gerhard. 'Die 'Wirklichkeit' und das 'Wissen.' Ein Blick auf das sozialgeschichtliche Œuvre von Georges Duby.' *Historische Zeitschrift* 232 (1981): 61–91.

– 'Tria genera hominum. Zur Geschichte eines Deutungsschemas der sozialen Wirklichkeit in Antike und Mittelalter.' In *Institutionen, Kultur und Gesellschaft im Mittelalter*, edited by Lutz Fenske, Werner Rösener, and Thomas Zotz, 483–500. Sigmaringen: J. Thorbecke, 1984.

– 'Die funktionale Dreiteilung als Deutungsschema der sozialen Wirklichkeit in der ständischen Gesellschaft des Mittelalters.' In *Ständische Gesellschaft und soziale Mobilität*, edited by Winfried Schulze, 19–51. Munich: R. Oldenbourg, 1988.

– 'Die Entstehung politischer Stände im Spätmittelalter – Wirklichkeit und Wissen.' In *Institutionen und Ereignis: Über historische Praktiken und Vorstellungen gesellschaftlichen Ordnens*, edited by Reinhard Blänkner and Bernhard Jussen, 137–62. Göttingen: Vandenhoeck & Ruprecht, 1998.

Offler, Hilary S. 'Über die Prokuratorien Ludwigs des Bayern für die römische Kurie.' *Deutsches Archiv für Erforschung des Mittelalters* 8 (1951): 461–87. Repr. in idem, *Church and Crown in the Fourteenth Century*, no. V.

– 'Empire and Papacy: The Last Struggle.' *Transactions of the Royal Historical Society* 5th Ser. 6 (1956): 21–47. Repr. in idem, *Church and Crown in the Fourteenth Century* no. II.

– *Church and Crown in the Fourteenth Century: Studies in European History and Political Thought*. Edited by Anthony I. Doyle. Aldershot and Burlington, VT: Ashgate, 2000.

Oksenberg Rorty, Amélie. 'The Place of Contemplation in Aristotle's *Nicomachean Ethics*.' *Mind* 87 (1978): 343–58. Repr. in *Essays on Aristotle's Ethics*, 377–94.

– ed. *Essays on Aristotle's Ethics*. Berkeley, CA: University of California Press, 1980.

Olivieri, Luigi. 'Teoria aristotelica dell'opinione e scienza politica in Marsilio da Padova.' In *MPCI*, 223–35.

– 'Il tutto e la parte nel *Defensor pacis* di Marsilio da Padova.' *Rivista critica di storia della filosofia* 37 (1982): 65–74.

– *Pietro d'Abano e il pensiero neolatino. Filosofia, scienza e ricerca dell'Aristotele greco tra i secoli XIII e XIV.* Padua: Antenore, 1988.

O'Meara, Dominic. 'Der Mensch als politisches Lebewesen: zum Verhältnis zwischen Platon und Aristoteles.' In *Der Mensch - ein politisches Tier? Essays zur politischen Anthropologie*, edited by Otfried Höffe, 14–25. Stuttgart: Reclam, 1992.

– 'Man as Political Animal: On the Relation between Plato and Aristotle.' In idem, *The Structure of Being and the Search for the Good: Essays on Ancient and Early Medieval Platonism*, Aldershot and Brookfield, VT: Ashgate, 1998, no. III.

Oncken, William. 'Die Wiederbelebung der aristotelischen Politik in der abendländischen Lesewelt.' In *Festschrift zur Begrüßung der vierundzwanzigsten Versammlung deutscher Philologen und Schulmänner*, edited by Historisch-philologischer Verein zu Heidelberg, 3–18. Leipzig: W. Engelmann, 1865.

Orlandi, Giovanni. 'Note sul *De Magnalibus Mediolani* di Bonvesin de la Riva.' *Studi Medievali* 17 (1976): 863–906.

Ortalli, Gherardo. 'Ezzelino crudelissimo tiranno: genesi e sviluppo di un mito.' *La ricerca folklorica* 25 (1992): 89–98.

– 'Ezzelino: genesi e sviluppi di un mito.' In *Nuovi Studi Ezzeliniani*, edited by Giorgio Cracco, 2: 609–25. Rome: Istituto storico italiano per il Medio Evo, 1992.

– 'Fra leggenda e realtà: la lunga vita del mito ezzeliniano.' In *Ezzelini: Signori della Marca nel cuore dell'Impero di Federico II*, edited by Carlo Bertelli and Giovanni Marcadella, 215–19. Milan: Skira, 2001.

Osmond, Patricia J. '*Princeps Historiae Romanae*: Sallust in Renaissance Political Thought.' *Memoirs of the American Academy in Rome* 40 (1995): 101–43.

Ostwald, Martin. *Nomos and the Beginnings of the Athenian Democracy.* Oxford: Clarendon Press, 1969.

– 'Was There a Concept *agraphos nomos* in Classical Greece?' In *Exegesis and Argument: Studies in Greek Philosophy Presented to Gregory Vlastos*, edited by Edward N. Lee, Alexander P.D. Mourelatos and Richard M. Rorty, 70–104. New York: Humanities Press, 1973.

– *From Popular Sovereignty to the Sovereignty of Law: Law, Society, and Politics in Fifth-Century Athens.* Berkeley, CA: University of California Press, 1986.

Ottaviani, Didier. 'Le peuple en puissance: Marsile de Padoue.' In *De la puissance du peuple*, vol. 1: *La démocratie de Platon à Rawls*, edited by Yves Vargas, 43–55. Pantin: Le Temps des Cerises, 2000.

Ottosson, Per-Gunnar. *Scholastic Medicine and Philosophy: A Study of Commentaries on Galen's Tegni (ca. 1300–1450).* Naples: Bibliopolis, 1984.

Ovitt, Jr, George. *The Restoration of Perfection: Labor and Technology in Medieval Culture*. New Brunswick, NJ, and London: Rutgers University Press, 1987.

Pahta, Päivi. *Medieval Embryology in the Vernacular: The Case of De spermate.* Helsinki: Société Néophilologique, 1998.

– 'Medieval Andrology and the Pseudo-Galenic *De spermate.*' *Medicina nei Secoli* 13 (2001): 509–21.

Palmieri , Nicoletta, ed. *L'Ars Medica (Tegni) de Galien: Lectures antiques et médiévales.* Saint-Étienne: Publications de l'Université de Saint-Étienne, 2008.

Papageorgiou, C.I. 'Four or Five Types of Democracy in Aristotle?' *History of Political Thought* 11 (1990): 1–8.

Parel, Anthony J. *The Machiavellian Cosmos.* New Haven: Yale University Press, 1992.

Parisoli, Luca. *La philosophie normative de Jean Duns Scot: Droit et politique du droit.* Rome: Istituto Storico dei Cappuccini, 2001.

Parker, Robert. *Athenian Religion: A History.* Oxford: Clarendon Press, 1996.

Passerin d'Entrèves, Alessandro. *The Medieval Contribution to Political Thought: Thomas Aquinas, Marsilius of Padua, Richard Hooker*. Oxford: Oxford University Press, 1939. Repr. New York: Humanities Press, 1959.

Pattin, Adrian. *Pour l'histoire du sens agent: La controverse entre Barthélemy de Bruges et Jean de Jandun, ses antécédents et son évolution.* Leuven: Leuven University Press, 1988.

Pelzer, Auguste. 'Barthélemy de Bruges, philosophe et médecin du XIVe siècle (†1356).' *Revue néoscolastique de philosophie* 36 (1934): 459–74.

Pembroke, S.G. 'Oikeiōsis.' In *Problems in Stoicism*, edited by Anthony A. Long, 114–49. London: Athlone Press, 1971.

Pennington, Kenneth. *The Prince and the Law, 1200–1600: Sovereignty and Rights in the Western Legal Tradition*. Berkeley, CA: University of California Press, 1993.

Perelli, Luciano. 'La definizione e l'origine dello stato nel pensiero di Cicerone.' *Atti della Accademia delle Scienze di Torino, 2. Classe di Scienze Morali, Storiche e Filologiche* 106 (1972): 281–309.

– *Il pensiero politico di Cicerone: Tra filosofia greca e ideologia aristocratica romana.* Florence: La Nuova Italia, 1990.

Perfetti, Stefano. 'Immagini della *Repubblica* nei commenti medievali alla *Politica* di Aristotele: i casi di Alberto Magno e Tommaso d'Aquino.' In Vegetti and Pissavino, *I Decembrio e la tradizione della Repubblica di Platone tra Medioevo e Umanesimo*, 83–98.

Perocco, Daria. 'Albertino Mussato e l'*Eccerinis*.' In *Dal Medioevo al Petrarca,* 337–49. Florence: L.S. Olschki, 1983.

Pesenti, Tiziana. 'Per la tradizione del testamento di Pietro d'Abano.' In *MPCI*, 533–42.

Piaia, Gregorio. 'L'averroismo politico e Marsilio da Padova.' In *Saggi e ricerche su Aristotele, Marsilio da Padova, M. Eckhart, Rosmini, Spaventa, Marty, Tilgher, Omodeo, metafisica, fenomenologia ed estetica*, edited by Carlo Giacon, 33–54. Padua: Antenore, 1971.

– 'Beato Renano e il *Defensor pacis* agli inizi della Riforma.' *Studia patavina* 21 (1974): 28–79.

– 'La 'presenza' di Marsilio da Padova in Tommaso Campanella.' In *Logica e semantica ed altri saggi*, edited by Carlo Giacon, 183–98. Padua: Antenore, 1975.

– *Marsilio da Padova nella Riforma e nella Controriforma: Fortuna ed interpretazione*. Padua: Antenore, 1977.

– '"Averroisme politique": anatomie d'un mythe historiographique.' In Zimmermann and Craemer-Ruegenberg, *Orientalische Kultur und europäisches Mittelalter*, 288–300.

– '"Averroismo politico": anatomia di un mito storiografico.' In idem, *Marsilio e dintorni: Contributo alla storia delle idee*, 79–103. Padua: Antenore, 1999.

Pianka, Richard S. 'The Sovereignty of the plêthos in Aristotle's *Politics*.' In *Aristotelian Political Philosophy*, edited by Konstantinos I. Boudouris, 2: 116–24. Athens: International Center for Greek Philosophy and Culture, 1995.

Picherit, Jean-Louis G. *La Métaphore pathologique et thérapeutique à la fin du Moyen Age*. Tübingen: M. Niemeyer, 1994.

– 'Les références pathologiques et thérapeutiques dans l'œuvre de Christine de Pizan.' In *Une femme de Lettres au Moyen Age: Études autour de Christine de Pizan*, edited by Liliane Dulac and Bernard Ribémont, 233–44. Orléans: Paradigme, 1995.

Picquet, Théa. 'Rome: un modèle pour Florence?' *Rinascimento* 41 (2001): 285–301.

Piepenbrink, Karen. *Politische Ordnungskonzeptionen in der attischen Demokratie des vierten Jahrhunderts v. Chr. Eine vergleichende Untersuchung zum philosophischen und rhetorischen Diskurs*. Stuttgart: F. Steiner, 2001.

Pierpauli, José R. 'El origen de la comunidad política en la Edad Media: Alberto Magno–Tomás de Aquino y Marsilio de Padua.' *Rivista internazionale di filosofia del diritto* 78 (2001): 47–75.

Pincin, Carlo. *Marsilio da Padova, Il Difenditore della pace. Nella traduzione in volgare fiorentino del 1363*. Turin: Einaudi, 1966.

– *Marsilio*. Turin: Giappichelli, 1967.

Pine, Martin L. *Pietro Pomponazzi: Radical Philosopher of the Renaissance*. Padua: Antenore, 1986.

Pines, Shlomo. 'La philosophie dans l'économie du genre humain selon Averroès: une réponse à al-Fārābi?' In *Multiple Averroès*, edited by Jean Jolivet, 189–207. Paris: Les Belles Lettres, 1978.

– 'The Limitations of Human Knowledge according to Al-Fārābī, Ibn Bājja, and Maimonides.' In *Studies in Medieval Jewish History and Literature*, edited by Isadore Twersky, 1: 82–109. Cambridge, MA: Harvard University Press, 1979. Repr. in idem, *Collected Works*, vol. 4: *Studies in the History of Jewish Thought*, edited by Warren Z. Harvey and Moshe Idel, 404–31. Jerusalem: Magnes Press, 1997.

Pingree, David. 'The Sayings of Abū Ma'shar in Arabic, Greek, and Latin.' In *Ratio et superstitio*, edited by Giancarlo Marchetti, Orsola Rignani, and Valeria Sorge, 41–57. Louvain-la-Neuve: Fédération internationale des instituts d'études médiévales, 2003.

Pitkin, Hanna F. *Fortune Is a Woman: Gender and Politics in the Thought of Niccolò Machiavelli*. Chicago, IL, and London: University of Chicago Press, 1999.

Pocock, John G.A. *The Machiavellian Moment: Florentine Political Thought and the Atlantic Republican Tradition*. Princeton, NJ: Princeton University Press, 1975.

Podlech, Adalbert. 'Die Herrschaftstheorie des Johannes von Paris.' *Der Staat* 16 (1977): 465–92.

Polansky, Ronald. 'Aristotle on Political Change.' In Keyt and Miller, *A Companion to Aristotle's Politics*, 323–45.

Polizzi, Carlo. 'Rolandinus Paduanus professor gramatice facultatis.' *Quaderni per la storia dell'Università di Padova* 17 (1984): 231–2.

Pomian, Krzystof. 'Astrology as a Naturalistic Theology of History.' In Zambelli, *'Astrologi hallucinati,'* 29–43.

Poppi, Antonino. *Introduzione all'aristotelismo padovano*.Padua: Antenore, 1970.

Pratt, Vernon. 'The Essence of Aristotle's Zoology.' *Phronesis* 29 (1984): 267–78.

Preus, Anthony. 'Galen's Criticism of Aristotle's Conception Theory.' *Journal of the History of Biology* 10 (1977): 65–85.

Previté-Orton, Charles W. 'Marsilius of Padua: Part II. Doctrines.' *English Historical Review* 38 (1923): 1–18.

– 'Marsilius of Padua and the Visconti.' *English Historical Review* 44 (1929): 278–9.

– 'Marsilius of Padua.' *Proceedings of the British Academy* 21 (1935): 137–83.

Price, Anthony W. *Love and Friendship in Plato and Aristotle*. Oxford/New York: Clarendon Press/Oxford University Press, 1989.

– 'Friendship and Politics.' In *The Legacy of Aristotle's Political Thought*, edited by Carlos Steel. Brussels: Brussel Palais der Academiën, 1999.

Quaglioni, Diego. 'The Legal Definition of Citizenship in the Late Middle Ages.' In *City States in Classical Antiquity and Medieval Italy*, edited by Anthony Mohlo, Kurt Raaflaub, and Julia Emlen, 155–67. Ann Arbor, MI: University of Michigan Press, 1991.

– 'Il tardo Medioevo: confusione o pluralità di linguaggi politici?' *Il Pensiero Politico* 26 (1993): 79–84.

– 'Politica e diritto al tempo di Federico II: L'*Oculus pastoralis* (1222) e la "sapienza civile."' In *Federico II e le nuove culture*, 3–26. Spoleto: Centro italiano di studi sull'alto medioevo, 1995.

Quaß, Friedemann. *Nomos und Psephisma: Untersuchung zum griechischen Staatsrecht*. Munich: Beck, 1971.

Quillet, Jeannine. 'L'aristotelisme de Marsile de Padoue.' In *Die Metaphysik im Mittelalter, ihr Ursprung und ihre Bedeutung*, edited by Paul Wilpert, 696–706. Berlin: W. de Gruyter, 1963.

– 'L'organisation de la société humaine selon le Defensor Pacis de Marsile de Padoue.' In *Beiträge zum Berufsbewußtsein des mittelalterlichen Menschen*, edited by Paul Wilpert, 185–203. Berlin: W. de Gruyter, 1964.

– *La philosophie politique de Marsile de Padoue*. Paris: Vrin, 1970.

– 'Brèves remarques sur les *Questiones super Metaphysice Libros I–VI* (Codex Fesulano 161 f° 1ra–41va) et leurs relations avec l'aristotélisme hétérodoxe.' In *Auseinandersetzungen an der Pariser Universität im XIII. Jahrhundert*, edited by Albert Zimmermann, 361–85. Berlin: W. de Gruyter, 1975.

– 'L'aristotélisme de Marsile de Padoue et ses rapports avec l'averroïsme.' In *MPCI*, 81–142.

– 'Community, Counsel and Representation.' In *The Cambridge History of Medieval Political Thought, c. 350–c. 1450*, edited by James H. Burns, 520–72. Cambridge: Cambridge University Press, 1988.

– 'Présence d'Aristote dans la philosophie politique médievale.' *Revue de philosophie ancienne* 2 (1984): 93–102. Repr. in eadem. *D'une cité l'autre: Problèmes de philosophie politique médiévale*, 35–41. Paris: H. Champion, 2001.

Raaflaub, Kurt A. 'Contemporary Perceptions of Democracy in Fifth-Century Athens.' *Classica et mediaevalia* 40 (= *Aspects of Athenian Democracy*) (1990): 33–70.

Radice, Roberto. *'Oikeiosis': Richerche sul fondamento del pensiero stoico e sulla sua genesi*. Milan: Vita e Pensiero, 2000.

Rahe, Paul A. *Against Throne and Altar: Machiavelli and Political Theory under the English Republic*. Cambridge: Cambridge University Press, 2008.

Raimondi, Ezio. 'L'*Ecerinis* di Albertino Mussato.' In *Studi Ezzeliniani*, 189–203.

Rapisarda, Marco. *La signoria di Ezzelino da Romano*. Udine: Del Bianco, 1965.

Rashed, Marwan. *Die Überlieferungsgeschichte der aristotelischen Schrift De generatione et corruptione*. Wiesbaden: L. Reichert, 2001.

Ravegnani, Giorgio. 'Nota sul pensiero politico di Giorgio da Trebisonda.' *Aevum* 49 (1975): 310–29.

Rawson, Elizabeth. *The Spartan Tradition in European Thought*. Oxford: Clarendon Press, 1969. Repr. Oxford: Oxford University Press, 1991.

Reeves, Marjorie. 'Marsiglio of Padua and Dante Alighieri.' In Smalley, *Trends in Medieval Political Thought*, 86–104.

Renna, Thomas [J.]. 'The Populus in John of Paris' Theory of Monarchy, 1260–1303.' *Tijdschrift voor Rechtsgeschiedenis* 42 (1974): 243–68.

– 'Aristotle and the French Monarchy.' *Viator* 9 (1978): 309–24.

Rese, Friederike. *Praxis und Logos bei Aristoteles: Handlung, Vernunft und Rede in Nikomachischer Ethik, Rhetorik und Politik*. Tübingen: Mohr Siebeck, 2003.

Richter, Melvin. s.v. 'Despotism.' In *Dictionary of the History of Ideas: Studies of Selected Pivotal Ideas*, edited by Philip P. Wiener, 2: 1–18. New York: Charles Scribner's Sons, 1973.

Riedlinger, Helmut. 'Note sur les *Questions sur la Métaphysique* attribuées à Marsile de Padoue.' *Bulletin de la Societé Internationale pour l'Étude de la Philosophie Médiévale* 4 (1962): 136–7. Repr. in *Raimundi Lulli Opera Latina*, vol. 5: 154–155: *Opera Pariesiensia, anno MCCCIX composita*, edited by Helmut Riedlinger, 62–6. Palma de Mallorca: Maioricensis Schola Lullistica, 1967.

Riesenberg, Peter. 'Citizenship and Equality in Late Medieval Italy.' *Studia Gratiana* 15 (1972): 425–39.

– 'Citizenship at Law in Late Medieval Italy.' *Viator* 5 (1974): 333–46.

Rigon, Antonio. *Clero e città: 'Fratalea cappellanorum,' parroci, cura d'anime in Padova dal XII al XV secolo*. Padua: Istituto per la Storia Ecclesiastica Padovana, 1988.

Riklin, Alois. 'Die Venezianische Mischverfassung im Lichte von Gasparo Contarini (1483–1542).' *Zeitschrift für Politik* 37 (1990): 264–91.

Ritter, Joachim. s.v. 'Fortschritt.' In *Historisches Wörterbuch der Philosophie*, edited by Joachim Ritter, 1032–59. Basel and Stuttgart: Schwabe, 1972.

Roberts, Jennifer T. *Athens on Trial: The Antidemocratic Tradition in Western Thought*. Princeton, NJ: Princeton University Press, 1994.

Robinson, James M. 'The Tripartite Soul in the *Timaeus*.' *Phronesis* 35 (1990): 103–10.

Romer, Frank E. 'The *Aisymnēteia*: A Problem in Aristotle's Historical Method.' *The American Journal of Philology* 103 (1982): 25–46.

Ronconi, Giorgio. *Le origini delle dispute umanistiche sulla poesia (Mussato e Petrarca)*. Rome: Bulzoni, 1976.

Rosenthal, Erwin I.J. 'The Place of Politics in the Philosophy of Ibn Rushd.' *Bulletin of the School of Oriental and African Studies* 15 (1953): 246–78. Repr. in idem, *Studia Semitica*, vol. 2: *Islamic Themes*, 60–92.

– *Studia Semitica*, vol. 2: *Islamic Themes*. Cambridge: Cambridge University Press, 1971.

Rostock, Michael. *Die antike Theorie der Organisation staatlicher Macht: Studien zur Geschichte der Gewaltenteilungslehre*. Meisenheim am Glan: A. Hain, 1975.

Rothschild, Jean-Pierre. 'Les traductions hébraïques du *Liber de causis* latin.' Thèse de doctorat, Université Paris III, 1985.

– 'Les traductions du *Livre des causes* et leurs copies.' *Revue d'Histoire des Textes* 24 (1994): 393–484.

Rubinstein, Nicolai. *La lotta contro i magnati a Firenze. II – La prima legge sul 'sodamento'*. Florence: L.S. Olschiki, 1939.

– 'Political Rhetoric in the Imperial Chancery during the Twelfth and Thirteenth Centuries.' *Medium aevum* 14 (1945): 21–43.

– 'Some Ideas on Municipal Progress and Decline in the Italy of the Communes.' In *Fritz Saxl (1890–1948): A Volume of Memorial Essays from His Friends in England*, edited by James D. Gordon, 165–83. London and New York: T. Nelson, 1957.

– 'Marsilius of Padua and the Italian Political Thought of His Time.' In *Europe in the Late Middle Ages*, edited by John R. Hale, John R.L. Highfield, and Beryl Smalley, 44–75. Evanston, IL: Northwestern University Press, 1965. Repr. in idem, *Studies in Italian History in the Middle Ages and the Renaissance*, vol. 1: *Political Thought and the Language of Politics: Art and Politics*, edited by Giovanni Ciappelli, 99–130. Rome: Storia e letteratura, 2004.

– 'Political Theories in the Renaissance.' In *The Renaissance: Essays in Interpretation*, edited by André Chastel, 153–200. London and New York: Methuen, 1982.

– 'The History of the Word *politicus* in Early Modern Europe.' In *The Languages of Political Theory in Early-Modern Europe*, edited by Anthony Pagden, 41–56. Cambridge: Cambridge University Press, 1987.

Runciman, W.G. 'Origins of States: The Case of Archaic Greece.' *Comparative Studies in Society and History* 24 (1982): 351–77.

Ruppel, Walter. 'Politeuma. Bedeutungsgeschichte eines staatsrechtlichen Terminus.' *Philologus* 82 (1927): 268–312, 433–54.

Rus Rufino, Salvador. 'Aristotelismo político en la Europa Medieval y Moderna.' *Schede Medievali* 44 (2006): 19–76.

– 'Aristóteles y el aristotelismo: Una aproximación a la historia de la filosofía política europea medieval y moderna.' In *Historia, filosofía y política en la*

Europa Moderna y Contemporánea, 119–58. León: Universidad de León, Secretariado Publicaciones y Medios Audiovisuales, 2004.
– 'Significado e importancia de la *Política* de Aristóteles en la Europa Medieval y Moderna.' *Patristica et Mediaevalia* 26 (2005): 3–30.
Ruschenbusch, Eberhard. 'Πάτριος πολιτεία. Theseus, Drakon, Solon und Kleisthenes in Publizistik und Geschichtsschreibung des 5. und 4. Jahrhunderts v. Chr.' *Historia* 7 (1958): 398–424.
Russi, Luciano. 'L'idea di pace in Marsilio da Padova.' In *Prima di Machiavelli: Itinerari e linguaggi della politica tra il XIV e il XVI secolo*, edited by Gabriele Carletti, 87–106. Pescara: Edizioni Scientifiche Abruzzesi, 2007.
Ryffel, Heinrich. *ΜΕΤΑΒΟΛΗ ΠΟΛΙΤΕΙΩΝ: Der Wandel der Staatsverfassungen*. Bern: P. Haupt, 1949.
Sabbadini, Remigio. 'Postille alle "Epistole inedite di Lovato."' *Studi Medievali* 2 (1906–7): 255–62.
– *Le scoperte dei codici latini e greci ne' secoli XIV e XV*. Florence: G.C. Sansoni, 1967.
Sabetti, Alfredo. *Marsilio da Padova e la filosofia politica del secolo XIV*. Naples: Liguori, 1964.
Salkever, Stephen G. *Finding the Mean: Theory and Practice in Aristotelian Political Philosophy*. Princeton, NJ: Princeton University Press, 1990.
Salomon, Max. *Der Begriff der Gerechtigkeit bei Aristoteles: nebst einem Anhang über den Begriff des Tauschgeschäfts*. Leiden: A.W. Sijthoff, 1937.
Salvemini, Gaetano. 'Il *Liber de Regimine Civitatum* di Giovanni di Viterbo.' *Giornale storico della letteratura italiana* 41 (1903): 284–303. Repr. in idem, *Scritti di storia medievale*, vol. 2: *La dignità cavalleresca nel Comune di Firenze e altri scritti*, edited by Ernesto Sestan, 358–70. Milan: Feltrinelli Editore, 1972.
– *Magnati e popolani a Firenze dal 1280 al 1295*. Milan: Feltrinelli, 1966.
Salzer, Ernst. *Ueber die Anfaenge der Signorie in Oberitalien: Ein Beitrag zur italienischen Verfassungsgeschichte*. Berlin: Ebering, 1900. Repr. Vaduz: Kraus Repr., 1965.
Samir, Khalil. 'Les versions arabes de Némésius de Homs.' In *L'eredità classica nelle lingue orientali*, edited by Massimiliano Pavan and Umberto Cozzoli , 99–151. Rome: Istituto della Enciclopedia italiana, 1986.
Sasse Tateo, Barbara. *Tradition und Pragmatik in Bonvesins 'De magnalibus mediolani': Studien zur Arbeitstechnik und zum Selbstverständnis eines Mailänder Schriftstellers aus dem späten 13. Jahrhundert*. Frankfurt a. M and Bern/New York: P. Lang, 1991.
Schmeidler, Bernhard. *Italienische Geschichtsschreiber des XII. und XIII. Jahrhunderts: Ein Beitrag zur Kulturgeschichte*. Leipzig: Quelle, 1909.

Schmidt, Dagmar. '"Regimen politicum" – Republikanisches Denken in den Stadtstaaten Italiens. Die Rezeption der aristotelischen Staatsformenlehre im frühen Trecento.' *Jahrbuch für Philosophie des Forschungsinstituts für Philosophie Hannover* 8 (1997): 44–67.

Schmidt, James. 'A Raven with a Halo: The Translation of Aristotle's *Politics*.' *History of Political Thought* 7 (1986): 295–319.

Schmidt, Ernst A., and Manfred Ullmann. *Aristoteles in Fes: Zum Wert der arabischen Überlieferung der Nikomachischen Ethik für die Kritik des griechischen Textes*. Heidelberg: Winter, 2012.

Schmitt, Charles B. 'Aristotelianism in the Veneto and the Origins of Modern Science: Some Considerations on the Problem of Continuity.' In *Atti del convegno internazionale su Aristotelismo veneto e scienza moderna*. Padua: Antenore, 1983, 104–23. Repr. in idem, *The Aristotelian Tradition and Renaissance Universities*. London: Variorum Reprints, 1984, no. I.

Schmugge, Ludwig. *Johannes von Jandun (1285/89–1328): Untersuchungen zur Biographie und Sozialtheorie eines lateinischen Averroisten*. Stuttgart: A. Hiersemann, 1966.

Schofield, Malcolm. 'Cicero's Definition of *res publica*.' In idem, *Saving the City: Philosopher-Kings and Other Classical Paradigms*, 178–94. London and New York: Routledge, 1999.

– 'Epicurean and Stoic Political Thought.' In *The Cambridge History of Greek and Roman Political Thought*, edited by Christopher Rowe and Malcolm Schofield, 435–55. Cambridge: Cambridge University Press, 2000.

Scholz, Richard. 'Marsilius von Padua und die Idee der Demokratie.' *Zeitschrift für Politik* 1 (1907): 61–94.

– 'Politische und weltanschauliche Kämpfe um den Reichsgedanken am Hofe Ludwigs des Bayern.' *Zeitschrift für deutsche Geisteswissenschaften* 1 (1938): 298–316.

– 'Marsilius von Padua und Deutschland.' In Checchini and Bobbio, *Marsilio da Padova*, 3–35.

Schönberger, Rolf. 'Der Disput über die Ewigkeit der Welt.' In *Bonaventura, Thomas von Aquin, Boethius von Dacien, Über die Ewigkeit der Welt*. German translation by Peter Nickl. Frankfurt a. M.: Klostermann, 2000, vii–xxxii.

Schreiner, Klaus. '«Correctio principis». Gedankliche Begründung und geschichtliche Praxis spätmittelalterlicher Herrscherkritik.' In *Mentalitäten im Mittelalter: Methodische und inhaltliche Probleme*, edited by František Graus, 203–56. Sigmaringen: J. Thorbecke, 1987.

Schulthess, Peter, and Ruedi Imbach. *Die Philosophie im lateinischen Mittelalter: Ein Handbuch mit einem bio–bibliographischen Repertorium*. Zurich: Artemis & Winkler, 1996. Repr. Düsseldorf and Zurich: Patmos, 2000.

Schütz, Ludwig. *Thomas-Lexikon. Sammlung, Übersetzung und Erklärung der in sämtlichen Werken des h. Thomas von Aquin vorkommenden Kunstausdrücke und wissenschaftlichen Aussprüche*. Paderborn: F. Schöningh, 1895. Repr. Stuttgart-Bad Cannstatt: Frommann-Holzboog, 1983.

Schwöbel, Hermann O. *Der Diplomatische Kampf zwischen Ludwig dem Bayern und der römischen Kurie im Rahmen des Kanonischen Absolutionsprozesses, 1330–1346*. Weimar: Böhlau, 1968.

Seeskin, Kenneth, ed. *The Cambridge Companion to Maimonides*. Cambridge: Cambridge University Press, 2005.

Seidler, Eduard. *Die Heilkunde des ausgehenden Mittelalters in Paris: Studien zur Struktur der spätscholastischen Medizin*. Wiesbaden: Steiner, 1967.

Seligsohn, Rudolf. *Die Übersetzung der pseudo–aristotelischen Problemata durch Bartholomaeus von Messina. Text und textkritische Untersuchungen zum ersten Buch*. Berlin: E. Ebering, 1934.

Sestan, Ernesto. 'Le origini delle signorie cittadine: un problema storico esaurito?' *Bullettino dell'Istituto Storico Italiano per il Medio Evo e Archivio Muratoriano* 73 (1961): 41–69. Repr. in *La crisi degli ordinamenti comunali e le origini dello stato del Rinascimento*, edited by Giorgio Chittolini, 53–75. Bologna: Il Mulino, 1979. German trans. by Lilo de Negri, 'Die Anfänge der städtischen Signorien: ein erschöpfend behandeltes historisches Problem?' In *Altständisches Bürgertum*, vol 1: *Herrschaft und Gemeinverfassung*, edited by Heinz Stoob, 346–79. Darmstadt: Wissenschaftliche Buchgesellschaft, 1978.

Sezgin, Fuat, Mazen Amawi, Carl Ehrig-Eggert, and Eckhard Neubauer, eds. *Dominicus Gundissalinus (12th c.) and the Transmission of Arabic Philosophical Thought to the West: Texts and Studies*. Frankfurt a. M.: Institute for the History of Arabic-Islamic Science, Johann Wolfgang Goethe University, 2000.

Sezgin, Fuat, Mazin Amawi, Carl Ehrig-Eggert, and Eckhard Neubauer, eds. *Galen in the Arabic Philosophical Tradition: Texts and Studies*. Frankfurt a. M.: Institute for the History of Arabic-Islamic Science, Johann Wolfgang Goethe University, 2000.

Sgrilli, Paola. 'Retorica e società: Tensioni anticlassiche nella *Retorica* di Brunetto Latini.' *Medioevo Romanzo* 3 (1976): 380–93.

Shatz, David. 'Maimonides' Moral Theory.' In Seeskin, *The Cambridge Companion to Maimonides*, 167–92.

Shogimen, Takashi. 'Treating the Body Politic: The Medical Metaphor of Political Rule in Late Medieval Europe and Tokugawa Japan.' *Review of Politics* 70 (2008): 77–104.

Sieben, Hermann J. *Die Konzilsidee des lateinischen Mittelalters (847–1378)*. Paderborn: Schönigh, 1984.

Siegel, Rudoph E. *Galen's System of Physiology and Medicine: An Analysis of His Doctrines and Observations on Blood Flow, Respiration, Tumors and Internal Diseases*. Basel and New York: Karger, 1968.

Siegfried, Walter. *Der Rechtsgedanke bei Aristoteles.* Zurich: Schulthess, 1947.

Sigmund, Paul E. 'Law and Politics.' In *The Cambridge Companion to Aquinas,* edited by Norman Kretzmann and Eleonore Stump, 217–31. Cambridge: Cambridge University Press, 1993.

Sihvola, Juha. *Decay, Progress, the Good Life? Hesiod and Protagoras on the Development of Culture.* Helsinki: Societas Scientiarum Fennica, 1989.

Silberdick Feinberg, Barbara. 'Creativity and the Political Community: The Role of the Law-Giver in the Thought of Plato, Machiavelli and Rousseau.' *Western Political Quarterly* 23 (1970): 471–84.

Silk, Mark. 'Numa Pompilius and the Idea of Civil Religion in the West.' *Journal of the American Academy of Religion* 72 (2004): 863–96.

Silvano, Giovanni. *La 'Republica de' Viniziani': Ricerche sul repubblicanesimo veneziano in età moderna.* Florence: L.S. Olschki, 1993.

Simonetta, Stefano. *Dal difensore della pace al Leviatano: Marsilio da Padova nel Seicento inglese.* Milan: UNICOPLI, 2000.

– *Marsilio in Inghilterra: Stato e chiesa nel pensiero politico inglese fra XIV e XVII secolo.* Milan: LED, 2000.

Sinclair, Robert K. *Democracy and Participation in Athens.* Cambridge: Cambridge University Press, 1988.

Siniossoglou, Niketas. *Radical Platonism in Byzantium: Illumination and Utopia in Gemistos Plethon*. Cambridge: Cambridge University Press, 2011.

Siraisi, Nancy G. 'The *Expositio Problematum Aristotelis* of Peter of Abano.' *Isis* 61 (1970): 321–39.

– *Arts and Sciences at Padua: The Studium of Padua before 1350.* Toronto: Pontifical Institute of Mediaeval Studies, 1973.

– *Medieval and Early Renaissance Medicine: An Introduction to Knowledge and Practice.* Chicago, IL: University of Chicago Press, 1990.

– *Medicine and the Italian Universities, 1250–1600.* Leiden: Brill, 2001.

Skard, Eiliv. 'Nemesiosstudien: II. Nemesios und Galenos.' *Symbolae Osloenses* 17 (1937): 9–25.

Skinner, Quentin. 'The Italian City-Republics.' In *Democracy: The Unfinished Journey, 508 BC to AD 1993,* edited by John Dunn, 57–69. Oxford: Oxford University Press, 1992.

– 'The Vocabulary of Renaissance Republicanism: A Cultural longue-durée?' In *Language and Images of Renaissance Italy,* edited by Alison Brown, 87–110. Oxford: Clarendon Press, 1995.

Smalley, Beryl. 'Sallust in the Middle Ages.' In *Classical Influences on European Culture A.D. 500–1500*, edited by Robert R. Bolgar, 165–75. Cambridge: Cambridge University Press, 1971.

Smalley, Beryl, ed. *Trends in Medieval Political Thought*. Oxford: B. Blackwell, 1965.

Solmsen, Friedrich. 'Leisure and Play in Aristotle's Ideal State.' *Rheinisches Museum für Philologie* 107 (1964): 193–220. Repr. in idem, *Kleine Schriften*, 2: 1–28. Hildesheim: G. Olms, 1968.

Somfai, Anna. 'The Transmission and Reception of Plato's *Timaeus* and Calcidius's *Commentary* during the Carolingian Renaissance.' Diss., University of Cambridge, 1998.

Sorbelli, Albano. 'I teorici del Regimento comunale.' *Bullettino dell' Istituto Storico Italiano per il Medio Evo e Archivio Muratoriano* 59 (1944): 31–136.

Sørensen, Gert. 'The Reception of the Political Aristotle in the Late Middle Ages (from Brunetto Latini to Dante Alighieri). Hypotheses and Suggestions.' In *Renaissance Readings of the Corpus Aristotelicum*, edited by Marianne Pade, 9–25. Copenhagen: Museum Tusculanum, 2001.

Sorge, Valeria. 'L'aristotelismo averroistico negli studi recenti.' *Paradigmi* 50 (1999): 243–63.

Sourvinou-Inwood, Christiane. 'What Is *Polis* Religion?' In *The Greek City: From Homer to Alexander*, edited by Oswyn Murray and Simon Price, 295–322. Oxford: Clarendon Press, 1990. Repr. in Buxton, *Oxford Readings in Greek Religion*, 13–37.

– 'Further Aspects of *Polis* Religion.' In Buxton, *Oxford Readings in Greek Religion*, 38–55.

Spörl, Johannes. 'Das Alte und das Neue im Mittelalter. Studien zum Problem des mittelalterlichen Fortschrittsbewußtseins.' *Historisches Jahrbuch* 50 (1930): 297–341, 498–524.

Springborg, Patricia. *Western Republicanism and the Oriental Prince*. Cambridge: Polity Press, 1992.

Staehelin, Ernst. 'L'édition de 1522 du *Defensor pacis* de Marsile de Padoue.' *Revue d'histoire et de philosophie religieuse* 34 (1954): 209–22.

Staico, Ubaldo. 'L'aristotelismo politico nel Medioevo. Pensiero politico medievale e problema storiografico.' *Studi Senesi* 99 (1987): 261–322.

Stalley, Richard F. 'Aristotle's Criticism of Plato's Republic.' In Keyt and Miller, *A Companion to Aristotle's Politics*, 182–99.

– 'Plato and Aristotle on Political Unity.' In *La Repubblica di Platone nella tradizione antica*, edited by Mario Vegetti and Michele Abbate, 29–48. Naples: Bibliopolis, 1999.

Stark, Rudolf. 'Ciceros Staatsdefinition.' *La Nouvelle Clio* 6 (1954): 56–69. Repr. in *Das Staatsdenken der Römer*, edited by Richard Klein, 332–47. Darmstadt: Wissenschaftliche Buchgesellschaft, 3rd ed. 1980.

Steinmetz, Fritz. 'Staatengründung – aus Schwäche oder natürlichem Geselligkeitsdrang? Zur Geschichte einer Theorie.' In Steinmetz, *Politeia und res publica*, 181–99.

Steinmetz, Peter, ed. *Politeia und res publica: Beiträge zum Verständnis von Politik, Recht und Staat in der Antike.*Wiesbaden: F. Steiner, 1969.

– *Schriften zu den Politika des Aristoteles*. Hildesheim and New York: G. Olms, 1973.

Steinwerter, Artur. 'ΝΟΜΟΣ ΕΜΨΥΧΟΣ: Zur Geschichte einer politischen Theorie.' *Abhandlungen der Akademie Wien, phil.-hist. Klasse* 83 (1936): 250–68.

Steiris, Giorgos. 'The Formation of the Notion of Progress in the Philosophy of History from Augustine to Bodin.' *Epistēmonikē Epetēris tēs Philosophikēs Scholēs tou Panepistēmiou Athēnōn* 26 (2006): 195–212 [in Greek].

Stelling-Michaud, Sven. 'Le mythe du despotisme oriental.' *Schweizer Beiträge zur allgemeinen Geschichte* 18/19 (1960/61): 328–46.

Sternberger, Dolf. *Die Stadt und das Reich in der Verfassungslehre des Marsilius von Padua* (= Sitzungsberichte der Wissenschaftlichen Gesellschaft an der Johann-Wolfgang Goethe-Universität Frankfurt am Main). Wiesbaden: Steiner, 1981, 87–147. Repr. in idem, *Die Stadt als Urbild: Sieben politische Beiträge*. Frankfurt a. M.: Suhrkamp, 1985, 76–142.

Stocks, John L. 'ΣΧΟΛΗ.' *The Classical Quarterly* 30 (1936): 177–87.

Stoczkowski, Wiktor. *Explaining Human Origins: Myth, Imagination and Conjecture*. Translated by Mary Turton. Cambridge: Cambridge University Press, 2002.

Storia e cultura a Padova nell'età di Sant'Antonio. Padua: Istituto per la Storia Ecclesiastica Padovana, 1985.

Strange, Steven K., and Jack Zupko, eds. *Stoicism: Traditions and Transformations*. Cambridge: Cambridge University Press, 2004.

Strauss, Barry S. 'On Aristotle's Critique of Athenian Democracy.' In *Essays on the Foundations of Aristotelian Political Science*, edited by Carnes Lord and David K. O'Connor, 212–33. Berkeley, CA: University of California Press, 1991.

Strohmaier, Gotthard. 'Das Bild und die Funktion vorchristlicher griechischer Religion bei arabischen Autoren des Mittelalters.' In *Reflections on Reflections: Near Eastern Writers Reading Literature*, edited by Angelika Neuwirth and Andreas C. Islebe, 181–90. Wiesbaden: Reichert Verlag, 2006.

Struve, Tilman. *Die Entwicklung der organologischen Staatsauffassung im Mittelalter.* Stuttgart: Hiersemann, 1978.

– 'Die Funktion des Organismusvergleichs in den mittelalterlichen Theorien von Staat und Gesellschaft.' In *Soziale Ordnungen im Selbstverständnis des Mittelalters*, edited by Albert Zimmermann, 144–61. Berlin and New York: W. de Gruyter, 1979. Repr. in idem, *Staat und Gesellschaft im Mittelalter: Ausgewählte Aufsätze*, 12–28. Berlin: Duncker & Humblot, 2004.

Stuardi, Donatella Marocco. 'Sovrano e governo nel pensiero di Marsilio da Padova.' In *Studi politici in onore di Luigi Firpo*, edited Silvia Rota Ghibaudi and Franco Barcia, 1: 15–48. Milan: Franco Angeli, 1990.

Studi Ezzeliniani. Rome: Istituto storico italiano per il Medio Evo, 1963.

Sturges, Robert S., ed. *Law and Sovereignty in the Middle Ages and the Renaissance.* Turnhout: Brepols, 2011.

Stürner, Wolfgang. *Natur und Gesellschaft im Denken des Hoch- und Spätmittelalters: Naturwissenschaftliche Kraftvorstellungen und die Motivierung politischen Handelns in Texten des 12. bis 14. Jahrhunderts.* Stuttgart: Klett, 1975.

Suerbaum, Werner. *Vom antiken zum frühmittelalterlichen Staatsbegriff: Über Verwendung und Bedeutung von res publica, regnum, imperium und status von Cicero bis Jordanis.* Münster: Aschendorffsche Verlagsbuchhandlung, 1961.

Sullivan, Mary E. 'Democracy and the *Defensor Pacis* Revisited: Marsiglio of Padua's Democratic Arguments.' *Viator* 41 (2010): 257–69.

– 'The Bond of Aristotelian Language Among Medieval Political Thinkers.' In *Communities of Learning in the Middle Ages: Networks and the Shaping of Intellectual Identity in Europe, 1100–1500*, edited by Constant J. Mews and John N. Crossley, 213–28. Turnhout: Brepols, 2011.

Syros, Vasileios. 'The Principle of the Sovereignty of the Multitude in the Works of Marsilius of Padua, Peter of Auvergne and Some Other Aristotelian Commentators.' In Moreno-Riaño, *The World of Marsilius of Padua*, 227–48.

– *Die Rezeption der aristotelischen politischen Philosophie bei Marsilius von Padua: Eine Untersuchung zur ersten Diktion des Defensor pacis.* Leiden and Boston: Brill, 2007.

– 'Marsilius of Padua on Princely Virtues and Aristotle's Absolute Ruler.' *Archiv für mittelalterliche Philosophie und Kultur* 13 (2007): 212–29.

– 'Did the Physician from Padua Meet the Rabbi from Cordoba? Marsilius of Padua and Moses Maimonides on the Political Utility of Religion.' *Revue des Études Juives* 170 (2011): 51–71.

– 'Founders and Kings Versus Orators: Medieval and Early Modern Views on the Origins of Social Life.' *Viator* 42 (2011): 383–408.

– 'Shadows in Heaven and Clouds on Earth: The Emergence of Social Life and Political Authority in the Early Modern Islamic Empires.' *Viator* 43 (2012): 377–406.

Szegedy-Maszak, Andrew. 'Legends of the Greek Lawgivers.' *Greek, Roman and Byzantine Studies* 19 (1978): 199–209.

Tabacco, Giovanni. *The Struggle for Power in Medieval Italy: Structures of Political Rule*. Translated by Rosalind Brown Jensen. Cambridge: Cambridge University Press, 1989.

Tanner, Kathryn. *God and Creation in Christian Theology: Tyranny or Empowerment?* Oxford: B. Blackwell, 1988.

Taranto, Domenico. *Le virtù della politica: Civismo e prudenza tra Machiavelli e gli antichi.* Naples: Bibliopolis, 2003.

Taylor, Richard C. 'The *Liber de causis*: A Preliminary List of Extant mss.' *Bulletin de Philosophie Medievale* 25 (1983): 63–84.

– 'Remarks on the Latin Text and the Translator of the *Kalâm fi mahd al-khair / Liber de causis*.' *Bulletin de Philosophie Medievale* 31 (1989): 75–102.

– 'Averroes: God and the Noble Lie.' In *Laudemus viros gloriosos*, edited by Rollen E. Houser, 38–59. Notre Dame, IN: University of Notre Dame Press, 2007.

Thijssen, Johannes M.M.H., and Henk A.G. Braakhuis, eds. *The Commentary Tradition on Aristotle's De generatione et corruptione: Ancient, Medieval, and Early Modern*. Turnhout: Brepols, 1999.

Thomas, Heinz. *Ludwig der Bayer (1282–1347): Kaiser und Ketzer*. Regensburg and Graz: Friedrich Pustet/Styria, 1993.

Thompson, Augustine, *Cities of God: The Religion of the Italian Communes, 1125–1325*. University Park, PA: Pennsylvania State University Press, 2005.

Thorndike, Lynn. *A History of Magic and Experimental Science*, vols. 3 and 4: *Fourteenth and Fifteenth Centuries*. New York: Macmillan, 1923.

Thumfart, Alexander, and Arno Waschkuhn. *Staatstheorien des italienischen Bürgerhumanismus. Politische Theorie von Francesco Petrarca bis Donato Giannotti.* Baden-Baden: Nomos, 2005.

Tornero, Emilio. 'La función sociopolítica de la religión según Averroes.' *Anales del Seminario de Historia de la Filosofia* 4 (1984): 75–82.

Toscano, Antonio. *Marsilio da Padova e Niccolò Machiavelli*. Ravenna: Longo, 1981.

Toschi, Paolo. 'Ezzelino da Romano nella leggenda.' In *Studi Ezzeliniani*, 205–23.

Tosel, André, ed. *De la prudence des anciens comparée à celle des modernes: Sémantique d'un concept, déplacement des problématiques*. Paris: Les Belles Lettres, 1995.

Toste, Marco. 'Nobiles, optimi viri, philosophi. The Role of the Philosopher in the Political Community at the Faculty of Arts in Paris in Late Thirteenth Century.' In *Itinéraires de la raison*, edited by José F. Meirinhos, 269–308. Louvain-La-Neuve: F.I.D.E.M., 2005.

Tosti-Croce, Mauro, ed. *Il viaggio di Enrico VII in Italia*. Città di Castello: Edimond,1993.

Tracy, Theodore J. *Physiological Theory and the Doctrine of the Mean in Plato and Aristotle*. The Hague: Mouton, 1969.

Triantaphyllopoulos, Johannes. *Das Rechtsdenken der Griechen*. Munich: Beck, 1985.

Trillitzsch, Winfried. 'Seneca tragicus: Nachleben und Beurteilung im lateinischen Mittelalter von der Spätantike bis zum Renaissancehumanismus.' *Philologus* 122 (1978): 120–36.

Troilo, Erminio. 'Per l'Averroismo Padovano o Veneto.' *Atti del Reale Istituto Veneto di Scienze, Lettere ed Arti* (Venezia) Parte II: Classe di Scienze morali e lettere 99 (1939–1940): 273–98. Repr. in *Ibn Rushd in the Western Tradition: Texts and Studies*, edited by Fuat Sezgin, 3: 357–82. Frankfurt a. M.: Institute for the History of Arabic-Islamic Science at the Johann Wolfgang Goethe University, 1999.

– *Averroismo e aristotelismo padovano*. Florence: L.S. Olschki, 1939.

– 'L'averroismo di Marsilio da Padova.' In Checchini and Bobbio, *Marsilio da Padova*, 49–77.

– 'Lo spirito dell'averroismo padovano.' In *Il diritto dell'uomo al sapere e al libero uso di esso*, 43–74. Padua: Liviana, 1954.

Trude, Peter. *Der Begriff der Gerechtigkeit in der aristotelischen Rechts– und Staatsphilosophie*. Berlin: W. de Gruyter, 1955.

Tulumakos, Ioannes S. *Die theoretische Begründung der Demokratie in der klassischen Zeit Griechenlands: die demokratische Argumentation in der Politik des Aristoteles*. Athens: Papazisis, 1985.

Turley, Thomas. 'Silbert of Beck's Response to Marsilius of Padua.' *Carmelus* 52 (2005): 81–104.

– 'The Impact of Marsilius: Papalist Reactions to the *Defensor pacis*.' In Moreno-Riaño, *The World of Marsilius of Padua*, 47–64.

Ubl, Karl. *Engelbert von Admont: Ein Gelehrter im Spannungsfeld von Aristotelismus und christlicher Überlieferung*. Vienna and Munich: R. Oldenbourg, 2000.

Ubl, Karl, and Lars Vinx. 'Zur Transformation der Monarchie von Aristoteles bis Ockham.' *Vivarium* 40 (2002): 41–74.

Ullman, Berthold L. 'Hieremias de Montagnone and his Citations from Catullus.' *Classical Philology* 5 (1910): 66–82. Revised version in idem, *Studies in the Italian Renaissance*, 81–115. Rome: Storia e letteratura, 1955.

Urmson, James O. 'Aristotle's Doctrine of the Mean.' In *Essays on Aristotle's Ethics*, 157–70.

Uxkull-Gyllenband, Woldemar. *Griechische Kultur-Entstehungslehren*. Berlin: Simion, 1924.

Valois, Noël. 'Jean de Jandun et Marsile de Padoue, auteurs du *Defensor pacis*.' *Histoire littéraire de la France* 33 (1906): 528–623.

Vanderspoel, John. *Themistius and the Imperial Court: Oratory, Civic Duty, and Paideia from Constantius to Theodosius*. Ann Arbor, MI: University of Michigan Press, 1995.

Van Deusen, Nancy. 'The *Timaeus latinus* and Cusanus.' In *Mind Matters*, edited by Cary J. Nederman, Nancy Van Deusen, and E. Ann Matter, 217–31. Turnhout: Brepols, 2009.

Vasoli, Cesare. 'La *Politica* di Aristotele e la sua utilizzazione da parte di Marsilio da Padova.' In *MPCI*, 237–57.

– 'Il carattere 'naturale' dello Stato e la sua 'patologia' nella tradizione politica aristotelica.' In *Aristotelismo politico e ragion di Stato*, edited by A. Enzo Baldini, 53–65. Florence: L.S. Olschki, 1995.

Vansteenkiste, Clemens. 'Il *Liber de Causis* negli scritti di San Tommaso.' *Angelicum* 35 (1958): 325–74.

Vecchiarelli Scott, Joanna. 'Influence or Manipulation? The Role of Augustinianism in the *Defensor pacis* of Marsiglio of Padua.' *Augustinian Studies* 9 (1978): 59–79.

Vegetti, Mario. 'Anima e corpo.' In idem and Giuseppe Cambiano, *Il sapere degli antichi*, 201–28. Turin: Boringhieri, 1985.

Vegetti, Mario, and Paolo Pissavino, eds. *I Decembrio e la tradizione della Repubblica di Platone tra Medioevo e Umanesimo*. Naples: Bibliopolis, 2005.

Vendemiati, Aldo. 'Le inclinazioni naturali e il bene. Letture parallele della *Politica* di Aristotele da parte di Tommaso d'Aquino e Pietro d'Alvernia.' *Rivista di Filosofia Neo-Scolastica* 89 (1997): 299–316.

Ventura, Iolanda. 'Quaestiones and Encyclopedias: Some Aspects of the Late Medieval Reception of Pseudo-Aristotelian Problemata in Encyclopaedic and Scientific Culture.' In *Schooling and Society: The Ordering and Reordering of Knowledge in the Western Middle Ages*, edited by Alasdair A. MacDonald and Michael W. Twomey, 23–42. Leuven: Peeters, 2004.

Venturelli, Piero. 'Teorie e immagini del governo "misto" nel Cinquecento: i casi di Gasparo Contarini, Donato Giannotti, Paolo Paruta e Traiano Boccalini.' Diss., University of Bologna, 2009.

Venturi, Franco. 'Oriental Despotism.' *Journal of the History of Ideas* 24 (1963): 133–42.

Vile, Maurice J.C. *Constitutionalism and the Separation of Powers*. Oxford: Clarendon Press, 1967.

Villard, Renaud. 'Le héros introuvable: Les récits de fondation des cités en Italie: XIVe–XVIe siècle.' *Histoire, économie & société* 19 (2000): 5–24.

Vincenti, Eleonora. 'Matteo dei Libri e l'oratoria pubblica e privata nel '200.' *Archivio Glottologico Italiano* 54 (1969): 227–37.

Viroli, Maurizio. *From Politics to Reason of State: The Acquisition and Transformation of the Language of Politics, 1250–1600*. Cambridge: Cambridge University Press, 1992.

Voigtländer, Hanns-Dieter. *Der Philosoph und die Vielen: die Bedeutung des Gegensatzes der unphilosophischen Menge zu den Philosophen (und das Problem des argumentum e consensu omnium) im philosophischen Denken der Griechen bis auf Aristoteles*. Wiesbaden: Steiner, 1980.

Von Albertini, Rudolf. *Das florentinische Staatsbewusstsein im Übergang von der Republik zum Prinzipat*. Bern: Francke, 1955.

Von Fritz, Kurt. *The Theory of the Mixed Constitution in Antiquity*. New York: Columbia University Press, 1954. Repr. 1975.

Waechter, Kay. 'Der Gesetzesbegriff bei Marsilius von Padua: Positivismus mit naturgarantierter Rückversicherung.' In *Transformation des Gesetzesbegriffs im Übergang zur Moderne? Von Thomas von Aquin zu Francisco Suárez*, edited by Manfred Walther et al., 93–102. Stuttgart: F. Steiner, 2008.

Waldron, Jeremy. 'The Wisdom of the Multitude: Some Reflections on Book 3, Chapter 11 of Aristotle's *Politics*.' *Political Theory* 23 (1995): 563–84. Repr. in Kraut and Skultety, *Aristotle's Politics: Critical Essays*, 145–65.

Wallace-Hadrill, David S. *The Greek Patristic View of Nature*. Manchester/New York: Manchester University Press/Barnes & Noble, 1968.

Ward, John O. 'Renaissance Commentaries on Ciceronian Rhetoric.' In *Renaissance Eloquence: Studies in the Theory and Practice of Renaissance Rhetoric*, edited by James J. Murphy, 126–87. Berkeley, CA: University of California Press, 1983.

Waszink, Jan H. *Studien des Timaioskommentar des Calcidius*. Leiden: E.J. Brill, 1962.

Watt, John W. 'Julian's Letter to Themistius – and Themistius' Response?' In *Emperor and Author: The Writings of Julian 'The Apostate,'* edited by Nicholas J. Baker-Brian and Shaun Tougher, 91–103. Swansea: Classical Press of Wales, 2011.

Weijers, Olga, and Louis Holtz, eds. *L'enseignement des disciplines à la Faculté des arts (Paris et Oxford, XIIIe–XVe siècles)*. Turnhout: Brepols, 1997.

Weiss, Peter. 'Lebendiger Mythos: Gründungsheroen und städtische Gründungstraditionen im griechisch-römischen Osten.' *Würzburger Jahrbücher für die Altertumswissenschaft* n.s. 10 (1984): 179–208.

Weiss, Roberto. *The Dawn of Humanism in Italy: An Inaugural Lecture*. London: Lewis, 1947. Repr. New York: Haskell, 1970.

– *Il primo secolo dell' umanesimo: Studi e testi*. Rome: Storia e letteratura, 1949.

– 'Lovato Lovati (1241–1309).' *Italian Studies* 6 (1951): 3–28.

Weisser, Ursula. *Das "Buch über das Geheimnis der Schöpfung" von Pseudo-Apollonios von Tyana*. Berlin and New York: W. de Gruyter, 1980.

Welskopf, Elisabeth C. *Probleme der Musse im alten Hellas*. Berlin: Rütten & Loening, 1962.

West, Jason L.A. 'Distorted Souls: The Role of Banausics in Aristotle's *Politics*.' *Polis* 13 (1994): 77–95.

Wheeler, Marcus. 'Aristotle's Analysis of the Nature of Political Struggle.' *The American Journal of Philology* 72 (1951): 145–61. Repr. in Barnes, Schofield, and Sorabji, *Articles on Aristotle*, vol. 2: *Ethics and Politics*, 159–69.

Whitney, Elspeth. *Paradise Restored: The Mechanical Arts from Antiquity through the Thirteenth Century*. Philadelphia, PA: American Philosophical Society, 1990.

Wieland, Georg. 'Ethik und Metaphysik. Bemerkungen zur Moralphilosophie Roger Bacons.' In *Virtus Politica*, edited by Joseph Möller, 147–73. Stuttgart-Bad Cannstatt: Friedrich Fromann, 1974.

– 'Die Rezeption der aristotelischen *Politik* und die Entwicklung des Staatsgedankens im späten Mittelalter: Am Beispiel des Thomas von Aquin und des Marsilius von Padua.' In *Rechts- und Sozialphilosophie des Mittelalters*, edited by Erhard Mock und Georg Wieland, 67–81. Frankfurt a. M. and New York: P. Lang, 1990.

– 'Politik und Religion. Das Friedenskonzept des Marsilius von Padua.' In *Friedensethik im Spätmittelalter: Theologie im Ringen um die gottgegebene Ordnung*, edited by Gerhard Beestermöller and Heinz-Gerhard Justenhoven, 79–94. Stuttgart: W. Kohlhammer, 1999.

Wieruszowski, Helene. '*Ars dictaminis* in the Time of Dante.' *Medievalia et Humanistica* 1 (1943): 95–108. Repr. in eadem, *Politics and Culture in Medieval Spain and Italy*, 359–77.

– 'Brunetto Latini als Lehrer Dantes und der Florentiner.' *Archivio Italiano per la Storia della Pietà* 2 (1957): 171–98. Repr. in eadem, *Politics and Culture in Medieval Spain and Italy*, 515–61.

– *Politics and Culture in Medieval Spain and Italy*. Rome: Storia e Letteratura, 1971.

Winthrop, Delba. 'Aristotle on Participatory Democracy.' *Polity* 11 (1978): 151–71.

Wissink, Josef B.M., ed. *The Eternity of the World in the Thought of Thomas Aquinas and His Contemporaries*. Leiden: E.J. Brill, 1990.

Witt, Ronald [G.]. 'Brunetto Latini and the Italian Tradition of *Ars Dictaminis*.'

Stanford Italian Review 2 (1983): 5–24. Repr. in idem, *Italian Humanism and Medieval Rhetoric*, no. V.

– *'In the Footsteps of the Ancients': The Origins of Humanism from Lovato to Bruni*. Leiden: Brill, 2000.

– *Italian Humanism and Medieval Rhetoric*. Aldershot: Ashgate, 2001.

– 'The Arts of Letter-Writing.' In *The Cambridge History of Literary Criticism*, vol. 2: *The Middle Ages*, edited by Alastair Minnis and Ian Johnson, 68–83. Cambridge: Cambridge University Press, 2005.

– 'Rhetoric and Reform during the Eleventh and Twelfth Centuries.' In *Textual Cultures of Medieval Italy*, edited by William Robins, 53–79. Toronto: University of Toronto Press, 2011.

– *The Two Latin Cultures and the Foundation of Renaissance Humanism in Medieval Italy*. Cambridge: Cambridge University Press, 2012.

Wörner, Markus H. *Das Ethische in der Rhetorik des Aristoteles*. Freiburg i.Br. and Munich: K. Alber, 1990.

Wood, Neal. 'The Economic Dimension of Cicero's Political Thought: Property and State.' *Canadian Journal of Political Science* 16 (1983): 739–56.

– *Cicero's Social and Political Thought*. Berkeley, CA: University of California Press, 1988.

Wootton, David. *Paolo Sarpi: Between Renaissance and Enlightenment*. Cambridge: Cambridge University Press, 1983.

Wyduckel, Dieter. *Princeps legibus solutus: Eine Untersuchung zur frühmodernen Rechts- und Staatslehre*. Berlin: Duncker & Humblot, 1979.

Zabbia, Marino. 'Il Mito di Ezzelino. Le Cronache.' In *Ezzelini: Signori della Marca nel cuore dell'Impero di Federico II*, edited by Carlo Bertelli and Giovanni Marcadella, 227–31. Milan: Skira, 2001.

Zambelli, Paola, ed. *'Astrologi hallucinati': Stars and the End of the World in Luther's Time*. Berlin and New York: W. de Gruyter, 1986.

Zancarini, Jean-Claude. 'Gli umori del corpo politico. '"Popolo" e "plebe" nelle opere di Machiavelli.' In *La lingua e le lingue di Machiavelli*, edited by Alessandro Pontremoli, 61–70. Florence: L.S. Olschki, 2001.

Zanetti, Gianfrancesco. *La nozione di giustizia in Aristotele: Un percorso interpretativo*. Bologna: Il Mulino, 1993.

Zardo, Antonio. *L'Ecerinis di Albertino Mussato sotto l'aspetto storico*. Turin: Fratelli Bocca, 1889.

Zavadil, Jeffery. 'Anatomy of the Body Politic: Organic Metaphors in Ancient and Medieval Political Thought.' Diss., Arizona State University, 2006.

Zennari, Jacopo. 'Giacomo II da Carrara, signore di Padova 1345–1350.' *Bollettino del Museo Civico di Padova* 13 (1910): 101–23; 14 (1911): 1–55.

Zillig, Paula. *Die Theorie von der gemischten Verfassung in ihrer literarischen Ent-*

wickelung im Altertum und ihr Verhältnis zur Lehre Lockes und Montesquieus über Verfassung. Diss., University of Würzburg, 1916.

Zimmermann, Albert, and Ingrid Craemer-Ruegenberg, eds. *Orientalische Kultur und europäisches Mittelalter*. Berlin and New York: W. de Gruyter, 1985.

Zonta, Mauro. 'Traduzioni e commenti alla *Guida dei perplessi* nell'Europa del secolo XIII: a proposito di alcuni studi recenti.' *Maimonide e il suo tempo*, ed. Geri Cerchiai and Giovanni Rota, 51–60. Milan: Franco Angeli, 2007.

– 'Nemesiana Syriaca: New Fragments from the Missing Syriac Version of the *De natura hominis*.' *Journal of Semitic Studies* 36 (1991): 223–58.

Zorzi, Maria A. 'L'ordinamento Comunale Padovano nella seconda metà del secolo XIII. – Studio storico con Documenti inediti.' *Miscellanea di Storia Veneta* s. 4, 5 (1931): 1–248.

Index of Subjects

acts: *actus immanentes*, 8–9, 57–61; *actus transeuntes*, 8–9, 57–61, 70, 84–5
advice, 45
Aristotelianism / Aristotelian tradition, 4–5, 8, 14, 23, 28, 59, 106, 114–16
ars dictaminis, 45
astrology, 22, 72–3, 88, 103–4
astronomy, 104
Averroism, 19, 23–4

barbarians, 76, 82, 103
Byzantine political thought, 3, 30, 37–8, 64–5, 115–16

Capitaneatus, 102
causality / causes: efficient, 4, 6, 12, 26–7, 85, 91, 95, 106, 108, 112; final, 4, 6, 16, 25–8, 102
'Circle of Justice,' 9, 64–8
citizenship, 11, 48–9, 66, 76–9
city states (Italian), 50–1, 77–8, 115
community (political): aim, 7–8, 24, 29, 34, 46–7; founding, 7, 28–46, 92; parts, 8–9, 11–12, 14, 25, 27, 47–9, 50, 51–2, 53–4, 56–70, 76–8, 85, 93, 96, 106, 108–9, 112–13; sufficiency, 6, 11, 26, 28–9, 31, 35, 39, 43–4, 46–7, 55, 62, 74–5, 84–5, 98; tranquility, 6, 8, 27, 33–4, 47–52, 81, 84–5, 97; unity, 8, 53–6
consent, 7, 27, 36, 53, 91, 98–9, 101–2, 104–5, 112
constabiliaria (*Connétable de France*), 102
constitutions / constitutional forms: aristocracy, 8, 13, 37, 54, 81, 100–1; democracy, 11, 13, 37–8, 49, 52, 76–9, 93–4, 100–1; kingship, 13–14, 43–4, 54, 90–1, 101–5, 110–11; oligarchy, 13, 49, 52, 77, 95, 98, 100–1, 193; polity, 8, 13, 53, 101; timocracy, 100; tyranny, 13, 19–20, 38, 44, 51, 82, 90, 100–3, 105, 112
contemplation / contemplative life, 47–8
counsel. *See* advice

Defensor minor, 17–18
Defensor pacis: authorship, 16; *editio princeps*, 17; reception, 17
despotism, 100, 111

equitas, 35

eternity of the world, 24, 26

family, 35–6
friendship, 11, 28–9, 54, 82, 84
functional specialization, 5, 47, 56–7, 61–9, 77, 114–15

habitus, 80–1, 84
hierarchy of ends, 11, 48–9, 76
honorabilitas, 75, 78–9, 96, 101
household, 7, 34–6, 43–4, 65, 104

Islamic political thought/philosophy, 3, 5–6, 9–10, 14, 19, 23–4, 26, 30, 33, 37, 62–4, 65, 68–9, 71, 73, 74–5, 87–8, 90, 107, 110, 114–16, 189

Jewish political thought/philosophy, 3, 5–7, 9–10, 14, 19, 24, 33–4, 59–61, 68, 71–2, 89, 110, 114–16
justice: corrective, 34, 58, 83; distributive, 83–4

legislator humanus/legislation, 9, 11–14, 18, 24, 56–7, 58, 71, 74, 80–114
leisure, 8, 47–8, 56, 63–4, 71, 79, 91, 173, 188
Liber de causis, 107

mechanical arts, 9, 11, 58, 61, 70, 76–8, 91
medicine, 6, 15, 19, 21–3, 27, 68, 70, 85, 174–5
metaphors: astrological, 104, 112; biological/organic, 6, 8, 13–14, 27–8, 48–52, 55, 66, 68–9, 76, 100, 108–13
'Myth of Venice,' 37–9
mythology/myths, 70–3, 74, 80

Neoplatonism, 5, 13–14, 106, 214

oikeiosis, 28, 98
oratory. *See* rhetoric

peace, 6–8, 44, 46–52, 116
podestà/podestà literature, 45
Prehumanism, 19–20, 45
priests, 9–10, 17–18, 52, 61–3, 70–5, 98, 113
progress, 12, 87–9
prudence, 7, 11–13, 36, 38, 42, 47, 70, 79, 81, 87–91, 96–7, 109, 112, 116

religion, 5, 10–11, 24, 29, 59, 65, 70–5, 80, 82, 104, 115
rhetoric, 7, 36–46, 63–4, 86, 93
ruler: appointment and duties/function, 7, 11–14, 24, 31, 33–4, 36, 38, 40–1, 43, 53–4, 56, 60, 62–7, 74, 79, 84–7, 89–91, 97–8, 100–16; qualities and virtues, 47, 78–9, 109–12

Sabians, 10, 71–2
slaves/slavery, 11, 16, 65, 77, 97
social/civil life, 4, 6–8, 10, 12, 24–5, 27–46, 50–1, 68, 70, 74, 83–4, 86, 92, 97–8, 103, 109, 111, 114
sovereignty,12, 78, 86, 89, 91–9, 106
Stoics/Stoicism, 197
strife, 3, 31, 33, 35, 44, 46, 50–1, 67, 70, 84–5, 91, 109

teleology, 4, 6, 25–8, 102

valencior pars, 12, 26–7, 54, 91–4, 106, 108
village, 35, 43, 46
vulgus, 75–6, 78, 92, 96, 101

Index of Places and Proper Names

Abelard, Peter, 123
Abraham, 62
Abraham (ben Meir) ibn Ezra (Avenarius), 22
Abravanel, Isaac, 89, 110
Abū Ma'shar (Albumasar), 73
(Pseudo-) Adam of Bocfeld, 107
Aegidius Romanus. *See* Giles of Rome
Agamemnon, 102
Albert the Great (Albertus Magnus), 24, 78, 89, 107
Al-Bīrūnī, 33
Alexander the Great, 73
Al-Fārābī, 10, 19, 24, 37, 70–1, 74, 115, 188
Al-Ghazzālī, 71
Ali ibn Ridwān (Haly), 22
Amphion, 46, 165
Aquinas, Thomas, 9, 24, 34, 37, 58–9, 88–9, 107
Ardashīr, 65, 183
Augustine, 6, 28–9, 42
Averroes, 10, 19, 23–4, 26, 62, 71, 74, 75, 87–9, 90, 110, 114–15, 188
Avicenna, 5, 10, 63, 88–9

Bacon, Roger, 5, 10, 63, 73, 88–9, 107
Bagolinus, Hieronymus, 110
Bartholomew of Bruges, 23
Bartholomew of Messina, 21
Belus, 43
Bodin, Jean, 124
Boncompagno da Signa, 163
Bruni, Leonardo, 121
Buridan, John, 97

Campanella, Tommaso, 191
Cangrande I della Scala. *See* Della Scala, Cangrande I
Cassiodorus, 166
Cecco d'Ascoli, 73
Ceffi, Filippo, 163
Chalcidios, 63
Charles IV, 15, 23
Christine de Pizan, 10, 66
Cicero, Marcus Tullius, 5–8, 14, 28–30, 36, 39–46, 48, 53, 114
Clement VI (Pope), 18
Cleovoulos, 30
Colonna, Giacomo (Sciarra), 17
Contarini, Gasparo, 38
Cornarius, Janus, 109
Cromwell, Thomas, 17

Cyrus, 37

da Carrara, Giacomo, 20
d'Alessandria, Benzo, 50
da Reggio, Niccolò, 219
da Montagnone, Geremia, 51
da Nono, Giovanni, 51
da Vignano, Giovanni, 163
della Scala, Cangrande I, 16, 20, 21, 51
de' Libri, Matteo, 163
del Medigo, Elia (Elijah), 24
Democritos, 29
de Pizan, Christine. *See* Christine de Pizan
Duns Scotus, John. *See* John Duns Scotus

Engelbert of Admont, 43
Ezzelino III da Romano, 19–20, 31, 51

Faba, Guido, 163
Felicianus, Johannes Bernardus, 109
Forzate, Giovanni, 52

Galen, 7, 19, 21–2, 66, 109–10, 148
Gemistos Plethon, George, 64–5
Gerard of Cremona, 22, 107
Gerson, Jean, 66
Giannotti, Donato, 38–9
Giles of Rome (Aegidius Romanus), 43–4, 107, 110, 123
Grotius, Hugo, 124
Guicciardini, Francesco, 68, 115
Guinterius Andernacus, Johannes, 109
Gundissalinus, Dominicus, 5, 10, 63, 188

Haly. *See* Ali ibn Ridwān
Henry VII, 19, 21
(Pseudo-) Henry of Ghent, 107, 123
Hesiod, 70
Hippocrates, 21, 68, 73
Hobbes, Thomas, 124
Hugh of St Victor, 188

Ibn Qutaybah, 65
Ibn Rushd. *See* Averroes
Ibn Sīnā, *See* Avicenna
Ikhwān al-Ṣafā', 73
Isocrates, 172

Jesus, 16, 73
Joan I of Navarre, 23
John XXII (Pope), 15–17, 23, 125
John Duns Scotus, 42
John Henry of Luxembourg, 17
John of Göttingen, 23
John of Jandun, 6, 16, 19, 21–4, 58
John of Linerius, 104
John of Paris (Quidort), 42–3
John of Salisbury, 112–13
John of Spain, 73
John of Viterbo, 45

Latini, Brunetto, 45–6
Leo VI, 65
Lovato Lovati, 20
Louis I, margrave of Brandenburg (Louis V, Duke of Bavaria), 17
Louis IV of Bavaria, 16–17, 21, 23–4, 125, 127
Lycourgos, 30, 36, 39, 90

Machiavelli, Niccolò, 10, 37, 67–8, 95, 115–16
Magister, Thomas, 64
Maimonides, Moses, 7, 9–10, 19, 24, 33–4, 59–61, 68, 71–2, 115

Manegold of Lautenbach, 189
Manfred of Sicily, 21
Mantinus (Mantino), Jacob, 24
Manuel II Palaiologos, 64
Marshall, William, 17
Matteo I Visconti, 15
Maultasch, Margaret, 17
Mézières, Philippe de, 66
Michael Scotus, 110, 217
Moḥammed, 73
Moroni, Simone, 104
Moses, 37, 73
Mussato, Albertino, 6, 15, 19–21, 51–2, 104

Nebuchadrezzar, 73
Nemesios of Emesa, 7, 31–3
Nicholas V (Pope), 37
Nicolas de Vaudémont, 13, 97–8
Ninus, 43

Origen, 30

Peter of Abano, 6, 15, 21–3, 27, 59, 73, 103–4, 110, 112, 167, 174–5
Peter of Auvergne, 13, 58, 96–7, 107, 111–12
Peter of Corbara, 17
Philoponos, John, 110
Phrynes, 87
Pittacos, 30
Plato, 5–6, 9–10, 24, 29, 37–8, 53, 61–4, 68–9, 71, 76, 84, 112, 114, 172, 197
Plotinos, 107
Plutarch, 30
Pomponazzi, Pietro, 10, 73–4, 115
Proclos, 107, 213
Protagoras, 29
Ptolemy of Lucca (Tolomeo da Lucca), 7, 34, 78, 103

Pythagoras, 70

Raniero da Perugia, 163
Rhenanus, Beatus, 17
Robert of Anjou, 16
Rolandino of Padua, 20, 104
Romulus, 37, 39

Sallust, 51
Samuel ben Judah, 24
Sarpi, Paolo, 10–11, 74, 115
Scipio Aemilianus, 40
Scotus, Michael. *See* Michael Scotus
Seneca, 20, 172
Shem-Ṭov ben Joseph ibn Falaquera, 68–9
Siger of Brabant, 23, 107
Solon, 30, 90, 94
Sylvius, Andreas, 110

Tantalos, 10, 72
Themistios, 7, 30–1, 33
Theodoros II Palaiologos, 64
Theseus, 36–7
Thierry of Chartres, 44–5
Timotheos, 87
Tommaso da Capua, 163

Vias, 30
Villani, Giovanni, 104

William of Moerbeke, 4, 75, 89, 92, 107, 111, 121, 213

Xenophon, 193

Zoroaster, 73

www.ingramcontent.com/pod-product-compliance
Lightning Source LLC
LaVergne TN
LVHW090151080826
844660LV00013B/766/J

* 9 7 8 1 4 4 2 6 4 1 4 4 0 *